VISUAL QUICKSTART GUIDE

DREAMWEAVER 3

FOR WINDOWS AND MACINTOSH

J. Tarin Towers

 Peachpit Press

macromedia®
PRESS

Visual QuickStart Guide
Dreamweaver 3 for Windows and Macintosh
J. Tarin Towers

Peachpit Press
1249 Eighth Street
Berkeley, CA 94710
(510) 524-2178
(510) 524-2221 (fax)
www.peachpit.com

Published by Peachpit Press in association with Macromedia Press

Peachpit Press is a division of Addison Wesley Longman

Visit this book's Web site at: www.peachpit.com/vqs/dreamweaver

Editor: Cary Norsworthy
Copy Editor: Valerie Perry
Tech Editor: VernonViehe
Production Coordinator: Amy Changar
Compositor: Owen Wolfson
Indexer: Karin Arrigoni, Write Away

ISBN: 0-201-70240-1

0 9 8 7 6 5 4 3 2 1

Printed and bound in the United States of America

♲ Printed on recycled paper

*To Sean Porter,
for the pitchfork.*

Acknowledgements

I'd like to thank everyone who helped me with this book: Cary Norsworthy, my editor and reluctant dictator, for laughing while cracking the whip; Marjorie Baer for diligence and patience; David Van Ness for the initial design; Amy Changar and Owen Wolfson (for gluing the electrons onto the pages and making it look great); Eric Ott and Alisse Berger at Macromedia for helping me get the stuff I needed; Vernon Viehe, who did the Tech Review at Macromedia; Christian Cosas, Amy Franceschini, Zhenia Timerman, Dave Eggers, and Jamie Zawinski, for lending me their art; the good folks behind the scenes at Macromedia, who wrote an even better program, and many, many faithful readers who sent in comments, encouragement, questions, and suggestions. I'd also like to thank Brian Matheson, Sean Porter, jwz, all my friends who are geeks, and all my friends who aren't.

TABLE OF CONTENTS

Chapter 17: Automating Dreamweaver   401

TABLE OF CONTENTS

INTRODUCTION

Welcome to the *Dreamweaver 3 for Windows and Macintosh: Visual QuickStart Guide*! Dreamweaver is exciting software: it's simple to use and it's one of the very best WYSIWYG (What You See Is What You Get) editing tools to ever come down the pike.

Dreamweaver isn't just another visual HTML tool. It does do what all the best editors do: creates tables, edits frames, and switches easily from page view to HTML view.

But Dreamweaver goes way beyond the other editors to allow you to create Dynamic HTML (DHTML) gadgets and pages. Dreamweaver fully supports Cascading Style Sheets (CSS-1) as well as layers and JavaScript behaviors. It even includes its own DHTML animation tool: Timelines. And a fully-fledged FTP client, complete with visual site maps, is built right in.

What's New?

Dreamweaver 3 introduces several new features that simplify page production. And this book includes four new chapters to keep up. The last chapter in the Dreamweaver 2 book was about setting up and managing Web sites using the Site window. I've moved coverage of how to set up a local site to the new Chapter 3. Chapter 20 includes new site-management features, such as design notes and the streamlined site updating features.

Dreamweaver's new features include the following:

Quick Tag Editor (Chapter 4): If you'd like to be able to add, edit, or remove tags while staying in the Document window, the Quick Tag editor will be your new friend. Chapter 4 is new, too, and it's all about HTML.

Clean Up Word HTML (Chapter 4): They figured out that Word always makes the same mistakes when it saves files as HTML, and they figured out how to fix them, too.

Special Characters (Chapter 6): Dreamweaver now includes direct support for special characters (such as ©) in the Objects palette and the Insert menu.

HTML Styles (Chapter 7): Because CSS hasn't yet taken off the way experts predicted, formatting text with font tags is still what most webmasters prefer. With HTML styles, you can save sets of text properties as reusable, named styles in the HTML styles inspector.

Navigation Bars (Chapter 9): Dreamweaver now offers a dialog-box level method for inserting button rollovers that can have up to four different visible states.

E-mail Links (Chapter 9): A new Insert menu object is a dialog box for inserting e-mail links. New menu items for Insert > Link and Remove > Link appear there, too.

Who Should Use This Book?

No matter what your level of Web experience, you can use Dreamweaver and this book. I'm assuming you've used some sort of page-creation tool before, even if it's just a text editor. You should use this book if you're:

- ◆ An absolute beginner who wants an editor that writes great HTML.

- ◆ A graphic designer who's used to using document editors like Director, PageMaker, or Photoshop, but who isn't as proficient with HTML.

- ◆ An HTML expert who likes to hand code but wants automation of simple tasks.

- ◆ Frightened of Dynamic HTML.

- ◆ Someone who needs to learn Dreamweaver quickly.

Browsers Beware

I use sidebars to point out "extra" information about specific features, including HTML tricks that aren't directly supported by Dreamweaver.

This sidebar is about browser wars. I've made every effort to be fair to both the powerhouse browsers, Netscape Navigator (which I usually call Navigator, or just NN) and Microsoft Internet Explorer (called MSIE, IE, or sometimes Explorer). I also point out important differences between them, which are most apparent when talking about 4.0 browsers.

Browsers are like sausage: No one should have to know how they're made. I was, however, employed for Netscape at one point; for Microsoft, I wrote reviews of bars and cocktail lounges. (Full disclosures are in vogue right now.)

When I wrote the first edition of this book, the browser wars made it seem likely that the year 2000 would bring, if not the apocalypse, then version 6.0 of something. Navigator is still on edition 4.7, and Explorer 5.0 added Netscape-level security, more user customization, and not much else.

Interestingly enough, the first version of Dreamweaver was lauded for the ease it granted Cascading Style Sheets and layers. Ironically, computer prices dropped so much that more people than ever started using 4.0 browsers—and these 4.0-only features were abandoned by a lot of designers for their clunkiness, their browser incompatibility, and their backwards noncompatibility.

Dreamweaver does make it easy to write 4.0 pages and save them as 4.0 code. But on a small farm in the middle of nowhere, my grandpa is surfing the Web using Windows 3.1 and a ball of twine.

Import/Export Table Data (Chapter 10): Import database or spreadsheet information into a table in Dreamweaver, or export table data from Dreamweaver into a data file.

Jump Menus (Chapter 12): Use a simple dialog box to insert JavaScript-driven navigation menus, with or without "Go" buttons.

New Behaviors (Chapter 15): Set new content for a layer or a frame when a user performs an event.

History Palette (Chapter 17): Dreamweaver now tracks your actions in the Document window, and not just for multiple Undos. In the History palette, you can redo any action, even on a different object than your initial selection. And you can save an action or set of actions as an entry in the Commands menu.

Objects Support (Chapter 18): Adding custom objects to the Insert menu and the Objects palette is easier than ever.

Customizable Menus (Chapter 18): By editing a single XML file, you can change the content of the menus on any palette or menu bar in Dreamweaver.

Customizable Dialog Boxes (Chapter 18): You can change the appearance of most of Dreamweaver's dialog boxes.

Design Notes (Chapter 20): Design notes are files that let you save comments, dates, and other, perhaps proprietary data about pages and media objects on your local site or in your workgroup's file server.

Synchronize Files (Chapter 20): It's even easier now to select and Get or Put the more recent files on a local or remote site.

Improved Site Updating (Chapters 3, 9, 17, and 20): Loads of features, either new or streamlined, make it easier to keep your site—and its links and objects—up-to-date.

QuickStart Conventions

If you've read a previous *Visual QuickStart Guide*, you know that this book is made up of two main components: numbered lists that take you step by step through the things you want learn, and illustrations that show you what the heck I'm talking about.

I explain what needs to be explained, but I don't pontificate about the acceleration of information technology or wax dramatic about proprietary tags.

✔ Tips

- In every chapter, you'll find tips like these that point out something extra handy.

- Code in the book is set off in `code font`.

- Sometimes you can find extra tidbits of info in the figure captions, too.

What's in this Book

Here's a quick rundown of what I cover in this book.

Dreamweaver Basics

In the first four chapters I introduce you to HTML and the Dreamweaver interface. If you never want to look at any HTML when you use Dreamweaver, you don't have to; on the other hand, if you want to learn HTML, there's no better way than by creating a page and looking at the code you just made. The new Chapter 3 walks you through setting up a local site, so that all of Dreamweaver's site management, linking, and updating tools will work for you. The new History palette lets you repeat or undo almost anything. Chapter 18 introduces you to customizing Dreamweaver by editing object files, menus, and other interface elements.

Web Page Basics

Chapters 5-7 talk about text and all the things you can do with it, and Chapter 9 describes linking in more detail than you thought possible. Chapter 8 gets you on your way with images—and Appendix A, on the Web site for this book, describes how to make client-side image maps with the image map editor.

Tables, Frames, and Forms

Chapters 10-12 are what most folks consider the "intermediate" range in HTML—10 is tables, 11 is frames, and 12 is forms, all of which are much easier to construct in Dreamweaver than by hand.

But Wait, There's More on the Web Site!

The companion Web site for this book contains lots and lots of links to developers' pages, handy shareware tools, and example sites, and because the page is on the Web, you don't have to type in a bunch of URLs. You'll also find online appendixes covering the image map editor, HTML preferences, and browser compatibility. I also include my own sample pages, along with some DHTML I made just for this book. (You can only see the DHTML stuff if you're using a 4.0 or later browser, but the site is open to everyone, and I made it all using Dreamweaver, naturally.)

Visit http://www.peachpit.com/vqs/dreamweaver and let me know what you think of the book and the Web site by e-mailing dreamweaver@tarin.com.

Dynamic HTML

Then we get to the Dynamic part of the book. The components of DHTML are covered in Chapters 13-16. Chapter 13 covers Cascading Style Sheets. In Chapter 14, you'll learn about layers and all that goes with them, including absolute positioning. Chapter 15 covers behaviors, a Chinese food menu way of putting together JavaScript actions—just choose one from column A and one from column B. And Chapter 16 discusses Timelines, Dreamweaver's DHTML animation tool.

Site Management

Chapter 17 discusses three ways of automating common tasks in Dreamweaver: libraries, templates, and history. Libraries are a site-management tool, whereas you use custom objects to modify Dreamweaver's Insert functions. The template feature in Dreamweaver allows you to create versatile templates with read-only design features, and you can update the design of pages based on these templates just by updating the template file. In the new Chapter 4, you'll even learn how to edit it in its own window; or, using the Quick Tag editor, how to edit it without even looking at the code, per se.

In Chapter 19, you'll learn everything you need to know about putting plug-ins and other multimedia content on your site. Appendix B on the companion Web site describes how to make your Web pages work and look the way you want them to in all kinds of browsers. And Chapter 20 is all about site management with Dreamweaver's Site window, a full-fledged FTP client.

HTML is HTML

Like the song, HTML remains the same, whether you construct it on a Mac or PC. Even better, Dreamweaver's Roundtrip HTML feature ensures that HTML you create outside the program will retain its formatting—although obvious errors, like unclosed tags, will be fixed.

The PC version of Dreamweaver comes with HomeSite, and the Mac version comes with BBEdit. You can set up either program to work with any HTML editor you like, however. See Appendix D, on the companion Web site for this book, to find out how to set up these editors and how Dreamweaver will treat your HTML.

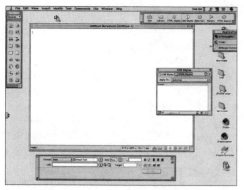

Figure 1 Dreamweaver's Document window and some of its floating windows, as seen on the Mac.

Figure 2 Dreamweaver's Document window and some of its floating windows, as seen on a PC. Not many differences other than the title bar and menu bar.

Special to Mac Users

I wrote this book on a PC, but this time around, I had a Mac on the same desk. And this time around, Dreamweaver wrote the program with a code base entirely specific to each platform. Much of the program is written in cross-platform languages like JavaScript, XML, and HTML, and the Mac version of Dreamweaver 3 was written *for* the Mac, not written for Windows and ported over.

The main difference between the Mac and Windows flavors in previous versions of Dreamweaver was that the Mac, having only one menu bar, featured a Sites menu in the Document window. Now Windows features the same menu. The differences are negligible, as you can see in **Figures 1** and **2**.

There are some basic platform differences that will cause the screen shots to look slightly different. Windows windows (ha ha) have a menu bar affixed to each and every window, whereas the Mac menu bar is always at the top of the screen, and it changes based on the program you choose from the Application menu (the one in the upper left of the Mac screen, next to the clock).

Windows windows close by clicking on the close box on the upper right, whereas close boxes on the Mac are on the upper left. Occasionally, buttons will have different names. For instance, in some dialog boxes, the button says Browse in Windows and Choose on the Mac. They're always close enough.

INTRODUCTION

Keyboard conventions

When I refer to key commands, I put the Windows command first and the Mac command in parentheses, like this: Press Ctrl+L (Command+L)

I use this format for some other differences, too, like system fonts:

The source code uses the Courier New (Courier) font face.

Mouse conventions

Some Mac mice have more than one button; some don't. For that matter, some folks don't really use mice at all, they have those touch-pad and stylus thingies. That said, I do refer to right-clicking a lot. On a Windows machine, when you click the right rather than the left mouse button, a contextual pop-up menu appears (**Figure 3**).

Pop-up menus, or context menus, are available in some Mac systems. To make a pop-up menu appear on a Mac, or in system 8.x, try Ctrl+clicking. Your mileage may vary depending on your system configuration. Options available from pop-up menus are always available as menu bar options, too, so you'll never miss functionality in Dreamweaver even if you can't right-click.

And now... on to the book!

Figure 3 If you're a Windows user, right-click on an object to pop up a contextual menu. If you're a Mac user, just click on the object while holding down the Ctrl key. The pop-up menu will appear in a second or two.

GETTING STARTED

When you start Dreamweaver (**Figure 1.1**) for the first time, you'll see a main window, called the *Document window,* and several floating windows, called either *palettes* or *inspectors.*

The main components of Dreamweaver that I'll introduce in this chapter are the Document window, the HTML inspector, the Properties inspector, the Launcher, and the Objects palette.

Objects palette

Document window

Launcher

Properties inspector

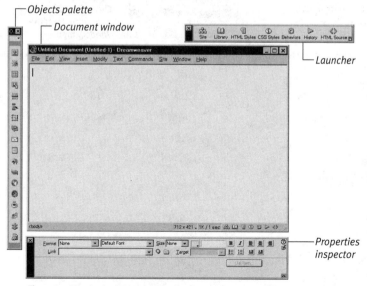

Figure 1.1 Here's the Dreamweaver work environment, complete with the floating windows you'll see on startup.

Dreamweaver Terminology

The various components that comprise Dreamweaver are called windows, palettes, and inspectors. Although all of these items are available from the Window menu (**Figure 1.2**), they are not all called windows.

A *window,* in Dreamweaver, is a stand-alone screen element that will show up on the Windows status bar (the Mac doesn't display windows separately in the Applications menu). The Document window is one example of a window, and the Site window is another.

You can have multiple document windows open; the filename for each will appear at the bottom of the Window menu (**Figure 1.3**).

The miniature, floating windows that are used to adjust particular sets of properties are called either *inspectors* or *palettes.* These are similar to the palettes and inspectors you may have used in other multimedia creation programs, such as Photoshop, PageMaker, or Director.

In general, an inspector changes appearance based on the current selection, whereas a palette controls elements, such as styles or library items, that are available to the entire current site.

You can control your workspace by moving any of these windows, or by closing them to get rid of them altogether.

✔ Tips

- To view or hide any window, palette, or inspector, select its name from the Window menu.

- Keyboard shortcuts for each palette are listed in the Window menu.

- Read the sidebar *Stacking Palettes,* later in this chapter, to find out how to save screen space.

Figure 1.2 You can open any of Dreamweaver's windows, palettes, and inspectors from the Document window's Window menu.

Figure 1.3 When you're working with multiple documents, each will appear in its own Document window. Each of these will be accessible from the Window menu.

Open documents

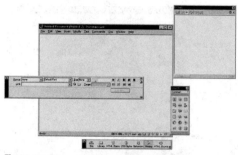

Figure 1.4 Dreamweaver remembers window positions; if this is where your palettes are when you exit the program, this is where they'll be when you open Dreamweaver again the next time.

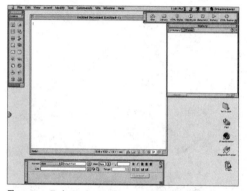

Figure 1.5 To have Dreamweaver clean up your workspace, select Arrange Floating Palettes from the Window menu bar.

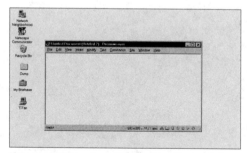

Figure 1.6 To hide all palettes for an uncluttered view of your workspace, press F4. Since Dreamweaver remembers where everything was (and which palettes were open), press F4 again to bring it all back.

To close any window:

◆ Just click on the X in the upper-right corner (Windows). On a Mac, click on the close box in the upper-left corner.

✔ Tips

■ Dreamweaver will remember where your windows are when you exit the program. When you start Dreamweaver again, your window preferences will remain the way they were when you last exited (**Figure 1.4**).

■ To move the floating windows back to their original, default positions, select Window > Arrange Floating Palettes from the Document window menu bar (**Figure 1.5**).

■ You can hide all of the floating windows, select Window > Hide Floating Palettes from the Document window menu bar, or press F4 (**Figure 1.6**).

DREAMWEAVER TERMINOLOGY

To change floating window preferences:

1. From the Document window menu bar, select Edit > Preferences. The Preferences dialog box will appear.

2. In the Category box at the left of the window, click on Floating Palettes. The Floating Palettes panel of the dialog box will come to the front (**Figure 1.7**).

3. This panel of the dialog box includes a checkbox for every floating window that's a part of Dreamweaver. Each window will always appear layered over the Document window (as well as the Site window and the HTML inspector), unless you uncheck its checkbox here.

   To neutralize a window's floating super-power, uncheck its checkbox.

4. When you're done, click on OK to close the Preferences dialog box and return to the Dreamweaver window.

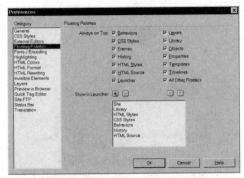

Figure 1.7 The Floating Palettes panel of the Preferences dialog box lets you disable the "always on top" feature of any of Dreamweaver's floating windows.

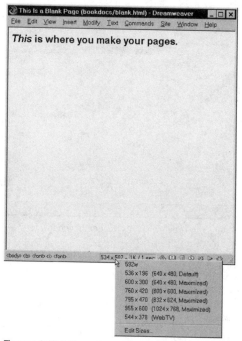

Figure 1.8 Click the arrow on the window size indicator to select a common, preset window size.

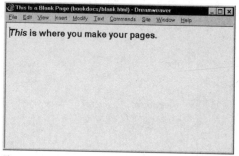

Figure 1.9 You can make the status bar go away if you want more screen space.

The Document Window

The Document window (shown in detail on the next page in **Figure 1.11**) is the main center of activity in Dreamweaver. Since Dreamweaver is a WYSIWYG HTML tool, the Document window approximates what you'll see in a Web browser window.

The *title bar* displays the filename and the title of the current Web page.

All Dreamweaver menu commands are available from the Document window *menu bar*.

The *body* of the HTML document is displayed in the main viewing area of the Document window. The *status bar* indicates three things about the current document:

◆ The *tag selector* displays all the HTML tags that apply to the current selection.

◆ The *window size indicator* displays the current size of the Document window. The numbers will change if you resize the document window; you can select a preset window size by clicking the down arrow in this area to display a pop-up window (**Figure 1.8**).

◆ The *download stats* area displays the total size, in K (kilobytes), of the current page, and the amount of time it would take to download over a 28.8 Kbps modem.

The *Launcher bar,* also in the status bar, includes the same buttons as the Launcher, which is discussed later in this chapter in the section called *The Launcher.*

To hide the status bar:

◆ From the Document window menu bar, select View > Status bar.

The status bar will disappear (**Figure 1.9**).

✔ Tip

- You can resize the Document window as you would any other window: by clicking on the lower-right corner and dragging to make the window larger or smaller. I show the Document window in many different sizes throughout this book, depending on the kind of content I'm discussing at the time. As you can see in **Figures 1.10** and **1.11**, the Mac and Windows versions of Dreamweaver are near-identical.

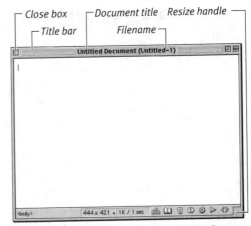

Figure 1.10 Dreamweaver's Document window for the Mac.

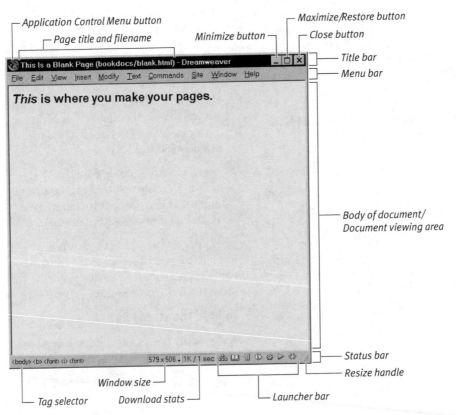

Figure 1.11 The Document window is where you compose your pages. This is the Windows version.

Measurements in pixels
The zero point

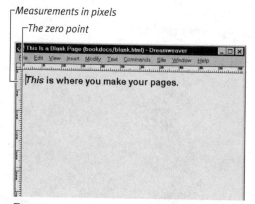

Figure 1.12 View the rulers to get an idea of how big your ideas are. Pixels are the default ruler unit.

Dragging the zero point to 100 x 100 pixels

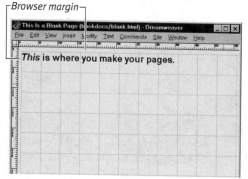

Figure 1.13 Click on the zero point and drag it to a new location to change the ruler origins.

Browser margin

Figure 1.14 To get even more precise measurements, turn on the grid.

Customizing the Document Window

You can turn on and off several options in the Document window to make composing pages easier.

You can display a ruler on the top and left sides of the screen to make incremental measurements, such as sizing tables or images, easier. You can also choose to display a grid that you can use in positioning objects.

To view the Rulers:

◆ From the Document window menu bar, select View > Rulers > Show.

The rulers will appear (**Figure 1.12**).

To change Ruler units:

◆ From the Document window menu bar, select View > Rulers > and then choose Pixels, Inches, or Centimeters.

The ruler measurements will change.

By default, the rulers' zero points, or starting point for measurements, start at the top, left corner.

To change the zero point:

◆ Click on the zero point (**Figure 1.13**), and drag it into the window. When the point is where you want it to be, let go of the mouse button.

Now, when you look at the rulers, the measurements will reflect the new zero point. If you change your mind, you can reset the zero point to its original position.

To view the grid:

◆ From the Document window menu bar, select View > Grid > Show.

The grid will appear (**Figure 1.14**). You can make items that are affected by absolute positioning snap to the grid lines, if you want.

To reset the zero point:

◆ From the Document window menu bar, select View > Rulers > Reset Origin (see **Figure 1.15**).

To turn on the "snapping" option:

1. Show the grid, if necessary.

2. From the Document window menu bar, select View > Grid > Snap To.

Now layers that you drag in the Document window will snap to the grid (see Chapter 14).

To change grid settings:

1. From the Document window menu bar, select View > Grid > Settings. The Grid Settings dialog box will appear (**Figure 1.16**).

2. The Visible Grid checkbox is the same as the View > Grid > Show menu option, and the Snapping checkbox is the same setting as View > Grid > Snap to Grid.

3. To change the spacing of the grid lines, type a number in the Spacing text box, and choose a unit from the Spacing drop-down menu: Pixels, Inches, or Centimeters.

4. To change the color of the grid lines, click on the Color button, and the Color palette will appear. Click on a color to choose it.

5. To display dotted rather than solid lines, click on the Dots radio button.

6. To change the snapping settings, type a number in the Snap Every text box, and then choose a unit (Pixels, Inches, or Centimeters) from the drop-down menu.

7. To view your changes before you return to the Document window, click on Apply.

8. To accept the changes, click on OK. The Grid Settings dialog box will close, and you'll return to the Document window.

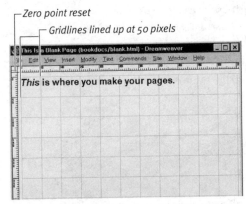

Figure 1.15 I reset the zero point to match the grid measurements; notice how the 50-pixel line matches up to the second vertical grid line.

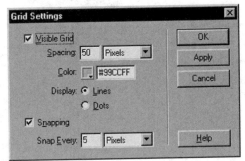

Figure 1.16 Control the grid by changing the Grid settings.

✔ Tip

■ Rulers and grids are most useful for positioning tables and layers, discussed in Chapters 10 and 14. Both elements can provide visual guidelines for sizing and laying out content.

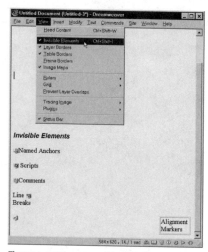

Figure 1.17 When you view invisible elements, you may see all kinds of little icons that weren't visible before.

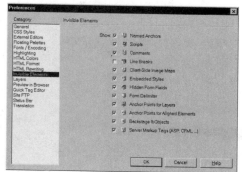

Figure 1.18 You can choose not to view certain invisible elements when you want to see some, but not all, of them.

✔ Tips

- Each of these invisible elements is discussed in the chapter that covers the topic to which it's related.

- **Figure 1.18** is also a handy reference for what the symbols stand for.

- Click on an invisible element icon to examine it with the Properties inspector.

Invisible Elements

Dreamweaver's Document window approximates what you'd see in a Web browser window; it tries to replicate the way a browser would interpret HTML.

One exception to this is invisible elements. These elements would not be visible to a Web browser, but you may have occasion to display them in order to select or move them.

To view invisible elements:

◆ From the Document window menu bar, select View > Invisible Elements.

Any invisible elements on the current page will show up in the form of little icons (**Figure 1.17**).

To change invisible element preferences:

1. From the Document window menu bar, select Edit > Preferences. The Preferences dialog box will appear.

2. In the Category box at the left of the Preferences dialog box, click on Invisible Elements. The Invisible Elements panel of the dialog box will appear (**Figure 1.18**).

3. The Invisible Elements panel of the dialog box displays all the invisible elements that will become visible when you select View > Invisible Elements.

   Each invisible element has a corresponding checkbox. Line breaks are deselected by default.

4. To deselect any element, click on its checkbox to remove the checkmark.

   To select any element without a checkmark, click on its checkbox.

5. When you're finished, click on OK to close the Preferences dialog box.

The HTML Inspector

The HTML inspector (**Figure 1.19**) shows
the HTML code for the current page.
Dreamweaver always adds the code shown
in **Figure 1.19** to a new Web page.

To view the HTML inspector:

◆ From the Document window menu bar,
select Window > HTML

or

Click on the HTML button on the
Launcher

or

Press F10.

In any case, the HTML inspector will appear.
If you change windows to view a different
document, the HTML inspector will update
to show the code of the current page.

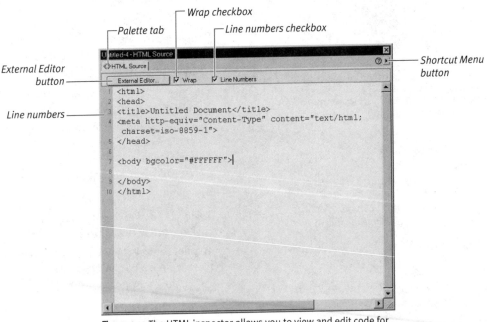

Figure 1.19 The HTML inspector allows you to view and edit code for
the pages in the Document window.

To close the HTML inspector:

◆ Click on the HTML button on the Launcher

or

Press F10.

The HTML inspector will close, returning you to the Document window. (Don't press Ctrl + W (Command + W)—as I do by reflex to close a window—because Dreamweaver will close the Document window as well.)

Any changes that you make to the code in the HTML inspector will be shown in the Document window when you close the HTML inspector, and any changes that you make in the Document window will be automatically updated in the HTML inspector.

✔ Tips

■ Select the Wrap checkbox to make the text wrap within the window.

■ Line numbers are indicated along the left side of the window.

About HTML

Chapter 4 is new to this edition of the book; it's called *Editing HTML*. It presents an intro to HTML. Although you never, ever have to look at the code if you don't want to, you can learn a lot about HTML by working in the Document window and then checking what the code is doing in the HTML inspector.

Unlike many Web page apps, Dreamweaver doesn't use made-up tags, nor does it rewrite your painstaking code. It does offer tools to help you clean up bad code or fix common errors, and it even synchronizes with other editors.

Chapter 4 discusses these tools, as well as the new Quick Tag editor, which allows you to change or insert single tags without leaving the Document window. It also describes how you can set Dreamweaver's preferences to set the rewriting and formatting options for your code.

Selecting Objects

Selecting objects in the Document window is similar to selecting them in any other program:

◆ To select a word, double-click on it.

◆ To select a line of text, click to the left of it to highlight it, or press Shift+Arrow to select a few characters at a time.

◆ To select an image, click on it.

◆ To select a table, right-click on it (Ctrl + click or click and hold down the mouse button on the Macintosh), and from the pop-up menu that appears, choose Table > Select Table.

When an item is selected, you can cut, copy, delete, or paste over it. You can also modify it with the Properties inspector.

If you select an item in the Document window and then open the HTML inspector, the item will remain selected in the HTML inspector, which is really handy for finding things in particular table cells or on pages with a lot of content (**Figure 1.20**).

Similarly, if you select some code in the HTML inspector and then return to the Document window, the objects you selected will appear highlighted in the Document window.

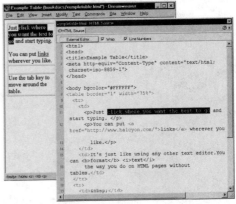

Figure 1.20 The Document window and the HTML inspector offer parallel selection: highlight code in one window, and it will also be selected in the other.

cell selected · code for cell selected

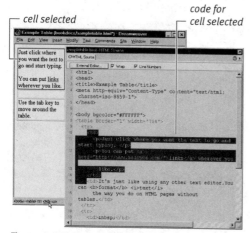

Figure 1.21 Click on one of the tags in the tag selector in the Document window's status bar to select the tag and everything it encloses. The tag I selected was <td>, a table cell.

To select code:

1. To select all the code and content that appears between a particular set of tags, first click on a word or image on the proper area of the page.

2. Click on the appropriate tag in the tag selector that appears in the Document window's status bar (**Figure 1.21**).

For instance, to select an entire paragraph, you can click on a word within the paragraph and then click on the <p> tag on the tag selector. This makes selecting links <a>, tables <table>, and the entire body of a page <body> easier.

✔ Tip

- You can also select a line of code in the HTML inspector by clicking on one of the line numbers in the left margin.

The Properties Inspector

The Properties inspector is a handy tool that changes appearance depending on which object is currently selected.

To display the Properties inspector:

1. From the Document window menu bar, select Modify > Selection Properties or Window > Properties, or press Ctrl + F3 (Command + F3). The Properties inspector will appear (**Figure 1.22**).

2. To display the entire Properties inspector, click on the expander arrow in the bottom-right corner of the Properties inspector (**Figure 1.23**).

If no object is selected, the Properties inspector will display text properties (**Figure 1.24**).

To modify object properties:

1. Select the object you wish to modify.

2. Display the Properties inspector, if necessary.

3. Based on your choices: click on formatting buttons, make menu selections from the drop-down menus, type numbers or names in the text boxes, and select checkboxes or radio buttons.

4. Some of your choices will be applied immediately; to make sure properties are applied to the selection, click on the Apply button (shown in **Figure 1.22**).

✔ Tips

■ All Properties inspectors except text have an Apply button (**Figures 1.22, 1.23**).

■ You can also display the Properties inspector by double-clicking on some objects.

— Apply button

Figure 1.22 The Properties inspector changes appearance depending on what item is selected. Image properties are shown in this figure.

— Apply button   *Expander arrow —*

Figure 1.23 Click on the expander arrow, and the Properties inspector will expand to show more options. This figure shows table properties.

Figure 1.24 Text properties are the ones you'll see most often.

There's an Apply Button?

Dreamweaver relies on an element that you may have seen in page layout programs such as PageMaker and Quark Express. These applications use inspectors that work like the Properties inspector; when you select an element, the inspector shows you the properties for that element. Therefore, the Properties inspector changes appearance with each subsequent selection.

Dreamweaver's Properties inspector also features a button called the Apply button, which changes appearance along with the inspector itself. When you modify an element, you can click on the Apply button to (guess what?) apply your changes.

If you select text, you won't see an Apply button, but if you select any other element, such as an image, a table cell, a Flash movie, a radio button in a form field, or a layer, the Apply button appears, displaying a graphic of the element that you selected. Usually, the name of the object—for example, Image or Radio Button—appears below the graphical button. In the case of an image, the Apply button appears as a tiny thumbnail of the image that you've selected.

The Apply button isn't labeled Apply as such; it bears the name of its object, instead.

Any time you make a change in the Properties inspector, you can click on the Apply button, or you can press Enter (Return) to apply your changes.

THE PROPERTIES INSPECTOR

The Launcher

The Launcher (**Figure 1.25**) provides an easy, one-click way to open some auxiliary windows in Dreamweaver. Click on the Launcher button, and the window will open. Click on the same button, and the window will close.

You can't minimize the auxiliary windows and palettes in Dreamweaver, but you can pop them open and closed easily with the Launcher.

Site

The Site button opens the Site window (Chapters 3 and 20), which you can use to make a local site on your hard drive that's parallel to the directory structure of the site on your Web server.

Library

The Library (Chapter 17) is a collection of HTML elements that can be shared from page to page.

HTML Styles

The HTML Styles button (Chapter 7) opens the palette by the same name, which lets you create text styles as you do in programs like Word or Quark.

Styles

The Styles button opens the CSS Styles palette, which keeps track of any custom style sheets you add to a page or site. Style sheets are explained in Chapter 13.

Behavior

The Behaviors button opens the Behaviors inspector (Chapter 15), which is used to set up JavaScript actions and test their compatibility with different generations of browsers.

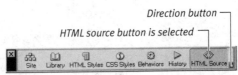

Direction button

HTML source button is selected

Figure 1.25 Click on one of the Launcher buttons to pop open the associated window. Note how the HTML Source button looks "pushed in."

History

The History palette, opened by pressing this button, keeps track of each action that you perform in Dreamweaver. It's discussed later in this chapter, as well as in Chapter 17.

HTML

Clicking on the HTML Source button opens the HTML inspector, which was discussed earlier in this chapter. We'll be using the HTML inspector throughout this book.

Launcher Tips

- Click on the Direction button to change the orientation of the Launcher.

- If you close the Launcher and wish to open it again, select Window > Launcher from the Document window menu bar.

- Even when the Launcher window is closed, a mini version of the Launcher will be visible in the bottom-right corner of the Document window, as seen in **Figure 1.11**.

- When a Dreamweaver window is open, its Launcher button will look like it's "pushed in" (**Figure 1.25**).

- In the Launcher bar in the Document window status bar, any active features will be "lit up."

- If you don't want the Launcher to appear in the status bar for some reason, you can change this preference. From the Document window menu bar, select Edit > Preferences. The Preferences dialog box will appear. In the Category list box, select Status Bar. In the Status Bar panel of the dialog box, deselect the checkbox marked *Show Mini-Launcher in Status Bar*. You can always reselect it later.

THE LAUNCHER

The Launcher, by default, contains the buttons described on the previous page. You can add buttons for additional palettes that you use a lot, or you can remove buttons for features that you don't use as often.

To add or remove buttons:

1. From the Document window menu bar, select Edit > Preferences. The Preferences dialog box will appear.

2. In the Category box at the left, select Floating Palettes. That panel of the dialog box will appear (**Figure 1.26**).

3. To add a button to the Launcher, click on the + (Plus) button in the Show in Launcher area of the dialog box. A pop-up menu will display the names of the palettes that don't currently have buttons in the Launcher (**Figure 1.27**).

4. Select the name of the item you want to add to the Launcher. The menu will close, and the palette's name will appear in the Show in Launcher list box.

5. To remove a button from the Launcher, select its name in the Show in Launcher list box.

6. Click on the - (Minus) button. The item will be removed from the Launcher.

7. When you're finished, click on OK to close the Preferences dialog box and return to the Document window.

You'll see your additions in the Launcher, and also notice that your subtractions are gone (**Figure 1.28**).

✔ Tip

■ If you remove a button, you can put it back later by following steps 1–4.

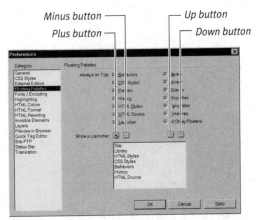

Minus button — Plus button — Up button — Down button

Figure 1.26 The Floating Palettes panel of the Preferences dialog box.

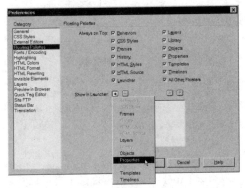

Figure 1.27 Click on the + button, and a menu will display those palettes that aren't currently in the Launcher.

Figure 1.28 I removed the Behaviors button and added the Properties (inspector) button.

Figure 1.29 All possible buttons are now in the Launcher, as well as in the mini-Launcher in the Document window status bar. I also clicked the Direction button to make the Launcher vertical.

Redecorating the Launcher

You can rearrange the order of the buttons, too.

1. Follow steps 1 and 2 on previous page.

2. In the Show in Launcher list box, click on an item whose position you want to move.

3. Click on the Up arrow to move it up through the list, or click on the Down arrow to move it down through the list.

Figure 1.29 shows a Launcher with all of the buttons in it, and in **Figure 1.30**, they're rearranged.

Figure 1.30 I rearranged the buttons in the Launcher, in order from my most-used to least-used button.

The Objects Palette

The Objects palette (**Figure 1.31**) offers shortcut buttons for placing common items on pages in the Document window.

To view or hide the Objects palette:

◆ From the Document window menu bar, select Window > Objects or press Ctrl + F2 (Command + F2). The Objects palette will appear.

The Objects palette consists of six panels: Common, Forms, Head, Invisibles, Characters, and Frames,

To change Objects palette panels:

◆ Click on the menu arrow at the top of the Objects palette. A pop-up menu will appear (**Figure 1.32**).

From the pop-up menu, choose Common, Forms, Head, or Invisibles.

The Objects palette will display the panel you chose.

To insert an object:

1. With both the current page and the Objects palette in view, click on the icon for the object you wish to insert.

2. If Dreamweaver needs more information to insert the object, a dialog box will appear.

3. Fill out the dialog box, if necessary, and then click on OK.

The object will appear in the Dreamweaver window.

To select and modify an object:

1. You can select most objects by highlighting them or clicking on them and the Properties inspector will display its properties.

2. Refer to the chapter in which the object is discussed for information about object properties.

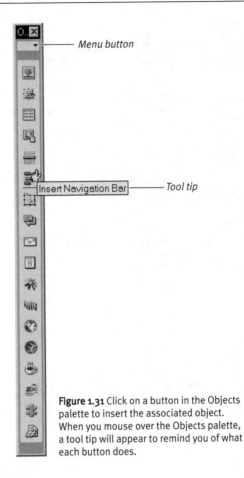

Menu button

Tool tip

Figure 1.31 Click on a button in the Objects palette to insert the associated object. When you mouse over the Objects palette, a tool tip will appear to remind you of what each button does.

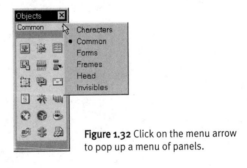

Figure 1.32 Click on the menu arrow to pop up a menu of panels.

THE OBJECTS PALETTE

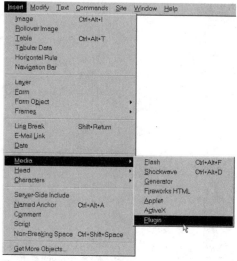

Figure 1.33 Objects available from the Insert menu.

Figure 1.34 Special Characters

Figure 1.35 Common elements

Dreamweaver Objects

All of the objects available to the Objects palette are also accessible from the Insert menu (**Figure 1.33**). The panels in the Objects palette are *Characters, Common, Forms, Frames, Head,* and *Invisibles. Characters* (**Figure 1.34**) are special text symbols such as copyright marks and Euro signs. Chapter 5 describes them. *Common elements* (**Figure 1.35**) include (from left to right):

- ◆ Images (Chapter 8)
- ◆ Rollover Images (Chapter 15)
- ◆ Tables (Chapter 10)
- ◆ Tabular Data (Chapter 10)
- ◆ Horizontal Rules (Chapter 6)
- ◆ Layers (Chapter 14)
- ◆ Line Breaks (Chapters 2 and 6)
- ◆ E-mail Links (Chapter 9)
- ◆ Date (Chapter 2)
- ◆ Flash Movies (Chapter 19)
- ◆ Shockwave Director Elements (Chapter 19)
- ◆ Fireworks HTML (Chapters 8 & 9)
- ◆ Applets (Chapter 19)
- ◆ ActiveX Controls (Chapter 19)
- ◆ Plug-ins (Chapter 19)
- ◆ Server-Side Includes (Chapter 15)

Form elements (**Figure 1.36**) appear on pages that feature interactive forms, which are discussed in Chapter 12. *Frame elements* (**Figure 1.37**) are actually prefab frames layouts and are described in Chapter 11. *Head elements* (**Figure 1.38**) are discussed on the Web site for this book.

Invisible elements (**Figure 1.39**) are:

◆ Named Anchors (Chapter 9)

◆ Comments (Chapter 4)

◆ Scripts (Chapter 15)

◆ Nonbreaking Spaces (Chapter 6)

Figure 1.36 The Form Elements panel of the Objects palette lets you drop forms and form fields onto your pages.

Figure 1.37 Frame elements

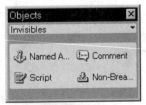

Figure 1.38 Head elements

Figure 1.39 Invisible elements

DREAMWEAVER OBJECTS

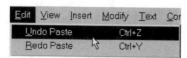

Figure 1.40 From the Edit menu, you can see what your last action was, so you can Repeat it or Undo it.

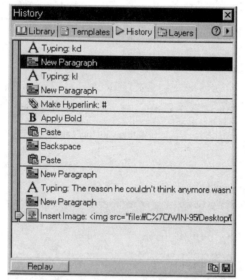

Figure 1.41 The History palette contains a list of the previous actions you performed during this session of Dreamweaver (before a Quit). You can repeat any one of them by selecting it and then clicking Replay.

About History

Dreamweaver stores the actions that you perform in a History file, similar to how a Web browser stores the sites you visit.

Dreamweaver 3 now supports multiple levels of Undo. For example, suppose you accidentally backspace to delete a table, and then you paste an image on the page. A single undo would un-paste the image. A second undo brings back the table.

To undo an action:

◆ Press Ctrl+Z (Command+Z)

or

From the Document window menu bar, select Edit > Undo [Action Name].

You can also repeat your last action.

To repeat an action:

◆ Press Ctrl+Y (Command+Y)

or

From the Document window menu bar, select Edit > Repeat [Action Name] (**Figure 1.40**).

You can also repeat any action you have performed while Dreamweaver is open.

To use the History palette:

1. From the Document window menu bar, select Window > History. The History palette will appear (**Figure 1.41**).

2. In the History palette is a list of actions you have performed. Click on an action, and then click on Replay to repeat the action.

You can also combine and even save actions. The History palette is described in more detail in Chapter 17.

ABOUT HISTORY

✔ Tips

- You can create custom objects and even add panels to the Objects palette. See Chapter 18 to find out how.

- You can view text in addition to (**Figure 1.39**) or instead of (**Figure 1.38**) images on the Objects Palette. View the Preferences dialog box (Edit > Preferences), and click on General. From the Objects Palette drop-down menu, select the option you want, and click on OK to apply your changes.

Drag to here

Click and grab here

Figure 1.42 Click on the name tab of the palette and drag it onto another. In this case, I'm dragging the HTML Source palette onto the History palette.

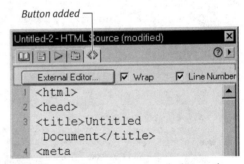

Button added

Figure 1.43 Now five palettes are stacked up, so they only take up the space of a single palette.

Stacking Palettes

You can stack any of Dreamweaver's palettes *except* the Properties inspector on top of one another to save screen space. In **Figure 1.41**, the History palette is stacked with several other palettes.

To stack a palette, click on its tab, drag on top of another palette (**Figure 1.42**), and let go. Names (or symbols, if space is tight) for the palettes will appear as tabs that you can click on to change from one palette to the next (**Figure 1.43**).

To unstack a palette, click on its tab and drag it off the stack.

BASIC WEB PAGES

Figure 2.1 The McSweeney's Web site (www.mcsweeneys.net) uses mostly text, but it still looks snappy.

Figure 2.2 Jamie Zawinski's home page (www.jwz.org) uses text and a few images, laid out in a table.

In the last chapter, we got acquainted with the Dreamweaver interface. This chapter describes how to use the Document window to create and save Web pages (**Figures 2.1–2.3**).

Most of the material in this chapter will be a review for people who have used nearly any document creation software at all. We'll also learn how to adjust the properties of a page, including the title and the page background.

This chapter also describes how to select and use colors in Dreamweaver. I'll refer to this material throughout the book.

In this chapter, we'll learn how to:

- ◆ Open a page
- ◆ Create a new page
- ◆ Save your work
- ◆ Save a copy of your page
- ◆ Adjust the page properties
- ◆ Preview the page in a browser
- ◆ Print the page from the browser
- ◆ Close the file

✔ Tips

- In this edition of the book, I've cut the basic rundown of putting content on your pages from this chapter. You can still find out what you need to know about text and images in the chapters about those things.

- A *file* is a chunk of related data stored by computer media—programs are also files. A *document*, loosely speaking, is a computer file created by a program such as a text editor or a word processor. An *HTML document* or *HTML file*, then, is a document that is written in the Hypertext Markup Language. A *Web page* (sometimes called simply a page in this book) is an HTML file that's intended for consumption on the Web. A *Web site* is a collection of Web pages, generally located on the same server. Finally, a *server* is a computer on the Internet that stores files and delivers them to other computers that request the files. A *Web server* specializes in Web pages.

- To find out about creating a local site and saving files within its framework, read Chapter 3.

Figure 2.3 Klaud Design (www.klaud.com) is the home of designer Zhenia Timerman.

Figure 2.4 Use the Open dialog box to select a file on your computer to open in the Document window. By default, the Open dialog box first looks in the last folder that you opened.

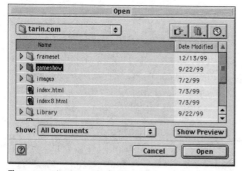

Figure 2.5 The Open dialog box looks a little different on the Mac, but it works the same way.

Figure 2.6 Open the last four files that you've edited in Dreamweaver by selecting their names from the File menu.

Opening and Creating HTML Files

If you have previously created HTML files you want to update with Dreamweaver, you can open them with Dreamweaver.

To open a file:

1. From the Document window menu bar, select File > Open. The Open dialog box will appear (**Figure 2.4**).

2. If the file extension is not .htm or .html (you're opening a .cgi or .asp file, for instance), select All Types from the Files of Type list box. (On the Mac, select All Documents from the Show drop-down menu. See **Figure 2.5**.)

3. Browse through the files and folders on your computer until you find the file you want to open.

4. Select the file by clicking on its icon. The filename will appear in the File name list box.

5. Click on Open. The file will appear in a new Document window.

Of course, sooner or later you'll also want to open files you create with Dreamweaver.

✔ Tips

■ You can open the last four files you viewed with Dreamweaver by selecting them from the File menu (**Figure 2.6**).

■ Chapter 4 discusses Roundtrip HTML, which affects how Dreamweaver treats HTML files created in other programs.

To create a new file:

◆ From the Document window menu bar, select File > New, or press Ctrl + N (Command + N). A new, blank document will appear.

When you open a file in Dreamweaver, a new Document window will open that contains the selected file. If you'd rather have Dreamweaver reuse the same window, you can change the window preferences.

To change the Open prefs (Windows only):

1. From the Document window menu bar, select Edit > Preferences. The Preferences dialog box will appear (**Figure 2.7**).

2. In the Category list box click on General. The General panel will move to the front.

3. Identify the checkbox marked *Open Files in New Window*. To turn off this option, deselect it.

4. Click on OK to close the dialog box and return to the Dreamweaver window.

✔ Tip

■ If you change your preferences to have only one Document window open, it will only contain one document (unlike some other programs that use the same window to hold multiple documents).

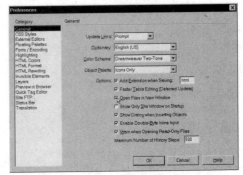

Figure 2.7 If you only want one Document window open at a time, you can change Dreamweaver's preferences. This is a good solution for computers without much built-in memory.

Text from Other Sources

When you paste text from another program, such as an e-mail or word-processing program, it will lose all its formatting, including paragraph breaks.

One way to keep this from happening is to use a word-processing program to save the text as HTML. Many word processors, including Microsoft Word, Nisus Writer, and Corel WordPerfect, include HTML conversion extensions (try File > Save as HTML, or consult the program's help files).

While these programs write atrocious HTML in some cases, they're just fine for coding paragraph and line breaks.

Another good shortcut is Microsoft Excel's Save as HTML feature, which saves spreadsheets as not-too-terrible HTML tables.

No matter what other program you use to create an HTML file, you can easily clean up the big boo-boos by selecting Commands > Clean Up HTML (or Clean Up Word HTML) and selecting which common mistakes you want to correct. Chapter 4 describes Roundtrip HTML in more detail.

Figure 2.8 Type a filename for your Web page in the File name text box, then click on Save to save it.

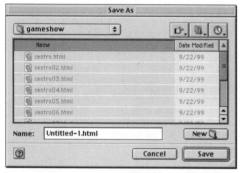

Figure 2.9 The Mac view of the Save As dialog box.

Dial the Right Extension

By default, PCs will save HTML files with the .htm extension, and Macs will save them with the .html extension. If you want to use a different extension, change the preferences. From the Document window menu bar, select Edit > Preferences, and select the General category. In the Add Extension When Saving text box, type your preferred file extension, whether it's html, cgi, or asp. You'll need to specify any exceptions to this extension by typing the full filename, such as dork.html, when you save a file.

Saving Your Work

If you're creating more than just an afternoon's entertainment, you'll want to save the work you do to the Web pages you make.

To save the current page:

1. From the Document window menu bar, select File > Save, or press Ctrl+S (Command+S). The Save As dialog box will appear (**Figures 2.8, 2.9**).

2. Make sure the Save In list box indicates the proper location in which to save the file. If not, browse through the folders on your computer until you find the one in which you want to save your work.

3. Type a name for your file in the File Name text box. The name cannot include any spaces, but you can use underscores (as in main_page.html).

4. Click on Save. The Save As dialog box will close, and you'll return to the Document window.

To save all open files:

1. From the Document window menu bar, select File > Save All.

2. All the named files that have been changed since the last time you saved will be saved now.

3. A Save As dialog box will appear for all open files that have not been named and saved.

Saving a Copy of a File

If you want to use a page as a template for another, similar page, you can save a copy of the page with a different filename. Guidelines for using Dreamweaver templates and creating custom templates are in Chapter 17.

To save a copy of a page:

1. Open the page in the Document window, if it's not there already.

2. From the Document window menu bar, select File > Save As. The Save As dialog box will appear (**Figure 2.10**).

3. Type a filename for the new page in the File Name text box.

4. Click on Save. The Save As dialog box will close and return you to the Document window.

The Document window will now display the copy of the file, as indicated by the filename in the Document window's title bar.

To close a page:

◆ Click on the close box, or select File > Close from the Document window menu bar.

Occasionally, you may open a page, make a few changes, and realize that something has gone horribly wrong. Or you may be fooling around with a document you have no intention of saving. In those instances, you can close without saving the changes.

To close without saving:

1. From the Document window menu bar, select File > Close. A dialog box will appear asking you if you want to save your changes (**Figure 2.11**).

2. Click on No. The dialog box will close, and a new, blank document will appear in the Document window.

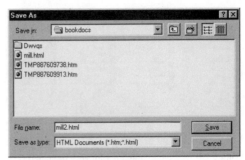

Figure 2.10 You use the same Save As dialog box to save a copy of a file as you do to save it in the first place. In this figure, we're saving the file mill.html as mill2.html, so we'll have two versions of the same file.

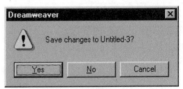

Figure 2.11 To close a file (such as a template, for example) without saving the changes, click on No when this dialog box appears.

Dreamweaver Templates versus Copying Files

You may be used to creating a Web page and then saving copies of it over and over in order to create many pages based on the design of the first.

Dreamweaver has a built-in template feature, described in Chapter 17. Dream Templates, as they're called, have their pros and cons. In those templates, you need to designate areas of the page that can be changed. Everything else on the page is fixed, and only those marked areas are editable.

This is a great idea for locking pages and giving basic data entry work to temps or interns (or marketing). On the other hand, sometimes it's just easier to do it the old-fashioned way and skip the fancy stuff.

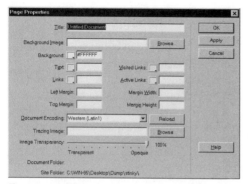

Figure 2.12 The Page Properties dialog box allows you to set options that apply to an entire page.

※ It's the Year 2000! Where's My Jet-pak? - Netscape

Figure 2.13 The title you choose for your Web page will be displayed in the Web browser's title bar.

About Document Encoding

If you're composing Web pages in a language that uses a non-Western (non-Latin) alphabet, you probably browse the Web using Document encoding for that language. Languages such as Chinese, Cyrillic, Finnish, Greek, Japanese, Korean, and some Eastern European languages use special text encoding to display fonts that can interpret and display the characters that language uses.

To set the encoding for your page so that Web browsers can load the proper set of fonts, select your language from the Document Encoding drop-down menu in the Page Properties dialog box.

To find out how to change the encoding for the entire program, see Chapter 4.

Page Properties

Page properties are elements that apply to an entire page, rather than to just an object on the page. *Visual properties* include the page's title, a background color or image, and the text and link colors. Other page properties include the document encoding and the site folders, if any.

To view page properties:

◆ From the Document window menu bar, select Modify > Page Properties or press Ctrl+J (Command+J). The Page Properties dialog box will appear (**Figure 2.12**).

To change the document title:

1. Open the Page Properties dialog box.

2. In the Title text box, type the title of your page.

3. Click on OK to close the Page Properties dialog box, or leave the dialog box open to modify other properties.

✔ Tips

■ The page title is stored in the document's <head> tag.

■ Unlike some other page creation tools, Dreamweaver doesn't prompt you to give your pages a title—in fact, it titles all your pages "Untitled Document" until you change the Page Properties.

■ The title you give your page will be displayed in the Web browser's title bar (**Figure 2.13**).

■ Choose a good title for your page, something more descriptive than "My Home Page." Many search engines use the words in the page title to index pages.

Colors and Web Pages

In Web pages, each color you can use is represented by a *hex code*, a six-digit number that represents a particular color.

There are many different color selections you can make for your Web pages, including background color, text color, link color, active link color, and visited link color. You can also choose colors for text selections, table backgrounds, table borders, frame borders, and layers.

This isn't even counting any colors that appear in images you add to your pages.

In general, it's a good idea to keep a fixed color scheme in mind while planning your pages. It's an even better idea to plan text and background colors with readability in mind; if you clash yellow text with an orange background, it may look striking, but no one will stick around to read a page that gives them a headache.

Choosing Color

You can choose from millions of colors or only Web-safe ones using the Color dialog box, which you can get to by clicking on the Color button on the Colors palette (**Figure 2.14**). Mac and Windows versions of the dialog box are quite different; we'll look at both in detail.

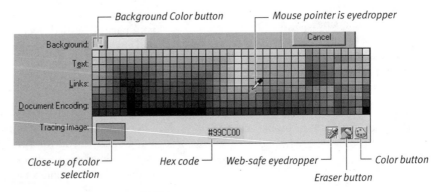

Background Color button — — *Mouse pointer is eyedropper*

Background: Cancel

Text:

Links:

Document Encoding:

Tracing Image: #99CC00

Close-up of color selection — — *Hex code* — — *Web-safe eyedropper* — *Eraser button* — *Color button*

Figure 2.14 Click on the Background Color button and the Colors palette will appear—then just click on a color to select it. That includes colors not only in the palette but anywhere on your desktop.

Color button

Background:	#FFFFFF	Cancel
Text:		
Links:		
Left Margin:		
Top Margin:	#999900	

Figure 2.15 Click on the Color button on the Colors palette to open the Color dialog box.

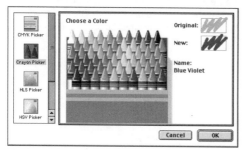

Figure 2.16 The Crayon picker, in the Color dialog box for the Mac. Click on a crayon to choose a color.

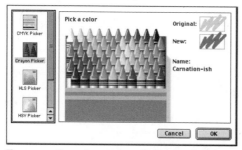

Figure 2.17 If you choose a non-Web safe color when using the Crayon Picker, the name will end in -ish.

Colors for the Mac

The standard Color dialog box for the Mac looks somewhat different. It offers several different tools for selecting colors: CMYK Picker, Crayon Picker, HLS Picker, HSV Picker, HTML Picker, and RGB Picker. You can use any of these tools by clicking on it in the list box at the left of the dialog box.

You open the Mac Color dialog box the same way you do the Windows one: On the Colors palette, click on the Color button (**Figure 2.15**).

The easiest color picker to use is the Crayon Picker (**Figure 2.16**).

To use the Crayon Picker:

◆ Click on a crayon in the box. The color that you choose will appear in the New color swatch, and its cutesy name will appear in the Name area.

✔ Tip

■ The crayons are all Web-safe colors. If you select a non-Web safe color with another picker, a name such as "Carnation-ish" will appear (**Figure 2.17**), indicating an inexact match to the closest Web-safe color.

You can select a color in any picker and make it a Web-safe color with the HTML picker.

To use the HTML Picker:

1. When you click on the HTML Picker button, the HTML Picker will appear (**Figure 2.18**) and convert any prior color selection into a Web-safe color.

2. To change colors within the Web-safe continuum, click on the Hex pairs (00, 33, and so on) on the R, G, or B color sliders. (RGB stands for red, green, and blue.) The hex code will appear in the HTML text box.

✔ Tip

■ To select a non-Web-safe color, deselect the Web color checkbox, and use the sliders to select whatever color you like.

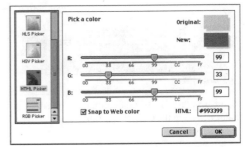

Figure 2.18 The HTML Picker, in the Color dialog box for the Mac. These colors are Web safe unless you turn off the Web Color checkbox.

Browser-safe Colors

You may have heard something about browser-safe color schemes. There are 216 colors that Netscape and Microsoft browsers on both Windows and Macintosh platforms use, and these colors are called "browser safe." The colors in the browser safe area all contain a 00, 33, 66, 99, CC, or FF pair in their hex code.

The Colors palette that you'll see when you click on any color selection button (**Figure 2.14**), in a dialog box or in the Properties inspector, is comprised of these browser-safe colors, some of which repeat in the palette's 351 squares. If you're planning your page around browser-safe colors, the Colors palette is a good place to start.

Additionally, you'll notice that the pointer for the Colors palette is an eyedropper rather than a regular pointer. You can use the eyedropper to select any color you can see inside the Dreamweaver window, including colors in images.

If the Eyedropper button 🖊 is pushed in before you click your selection, Dreamweaver will convert the color you picked into a Web-safe color, automatically.

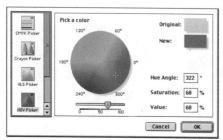

Figure 2.19 The HSV (Hue Saturation Value) Picker, in the Color dialog box for the Mac.

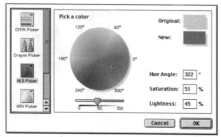

Figure 2.20 The HSL Picker (Hue Lightness Saturation), in the Color dialog box for the Mac, is quite similar to the HSV picker.

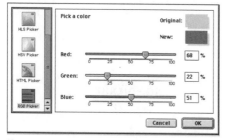

Figure 2.21 The RGB Picker (again in the Mac Color dialog box) uses the Red-Green-Blue values of visible light.

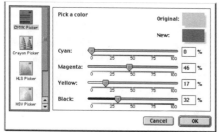

Figure 2.22 The CMYK (Cyan, Magenta, Yellow, and Black) Picker resembles the RGB picker, both on the Mac. Printers' inks use these four colors.

The standard color picker that's similar to the Windows Color dialog box is the HSV Picker (**Figure 2.19**). HSV stands for hue, saturation, and value. For those of you unversed in color theory, a *hue* is a specific named color, such as blue or red; the *saturation* is the difference between a given tone and the nearest gray; and the *value* is the relative lightness (tint) or darkness (shade) of the color.

To use the HSV Picker:

1. Click on a color in the color wheel. Your selection will be displayed in the New color box. That sets the hue and saturation.

2. Adjust the slider bar to make the color lighter (towards 100) or darker (towards 0). That's the value.

3. You can fine-tune any of the values by typing a number in its text box.

The HSL Picker (**Figure 2.20**) works the same way; the letters stand for hue, lightness, and saturation.

RGB and CMYK are two ways of measuring color by its components. RGB is red-green-blue; those are the primary components of white in visible light (as opposed to paint, where we think of the primaries as red, blue, and yellow). The CMYK scale is cyan, magenta, yellow, and black; these are the primary colors for ink, and most color graphics are printed using layers of these colors.

In both RGB (**Figure 2.21**) and CMYK (**Figure 2.22**), all colors can be represented by how much of each primary color they contain. You'll mostly want to use these pickers if you have the color values already—from Photoshop or Fireworks, for example.

In any case, you can type values in the color's text box or use the sliders to increase or decrease the amount of each primary color.

COLORS AND WEB PAGES

Modifying the Page Background

By default, Dreamweaver will set the background color of your page as plain white. You can choose a different background color, or use a background image instead.

To set the background color:

1. Open the Page Properties dialog box.

2. In the Background text box, type the hex code for the color you wish to use.

   or

   Click on the Background color button. The Colors palette will appear (**Figure 2.23**). Click on a color with the eyedropper to select it.

   or

   In the Colors palette, click on the Color button: 🎨. The Color dialog box will appear (**Figure 2.24**).

To use the Color dialog box (Windows):

1. You can choose one of the preselected colors by clicking on it, or you can select a slot for a custom color by first clicking on one of the Custom Colors boxes at the left of the dialog box.

2. In the Color dialog box, click on a hue (color) in the large colors box, and then click on a shade (lighter or darker) in the narrow panel to the right of that. The combination of your clicks will be displayed in the Color|Solid box.

3. To select this color, click on the Add to Custom Colors button. Your color will appear in the box you selected in Step 1.

4. Click on OK to close the Color dialog box. The hex code for the color you chose will appear in the Background Color text box.

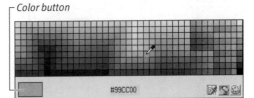

Figure 2.23 The Colors palette opens when you click on any Color button on a dialog box or on the Properties inspector.

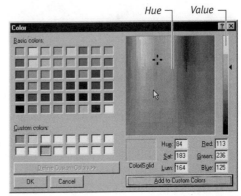

Figure 2.24 The Color dialog box. (1) Select a predefined color, or select an empty Custom Colors box. (2) Select a hue and (3) a shade. (4) click on the Color|Solid box and (5) click on Add to Custom Colors. (6) Click on OK.

Color-pickin' Tips

◆ When you open the Colors palette (**Figure 2.15**), the mouse pointer turns into an eyedropper that you can use to select a color inside or outside the Colors palette.

◆ If you have the Colors palette open and decide that you'd rather not change the color just now, click on the Eraser button 🖌 to return the color value to default, or click in a non-active area to close with no change.

◆ Read the sidebar called *Browser-safe Colors*, earlier in this chapter, to find out more.

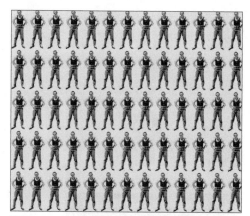

Figure 2.25 A tiled background image. The image repeats from left to right and then down the page.

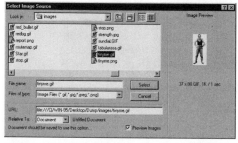

Figure 2.26 The Select Image Source dialog box, like an Open dialog box, lets you browse through your computer's files to select an image. The Image Preview at the right also displays the image's dimensions, file size, and download time.

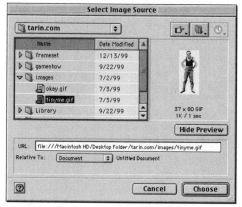

Figure 2.27 The Select Image Source dialog box on the Mac also offers a preview of the image; click on Show Preview to view it or Hide Preview to hide it.

Background images are supported by most browsers created after Netscape Navigator 2. A background image can consist of one large image, but more frequently, it's a smaller image that the browser window tiles so that it repeats in a contiguous pattern across and down the browser window (**Figure 2.25**).

To set a background image:

1. Open the Page Properties dialog box by selecting Modify > Page Properties from the Document window menu bar.

2. In the Page Properties dialog box, type the pathname of the image you wish to use.

   or

   Click on the Browse (Choose) button. The Select Image Source dialog box will appear (**Figures 2.26 and 2.27**). This is similar to the Open dialog box.

3. Browse through the files and folders on your computer until you find the GIF or JPEG image that you want to use. Click on the file icon so that the image's pathname appears in the URL text box.

4. Click on Select (Open) to close the Select Image Source dialog box and return to the Page Properties dialog box, where you'll see the pathname of the image in the Background Image text box.

5. Click on OK to close the Page Properties dialog box and return to the Document window, where your image will appear as the page background.

✔ Tip

■ You can set both a background image and a background color. The image will override the color in most cases, and the color will show up in browsers that support background colors but not background images. To find out about Tracing Images, see Chapter 14.

MODIFYING THE PAGE BACKGROUND

Setting the Text Colors

By default, the text color of a Web page is black; obviously, you'll want to use a different color for pages with darker backgrounds. You can also set colors for the links on your pages. Be sure to use colors that will be legible on the background color or image you're using.

To set the text colors:

1. Open the Page Properties dialog box by pressing Ctrl+J (Command+J).

2. In the Text text box, type (or paste) the hex code for the color you wish to use.

   or

   Click on the Text Color button. The Colors palette will appear (**Figure 2.28**). Click on a color with the eyedropper to select it.

   or

   In the Colors palette, click on the Color button. The Color dialog box will appear (**Figures 2.15 and 2.24**). Follow the instructions in the section called *Modifying the Page Background,* earlier in this chapter, and then click on OK.

3. Repeat steps 1 and 2 for the link colors, if you wish.

4. Click on OK to close the Page Properties dialog box, where your new text (colors) will be visible (**Figure 2.29**).

✔ Tips

- More details about what link colors are and how they work are available in Chapter 9.

- You can find out how to make selected portions of text a different color in Chapters 5 and 13.

- You can also type the *name* of a color, such as red or silver, in a color text box.

Figure 2.28 Click on the Text color button on the Page Properties dialog box.

Figure 2.29 Make sure your text color is visible and readable on your background color.

Converting Other Color Numbers into Hex

Colors are definable by a three-number sequence of hue, saturation, and value , or by another three-number sequence: the red-green-blue, or RGB, ratio. There are boxes for these numbers in the Color dialog box (**Figure 2.24**).

You can get the RGB sequence of a particular color from an image editor, like Photoshop or Paint Shop Pro, and then duplicate the color by typing the correct numbers into the right boxes in the Color dialog box. Then, of course, you should jot down that hex code for further reference. (You can copy RGB numbers *into* an image editor, too, if you want to duplicate a background color in an image for some reason.)

SETTING THE TEXT COLORS

Figure 2.30 Select File > Preview in Browser and then select a browser. Find out how to add browsers to your list on the Web site for this book.

Figure 2.31 Preview your page in a browser, no matter what state of the design process you've reached, to find out what it really looks like.

Previewing in a Browser

While Dreamweaver is pretty much WYSIWYG (what you see is what you get), there are some tags it doesn't support. Additionally, Dreamweaver's representation of HTML is a kind of fusion of Navigator and Explorer. To find out how your page looks in a particular browser, you need to actually use that browser to view your page.

To view your page in a browser:

1. With the page you want to preview in the Document window, select File > Preview in Browser > Browser Name from the menu bar (**Figure 2.30**), or press F12.

   ◆ If the browser isn't open yet, Dreamweaver will launch it and load the current page (**Figure 2.31**).

   ◆ If the browser is already open, Dreamweaver will load the current page into the last window you used in that browser.

2. To make changes, return to the Document window by using the Taskbar (the Applications menu on the Mac).

✔ Tips

■ Dreamweaver creates a temp file that it uses as the browser preview file. Pressing Reload or Refresh in the browser window may not show the most current version of the file. Instead, you'll need to repeat the steps for previewing.

■ For more details on previewing, and to find out how to add and remove browsers from the preview list, refer to the book's Web site.

■ You can also use the browser itself to open a saved file on your hard drive. Choose File > Open Page from the browser's menu bar.

Printing from the Browser Window

Dreamweaver's Document window does not include a Print command. You can, however, print a file after you preview it in the browser window.

To print a file:

1. Preview the file in the browser window as described in the previous section.

2. From the Web browser's menu bar, select File > Print. The Print dialog box will appear.

3. Verify the number of copies, the destination printer, and the pages to print in the Print dialog box.

4. Click on OK. The browser will send the document to the printer.

You can return to Dreamweaver by using the Windows Taskbar (the Applications menu on a Mac).

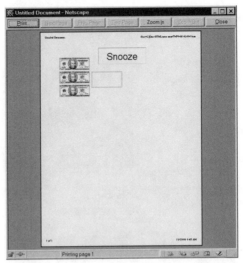

Figure 2.32 Navigator's Print Preview feature lets you see what you're getting before you send it to the printer. Good thing, because white text won't print on white paper (this is the same page we saw in Figure 2.31). You can change printing options in your browser. See the sidebar below.

Fancy-Schmancy Printing Options

Both Netscape Navigator and Microsoft Internet Explorer offer some convenient printing options. Navigator (Windows only) offers the File > Print Preview command (**Figure 2.32**). Navigator's Page Setup dialog box (File > Page Setup) offers options for printing backgrounds, black text (instead of printing a background in order to show text), and headers. (On the Mac, open the Page Setup dialog box and select Browser from the Options drop-down menu.) Internet Explorer's Print dialog box (File > Print) lets you choose frame printing options. You can also print a table of all the links on a given page, or print each page linked from that page.

SETTING UP A LOCAL SITE

What you probably want to do with this book is jump to the fun parts and start making Web pages. You can skip this chapter and make Web pages willy-nilly, but if you do, you'll miss out.

This chapter describes how to set up Dreamweaver so that it helps you manage a set of pages as a local site. A *local site* is a collection of pages on your computer that are destined to be part of a site on the Internet.

Sometimes half the battle of creating a Web site is figuring out where all the files are. If they're scattered all over your hard drive, you need to locate them, check all the links and image locations, upload the files, and then check all the links again.

Dreamweaver's file management tools don't preclude having to check your links, but they do make it easier to administer things.

Every time you create a link from one of your pages to another, Dreamweaver keeps track. Dreamweaver can help you manage your links so that if you move or rename a file, all links to that page will be updated.

About the Site window

Dreamweaver's Site window (**Figure 3.1**) is both a file-management tool and a full-fledged FTP client that helps you put your site online.

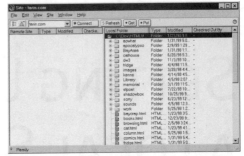

Figure 3.1 The Site window operates both as a local site management and site planning tool as well as an FTP client. This is the local site view. In Chapter 20, I'll discuss the remote site view and the site map view.

What's Where

This short chapter will teach you how to set up a local site—or several. First, you'll get acquainted with the Site window. Then, you'll designate a folder on your computer as the *site root folder*. You'll find out how to add, edit, and delete sites. And we'll look at some tips for file management in the Site window.

Chapter 9 describes everything you need to know about link management, including checking links, from a single page to an entire site. You need to set up a local site as described in this chapter as a prerequisite for using the fancy link tools described in Chapter 9.

Chapter 20, the last chapter in this book, covers preparing your site for prime time and then putting it up on the Internet. You'll learn to use the Site window as an FTP tool to download and upload files. Chapter 20 also describes some site management tools such as the site map and design notes.

You'll find more tips on site management on the Web site for this book, including how to use <head> tags to your advantage.

Refresh button

Figure 3.2 The Site window is a combination file management tool and FTP client.

The Site window

In the Site window, you designate a folder, or *directory,* on your computer or local network as a local site. This folder becomes the site root folder, and Dreamweaver uses its location to code relative links, including the paths for images. *Relative links,* which are described more fully in Chapter 9, are efficient shortcuts to pages within the same Web site.

Managing files in local and remote sites takes place in the Site window (**Figure 3.2**).

To view the Site window:

◆ From the Document window menu bar, select Window > Site Files.
or
Press F5.

Either way, the Site window will appear (**Figure 3.2**). When you first view the Site window, it will be empty. Before you can begin working with a local site, you must set one up on your computer.

✔ Tips

- All the column headings are also buttons; click on any one of them to sort the directory contents by that criteria.

- You can drag the borders between the column buttons to adjust the column width.

THE SITE WINDOW

Setting Up a Local Site

You can base a local site on the contents of an existing Web site, or you can set up a local site before any version of it exists at all. Before you do either, you need to pick a root directory (a home folder) for your local site.

To designate a new local site root:

1. From the Document window menu bar, select Site > Define Sites.

   or

   From the Site window's local site drop-down menu, select Define Sites. Either way, the Define Sites dialog box will appear (**Figure 3.3**).

2. Click on New to open the Site Definition dialog box (**Figure 3.4**).

3. Type the pathname of the local site root folder in the Local Root Folder text box.

   or

   Click on the folder icon. The Choose Local Folder dialog box will appear (**Figures 3.5** and **3.6**).

4. You can select an existing folder or create a new one:

   - To select an existing folder, click on its icon, click on Open, and then click on Select to close the Choose Local Folder dialog box and return to the Site Definition window.

   - To create a new folder, click on the New Folder button and type a name for the new folder. Double-click on its icon to select it and return to the Site Definition window.

5. In the Site Definition dialog box, type a site name in the Site Name text box.

6. Click on OK to close the dialog box.

The rest of the options in the Site Definition dialog box are explained in Chapter 20, *Managing Your Web Sites*.

Figure 3.3
The Define Sites dialog box lets you manage multiple local and remote sites.

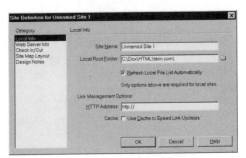

Figure 3.4 Set up local sites and connection information in the Site Definition dialog box.

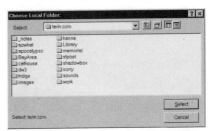

Figure 3.5 Use the Choose Local Folder dialog box to select a folder to serve as the site root for your new local site.

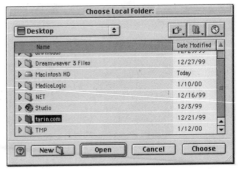

Figure 3.6 The Mac view of the Choose Local Folder dialog box. Click on Choose instead of Select.

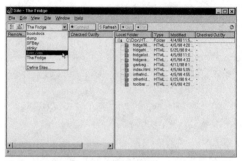

Figure 3.7 I have several different local sites set up for different projects in progress.

Figure 3.8 After you click on OK in the Site Definition dialog box, this dialog box (or another, similar one) will appear, confirming whether you'd like to create the cache.

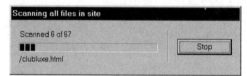

Figure 3.9 While the cache is being created, a dialog box will appear informing you of Dreamweaver's progress.

✔ Tips

- A new local site may or may not have any documents in it when you create it. You can create a local site based on an existing folder that's chock full of docs, or you can create a blank folder and download part or all of an existing site into it.

- Or, you can create a blank folder for a site that doesn't have any docs at all yet—because you're going to create them. I recommend setting up a local site at the point you begin using Dreamweaver, even if you haven't created a single page yet.

- You can create as many local sites as you want. I have different local sites for different parts of my main remote site (**Figure 3.7**).

- Dreamweaver can create an index, called a *cache,* of your local sites, which allows it to perform faster searches when you find or replace text (see Chapter 5). The cache also remembers when you link one file to another on your local site. You can then update a link site-wide when you move or rename a file (see *To rename a file,* later in this chapter; the process is described in further detail in Chapter 20). To create a local cache in which Dreamweaver stores information about the local site root, relative links, and filenames, simply leave the Cache checkbox checked in the Site Definition dialog box.

- When you create a site and click on OK in the Site Definition dialog box, a dialog box will tell you that the cache will be created (**Figure 3.8**). Creating the cache will take a few seconds (**Figure 3.9**).

- Remember that everything having to do with a remote site, including how to put your pages on the Web, is discussed in Chapter 20. That chapter also describes how site maps and design notes work.

It's All Relative

You may have noticed that Dreamweaver is picky about coding *relative paths* (aka relative links or relative URLs).. When you insert an image or a link to a local file on a page in Dreamweaver, a dialog box appears notifying you that the link will use a `file:///` path until you save the page. When you do so, Dreamweaver converts these `file:///` paths into the same relative paths that will be used online.

When you create a local site in Dreamweaver, it codes site-root relative paths based on the directory structure of the local sites. Take this example: Your local site root is `C:\HTML`. The current page is in `C:\HTML\Bubba`, and your images folder for the project is `C:\HTML\Images\Current`. When you save the page, Dreamweaver will make a relative link like this one:

```
<img src="/Images/Current/Bubba.gif">
```

Using local sites in Dreamweaver is easier than hand-coding relative links. I designate each project folder on my computer as a separate local site. Then, when I put the files online, the links remain intact.

You can choose to have Dreamweaver update all relative links when you perform a Save As, rename a page, or move a page into a different folder. You set this option in the Preferences dialog box. Press Ctrl+U (Command+U) to view the Preferences dialog box, and click on General to bring that panel to the front. From the Update Links drop-down menu, select Prompt, Always, or Never, and then click on OK to close the Preferences dialog box. See Chapter 9 for more about relative links.

To speed Dreamweaver in storing and updating the paths for relative links and filenames, make sure the Cache checkbox in the Site Definition dialog box is checked.

Figure 3.10 Select Site > Define Sites from the Site window menu bar (or the Document window menu bar).

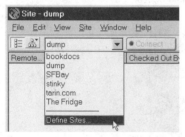

Figure 3.11 This drop-down menu allows you to switch from local site to local site; it also offers the quickest Define Sites menu option.

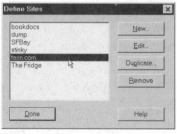

Figure 3.12 In the Define Sites dialog box, select the name of the site you want to edit.

Figure 3.13 Do you really want to delete this site? If so, click on Yes. No files will be deleted, but the site will be removed from Dreamweaver's list of local sites.

Editing and Deleting Local Sites

You can edit a local site if the information changes, or delete a local site that you're no longer using.

To edit a local site:

1. From the Document window menu bar or the Site window menu bar, select Site > Define Sites (**Figure 3.10**).

   or

   In the Site window, select Define Sites from the [site name] drop-down menu (**Figure 3.11**).

   Either way, the Define Sites dialog box will appear.

2. In the dialog box, select the name of the site you want to edit (**Figure 3.12**).

3. Click on Edit. The Site Definition dialog box will appear.

4. Make any necessary changes to the information in the Site Definition dialog box.

5. When you're done, click on OK to return to the Site window.

To delete a site:

1. Follow steps 1 and 2, above, to display the site information for the site you want to delete.

2. Click on Remove. A dialog box will appear, asking if you really want to do that (**Figure 3.13**). Click on Yes.

Dreamweaver will remove the site from the listing of local sites in the Site window, but it will not delete any files or folders from any remote or local site.

Site Window Tips & Shortcuts

You can perform a lot of common Dreamweaver file tasks with a couple of clicks.

To open a file:

1. In the Site window, view the local or remote site the file resides in.

2. Double-click on it. The file will open in the Document window (**Figure 3.14**).

To preview a file:

1. In the Site window, view the local or remote site the file resides in.

2. Right-click (Ctrl+click) on the file. From the pop-up menu that appears (**Figure 3.15**), choose Preview in Browser > [Name].

   or

   From the menu bar, select File > Preview in Browser > [Browser name]. The file will open in the selected browser.

To create a new folder:

1. In the Site window, click where you want the new directory to appear.

2. From the Site window menu bar, select File > New Folder (on the Mac: Site > Site Files View > New Folder). A new folder will appear.

3. Type a name for the folder, and you're done (**Figure 3.16**).

To delete a file or folder:

1. Right-click (Ctrl+click) on the file or folder you want to delete.

2. From the pop-up menu that appears (**Figure 3.15**), choose Delete. A dialog box will appear to confirm your choice; click on OK to delete the file.

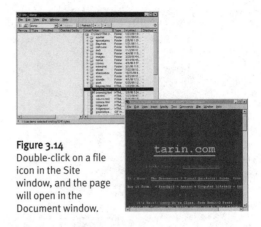

Figure 3.14 Double-click on a file icon in the Site window, and the page will open in the Document window.

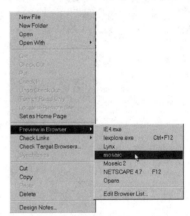

Figure 3.15 The pop-up menu for files in the Site window offers lots of handy shortcuts. Just right-click on a file or folder. Mac users: Ctrl+click to pop up the menu.

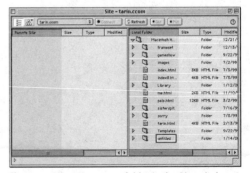

Figure 3.16 Creating a new folder in the Site window. Note that this is the Mac view of the Site window; it's pretty much the same as the one for Windows, yes?

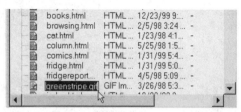

Figure 3.17 When a box appears around the filename, you can type the new filename.

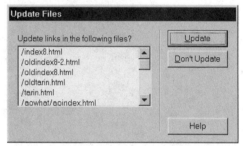

Figure 3.18 Once Dreamweaver knows about your links, either through a cache or by scanning the site, the Update Files dialog box will appear, and it will tell you which pages link to the renamed or moved page.

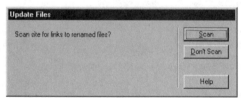

Figure 3.19 If you haven't created a cache for your site, this dialog box will appear and ask you whether you wish to scan for links to a renamed or moved file.

To rename a file:

1. Right-click (Ctrl+click) on the file, and from the pop-up menu that appears, select Rename. A box will appear around the filename (**Figures 3.16** and **3.17**).

2. Type the new filename and press Return. A dialog box will appear while Dreamweaver scans for links to this file. If it finds any affected files, the Update Files dialog box will appear, asking if you want to update links in that set of files (**Figure 3.18**).

   You may instead get a dialog box that asks you whether you wish to scan for files (**Figure 3.19**). If this dialog box appears, click on Scan to look for affected pages.

3. Click Update, and Dreamweaver will change links in any files that link to the page you renamed.

✔ Tip

■ There are also menu options for each of these shortcuts. Open, Preview, Check Target Browsers, Delete, New Folder, and many other options are available under the File menu on the Site window menu bar. On the Macintosh, the menu command for some options is Site > Site Files View > [...].

SITE WINDOW TIPS & SHORTCUTS

Moving files

You can also use the Site window like a file manager to move files around.

To move files from folder to folder:

1. View the file(s) you want to move by displaying their directory information. For multiple files, hold down Ctrl (Command) while clicking. To select contiguous files, hold down Shift while clicking.

2. Click on the selected file(s) or folder(s), hold down the mouse button, and drag them to a new location. See steps 2 and 3 under *To rename a file* at the top of the previous page to find out about updating links to renamed or moved files.

To toggle between local sites:

◆ In the Site window, select the name of the site you want to display from the Sites drop-down menu. The Site window will display the files and folders in the site you selected.

✔ Tips

■ Folders on local and remote sites that contain files will be indicated by a + next to the folder. To display the contents of the folder, double-click on it (**Figure 3.20**), or click on the + sign. On the Mac, an arrow appears instead of a + sign.

■ If you are connected to a remote site when you switch sites in the Site window, Dreamweaver will automatically disconnect you from the remote site, even if the two local sites are on the same server. Just reconnect to establish contact with the server again. See Chapter 20 to find out how to set up remote site information and connect to a server.

Figure 3.20 Folders with hidden contents have a plus sign to the left of them. Folders with their contents displayed have the files indented under them. To open or close a folder, double-click on it. The Mac uses blue arrows instead of plus signs.

EDITING HTML

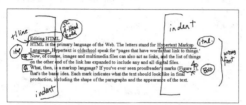

Figure 4.1 Marking up a page with HTML is just like marking up a page by hand with proofreader's marks.

HTML is the primary language of the Web. The letters stand for *HyperText Markup Language*. Hypertext is oldschool speak for "pages that have words that link to things." Now, of course, images and multimedia files can also act as links, and the list of things on the other end of the link has expanded to include any and all digital files.

What, then, is a markup language? If you've ever seen proofreader's marks (**Figure 4.1**), that's the basic idea. Each mark indicates what the text should look like in final production.

HTML evolved from a language called SGML (Standard Generalized Markup Language). In ye olden days of digital book and CD-ROM production, an editor used little pieces of SGML code called *tags* to mark, say, where the italics in a sentence started and stopped. Microsoft Word uses similar tags in its language, RTF (Rich Text Format), to indicate the formatting the user creates with buttons and menus.

A tag generally has two parts: an opening and a closing (**Figure 4.2**). The stuff in between any tags is what the tag modifies, whether that's text, images, or other tags. Tags generally operate in pairs, like quotation marks and parentheses do, and they can be overlapped, or *nested*, just like multiple sets of quotation marks (**Figure 4.3**).

For instance, you may have a sentence with a link in it. All the text, including the link, may be included in a paragraph tag. The paragraph may be in a table cell, which is in a table row, which is in a table (**Figure 4.4**). The table, and everything else on the page, is included in the basic tag structure of a page, which tells the Web browser that this is a bona fide Web page and where to go from there.

The browser reads all the tags on a page and then draws the page, filling in the contents and shaping the text based on what the tags have to say.

HTML is an easy language to learn because the tags it uses are self-explanatory for the most part (see **Table 4.1**). P is for paragraph, B is for bold, I is for italic, IMG means image, and so on. Not all the tags are that transparent, but if you follow along in the HTML Inspector as you modify your page, you can pick up quite a bit.

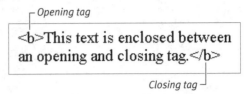

Figure 4.2 This text is enclosed by the two halves of a tag. The tag in this case is the <b> tag, which marks text as bold.

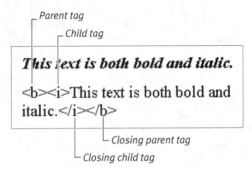

Figure 4.3 Notice that the tags envelop the text in order. The opening <i> tag is closest to the text, as is the closing <i> tag. The <b> tag envelops the <i> tag in the same way, and is called the *parent* tag for that reason.

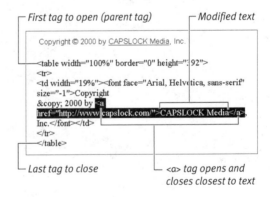

Figure 4.4 Here, the code gets more complex. The highlighted tag is the <a> tag, which makes a link. Notice that the <a> tag includes an attribute, href, which means that it's a Web link, and a value (in quotation marks), which is the address of the Web site. Moving outward from the <a> tag are the following tags: <font>, which designates a font face and size; <td>, a table cell; <tr>, a table row; and <table>, which defines the entire table. Most tables have more than one cell and more than one row, but this is simplified for illustration.

Head contents

Page title

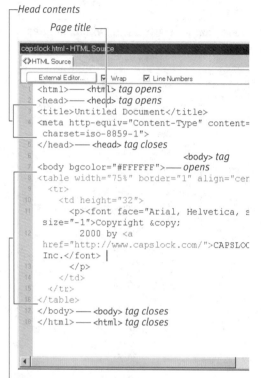

```
capslock.html - HTML Source
<>HTML Source
  External Editor...   ☑ Wrap    ☑ Line Numbers
1  <html>── <html> tag opens
2  <head>── <head> tag opens
3  <title>Untitled Document</title>
4  <meta http-equiv="Content-Type" content=
   charset=iso-8859-1">
5  </head>── <head> tag closes
6                              <body> tag
7  <body bgcolor="#FFFFFF">── opens
8  <table width="75%" border="1" align="cer
9    <tr>
10     <td height="32">
11       <p><font face="Arial, Helvetica, s
   size="-1">Copyright &copy;
12         2000 by <a
   href="http://www.capslock.com/">CAPSLOC
   Inc.</font> |
13       </p>
14     </td>
15   </tr>
16 </table>
17 </body>── <body> tag closes
18 </html>── <html> tag closes
```

Page contents

Figure 4.5 The table and its contents from Figure 4.4 are shown here in the context of the code for an entire page. The first tag on a Web page is <html> and the closing tag is </html>. All visible contents are enclosed within the <body> tag. The <head> tag, at the top of every Web page, contains defining information for the page, such as the language it's in and the title of the page.

Figure 4.6 Viewing the source of a Web page reveals the code behind it. From your browser's menu bar, select View > Page Source (or its equivalent command). To save the page for use in Dreamweaver, from the page source's menu bar, select File > Save As.

The best way to learn about Web pages is to view the source of pages on the Web that you like. You can save the page and open it in Dreamweaver to learn more. From your browser's menu bar, select View > Source, and you'll get a text window that shows you what's going on behind the scenes (**Figure 4.6**).

In most chapters of this book, I discuss specific tags and how they work (**Table 4.1**). In order to feel comfortable working directly with the code, you need to stop thinking of HTML as a programming language. It's really not. It's more of an electronic shorthand for Post-It notes and highlighter pens.

In this chapter, I'll continue to introduce the basic principles of HTML. You'll find out how to edit pages in the HTML inspector (**Figure 4.5**), as well as in the Quick Tag editor. You'll also find out how to clean up HTML mistakes made by software or humans.

Appendix D on the Web site for this book offers copious details about HTML preferences and about using external HTML editors in conjunction with Dreamweaver.

Table 4.1 introduces some common tags we'll be seeing over the course of the book. **Table 4.2** shows you what an *attribute* is—it's like an adverb that modifies the action of the tag.

Table 4.1

Common HTML tags

TAG	NAME	USE	ALWAYS CLOSED?
<HTML>	HTML	Document	Y
<HEAD>	Head	Document	Y
<TITLE>	Page Title	Document	Y
<BODY>*	Body	Document	Y
<H1>, <H2>...<H7>	Headings	Text Block	Y
<P>	Paragraph	Text Block	N
<BLOCKQUOTE>	Blockquote	Text Block	Y
<CENTER>	Center	Text Block	Y
<PRE>	Preformatted Text	Text Block	Y
 	Line Break	Text	N
<I>	Italic	Text	Y
<B>	Bold	Text	Y
<TT>	Teletype	Text	Y
<FONT>*	Font	Text	Y
<UL>	Bulleted List	List	Y
<OL>	Numbered List	List	Y
<LI>	List Item	List	N
<DL>	Definition List	List	Y
<DD>, <DT>	Definition Items	List	Y
<A>*	Anchor	Links	Y
<IMG>*	Image	Image Paths	N
<TABLE>*	Table	Table	Y
<TR>	Table Row	Table	Y
<TD>	Table Cell	Table	Y
<FORM>*	Form	Form	Y
<INPUT>*	Form Field	Form	N
<SELECT>*	Form Menu	Form	Y

Indicates Tags that usually take attributes

Table 4.2

Tags That Take Attributes, with Examples

TAG	EXAMPLE
<A>	<a HREF="http://www.nasa.gov"> Mars-2, Earth-0</a>
<BODY>	<BODY bgcolor="#FFFFFF" link="#FF3300" vlink="#CC99CC" alink="#0000FF">Your entire visible page goes here.</BODY>
<IMG>	<IMG SRC="/images/doggie.gif">
<FONT>	<FONT FACE="Courier, Courier New" COLOR="red" SIZE="+2">This text will appear in Courier, in red, and two sizes larger than normal text. </FONT>
<TABLE>	<TABLE width="100%" border="1" align="center" cellpadding="10" cellspacing="5">There must be rows and cells within opening and closing table tags.</TABLE>

Roundtrip HTML

Dreamweaver was designed for use by both codephobes and codephiles. If you never want to see a line of code in your life, you don't have to.

On the other hand, if you know how to tweak HTML to make it work for you, you've probably experienced the frustration of opening a page in a WYSIWYG editor and having it munged to bits by the purportedly helpful code engine of a program like FrontPage.

Dreamweaver writes valid code in the first place, and it uses no proprietary tags other than the JavaScript it writes (see Chapter 15). On the other hand, if you want to use mildly illegal code (such as wrapping a single <font> tag around an entire page instead of each paragraph), Dreamweaver can be coaxed into letting that slide.

Dreamweaver will not remove proprietary tags. Some made-up tags may be valid XML template markup created for a database application (see Chapters 17 & 18). If you write HTML improperly in the HTML inspector, however, Dreamweaver will mark tags that are unclosed, missing quotation marks, or badly overlapped in both the HTML inspector Document window (**Figure 4.7**). Click on the yellow mark in the either window to read a brief description of the error in the Properties inspector. Dreamweaver does have corrective features, which you can modify or turn off (see *Cleaning Up HTML*, later in this chapter). And you can use Dreamweaver simultaneously with an external editor. This group of features together comprises what Macromedia calls *Roundtrip HTML*.

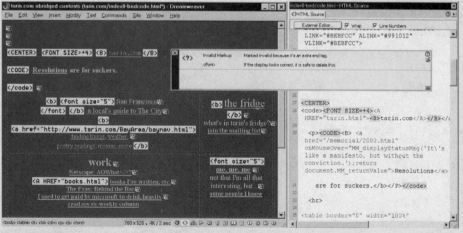

Figure 4.7 If you forget to close a tag, or if you overlap two tags improperly, Dreamweaver will mark the bad tags in yellow in both the HTML inspector and the Document window, with descriptions available from the Properties inspector. I went a little overboard here making errors.

Using the HTML Inspector

The HTML inspector (**Figure 4.8**) lets you both view and edit the HTML code for a page. While the Document window shows you the WYSIWYG or browser view of a page, the HTML inspector displays the code that makes the page look like that in the first place.

To view the HTML inspector:

◆ From the Document window menu bar, select Window > HTML Source.

or

Press F10.

or

Click on the Launcher or mini-Launcher's Show HTML Source button (**Figure 4.9**).

About selections

As I described in Chapter 1, any selections you make in the Document window will also be made in the HTML inspector (**Figure 4.10**), and vice versa.

Shortcut button for Find and Replace features

Filename

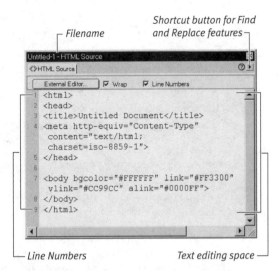

Line Numbers   *Text editing space*

Figure 4.8 The HTML inspector is Dreamweaver's built-in HTML code editor.

HTML Source button (mini-Launcher)

HTML Source button (Launcher)

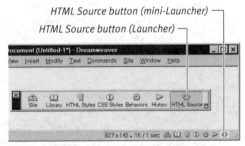

Figure 4.9 Click on the HTML Source button on the Launcher or mini-Launcher to view the HTML inspector.

The same text is highlighted in both views.

Figure 4.10 When I select text in the Document window, the HTML inspector also highlights the selection.

Wrap checkbox unchecked

Figure 4.11 I unchecked the Wrap checkbox. Even with the HTML inspector really, really wide, long lines of code scroll offscreen horizontally.

Numbered lines wrap onto unnumbered ones.

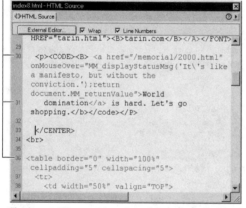

Figure 4.12 When text is wrapped, long lines of code, such as lines 30, 31, and 36 here, may wrap over onto unnumbered lines.

About wrapping

The text wraps to the window width in the HTML inspector. This is *soft wrapping*—no line breaks are inserted. You can toggle wrapping on and off by checking the Wrap checkbox (**Figure 4.11**). For more on wrapping preferences, see *Setting HTML Preferences,* later in this chapter.

About line numbers

Each line of code is numbered in the HTML inspector. A line of code may wrap over into an unnumbered line (**Figure 4.12**). Line numbers can be useful for discussing pages with your colleagues, as in, "Hey, Steph, the table I'm having trouble with starts on line 47." Line numbers—sans wrapping—should be the same in Dreamweaver and in line editors such as vi.

✔ Tips

- To select a line of code, click on its line number. To select a wrapped line in its entirety, turn off wrapping temporarily before you select the line number.

- The HTML inspector features a Find and Replace shortcut menu button (**Figure 4.8**). For full instructions on using the Find and Replace features of Dreamweaver, see Chapter 5.

Using the Quick Tag Editor

Describing how to use the Quick Tag editor is much harder than actually using it. The QT editor, as I'll call it, allows you to insert or edit HTML code without leaving the Document window. That means you save some time because you don't have to switch back and forth between the Document window and the HTML inspector in order to fine-tune your code.

It's true that there are instances you may find it easier to simply type the code you want in the HTML inspector. But if you're learning HTML as you go, the QT editor offers shortcuts and safeguards that virtually guarantee clean code, even if you've never written a line of HTML.

The QT editor (**Figure 4.13**) offers several different modes in which you can work with HTML. Which mode you work in depends on what items you select (text, tag, object, and so on) before you open the editor.

No matter what selection you make, though, you open the QT Editor in one of two ways.

To open the QT editor:

◆ Click on the QT editor button on the Properties inspector (**Figure 4.14**).

or

Press Ctrl+T (Command+T).

You'll see a typing area, and the words *Edit HTML, Insert HTML,* or *Wrap Tag.* Those are the names of the edit modes.

To close the QT editor:

◆ Simply press Enter (Return).

To move the QT editor:

1. Click on its selection handle; that's the gray part of the Editor (**Figure 4.15**).

2. Drag it wherever you like (**Figure 4.16**).

Figure 4.13 The Quick Tag Editor. Pretty unassuming looking, yes?

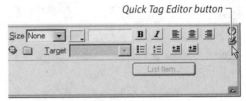

Figure 4.14 Click on the Quick Tag Editor button on the Properties inspector to pop open the editor.

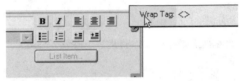

Figure 4.15 Click on the gray selection handle to drag the Editor away from the Properties inspector.

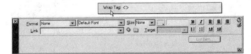

Figure 4.16 You can drag the Editor wherever you like.

Figure 4.17 The Quick Tag Editor in Wrap Tag mode. Use this mode to insert a tag around some text or another object.

Figure 4.18 The Quick Tag Editor in Insert HTML mode. Use this mode to insert more than one tag.

Figure 4.19 The Quick Tag Editor in Edit Tag mode. Use this mode to edit existing code.

Font tag selected

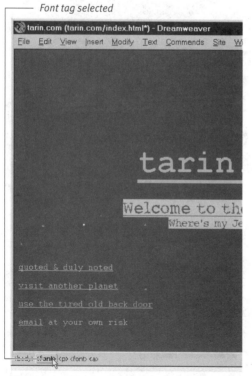

Figure 4.20 Click on a tag in the tag selector to highlight the entire tag and its contents. Right-click (Ctrl+click) on a tag in the tag selector to pop up a menu of editing options.

Working in Wrap Tag mode

Wrap Tag mode (**Figure 4.17**) allows you to select an object or some text and then wrap a tag around it. For instance, if you select some unformatted text and then enter the <center> tag in the QT Editor, the tag will open at the beginning of your selection and close at the end of it, and your text will be centered.

✔ Tips

- In Wrap Tag mode, you can only enter one tag at a time.

- The editor opens in Wrap Tag mode if you select text or an object rather than a tag.

Working in Insert HTML mode

Insert HTML mode allows you to insert as much HTML as you want at the insertion point. You can insert multiple tags if you like.

✔ Tips

- Insert HTML mode is the default Quick Tag editor mode if you haven't selected a specific object or tag (**Figure 4.18**).

- If you only insert an opening tag with Insert HTML mode, the closing tags will be inserted for you if they're required. You can move them afterward, if you like.

Working in Edit Tag mode

To edit an existing tag, you'll use Edit Tag mode (**Figure 4.19**). You can change the tag itself; or add, delete, or change its attributes.

✔ Tips

- If you select the contents of the tag, but not the whole tag, the QT editor will second-guess you and select the entire tag.

- The best way to select an entire tag is by clicking on it in the tag selector in the lower-left corner of the Document window (**Figure 4.20**).

To insert a tag using the QT editor:

1. In the Document window, select the text or object to which you want to apply a tag in Wrap Tag mode (**Figure 4.21**).

   or

   To work in Insert HTML mode, click where you want to insert the code.

2. Open the Quick Tag editor by clicking on the Quick Tag editor button, or by pressing Ctrl+T (Command+T).

   If the QT editor does not open in your preferred mode, press Ctrl+T (Command+T) again, until the QT editor shows the mode you desire.

3. After a second or two, the Tag Hints menu will appear (**Figure 4.22**).

   Select a tag from the menu by double-clicking it or pressing Enter (Return)

   or

   Type a few characters of your tag, and the menu will scroll to the closest tag alphabetically, so you can select it

   or

   If you wish to type code directly, instead of choosing it from the menu, click within the brackets to dismiss the Tag Hints menu.

4. Either way, when the tag you like appears in the brackets in the QT editor, you can do one of two things.

   ◆ To insert the tag as is, press Enter (Return).

   ◆ To add attributes to the tag, type a space. After the space, the Tag Hints menu will appear again (**Figure 4.23**).

5. Follow steps 3–5 for each attribute you wish to put in the tag (**Figure 4.24**).

Figure 4.21 Select the text or object you want to wrap a tag around, or just click in the Document window to use Insert HTML mode.

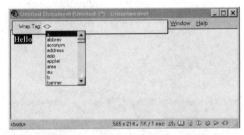

Figure 4.22 If you pause while typing, the Tag Hint menu will appear.

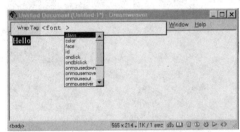

Figure 4.23 Type a space after the tag name to add an attribute, and the Tag Hint menu, which lists the available attributes for that tag, will appear.

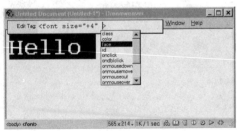

Figure 4.24 You can continue to add attributes by typing a space after each one.

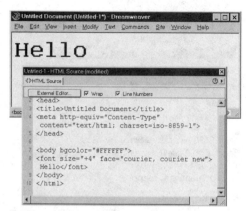

Figure 4.25 I did not add the closing </font> tag, but Dreamweaver did it for me. This happens both in Wrap Tag and Insert HTML mode.

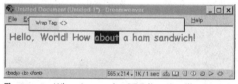

Figure 4.26 I selected just part of the text that's surrounded by a <font> tag.

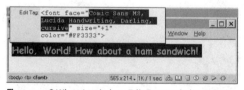

Figure 4.27 When I open the QT Editor, it will appear in Wrap Tag mode because I didn't select an entire tag.

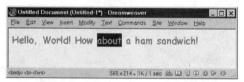

Figure 4.28 When I switch to Edit Tag mode by pressing Ctrl+T (Command+T), the Editor will select the entire tag's worth of text.

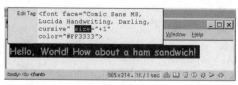

Figure 4.29 Press Tab to hop from one attribute to the next within the tag and the editor.

6. When you're finished, press Enter (Return) to close the QT editor and apply the code to the selection. Dreamweaver will close any tags you opened (**Figure 4.25**).

To edit a tag using the QT editor:

1. In the Document window, select the tag you wish to edit. (Click the text or object, and then click the appropriate tag in the tag selector). If you don't select an entire tag (**Figure 4.26**), Dreamweaver will select the whole tag, and possibly its parent tag.

2. Open the Quick Tag editor (**Figure 4.27**) by clicking on the QT editor button, or by pressing Ctrl+T (Command+T).

3. If the QT Editor does not open in Edit Tag mode, press Ctrl+T (Command+T) once or twice more (**Figure 4.28**).

4. You can edit the tag itself, or any attribute of the tag. To scroll through the attributes of the tag, press Tab (**Figure 4.29**); to move backward, press Shift+Tab.

continues on next page

5. With the tag name or an attribute name selected, you can type over it to change it. If you pause while typing, the Tag Hints menu will appear (**Figure 4.30**).

6. Select a tag from the menu by double-clicking it or pressing Enter (Return).

   or

   If you wish to type code directly instead of choosing it from the menu, click within the brackets or press Esc to dismiss the Tag Hints menu.

7. To add attributes to the tag, type a space. After the space, the Hints menu will appear again, listing available attributes for the tag, or available values for the attribute.

8. When you're finished, press Enter (Return) to close the QT editor and apply the code to the selection (**Figure 4.31**).

✔ Tip

■ If you Tab or Shift+Tab after you've edited an attribute, your changes will be applied to the tag immediately. To disable this feature, see Appendix D on the Web site for this book.

Figure 4.30 After you press Tab, your edits, if any, will be applied to the tag. If you pause while editing, the Tag Hint menu may reappear.

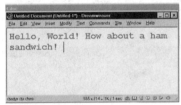

Figure 4.31 Now I'm all done. I changed two of three font tag attributes.

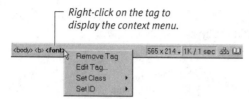

Right-click on the tag to display the context menu.

Figure 4.32 Right-click (Ctrl+click) on the tag in the status bar, and select Remove Tag from the menu that appears.

Selecting Parent and Child Tags

While you're editing tags, you may find it difficult to select a tag for whatever reason. You can toggle from the tag you've selected with the QT Editor to its immediate surrounding tag, called the _parent tag_, or to the immediate tag it envelops, called the _child tag_. This works whether you're working in the QT Editor or just in the Document window.

To select the parent tag:

◆ Press Ctrl+Shift+< (Less Than); on the Mac, it's Command+Shift+< (Less Than).

_or_

From the Document window menu bar, select Edit > Select Parent Tag.

To select the child tag:

◆ Press Ctrl+Shift+> (Greater Than); on the Mac, it's Command+Shift+> (Greater Than).

_or_

From the Document window menu bar, select Edit > Select Child Tag. If there is no child tag inside the selected tag, the tag will simply remain selected.

Removing a tag

You can also delete tags from within the Document window. Dreamweaver watches your back and won't let you remove some tags; for instance, the body tag is required.

To remove a tag:

1. Click on the object or text affected by the offending tag.

2. Right-click on the tag you wish to remove in the tag selector in the lower-left corner of the Document window (**Figure 4.32**).

3. From the pop-up menu that appears, select Remove Tag. The tag will be deleted.

About the Hints Menu

The Hints menu will appear after a few seconds when you open the tag selector. It's a regular old drop-down menu. To select a tag, scroll through the menu using the scrollbars or arrow keys, or type a few letters of the tag, and the menu will scroll down alphabetically. For example, type cen, and the menu will scroll to center. To enter a selection, press Enter (Return), or double-click the entry.

If you pause for a few seconds while editing or entering a tag or an attribute, the Hints menu will come back. The Hints menu will also appear for attributes of a tag if you type a space after the tag.

If you select the name of an attribute, available standard values for that attribute will appear. For example, the tag <td> (table cell) offers several attributes, including align. If you select the align attribute, the Hints menu will offer left, center, and right as available values. On the other hand, another attribute of the td tag is bgcolor. If you select that attribute, every code for every color will not appear. You'll have to type the hex code yourself, or save your changes and then select the color using the Properties inspector.

To make the Hints menu go away, click the QT Editor, press Esc, or just keep typing. If the Hints menu doesn't appear when you want it to, I'm afraid you'll have to close the QT editor and try it again, or just type the tag or attribute.

The Tag Hints menu contents are in a file called TagAttributeList.txt, inside Dreamweaver's Configuration folder. You can add tags, attributes, or values to this file, or you can delete esoteric tags you don't use. Make a backup of this file before you edit it.

To set preferences, see Appendix D on the book's Web site.

Figure 4.33 Leave a message for yourself or for future producers of the page by using the Insert Comment dialog box. Dreamweaver enters the brackets for you.

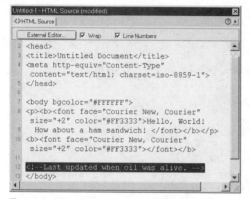

Figure 4.34 The comment appears in the HTML inspector, but not in the Document window.

Figure 4.35 You can view or edit your comment in the Properties inspector by clicking on the Comment icon.

Figure 4.36 You can view or edit your comment in the QT Editor by clicking on the Comment icon and pressing Ctrl+T (Command+T).

Inserting Comments

Comments are notes you want to leave for yourself in the code that won't show up in the browser window. You might want to add a reminder of when you created the file, when you last updated it, or who made the last revision.

You can also use comments to demarcate sections of a document, such as where a table begins and ends, or what part of the document constitutes the footer and copyright notice.

Comments look like this:

```
<!-- You can't see me -->
```

To add a comment:

1. In the Document window, click to place the insertion point in the area where you want the comment to appear.

2. From the Document window menu bar, select Insert > Comment

   or

   On the Objects palette (Invisibles panel), click on the Comment button.

3. The Insert Comment dialog box will appear (**Figure 4.33**).

4. Type the text you want to include in the comment in the Comment text box.

5. Click on OK to close the dialog box.

If you have invisible element viewing turned on (View > Invisible Elements), you'll see the comment icon: 🖐.

Otherwise, you can look at the comment in the HTML inspector (**Figure 4.34**).

✔ Tip

- You can view or edit the comments later on by selecting the Comment icon and viewing the Properties inspector (**Figure 4.35**) or the Quick Tag editor (**Figure 4.36**).

Setting HTML Preferences

If you work somewhere that has a house HTML style guide, it's probably specific about things like indenting (or not), tag case (upper or lower), and how text is wrapped. In production groups, the interaction of individual coders' pages with the entire site and with vi and CVS (two tools used in Unix environments) has a lot to do with these standards. Even if you work for yourself, setting up these standards is a good idea.

✔ Tip

■ More HTML preferences, including HTML Color preferences, Quick Tag editor preferences, and External Editor preferences, are discussed in Appendix D on the Web site for this book. HTML Cleanup preferences are discussed later in this chapter.

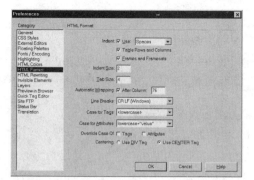

Figure 4.37 The HTML Format panel of the Preferences dialog box lets you get nitpicky about how your code is constructed.

To change HTML Format preferences:

1. From the Document window menu bar, select Edit > Preferences. The Preferences dialog box will appear.

2. In the Category box at the left of the dialog box, click on HTML Format. That panel of the dialog box will appear (**Figure 4.37**).

3. To turn off indenting altogether, uncheck the Indent checkbox.

   To use Spaces or Tabs for indent, select that option from the Use drop-down menu.

   For more on indenting, see the sidebar, *HTML Format Details*, on the next page.

4. You can have Dreamweaver automatically wrap text in the HTML inspector by checking the Automatic Wrapping checkbox.

   For more on wrapping, see *HTML Format Details*.

5. To set the format for line breaks, select Windows, Macintosh, or Unix from the Line Breaks drop-down menu.

   For more on line breaks, see the sidebar, *HTML Format Details*.

6. To set the case for tags, select lowercase or UPPERCASE from the Case for Tags drop-down menu.

   For more on tag case, see the sidebar, *HTML Format Details*.

7. To set the default tag for centering text, click the Use DIV Tag or Use CENTER Tag radio button.

   These tags are described in detail in Chapters 6 and 14.

8. When you're all set, click on OK to save your changes and close the Preferences dialog box.

HTML Format Details

Good code is nitpicky, right? This sidebar describes some of the nitpickier details and rationales for indenting, wrapping, line breaks, and tag case. Use this sidebar in conjunction with the steps on the previous page.

◆ **Indenting:** By default, Dreamweaver indents certain elements of HTML; the rows and cells in a table, for example. *Not* indenting may save some download time on very large pages.

To set an indent size (the default is two spaces or two tabs), type a number in the Indent text box. To set the tab size, because tabs in HTML *are* spaces, type a number in the Tab text box.

Some production teams indent on frameset pages even if they don't do so anywhere else. (It makes working with nested framesets easier.) To turn on indenting specifically for Frames and Framesets, check that box.

◆ **Wrapping:** To wrap within the HTML inspector window automatically, check the Automatic Wrapping checkbox. To turn off autowrapping, uncheck it. (You can wrap individual pages differently in the HTML inspector itself.)

The default column width for text-based programs like vi and Telnet is usually 76 or 80 columns (a *column* in this context is the number of monospace characters across a window). To set a different width, type it in the After Column text box.

◆ **Line Breaks:** Line breaks are done differently on different platforms. Because they're actually characters, a line-break character may show up in Unix if a Mac or Windows line break is inserted. If you work with pages that will be checked in to a document management system like CVS, be sure to check with the style guide or an engineer to verify your choices here.

◆ **Tag Case:** Folks are especially picky about whether tags and attributes are written in UPPERCASE or lowercase.

To set the case for attributes (the case can be the same or different from tag case), select lowercase or UPPERCASE from the Case for Attributes drop-down menu.

(Attribute values are always lowercase, as in `<TD ALIGN="center">`.)

You can have Dreamweaver override the tag and attribute case for documents that were produced in other applications or before you edited preferences.

To change the case of older documents opened in Dreamweaver, check the Tags and/or Attributes checkbox in the Override Case Of line.

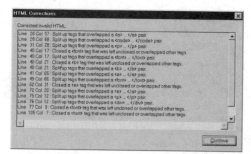

Figure 4.38 When you open a file with errors in it, you can get a prompt like this one that tells you what's being fixed. This is the file that I trashed in Figure 4.7.

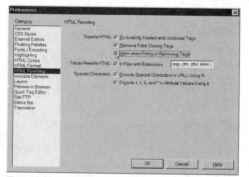

Figure 4.39 The HTML Rewriting panel of the Preferences dialog box. The Warn When Fixing or Removing Tags checkbox is turned off by default; check it if you want to see Figure 4.38.

Nesting Instincts

Valid, by-the-spec HTML asks that `<font>` tags be nested inside `<p>` tags. This means that each paragraph contains its own font formatting. This can take up quite a bit of room and add significant download time to large pages.

If you want to cheat on this, which the browsers allow, then turn off the Fix Unvalidly Nested and Unclosed Tags option. Then, you can use a single `<font>` tag to modify as many blocks of text as you desire.

Cleaning Up HTML

For the most part, Dreamweaver writes passable, clean code. If you modify the code, Dreamweaver usually avoids changing it back. On the other hand, some applications (most notably Microsoft products) write hideous code that begs intervention from the UN.

Dreamweaver offers several handy shortcuts for cleaning up gnarly code. You may have handwritten the code half-smashed on No-Doz and Jolt cola, or an intern may have demonstrated his or her lack of brilliance all over your site, or you may have produced pages in a lackluster editor.

Dreamweaver even makes some common errors that are easily fixed. There are three ways to clean up your code: opening a file, using the Clean Up HTML command, and using the Clean Up Word HTML command.

What Dreamweaver does on opening a file

Dreamweaver makes certain revisions to a page when it's opened in the first place. To get a prompt when these changes occur (**Figure 4.38**), or to turn off some of the automatic corrections, you can modify the preferences. If you're a beginning coder, it's best to leave most of these options as is.

To modify the auto-cleanup prefs:

1. From the Document window menu bar, select Edit > Preferences. The Preferences dialog box will appear.

2. In the Category list at the left, select HTML Rewriting. That panel of the dialog box will appear (**Figure 4.39**).

3. To see a prompt when Dreamweaver modifies your code, check the Warn When Fixing or Removing Tags checkbox.

4. For assistance in modifying the other attributes, see Appendix D on the Web site for this book.

Performing additional clean-up

Aside from Dreamweaver's automatic cleanup functions, you can have it perform more specific code-massaging at any point.

To clean up HTML code:

1. From the Document window menu bar, select Commands > Clean Up HTML. The Clean Up HTML dialog box will appear (**Figure 4.40**).

2. Dreamweaver lets you remove the following boo-boos (**Figure 4.41**):

   ◆ Empty Tags (Lines 8 and 9)

   ◆ Redundant Nested Tags (Line 11)

   ◆ Non-Dreamweaver HTML Comments (regular comments not inserted by the program; Line 13)

   ◆ Dreamweaver HTML Comments (This box may not appear. This option removes comments Dreamweaver inserts with scripts and the like).

   ◆ Specific Tags (any specified tag; Line 15). You must type the tag in the text box. Type tags without brackets, and separate multiple tags with commas. For example: `blink, u, tt`).
   Check the box beside the garbage you want to be removed.

3. Even Dreamweaver is guilty of redundancy when coding `<font>` tags (**Figure 4.42**). To combine all redundant font tags, check the Combine Nested `<font>` Tags When Possible checkbox.

4. To see for yourself the errors Dreamweaver catches, check the Show Log on Completion checkbox.

5. Ready? Click on OK. Dreamweaver will scan the page for the selected errors, and if you chose to display a log, it will return a list of what it fixed (**Figure 4.43**).

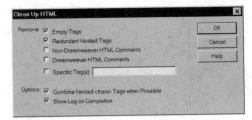

Figure 4.40 Choose which elements to clean up in the Clean Up HTML dialog box.

Figure 4.41 This "page" is really just a catalog of errors to be fixed.

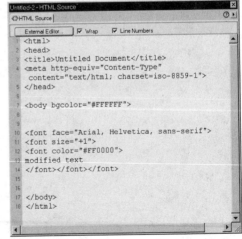

Figure 4.42 The three font tags on line 14 can be easily combined into a single font tag using the Clean Up HTML command.

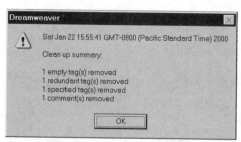

Figure 4.43 After cleaning up the stuff in Figure 4.41, this dialog box shows what was done.

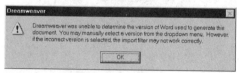

Figure 4.44 This dialog box will appear if you use Clean Up Word HTML to fix a file that wasn't created with Word, or that was created with an ancient version.

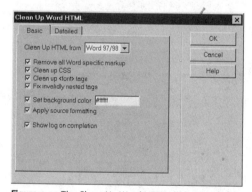

Figure 4.45 The Clean Up Word HTML dialog box for Word 97/98.

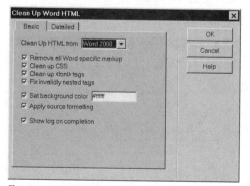

Figure 4.46 The Clean Up Word HTML dialog box for Word 2000.

Cleaning Up Word HTML

Most text documents, for better or worse, are prepared in Microsoft Word at one stage or another in the production process. Word (95, 97, 98, 00) offers a timesaving Save As HTML feature that puts in paragraphs, line breaks, links, and most text formatting. But it does it so badly!

Fortunately, the errors Word makes when converting pages to HTML are *consistently* bad. The Dreamweaver team figured out the error patterns and wrote a widget to fix most of them.

To clean up Word HTML:

1. In the Document window, open the page you saved as HTML using Word.

2. From the Document window menu bar, select Commands > Clean Up Word HTML.

   Dreamweaver will read the document info to determine which version of Word was responsible for the damage. If it can't detect this information, a warning will appear (**Figure 4.44**). Your document may not have been prepared in Word; you might want to run it through twice.

   In any case, the Clean Up Word HTML dialog box will appear, perhaps after you click on OK to dismiss the dialog (**Figure 4.45** and **Figure 4.46**).

3. If Dreamweaver detects the version of Word used to save the HTML, it will appear in the Clean Up HTML From drop-down menu. If not, select your version. (For Word 95, select Word 97/98). You may get a warning that the version is different from what Dreamweaver detected.

   continues on next page

4. The following options are available for fixing. For more details about Word-specific markup, see the sidebar, *Detailed Word Markup*.

♦ Remove all Word Specific Markup (tags that aren't standard HTML tags)

♦ Clean Up CSS (fixes modifications made using Cascading Style Sheets)

♦ Clean Up <font> tags (consolidates redundant text formatting)

♦ Fix Invalidly Nested Tags (rearranges tags nested in nonstandard order)

♦ Set Background Color. (Type the hex code in the text box. #ffffff is white. If you don't know the hex code, skip this one and apply the background color later.)

♦ Apply Source Formatting. (Makes modifications to the indenting, line breaks, and case selections. See *Setting HTML Preferences*, earlier in this chapter.)

5. To see a dialog box describing the fixes Dreamweaver made, make sure the Show Log on Completion checkbox is marked.

6. Ready? Click on OK. Dreamweaver will make the selected revisions and display a log if you asked it to do so (**Figure 4.47**).

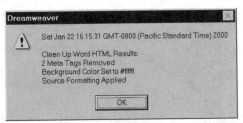

Figure 4.47 This dialog box is a log of the changes that were made using the Clean Up Word HTML command.

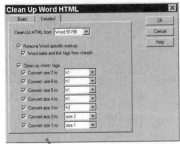

Figure 4.48 The Detailed panel of the Clean Up Word HTML dialog box for Word 97/98.

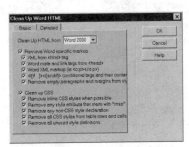

Figure 4.49 The Detailed panel of the Clean Up Word HTML dialog box for Word 2000.

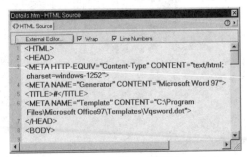

Figure 4.50 Word inserted these META tags; the two META NAME tags will be removed.

Detailed Word Markup

Word makes some singular, usually unnecessary additions to standard HTML code when you save out a Word file as HTML. If any of this proprietary code is something you want to address on your own, you can ask Dreamweaver not to remove it.

In the Clean Up HTML dialog box, click on the Detailed tab. That panel will come to the front (**Figure 4.48** and **Figure 4.49**).

In all versions of Word, the program applies its own <meta> and <link> tags in the head of the document. If these are useless to you, check the Word Meta and Link Tags from <head> checkbox (**Figure 4.50**).

◆ **Word 97/98:** Word 97 and 98 make peculiar choices when it comes to font sizes. To convert Word's font size choices to your own, click the checkbox for the font size, and then select a heading size or font size from the associated drop-down menu. For example, a wise choice would be to assign size 3 text to the default size in Dreamweaver. If you want to keep Word's size assignment, select Don't Change.

◆ **Word 2000:** Word is getting ahead of itself in using XML, or in other words, it includes proprietary code for perfectly vanilla HTML functions. It also makes a few more booboos.

To remove XML from the opening <html> document tag, check that box.

To remove other Word HTML markup (in the form of proprietary tags), check the Word XML Markup checkbox.

To remove pseudo-code, check the <![if ...]><![endif] Conditional Tags and Their Contents checkbox.

To remove both empty paragraphs and extra margins, check that box.

These details can be modified at any point before step 6.

WORKING WITH TEXT

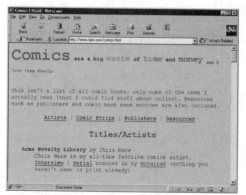

Figure 5.1 You can use different sizes, colors, and text styles on a single Web page, or even in a single paragraph.

What's Where

This chapter covers font sizes, font faces, text styles, font colors, special characters, finding and replacing text, and spell checking. Comments are covered in Chapter 4.

Chapter 6 covers all the basics of laying out blocks of text: paragraphs versus line breaks, headings, preformatted text, numbered lists, bulleted lists, definition lists, paragraph alignment, divisions, indent and outdent, nonbreaking spaces, and horizontal rules.

Text comes in all shapes, sizes, and colors— or at least it can do so on Web pages (**Figure 5.1**). In this chapter, we'll go over the very basic ways of working with text for very beginners. We'll find out how to accomplish rudimentary typographical changes: font size, font face, and font color, as well as various text styles. You can also add invisible text remarks, called *comments,* as annotations to your documents. And we'll also see how you can use Dreamweaver's word-processing tools, such as find-and-replace and spell check.

Basically, this chapter covers changes that you can make on the character level—that is, to individual words or groups of words. There's a lot more you can do with text, of course. If you want to learn more about automating your frequently used attributes, Chapter 7 addresses a new feature in Dreamweaver 3, HTML Styles, which allows you to define sets of text characteristics that you can then apply to either the character or the paragraph level of text. Web pages created using this feature are compatible with both newer and older browsers.

Chapter 13 also deals with manipulating text, using a feature of Dynamic HTML called *cascading style sheets (CSS)* to manipulate text over the course of a page or an entire site. This feature is compatible with Netscape and MSIE browsers version 4.x or later.

Placing Text

There are several ways to put text on your pages with Dreamweaver (**Figure 5.2**).

To put text on your page:

◆ Just start typing in the Document window!

or

◆ Select some text from another program or window, copy the text to the clipboard (usually by pressing Ctrl+C (Command+C)), return to the Dreamweaver window, and paste it there by pressing Ctrl+V (Command+V).

or

◆ Convert a text file or word-processed document to HTML, and then open it with Dreamweaver.

Once you have text on your Web page, you can treat it like you do in any other text editor. You can highlight the text and then copy, cut, delete, or paste over it. Use these commands:

◆ Copy: Ctrl+C (Command+C)

◆ Cut: Ctrl+X (Command+X)

◆ Paste: Ctrl+V (Command+V)

◆ Clear: Delete/Backspace

✔ Tips

■ If you copy text from another source and paste it into the Document window, it will not retain any formatting you've given it—including paragraph breaks. See Chapter 6 for information on using preformatted text.

■ If you want to copy some formatted text, but not the formatting, select the text, and then choose Edit > Copy Text Only from the Document window menu bar.

■ To paste text you've copied without any formatting, choose Edit > Paste as Text.

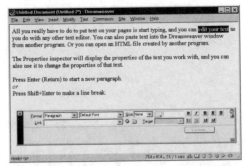

Figure 5.2 You can use the Dreamweaver Document window to type and edit text as you do with any other text editor.

Mom, What's Deprecated?

Custom style sheets are so nifty that they're making obsolete a lot of the physical font manipulations people have been so happy about for a while—most of the stuff in this chapter. The <font> tag, for instance, is eventually going to die quietly, along with its attributes—a process called *deprecation* (meaning the tags are being phased out of the HTML standard).

On the other hand, this won't be a quick or easy death. Tons of people still use Navigator and Explorer 2–4, and all the browsers that have been revamped in the same time period still support the <font> tag. And people who use versions of Navigator earlier than 4, and versions of Explorer earlier than 3, can't see all the wonderful things that style sheets can do.

If you want to design for a wide audience, you need to be able to use these deprecated tags for the older generation browsers, and find out how to get along without them in the newest incarnations. While the deprecated tags may eventually be phased out, they won't die until no one on earth is surfing with an out-of-date browser: not a likely prospect, unless the earth loses all electrical power tomorrow.

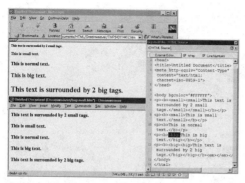

Figure 5.3 The big and small tags can be used for relative size changes. Note that the size changes show up in the browser window, but not in Dreamweaver's Document window.

Changing Font Size

There are several ways to indicate font size in HTML. Using style sheets (see Chapter 13), you can set a font size in points, like you do in word-processing and page-layout programs.

Without style sheets, however, you set font sizes relative to a base size. This base size is not something you can fix exactly, because every user has the option of customizing the basic font size in their browser program to whatever size they choose. The font sizes that you set will be relative to this basic font size, which is usually 12 or 14 points.

There are two separate scales you can use to determine size: the "absolute" 1–7 scale (which is still relative to the user's preferences) and the relative-to-base-font scale. Some folks also prefer using the very relative `<big>` and `<small>` tags.

Figure 5.3 demonstrates the use of the `<big>` and `<small>` tags. Nesting these tags isn't an HTML convention directly supported by Dreamweaver, but it works in browsers that support the tags.

To use these tags, simply nest your text within them:

```
<big>this is big text</big>
<small>this is small text</small>
```

If you're not comfortable adding code to your pages by hand, you may want to go back and read Chapter 4.

Language Encoding

Not everyone makes Web pages in the English language, and Dreamweaver addresses that. Western encoding is what most European languages use, and you can also set the encoding as Japanese, Traditional Chinese, Simplified Chinese, Korean, Central European, Cyrillic, Greek, Icelandic for the Mac, or any other non-Western encoding set you have installed. To do this, open the Preferences dialog box by pressing Ctrl+U (Command+U), and then click on Fonts/Encoding to bring that panel to the front of the dialog box. Select your language group from the Default Encoding drop-down menu, and click on the language in the Font Settings list box to select a font group. In order to use non-Western encoding, you need to have the appropriate fonts installed; Asian languages in particular require a system that supports double-byte encoding.

You can also set encoding for a single page in the Page Properties dialog box (Modify > Page Properties).

To use the absolute scale:

1. Select the text whose size you want to change.

2. From the Document window menu bar, choose Text > Size > and then choose a number between 1 and 7 (**Figure 5.4**).

   or

   In the Properties inspector, click on the Size drop-down menu, and choose a number between 1 and 7 (**Figure 5.5**).

In either case, the size of your text will change (**Figure 5.6**).

✔ Tips

- If you choose size 3, you likely won't see any change in size, because size 3 is the default font size unless you specify otherwise.

- If you change font size and then change your mind, select the offending text, and then select Default from the Text > Size menu.

- To change the size of all the text on a page, select Edit > Select All (Ctrl+A/Command+A) from the Document window menu bar. Then follow the steps described earlier. Or, you can change the base font size, as described on the next page.

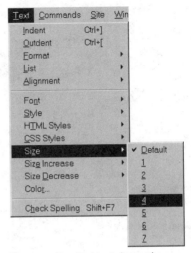

Figure 5.4 To adjust text size on the "absolute scale, select Text > Size > N from the Document window menu bar.

Figure 5.5 You can also choose a text size from the Properties inspector's Size drop-down menu.

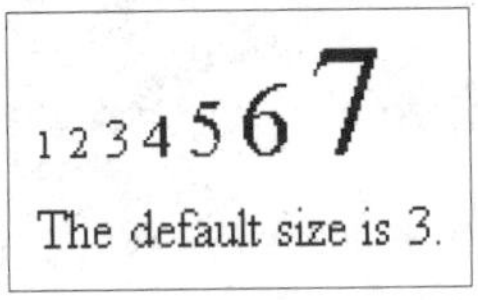

$$1\,2\,3\,4\,5\,6\,7$$

The default size is 3.

Figure 5.6 The absolute scale of text starts with the size 1 as the smallest available size and moves up to a maximum font size of 7.

CHANGING FONT SIZE

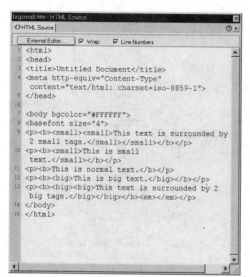

Figure 5.7 Here's the code for the page. You can see the <body> tag at line 7, and the inserted <basefont> code at line 8.

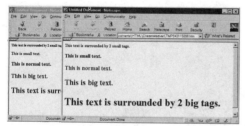

Figure 5.8 The page on the left is the same page we looked at in Figure 5.3. The page on the right is the same document, with the <basefont> code added. Note that the "normal" sized text is a size bigger, since I set the base font size to 4. Resetting the base font size works with the relative sizes I discuss in this chapter as well.

You can set a base font size other than 3 for your page, in which case all differing font sizes will be set relative to this new size.

To set the base font size:

1. Open the HTML inspector for your page by selecting Window > HTML from the Document window menu bar (or by pressing F10).

2. At the top of the document, locate the <body> tag.

3. Directly after the <body> tag, but before any other text, type the following line of code:

   <basefont size="n"> where *n* is a number between 1 and 7. Your code would look something like this:

   ```
   <body>
   <basefont size="4">
   ```

   although there may be other stuff inside the <body> tag (**Figure 5.7**).

4. Press Ctrl+S (Command+S) to save the changes to the code.

5. Close the HTML inspector by pressing F10.

Since Dreamweaver doesn't directly support the basefont tag, you won't see any size changes in the Dreamweaver window. However, any size changes you make will be based on the basefont number you specified, rather than on the default basefont size of 3. (You didn't go to all that trouble to set a basefont of 3, did you?) You'll see the change to the basefont size when you preview the page in your Web browser (File > Preview in Browser), as shown in **Figure 5.8**. See Chapter 2 for details.

You can use relative font sizes whether or not you change the basefont size. The effects of relative font sizes are displayed in **Figure 5.9**.

To use relative font sizes:

Select the text whose size you want to adjust.

◆ To increase font size, select Text > Size Increase from the menu bar, and then choose a number from +1 to +7 (**Figure 5.10**).

◆ To decrease font size, select Text > Size Decrease from the menu bar, and then choose a number from –1 to –7.

◆ To either increase or decrease size, select a number from the Size drop-down menu on the Properties inspector (as shown in **Figure 5.5**)

◆ To see a menu of all font sizes, select the text and then right-click (Ctrl+click) on it, and then from the pop-up menu, select Size (**Figure 5.11**).

You'll see the size change immediately, but the actual size relative to any basefont size you've set won't show up properly until you preview the page in a browser.

✔ Tips

■ You can also type a font size, whether it's absolute or relative, in the Properties inspector or the Quick Tag Editor.

■ The Size drop-down menu doubles as a text box.

■ As there are only seven gradations of font size, in total, the actual deportment of the font will vary depending on the base-font size. In other words, if your basefont size is 5, and you set the size increase to +7, the font will not get any bigger than size 7 (**Figure 5.9**).

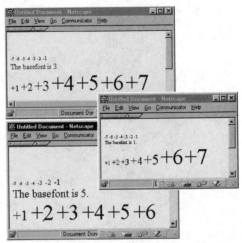

Figure 5.9 In these three examples, the basefont is 3, 1, and 5 (moving clockwise). Notice how none of the examples exceeds the maximum absolute size of 7 or the minimum absolute size of 1 (Figure 5.6).

Figure 5.10 To increase relative font size, select Text > Size Increase > N.

Figure 5.11 The context menu for selected text includes a great, big text size menu. Just right-click the text (Ctrl+click on the Mac).

Figure 5.12 In many browsers, the `<strong>` tag displays as bold and the `<em>` tag displays as italic. In Lynx, a text-only browser, all four tags are given the same emphasis. Other browsers, such as text-to-speech browsers, may interpret the `<strong>` and `<em>` tags differently.

Using Text Styles

You're probably used to using text styles, such as **bold**, *italic,* and underline in your word-processing program or page-layout tool. You can use these styles in HTML, too, to add emphasis or visual contrast to pieces of text.

There are two kinds of styles in HTML: physical and logical. *Physical styles* tell the text exactly how to look, while *logical styles* suggest an attribute and let the browser decide how to interpret it. For example, `<b>` (bold) is a physical style. On the other hand, `<strong>` (strong emphasis) is a logical style. While most graphical browsers display the `<strong>` tag as bold text, other software may treat it differently. Text-to-speech browsers, for instance, may read `<strong>` text with verbal emphasis.

Figure 5.12 contrasts the bold and strong tags, as well as the italic and emphasis tags.

✔ Tips

■ Text styles are not the same as style sheets. Text styles are one of the few font attributes that have not been deprecated, because there's more call to make them available to single words and not groups of layout elements. Style sheets, as explained in Chapter 13, offer even more text attributes than regular text styles, but not all browsers have style-sheet-processing capabilities.

■ Text styles as discussed in this section are also different from HTML styles, discussed in Chapter 7. HTML styles and CSS both allow you to create a set of attributes and combine a text style, such as bold, with another text attribute, such as color or font face.

The most common text styles in any document are **bold** and *italic*. You can also underline text (see Tips, below).

To make text bold:

1. In the Document window, select the text you'd like to make bold.

2. In the Properties inspector, click on the Bold **B** button. The text will become bold.

To italicize text:

1. In the Document window, select the text you'd like to make italic.

2. In the Properties inspector, click on the Italic *I* button. The text will become italic.

To underline text:

1. In the Document window, select the text you'd like to appear underlined.

2. From the Document window menu bar, select Text > Style > Underline. The text will become underlined.

✔ Tips

- If you prefer menu commands to the Properties inspector, you can select Bold and Italic from the Text > Style menu instead.

- The key commands for bold and italic are Ctrl+B (Command+B) and Ctrl+I (Command+I), respectively.

- Try to avoid underlining text that is not linked, unless the context demands it. Usability studies indicate that when users see underlined text, they assume it's a link to something.

- To remove a text style, reapply by repeating the key command, reselecting the menu command, or clicking again on the style button.

Physical Text Styles

Physical text styles (other than the ones on the previous page) are demonstrated in **Table 5.1**. Strikethrough and teletype are supported by Dreamweaver, and you can apply them by using the Text > Style menu.

Table 5.1

Physical Text Styles

Style	Appearance	Code Example
Strikethrough	~~strikes out text~~	<strike>strikes out text</strike>
Superscript	E=MC^2	E=MC²
Subscript	H$_2$O	H₂O
Typewriter or teletype	old fashioned monospace font	<tt>old fashioned</tt>

I Shot the Serif

Serifs are those curly things some fonts use at the ends of strokes in letters. They have their origins in ancient times when stonecutters had to make a terminating stroke in a letter in order to remove the chisel from the stone.

A *sans serif* font, then, is a font without any serifs. As illustrated in **Figure 5.14**, sans serif fonts, such as Arial and Verdana, have a different look than serif fonts.

Mono refers to a *monospace* font, which is the same as a fixed-width font. In a *fixed-width font*, each letter occupies the same amount of space. Most e-mail and Telnet programs use monospace fonts.

A *proportional font* is a font that's designed so that each letter, or character, takes up only as much space as it needs. Letter combinations such as *fi* and *th* fit together, rather than standing apart.

Proportional fonts are used for body text on most Web pages, while fixed-width fonts are used for the text typed into forms and for several text styles, such as teletype, code, and citation. Preformatted text, as described in Chapter 4, also employs a fixed-width font.

Courier New (Courier), used in **Figure 5.14**, is the most popular fixed-width font. Some browsers, however, allow their users to change their proportional and fixed-width fonts so that the choices don't necessarily correspond to their character.

Logical Text Styles

The logical styles that Dreamweaver supports are shown in **Figure 5.13** as displayed by most browsers. If you have a special concern as to how they're used in other browsers, you'll need to load the page into that browser.

To use a logical style:

1. In the Document window, select the text whose style you'd like to change.

2. From the Document window menu bar, select Text > Style > and then choose an item from the list. The text will change appearance to reflect your choice.

✔ Tip

■ To use a style that Dreamweaver doesn't support, apply the style to the code. See Chapter 4 if you need help.

Style Name	Tag	Uses
Emphasis	<em>	indicates importance
Strong Emphasis	<strong>	indicates strong importance
Code	<code>	programming code and scientific equations
Variable	<var>	in tutorials, marks placeholders for user-defined text
Sample	<samp>	samples of code output
Keyboard	<kbd>	in tutorials, indicates text the user should input
Citation	<cite>	a citation or reference
Definition	<dfn>	marks the first use of a keyword in educational texts

Figure 5.13 This figure illustrates how the logical text styles supported by Dreamweaver are displayed in most browsers. There are many other such styles; these are merely some of the most common. To mark up text with any of these styles, select Text > Style > *N* from the Dreamweaver menu bar.

Old Style and Old Style Light

Some text styles are hardly used anymore, and you might wonder what they were ever used for in the first place. When the computer scientists at CERN invented the protocols now known as the Web, the Internet was used largely by scientists working for the government or universities. The Web Tim Berners-Lee envisioned was an updatable library of papers, theories, data findings, and discussion. That helps explain why tags such as <acronym>, <citation>, <code>, <keyboard>, <sample>, and <variable> appeared in the definition of the HTML Language, now under the care of the W3C (The World Wide Web Consortium). Most of these tags are illustrated in **Figure 5.13**. The <acronym> tag does not change the appearance of text, but the code looks like this:

```
The <acronym title="World Wide Web
Consortium">W3C</acronym> is located
in Switzerland.
```

As with many of these tags, the <acronym> tag is used rarely; it's included in the Quick Tag Editor Hints menu, but not in the menu bar. It would be convenient for indexers if all uses of acronyms carried the tag with the title attribute defined; however, its use isn't widespread enough to be practical. Of course, there's probably a research lab somewhere that loves it for in-house cataloguing. If you're out there, let me know.

Arial, Helvetica, sans serif

Times New Roman, Times, serif

Courier New, Courier, mono

Georgia, Times New Roman, Times, serif

Verdana, Arial, Helvetica, sans serif

Figure 5.14 These are the preset font combinations available in Dreamweaver. You can include any number of fonts in a font combination; the browser will try each one in turn, from left to right. Serif, Sans Serif, and Mono are not fonts, but types of fonts. See the sidebar, *I Shot the Serif,* earlier in this chapter.

Changing Font Face

Unless you specify a font face, any text on your pages will appear in the user's browser window in their browser's default font face. Most users probably have Times New Roman (Times) as their default proportional font, although some may have changed it.

When specifying font faces in HTML, keep in mind that not every user has every font installed—far from it. Additionally, fonts that come from the same typeface family can be named several different things (such as Arial, Helvetica, and Univers), particularly on different platforms (Times New Roman, Times, New York).

Luckily, when you're specifying font faces in HTML, you can offer several choices. The browser will check to see if the first suggested font is installed, and then the second, and so on. If none of the recommended display fonts are available, the text will be displayed in the user's default browser font—not the end of the world.

Dreamweaver offers several preset font combinations, shown in **Figure 5.14**. You can also define your own font combinations.

To define a font combination:

1. From the Document window menu bar, select Text > Font > Edit Font List.

   or

   In the Properties inspector (**Figure 5.15**), choose Edit Font List from the Font Face drop-down menu.

   In either case, the Font List dialog box will appear (**Figure 5.16**).

2. Dreamweaver's existing font combinations will appear in the Font List text box. All system fonts installed on your computer will appear in the Available Fonts list box.

3. Locate your first-choice font in the Available Fonts list box and click on it.

4. Click on the Left Arrow button 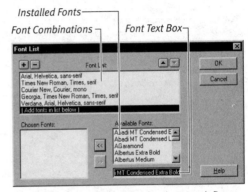, and the font's name will appear in the Chosen Fonts list box (**Figure 5.17**).

5. Repeat steps 3 and 4 for all the font faces you want to appear in this particular font combination.

6. To add the name of a font you don't own, type it in the text box below the Available Fonts list box. For example, you may have Bookman on your Mac, and to make Bookman Old Style your second choice, you need to type it here.

7. To remove a font you chose, click on the Right Arrow button ▶▶.

8. When you've chosen the right combination of fonts, click on the + button to add the font combination to the Font List list box.

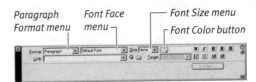

Paragraph Format menu — *Font Face menu* — *Font Size menu* — *Font Color button*

Figure 5.15 The Properties inspector allows you to set the font face for text, among other things.

Installed Fonts — *Font Combinations* — *Font Text Box* —

Figure 5.16 The Font List dialog box lets you define font combinations using any font on your computer.

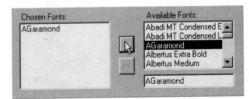

Figure 5.17 Select the font from the Available Fonts list box, then click on the left arrow button to move it to the Chosen Fonts list box.

CHANGING FONT FACE

Figure 5.18 I've added a font combination to the Font Face drop-down menu. You can select Edit Font List from the same menu to define your own font combinations.

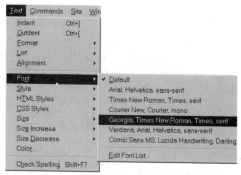

Figure 5.19 From the Document window menu bar, select Text > Font > and then choose a font combination from the menu bar. Any font combinations you added with the Font List dialog box will appear in this menu.

Figure 5.20 You can choose a font combination from the Properties inspector's Font Face drop-down menu.

9. When you're all done, click on OK to close the dialog box and return to the Document window. Your new font combination will be available in the Text > Font menu and in the Properties inspector's Font Face drop-down list (**Figure 5.18**).

✔ Tips

- There's no preview available in the Font List dialog box, and Dreamweaver doesn't allow you to display an individual font without adding it to the Font List. Therefore, it's advisable to view your font faces in another program (such as Word or PageMaker) so that you know what you're getting.

- You can change the order in which the font combinations appear in the list. Open the Edit Font List dialog box, and in the Font List list box, click on a font combination you'd like to move up or down in the list of fonts. Then click on the Up or Down Arrow buttons. When you're done, click on OK to close the Font List dialog box.

To set the face for an entire page:

1. With the document open in the browser window, select Edit > Select All from the Document window menu bar.

2. From the Document window menu bar, select Text > Font > and then choose a font group from the list (**Figure 5.19**).

or

In the Properties inspector, choose a font face group from the Font Face drop-down menu (**Figure 5.20**).

All the text on the page will change to the first installed font face on the list, unless it's formatted using a tag, such as <code>.

CHANGING FONT FACE

To set the face for selected text:

1. With the document open in the browser window, highlight the text whose font you wish to change.

2. From the Document window menu bar, select Text > Font > and then choose a font group from the list (**Figure 5.19**).

   or

   In the Properties inspector, choose a font face group from the Font Face drop-down menu (**Figure 5.20**).

The selected text will change to the first installed font face on the list.

✔ Tip

■ To remove any font face specifications, select the text whose font face you've changed, and then change the font face settings to Default Font, using either the Text > Font menu or the Properties inspector.

Basefont Face

You can set the basefont for a page, too, by adding the FACE attribute to the <basefont> tag. Follow the instructions in the section, *Setting the Basefont Size*, and to the base-font tag, add the attribute FACE ="Name". Your code will look something like this:

```
<basefont size="4" FACE="Arial">
```

Older versions of Explorer and some "third-party" browsers don't support this attribute; the worst that can happen is that the page's font face will still be the browser default.

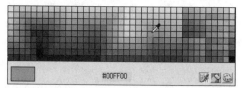

Figure 5.21 Click on the font Colors button, and then select a color by clicking on a color choice in the Colors palette. Note how the pointer becomes an eyedropper.

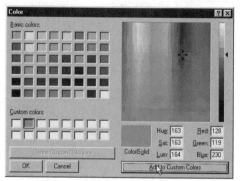

Figure 5.22 The Color dialog box offers a wider range of color choices. As described in Chapter 2, the Mac Color dialog box is somewhat different than this one, for the PC.

Color Recycling

Hex codes are defined in Chapter 2; in short, it's sufficient to say they have six (hex) digits.

To use the same color on another piece of text:

1. Select the hex code (including the # sign) from the Properties inspector's Color text box and copy it to the clipboard by pressing Ctrl+C (Command+C).

2. Select the next piece of text whose color you want to change.

3. Paste the hex code into the Properties inspector's Color text box, by pressing Ctrl+V (Command+V).

4. Press Enter (Return) and your text will change to that other color.

You learned how to set the text color for an entire page in Chapter 2. You can also set a different font color for specific pieces of text.

To change font color:

1. With your page open in the Document window, select the text whose color you want to change.

2. In the Properties inspector, type (or paste) the hex code for the color in the Color text box and press Enter (Return).

   or

   Click on the Colors button beside the Color text box. The Colors palette will appear (**Figure 5.21**). Click on a color to select it.

   or

   Click on the Colors button in the Colors palette 🎨. The Color dialog box will appear (**Figure 5.22**). Click on a hue and shade to choose a color, and click on OK to close the Color dialog box and return to the Page Properties dialog box. (For more details on using the Color dialog box, refer to Chapter 2.)

No matter the method you use, the color of the text will change to reflect your choice.

✔ Tips

- When you click on the Colors button on the Properties inspector, the cursor turns into an eyedropper. You can then click the eyedropper on any text or background color on the page, and the selected text will change to that color.

- To remove a font color you've set, select the text in question and then delete the hex code from the Font Color text box.

- To jump directly to the Color dialog box, select Text > Color from the Document window menu bar.

CHANGING FONT FACE

Special Characters in HTML

HTML is a language based on plain English text (also called ASCII), in which the characters you see on your keyboard are also the standard characters in the language. There are many other characters, however, that you may need to use on your pages. Special codes, called *escape sequences,* are used to reproduce these characters. The code for a copyright mark looks like this:

©

Dreamweaver now supports inserting these characters using a dialog box similar to Keycaps on the Mac or to Word's Insert Symbol feature.

Figure 5.23
Using the Special Characters panel of the Objects palette, you can add a special character to your text with a single click.

Those Wacky Characters

A few characters that aren't included in Dreamweaver's set of characters are the ampersand and the left and right angle brackets (greater-than and less-than signs). They require special codes because they are essential characters in HTML code that don't normally get printed in body text. Dreamweaver doesn't include them because you can type them in the Document window, and Dreamweaver will convert them in the background into code in the HTML inspector. If you're curious, those codes are:

&   &
<   <
>   >

A few other special characters not included by Dreamweaver are discussed on the Web site for this book.

Using the History palette described in Chapter 17, you can repeat a character without having to use the menu or dialog box. Also discussed in Chapter 17 is the Library, which is a good place to store updatable pieces of your site that get repeated from page to page, such as copyright notices.

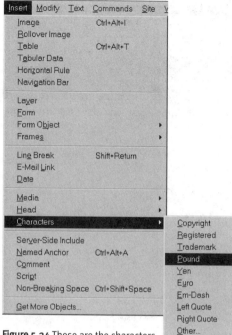

Figure 5.24 These are the characters available to insert using the Insert > Characters menu.

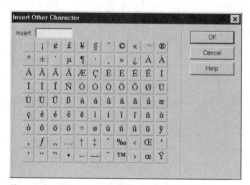

Figure 5.25 To insert a character other than the ones in the menu, select Other from the Insert > Characters menu, and this dialog box will appear.

To insert a special character:

1. In the Document window, click within the text where you want the special character to appear.

2. From the Document window menu bar, select Insert > Characters.

   If the character you want appears in the menu (**Figure 5.24**), select it. The character will appear in the Document window.

   or

   If the character you want doesn't appear in the menu, select Other. The Insert Other Character dialog box will appear (**Figure 5.25**).

3. When you see the character you want to use, click on it, and its escape sequence will appear in the Insert text box.

4. Click on OK to close the Insert Other Character dialog box and place the character on your page.

To insert special characters using the Objects palette:

1. In the Document window, click within the text where you want the special character to appear.

2. Click the menu button at the top of the Objects palette, and from the menu that appears, select Characters. The Objects palette will the display the special characters panel (**Figure 5.23**).

3. To insert a character, just click on it, or drag it onto the page. For more options, click on "Other," and see steps 2–4, above.

SPECIAL CHARACTERS IN HTML

91

Find and Replace

Dreamweaver can search your document and locate a particular piece of text. It can also replace one text string (a bunch of characters, whether they're code or words) with another.

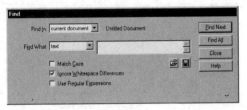

Figure 5.26 Type the text you want to find in the Find What text box.

To find a piece of text in the current page:

1. With the current page open in the Document window, select Edit > Find from the Document window menu bar, or press Ctrl+F (Command+F). The Find dialog box will appear (**Figure 5.26**).

2. Type what you're looking for in the Find What text box. This can be a whole word, a phrase, or part of a word.

3. To look for a particular case pattern (upper or lower), place a check mark in the Match Case checkbox.

4. To look for text and ignore spacing differences (i.e., to find both "tophat" and "top hat"), place a check mark in the Ignore Whitespace Differences checkbox.

5. Click on Find Next. If Dreamweaver finds what you're looking for, it will highlight the text in question on the current page (although you may have to move the Find dialog box to see it).

6. Click on Close to close the Find dialog box.

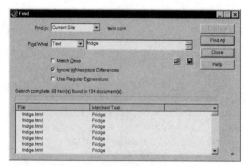

Figure 5.27 I selected Current Site from the Find In drop-down menu, and then clicked Find All. The dialog box expanded to show me a list of every instance of my search string. I can double-click any entry to open it.

✔ Tips

- If Dreamweaver can't find the text in question, a dialog box will appear telling you it didn't find the search item.

- To find the same item again (even on a different page), select Edit > Find Next from the Document window menu bar, or press F3.

- You can also use the Find command in the HTML inspector. Right-click the HTML inspector to see the pop-up menu.

- Click on Find All to pop up a list box containing all instances of your query (**Figure 5.27**).

Seek and Ye Shall Find

Dreamweaver includes some exhaustive search features for the current page, a local directory, or an entire local site. You can also use regular expressions and load or save searches.

To search an entire local site, a page from that site must be open. (See Chapter 3 for more) Select Current Site from the Find In menu to search the group of folders that comprises your site.

To search a local directory, select Folder from the Find In menu. Type the name of the directory in the text box, or click the folder icon to browse.

You can also choose what type of text to find by selecting one of these options from the Find What drop-down menu:

- **Text** Regular old text.
- **HTML Source** Searches text and tags.
- **HTML Tags** HTML tags and attributes, ignoring text not in tags.
- **Text (Advanced)** Defines a search for text within or outside tags. Additional menus include one that lets you choose "inside tag" or "not inside tag," and a menu to choose tags. Click on + to add additional search options for attributes.
- **Regular Expressions** are special text descriptors that let you refine a search. To enable regular expressions, select that checkbox. To find out more about Regular Expressions, see this book's Web site.

You can save a search query by clicking on the Disk icon. To load it later, click on the Folder icon and select the file.

To replace one piece of text with another:

1. From the Document window menu bar, select Edit > Replace, or press Ctrl+H (Command+H). The Replace dialog box will appear (**Figure 5.28**).

2. Type the text you want to destroy in the Find What text box.

3. Type the text you want to replace it with in the Replace With text box.

4. If you want to restrict the search to a specific case pattern (upper or lower), place a check mark in the Match case checkbox.

5. To look for text and ignore spacing differences (i.e., to find both "tophat" and "top hat"), place a check mark in the Ignore Whitespace Differences checkbox.

6. To supervise the search, click on Find Next, and when Dreamweaver finds an instance of the Find text string (the words or tags in the Find text box), it will highlight it in the document window. Then, you can click on Replace to supplant it with the text in the Replace text box.

   or

   To have Dreamweaver automatically replace all Find What text with the Replace With text, click on Replace All. A dialog box will appear informing you about how many replacements were made.

7. When you're all done, click on Cancel to return to the Document window.

✔ Tip

■ For advanced search tips see the previous page.

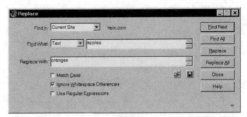

Figure 5.28 Type the text you want to find in the Find What text box, and the text you want to replace it with in the Replace With text box.

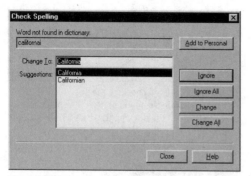

Figure 5.29 The Check Spelling dialog box allows you to ignore the unrecognized word, add it to your personal dictionary, or change it by typing it into the Change To text box or selecting a word from the Suggestions list box.

Checking Your Spelling

One nice thing about using a WYSIWYG editor to do HTML is that you can check the spelling on your pages without the spell checker constantly stopping to ask you about tags or URLs. You can check the spelling of an individual selection or an entire page.

To check the spelling of a page:

1. With the page in question open in the Document window, click to place the insertion point at the beginning of the page (or the place at which you'd like to begin the spell check).

2. From the Document window menu bar, select Text > Check Spelling, or press Shift+F7. The Check Spelling dialog box will appear (**Figure 5.29**).

3. When Dreamweaver finds the first questionable word, that word will appear in the Word Not Found in Dictionary text box. You have several options here:

   ◆ If the word is spelled correctly, click on Ignore.

   ◆ If the word is spelled correctly, and you think it might appear more than once on your page, click on Ignore All.

   ◆ If the word is misspelled, and the correct spelling appears in the Suggestions list box, click on the correct word, and then click on Change.

   ◆ If you think the word may be misspelled more than once, click on the correct word in the Suggestions list box, and then click on Change All.

continues on next page

♦ You can also manually correct the word by typing the correction in the Change To text box and then clicking on Change.

Make this choice for each word the spell check questions.

4. When the spell check reaches the end of the page, Dreamweaver may ask you if you want to check the beginning of the document (**Figure 5.30**). It's usually a good idea to click on Yes.

5. When the spell check is complete (including cases where there are no spelling errors), a dialog box will appear telling you so (**Figure 5.31**). It will also report the number of "errors." These errors include words not in the dictionary that you chose to ignore, such as an unusual proper name like Ronkowski or Gravity7. Click on OK to close this dialog box and return to the Document window.

✔ Tips

■ If a word is spelled correctly but is not in the dictionary, and you'd like to add this word to the custom dictionary, click on the Add to Personal button in the Check Spelling dialog box. The word will be added to your personal dictionary, and future spell checks will not question this word. Keep in mind, though, that you may also have to add variations on the word, such as plurals (*gorrillafishes*) or possessives (*Dorkface's*).

■ To spell check a single word or phrase, highlight the text in question, and then start the spell check as described in Step 1. If you want to skip the rest of the page, when the dialog box appears asking you if you want to check the rest of the document (shown back in **Figure 5.30**), click on No, and the spell check will go away.

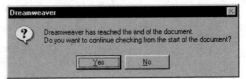

Figure 5.30 If you are checking the spelling of a selection, click on No. If you started the spell check partway through the document, click on Yes.

Figure 5.31 When the spell check is complete, you'll be told how many errors were found.

PARAGRAPHS AND LAYOUT

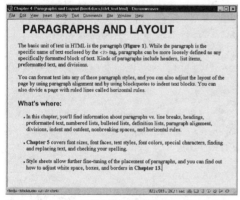

Figure 6.1 I converted this page into HTML by applying paragraph breaks, two kinds of headings, blockquotes, and a bulleted list. I also used the Arial font face for the headings, and applied the bold and <tt> styles in a few places, as described in Chapter 5. If I had wanted to replicate the exact layout of this page, I would have used tables, which are covered in Chapter 10.

The basic unit of text in HTML is the paragraph (**Figure 6.1**). While the paragraph is the specific name of text enclosed by the <p> tag, paragraphs can be more loosely defined as any specifically formatted block of text. Paragraph types include headers, list items, preformatted text, and divisions.

You can format text into any of these paragraph styles, and you can adjust the layout of the page by using paragraph alignment and by using blockquotes to indent text blocks. You can also divide a page with ruled lines called *horizontal rules.*

What's Where

In this chapter you'll find information about paragraphs versus line breaks, headings, preformatted text, numbered lists, bulleted lists, definition lists, paragraph alignment, divisions, indent and outdent, nonbreaking spaces, and horizontal rules.

Chapter 5 covers font sizes, font faces, text styles, font colors, special characters, finding and replacing text, and checking your spelling.

Style sheets allow further fine-tuning of the placement of paragraphs, and you can find out how to adjust white space, boxes, and borders in Chapter 13.

Paragraphs versus Line Breaks

Your elementary school English teacher probably told you that a paragraph contains a minimum of three sentences, and that longer paragraphs include a topic sentence. In HTML, the paragraph is simply a unit of text. Each paragraph is separated from other paragraphs by a blank line. **Figure 6.2** shows a page that consists of four paragraphs.

To make a paragraph:

1. In the Document window, type the text in the first paragraph. The text will wrap automatically.

2. At the end of the paragraph, press Enter (Return).

The line will be broken, and a line of blank space will be inserted between the paragraph and the insertion point (**Figure 6.3**).

To apply paragraph style to existing text:

1. Click within the block of text to which you want to apply paragraph tags.
   or
   Select several blocks of text by highlighting them.

2. In the Properties inspector, select Paragraph from the Format drop-down menu (**Figure 6.4**).

The paragraph style will be applied to the text. See *Paragraph Properties*, on the next page, to find out what this entails.

✔ Tip

■ You can also place the insertion point within an existing block of text and press Enter (Return) to insert a paragraph break.

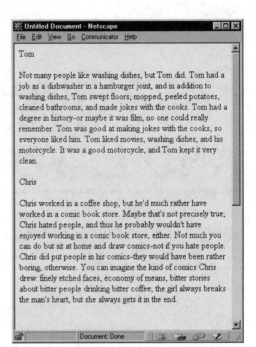

Figure 6.2 There are four paragraphs on this page: The single-word lines are paragraphs, too.

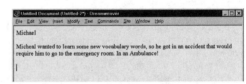

Figure 6.3 The text will wrap in the Document window—and in the browser window, as well—until you insert a paragraph break. When you press Enter (Return), the insertion point will skip a line of blank space and then start a new paragraph. Technically, there are three paragraphs on this page.

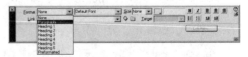

Figure 6.4 To easily surround text with paragraph tags, select the text and then choose Paragraph from the Properties inspector's Format drop-down menu.

Figure 6.5 The only way to break a line without adding white space, as you would in a poem, is to use a line break rather than a paragraph break. Press Shift+Enter (Shift+Return).

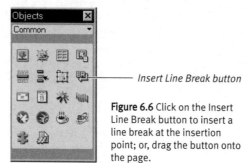

Insert Line Break button

Figure 6.6 Click on the Insert Line Break button to insert a line break at the insertion point; or, drag the button onto the page.

If you want to break the line without inserting a line of blank space, you can use a line break.

To make a line break:

1. In the Document window, type the text in the first paragraph. The text will wrap automatically.

2. At the end of the line you want to break, press Shift+Enter (Shift+Return).

The line will break, and the insertion point will begin at the next line (**Figure 6.5**).

You can also insert a line break using the Objects palette (**Figure 6.6**). You can then click the Insert Line Break button or drag the button to the page.

✔ Tip

■ You can achieve the same effect by selecting Insert > Line Break from the Document window menu bar.

Paragraph Properties

The tag for a paragraph is <p>. Technically, the <p> tag doesn't need a closing tag. However, if you surround a paragraph with <p> and </p> tags, as Dreamweaver does, that encloses the paragraph in the paragraph format. If you're used to hand-coding HTML, you may never have closed a paragraph with a </p> tag.

Until the introduction of style sheets, this wasn't an issue anyone worried about; however, style sheets allow you to change the properties of an enclosed tag, and defining the <p> tag's properties only does any good if you close your paragraphs with the </p> tag.

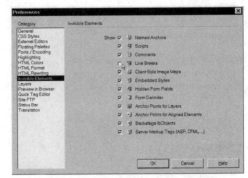

Figure 6.7 The Invisible Elements panel of the Preferences dialog box allows you to select which objects have visible markers when you view invisible elements.

What's My Line Break?

The tag for a line break is <br>. The <br> tag is one of those tags that doesn't need to be closed. You close your paragraphs with the </p> tag.

Line breaks are invisible on screen. By default, they aren't even visible with invisible-element viewing turned on (View > Invisible Elements). To view <br> tags as invisible entities, you'll need to change your preferences.

1. From the Document window menu bar, select Edit > Preferences. The Preferences dialog box will appear.

2. In the Category list box, click on Invisible Elements. That panel of the dialog box will become visible (**Figure 6.7**).

3. Check the box next to Line Breaks.

4. Click on OK to update your preferences and close the dialog box.

Now, line breaks will show up in the Document window as symbols: 🖼. You'll be able to select them to view their properties or edit them in Edit Tag Mode using the Quick Tag Editor. See *To add break properties,* later in this chapter, for details.

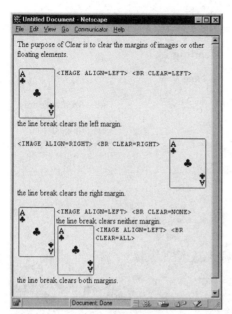

Figure 6.8 The CLEAR attribute of the break tag is demonstrated here in four possible permutations. The most obvious actions of the CLEAR attribute are visible when working with images aligned to the left or right margin—it stops the text from automatically wrapping the image. Refer to Chapter 8 for more on image alignment.

Quick Tag Editor button

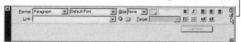

Figure 6.9 Click on the Quick Tag Editor button on the Properties inspector.

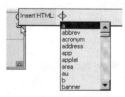

Figure 6.10 In a few seconds, the Quick Tag Editor will appear, in Insert HTML mode.

Figure 6.11 Type a space after the <br> tag, and the clear attribute will appear as the only option in the menu.

Figure 6.12 Options for the clear attribute will appear.

Break Properties

The break tag has a CLEAR attribute that can be used when combining text and floating elements, particularly floating images aligned at the left or right margin. In addition to LEFT, other CLEAR attributes are ALL, RIGHT, and NONE (**Figure 6.8**).

To add break properties:

1. Click to place the insertion point where you want a line break.

2. On the Properties inspector, click on the Quick Tag Editor button (**Figure 6.9**). The Quick Tag (QT) Editor will appear, in Insert HTML mode.

3. Mouse over the brackets so that the Tag Selector menu appears (**Figure 6.10**).

4. From the Tag Selector menu, select br. The QT Editor will now display the following text:

5. Type a space, and the QT Editor will pop up the clear attribute. Click on the menu (**Figure 6.11**).

6. Mouse over the clear attribute, and a menu containing the options left, right, and all will appear (**Figure 6.12**). Click on the attribute you want; if you want none, you'll need to type it in.

   The QT Editor should now display the following code:
   <br clear=*all*>
   where *all* may be another attribute.

7. Press Enter (Return) and the code will be inserted onto the page. You can view it in the HTML inspector, if you like.

✔ Tip

- If you view tags as invisible elements, as described on the previous page, you can select them in the Document window and edit them a little faster, in Edit Tag mode.

Headings

Think of headings (also called headers) as being the same as headlines in a newspaper. They're larger than the body text of an article and are generally bold. There is always a paragraph break between a heading and the text that follows.

There are six sizes, or levels, of headings (**Figure 6.13**). Heading 1 is the largest, and Heading 6 is often smaller than default body text.

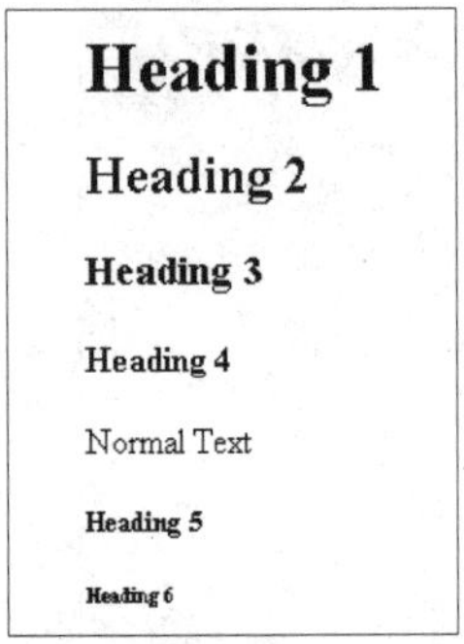

To format a heading:

1. Click within the line of text you want to make into a heading.

2. From the Document window menu bar, select Text > Format > and from the menu that appears (**Figure 6.14**), select a heading (size 1–6).

   or

   On the Properties inspector, select a heading (size 1–6) from the Format drop-down menu (**Figure 6.15**).

The text will become a heading: that is, there will likely be a size change; the text will become bold; and a blank line will be inserted after the heading (**Figure 6.16**).

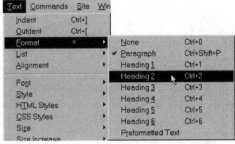

Figure 6.13 There are six levels of headings, from 1 (largest) to 6 (smallest). Heading 4 is the same size as the default font size.

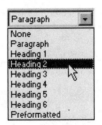

Figure 6.14 Choose a heading size, from 1 to 6, from the Text > Format menu.

Figure 6.15 You can also set headings using the Properties inspector's Format drop-down menu.

Figure 6.16 There are two paragraphs on this page; the first is in Heading 2 format, and the second is in Paragraph format.

HEADINGS

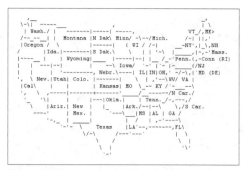

Figure 6.17 Someone worked very hard formatting this map of the United States in a text editor. (Pictures made with plain text are called *ASCII art*.)

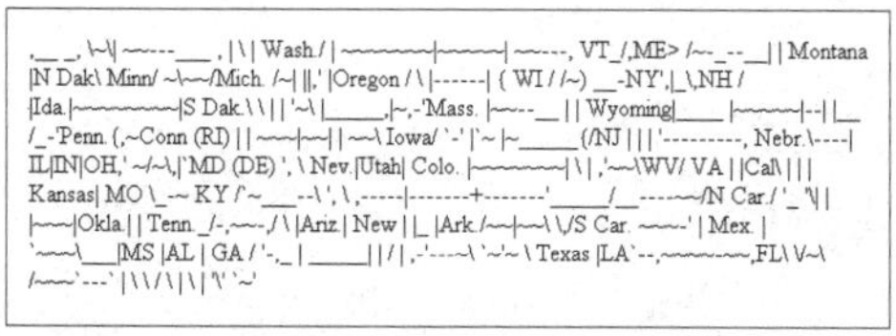

Figure 6.18 If you don't preserve the preformatted text, the picture looks like a jumble of characters.

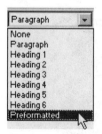

Figure 6.19 Select Preformatted from the Properties inspector's Format drop-down menu.

Preformatted Text

In general, when you paste text into the Document window, it doesn't retain any of its formatting. This includes line breaks, paragraph breaks, spacing, tabs, text-formatted tables, and the like.

If you have formatted text in another program and you wish it to retain its shape, you can insert it into the page's HTML as preformatted text. None of the other conventions of HTML will govern this text; for instance, in HTML, only one typed space will be displayed, even if you type 50 in a row. In preformatted text, any shaping of the text done with spaces or line breaks will be preserved.

Figure 6.17 shows a piece of ASCII art preserved with preformatted text, and **Figure 6.18** shows the same characters without the preformatted text format applied.

It's generally easier to set up the preformatted style before you paste in the text.

To place preformatted text:

1. In the Document window, click to place the insertion point where you want the preformatted text to begin.

2. From the Document window menu bar, select Text > Format > Preformatted Text.
   or

   On the Properties inspector, select Preformatted Text from the Format drop-down menu (**Figure 6.19**).

3. Now you can paste in the text from the other program whose formatting you wish to retain.

✔ Tip

■ You can also apply the Preformatted style to text already on a page, or type the work directly into Dreamweaver, although you may get better results using a text editor.

Div and Span

There are two other kinds of text blocks that you might run across: `<div>` and `<span>`. The `<div>` tag stands for division, and it's used to mark blocks of text that (generally) span more than one paragraph. You can't end the division within a paragraph, because the `</div>` closing tag automatically breaks the paragraph. The `<span>` tag, on the other hand, can be used to mark up an area of text within a single block of text, such as within a paragraph or blockquote.

These two tags are mostly used in conjunction with style sheets, but I'm pointing them out here because of their properties of breaking paragraphs (or not). In the section of this chapter called *Text Alignment*, we'll look more closely at the alignment properties of the `<div>` and `<span>` tags.

Preformatted Face

By default, the font used in preformatted text is the default monospace font, generally Courier or Courier New. The reason for this, as explained in Chapter 5, is that each character in a monospace font is the same width, which means that you can more easily control formatting of ASCII art or poetry (**Figure 6.20**).

You can change the font face, however, in addition to designating it as preformatted. Follow the steps in Chapter 5, in *Changing Font Face*, to change the face of the preformatted text. Or you can refer to Chapter 13 to find out how to change the attributes of the <PRE> tag.

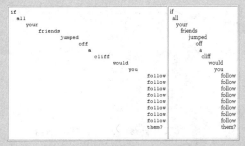

Figure 6.20 If you apply a non-monospace font to preformatted text, you'll get a different effect, because each character (including spaces) is not the same width.

Morning

wake up

feed the cat

make coffee

eat breakfast

brush teeth

shower

Figure 6.21 Type the items you want to make into a list.

Morning

1. wake up
2. feed the cat
3. make coffee
4. eat breakfast
5. brush teeth
6. shower

Figure 6.22 After the Ordered list style is applied, the list items will be numbered and indented from the left margin. A paragraph break is automatically applied before and after the list.

Morning

1. wake up
2. feed the cat
3. make coffee
4.
5. eat breakfast
6. brush teeth
7. shower

Figure 6.23 If you add or remove items from the list, it will automatically renumber itself.

Formatting Lists

Dreamweaver directly supports two kinds of lists: numbered lists, also called *ordered lists;* and bulleted lists, also called *unordered lists.* There is an additional kind of list called a definition list that is partially supported by Dreamweaver.

To make a numbered list:

1. In the Dreamweaver window, type (or paste) the items you'd like to make into a numbered list, *omitting the numbers* (**Figure 6.21**).

2. Select the list items.

3. From the Document window menu bar, select Text > List > Ordered List.

   or

   On the Properties inspector, click on the Ordered List button ⊞.

The list will become numbered (**Figure 6.22**).

To add an item to a numbered list:

1. To add an item to the end of a list, click to place the insertion point at the end of the last numbered line, and press Enter (Return). A new number will appear at the end of the list.

2. To add an item to the middle of the list, click to place the insertion point at the end of one of the lines, and press Enter (Return). A new number will appear in the middle of the list (**Figure 6.23**).

To remove an item from a numbered list:

1. Select the item to be removed, and press Delete (Backspace).

2. Press Delete (Backspace) again, and the numbered line will be removed.

The list will renumber itself to reflect any additions or subtractions from the list.

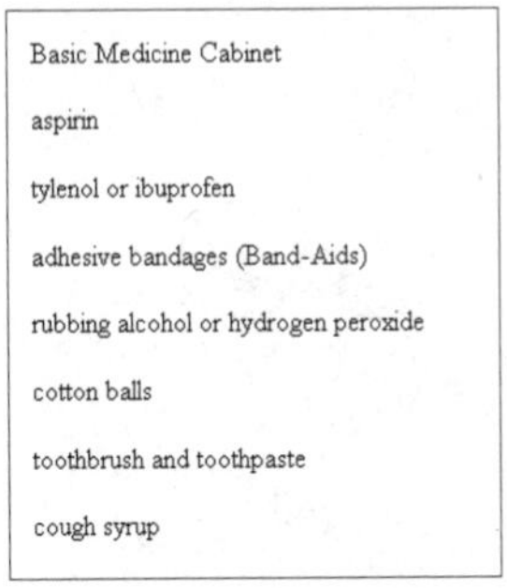

To make a bulleted list:

1. In the Dreamweaver window, type (or paste) the items you'd like to make into a bulleted list, *omitting any asterisks or other bullet placeholders* (**Figure 6.24**).

2. Select the list items.

3. From the Document window menu bar, select Text > List > Unordered List.

   or

   On the Properties inspector, click on the Unordered List button ⊞.

The list will become bulleted and indented (**Figure 6.25**).

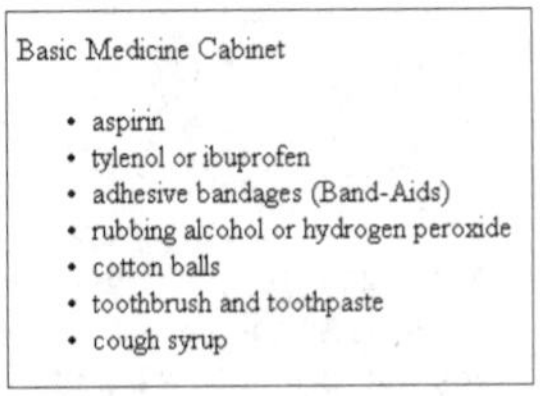

Basic Medicine Cabinet

aspirin

tylenol or ibuprofen

adhesive bandages (Band-Aids)

rubbing alcohol or hydrogen peroxide

cotton balls

toothbrush and toothpaste

cough syrup

Figure 6.24 Type the items you want to appear in the list, one to a line.

Basic Medicine Cabinet

- aspirin
- tylenol or ibuprofen
- adhesive bandages (Band-Aids)
- rubbing alcohol or hydrogen peroxide
- cotton balls
- toothbrush and toothpaste
- cough syrup

Figure 6.25 After you select the unordered list format, the list items will be single-spaced and indented, and bullets will be added.

Additional List Properties

Some additional list properties are available in Dreamweaver 3. See the Web site for this book for details on how to use them.

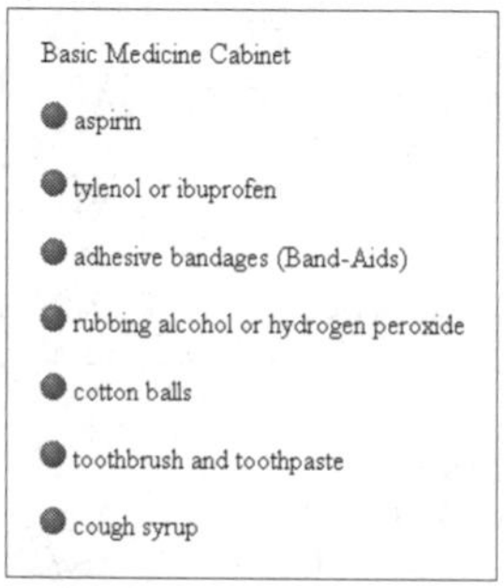

Basic Medicine Cabinet

● aspirin

● tylenol or ibuprofen

● adhesive bandages (Band-Aids)

● rubbing alcohol or hydrogen peroxide

● cotton balls

● toothbrush and toothpaste

● cough syrup

Figure 6.26 You can use tiny images on each line instead of making a bulleted list.

✔ Tips

- To convert a list back to paragraph style, reapply the style (select it from the menu bar or deselect the list button on the Properties inspector).

- If some extraneous text before or after the list gets added to the list, select the offending line of text and click on the corresponding list button to deselect it.

- You can also select Text > List > None from the Document window menu bar to clear list attributes from selected text.

- Lists can only be bulleted or numbered, not both (thank goodness). To convert a list from bulleted to numbered (or vice versa), select the list and then apply the other list format.

- By default, a paragraph break will be inserted both before and after the list. Press Enter (Return) twice to end the list.

- The items in the list will be single-spaced by default. To add a line of blank space between the list items, press Shift+Return (Shift+Return) *twice* after each list item.

- Other list options are available using style sheets; see Chapter 13.

FORMATTING LISTS

Images as Bullets

You may have seen a page that appears to use small images as bullets (**Figure 6.26**). This is not, in fact a bulleted list. Each image is placed on a line (you can copy and paste them with Dreamweaver), and then the lines can be optionally indented. (See *Indenting Text*, later in this chapter).

A third kind of list, called a *definition list,* is also supported by Dreamweaver. In a definition list, there are two kinds of list items: a definition term <dt>, and a definition <dd>.

As you'd find in a glossary, the definition is indented under the definition term(**Figure 29**). The items in a definition list don't have to be definitions; you can use the definition list style anywhere you want this sort of formatting.

To make a definition list:

1. Type the definition terms and the definitions in the Document window (**Figure 6.27**). Place each term and definition on a separate line, and omit any indentations.

2. Select the list items.

3. From the Document window menu bar, select Text > List > Definition List (**Figure 6.28**).

The list will be formatted so that every other item is a term and a definition (**Figure 6.29**).

✔ Tips

- If you're having trouble getting Dreamweaver to format the list properly, try selecting the text in the HTML inspector. Make sure you select all opening and closing tags (including <p> and </p> tags).

- If you want to format the definition list yourself, surround each *definition term* with <dt>and</dt>, and every *definition* with <dd>and</dd>.

- You can include more than one definition per definition term.

- This is an alternative way to indent blocks of text because they are indented only from the left margin, not from both margins (as opposed to blockquotes).

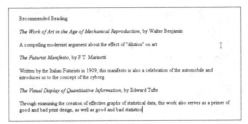

Figure 6.27 Type the terms and definitions, one to a line, in the Document window.

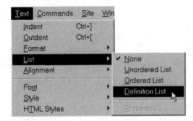

Figure 6.28 From the Document window menu bar, select Text > List > Definition List.

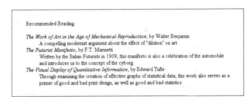

Figure 6.29 The list will be formatted so that every other item is a term or a definition. You can add other formatting and line breaks later.

Figure 6.30 You can align text to the left margin, the center of the page, or the right margin.

Terms of Alignment

Depending on what kind of text you're aligning—and how much—Dreamweaver may use different code. All default (unspecified) alignment is to the left margin.

The <center> tag can be used to center any element between the opening tag and the closing </center> tag.

Headers can be aligned by using the align attribute within the <Hn> tag. For instance: <H2 align=center>.

A similar attribute exists for paragraphs, although it's being deprecated (removed from the HTML standard). Dreamweaver, however, uses this code: <p align=right> The align attribute will end with the closing </p> tag.

For more than one line of text, Dreamweaver tends to use the <div> tag to define all the text with non-left alignment. For instance: <div align=center>centered text</div>.

As mentioned earlier in the chapter, the </div> tag creates a paragraph break. Centering applies to an entire division or paragraph; this includes line breaks within the <p> or <div>.

To align part of a paragraph or division, you can use the <span> tag to surround a few lines of text within a <p> or <div>:

```
<span align=right>
one line<br></span>
```

Text Alignment

As is the case with word-processing programs, you can align part or all of a page of text with the left margin, the right margin, or the center of the page (**Figure 6.30**).

To change the alignment of text:

1. Select the text whose alignment you wish to change. This can be a single paragraph, a heading, a list, or an entire page.

2. From the Document window menu bar, select Text > Alignment > and then Left, Right, or Center.

   or

   On the Properties inspector, click on the Left, Right, or Center alignment button.

The text will become aligned according to the option you selected.

✔ Tips

- When you're working with images, or with tables, there are more than three alignment options available. Refer to Chapter 8 or to Chapter 10 for more on these alignment options.

- Not all browsers support the relatively new <div> tag, which is what Dreamweaver uses for center alignment. You can set Dreamweaver's preferences to use the more backwards-compatible <center> tag for centering, or the more CSS-compatible <div align=center> tag. View preferences (Edit > Preferences), and select the HTML Format category. In that section of the dialog box, at the bottom, click on the radio button for either <div> or <center> as the default centering tag.

109

Indenting Text

There are no tabs in regular HTML; the kind of five-space paragraph indent used in other types of publishing is generally replaced by setting off each paragraph by a line of white space.

You can, however, indent an entire block of text. One way to accomplish this is by using definition lists (see *Formatting Lists,* earlier in this chapter). Or use the `<blockquote>` tag, which is what Dreamweaver does.

To indent a block of text:

1. In the Dreamweaver window, click within the paragraph you wish to indent; to select more than one paragraph, highlight the text you want to indent (**Figure 6.31**).

2. From the Document window menu bar, select Text > Indent.

   or

   On the Properties inspector, click on the Indent button ⬛.

Either way, the text will become indented (**Figure 6.32**).

✔ Tips

- You can repeat Step 2 for multiple indent levels (**Figure 6.33**).

- The `<blockquote>` tag indents text from both margins; to indent text from one margin only, use a definition list (see *Formatting Lists,* earlier in this chapter).

- You can also create an artificial indent by using nonbreaking spaces (see *The Nonbreaking Space*, later in this chapter).

- Tables are another way to create margins. See Chapter 10.

- Paragraph indents are available by using style sheets; see Chapter 13.

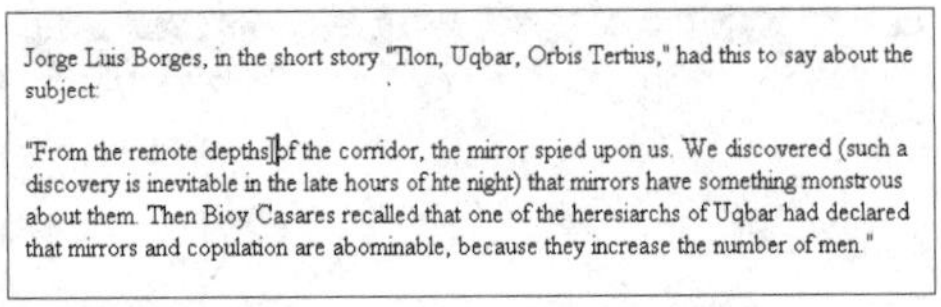

Figure 6.31 Click within the paragraph you want to indent.

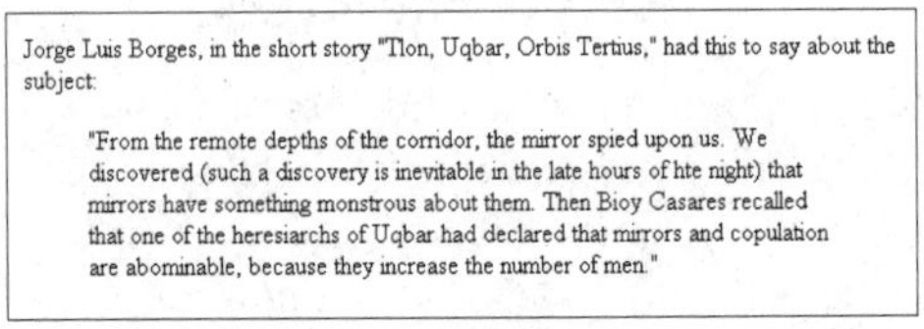

Figure 6.32 Dreamweaver indents text by applying the `<blockquote>` tag.

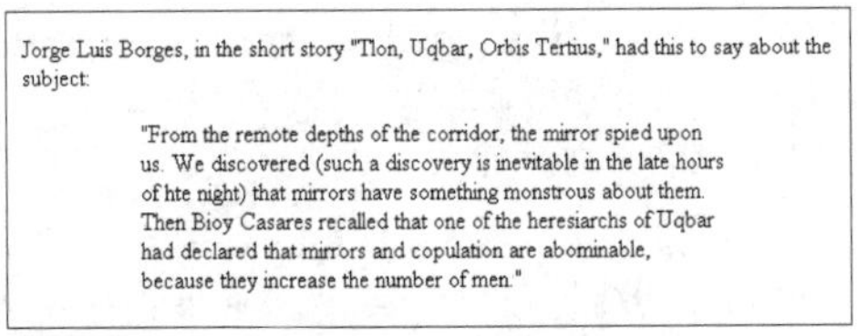

Figure 6.33 You can indent the paragraph more than one level; by doing so here, it becomes more apparent that blockquotes are indented from both margins.

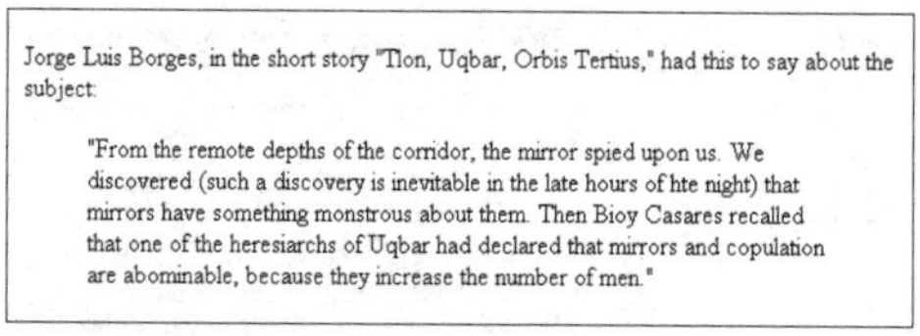

Jorge Luis Borges, in the short story "Tlon, Uqbar, Orbis Tertius," had this to say about the subject:

"From the remote depths of the corridor, the mirror spied upon us. We discovered (such a discovery is inevitable in the late hours of hte night) that mirrors have something monstrous about them. Then Bioy Casares recalled that one of the heresiarchs of Uqbar had declared that mirrors and copulation are abominable, because they increase the number of men."

Figure 6.34 You can remove a level of indent by clicking on the Outdent button. This often works for removing list formatting, too.

If you change your mind, you can remove one or more indent levels. Dreamweaver calls this "outdenting."

To remove a level of indent:

1. In the Dreamweaver window, click within the paragraph from which you wish to remove a level of indent; to select more than one paragraph, highlight the text.

2. From the Document window menu bar, select Text > Outdent.

   or

   On the Properties inspector, click on the Outdent button ⬚.

Either way, one level of indent will be removed (**Figure 6.34**).

✔ Tip

■ You can repeat step 2 until the text is at the margin, if you like.

Outdenting?

Here's a completely useless sidebar. The word *indent* derives from the Latin *in-* (in) + *dent* (tooth), meaning to bite into (in Middle English, the word *endenten* meant "to notch"). The text, then, bites its way into the page. Since you can't "unchew" something, this explains why "outdenting" isn't a conventional layout term.

I heard from a reader in Italy who suggested an alternate interpretation. He said to think of the indent as the tooth itself, in which case the outdent would be a space or gap between the teeth.

The Nonbreaking Space

In HTML, while spaces count as characters, they're shady ones. Only one simple spacebar-typed space will display in an HTML browser, even if you type 50 of them. There is an entity, however, called the *nonbreaking space*. This is part of a family of special characters that you can't type easily with ASCII text; each character is represented by a *control code* or *escape sequence*. The use of other special characters is described in Chapter 5.

Dreamweaver automatically puts nonbreaking spaces in the code where it thinks you need them; for instance, when you need more than one line of blank space, the nonbreaking space is used as an entity. Paragraphs can't be empty, and you can't line up <p> tags to create multiple paragraph breaks (they are also ignored).

Figure 6.35 shows a page and its code; while most of the page appears to be blank, it requires some behind-the-scenes code to work.

To insert a nonbreaking space:

1. Click to place the insertion point where you want the nonbreaking space.

2. From the Document window menu bar, select Insert > Nonbreaking Space.

   or

   On the Objects palette, view the Invisibles panel.

   Then, click on the Insert Nonbreaking Space button 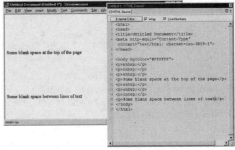.

   Either way, the Nonbreaking Space will "appear," albeit invisibly, on the page.

✔ Tips

- You can repeat the above steps to insert a string of nonbreaking spaces to create an artificial indent.

- A keyboard shortcut for inserting a nonbreaking space: Shift+Ctrl+spacebar (Shift+Command+spacebar).

Figure 6.35 As the code for this page indicates, the nonbreaking space is a useful placeholder.

Coding a Nonbreaking Space

If you're comfortable working directly with the code, you may want to insert a nonbreaking space exactly where you want it: between the <p> and </p> tags, or in a table cell, for example. To do so, follow these steps:

1. From the Document window menu bar, select Insert > Nonbreaking Space.

2. View the HTML inspector by selecting Window > HTML from the Document window menu bar.

3. Type the following characters:

4. When you close the HTML inspector, Dreamweaver will automatically convert the escape sequence into its visual equivalent, an ordinary-looking space.

If you take a look at the code, you'll see that the   sequence is still where you put it.

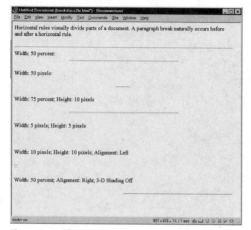

Figure 6.36 Horizontal rules can come in many different shapes and sizes; the first horizontal rule in this figure has the default attributes of 100 percent width, center alignment, and 3-D shading.

Apply button

Figure 6.37 You can change the appearance of a horizontal rule with the Properties inspector.

✔ Tip

■ You can also insert a horizontal rule by using the Common panel of the Objects palette, and clicking on the Insert Horizontal Rule button: 🔲.

Horizontal Rules

A horizontal rule is a line that runs across the page horizontally and provides an explicit rather than implied division between parts of a document (**Figure 6.36**). Some people swear by them; others think they're the scourge of HTML, but I'm going to show you how to make one, regardless.

To insert a horizontal rule:

1. Click to place the insertion point where you want the ruled line to appear.

2. From the Document window menu bar, select Insert > Horizontal Rule.

A ruled line will appear that is the width of the page, with a paragraph break before and after it.

To change the rule:

1. Select the horizontal rule and double-click it to display the Horizontal Rule properties in the Properties inspector (**Figure 6.37**).

2. To name the Horizontal rule, type a lowercase word in the Horizontal Rule text box.

3. To adjust the width, type a number, in either pixels or percent of window, in the W text box. Then, choose the unit of measure from the W drop-down menu.

4. To adjust the height, type a number (in pixels) in the H text box.

5. To adjust the alignment, choose Left, Center, or Right from the Align drop-down menu.

6. To remove the 3-D shading (also called the beveling), deselect the Shading check box.

7. Click on the Apply button to apply the changes to the horizontal rule.

CREATING HTML STYLES

7

When you're formatting text, it can get a little tedious applying the same formatting over and over again. Dreamweaver helps by allowing you to save sets of formatting, such as Bold + Arial + Heading 3 + Red, as a named HTML style.

HTML styles are similar to styles in Microsoft Word or Adobe PageMaker. They're a collection of text attributes that you can save and use again and again. HTML styles are also similar to cascading style sheets (see sidebar, this page).

Dreamweaver's tool for creating and applying HTML styles is the HTML Styles palette.

HTML Styles vs. CSS

The main difference between HTML styles and cascading style sheets (CSS) is that with CSS, discussed in Chapter 13, if you change a style, all instances of that style will be changed as well. For instance, if you create a style called A-Head, one of its attributes may be the color blue. In CSS, if you change its color to red, all uses of the A-Head style will turn red automatically. There is no automatic update in HTML styles.

If you change a style and want your changes to be applied to prior uses of the style, you'll need to reapply the new style to those portions of your text.

Why then, did Macromedia introduce HTML styles in Dreamweaver 3 instead of relying on CSS? Because CSS is not available to all browsers; because it acts differently in different browsers; and because Dreamweaver is for editing Web pages, not just style sheets. As long as people continue to use the old HTML text standards, why not make using them easier?

115

To view the HTML Styles palette:

◆ From the Document window menu bar, select Window > HTML Styles

or

Click on the HTML Styles button on the Launcher

or

Press Ctrl+F7 (Command+F7).

The HTML Styles palette will appear (**Figure 7.1**).

The HTML Styles palette comes pre-loaded in Dreamweaver 3 with several sample styles. You can use these styles on your own pages as is, or you can edit or delete them. You can also create your own HTML styles. I'll discuss how to do all of the above, but first, let's apply an existing style to some text.

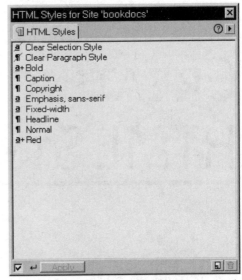

Figure 7.1 The HTML Styles palette lets you name and save a set of text formatting so that you can easily apply the formatting repeatedly.

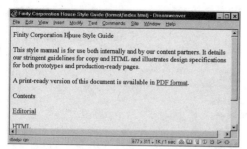

Figure 7.2 Click within the paragraph to which you want to apply a paragraph style.

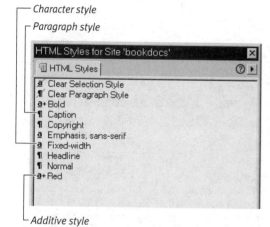

Character style
Paragraph style
Additive style

Figure 7.3 Paragraph styles are marked with a paragraph symbol, and character or selection styles are marked with the letter *a*. A plus sign indicates that the style is additive and that it will not remove other formatting from the selection.

Figure 7.4 I applied the Headline style to the selected paragraph.

Applying HTML Styles

HTML styles are either *paragraph-level* or *character-level* styles; that is, the style will either affect the way an entire paragraph looks, or it will affect only selected text. Character styles are also called *selection styles*.

To apply a paragraph style:

1. Click within the paragraph to which you want to apply the style (**Figure 7.2**).

2. In the HTML Styles window, click on a style marked by a paragraph symbol (**Figure 7.3**). Of the pre-loaded styles, Caption and Headline are two examples of paragraph styles.

   The text will change appearance: It will take on the characteristics of the selected style (**Figure 7.4**).

To apply a character style:

1. Select the text to which you want to apply the style (**Figure 7.5**).

2. In the HTML Styles window, click on a style marked by a character style symbol (**Figure 7.3**). Of the pre-loaded styles, Emphasis, Sans-Serif and Fixed Width are two examples of character styles.

   The text will change appearance and the style will be applied (**Figure 7.6**).

Additionally, applying a style can either clear previous style settings, or it can add its attributes on top of existing styles. *Additive styles* are marked in the HTML Styles palette by a plus sign (+).

For example, if you click in a paragraph and apply the Caption style, and then apply the Headline style to the same paragraph, that action will erase the Caption style and apply the Headline style. However, if you select text within the Headline-styled paragraph, and apply the Red style, the text will stay in Headline style, but it will also turn red.

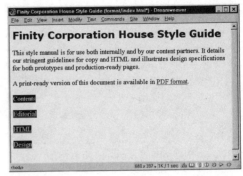

Figure 7.5 Select the text to which you want to apply the character style.

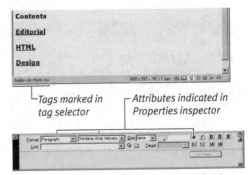

Figure 7.6 I applied the Emphasis, Sans-Serif style to the selected text. Note that the Properties inspector and the tag selector in the lower-left of the window show the new attributes of the selected text.

Figure 7.7 Click within the paragraph that contains the paragraph style you want to remove.

Figure 7.8 Click on Clear Paragraph Style in the HTML Styles palette, and the style is removed from the paragraph.

Figure 7.9 Select the text that contains the character style you want to remove.

Figure 7.10 Click on Clear Selection Style in the HTML Styles palette, and the style is removed from the selected text.

Removing Styles

There are two commands in the HTML Styles palette that make it easy to remove formatting from text that has an HTML style applied to it.

To remove a paragraph style:

1. In the Document window, click within the paragraph from which you want to clear an HTML style (**Figure 7.7**).

2. In the HTML Styles palette, click on Clear Paragraph Style. All formatting will be removed from the paragraph (**Figure 7.8**).

To remove a character style:

1. In the Document window, select the text from which you want to remove a selected style (**Figure 7.9**).

2. In the HTML Styles palette, click on Clear Selection Style. All formatting will be removed from the selection (**Figure 7.10**).

✔ Attention!

- When you use either the Clear Paragraph Style command or the Clear Selection Style command, all formatting will be removed. That means even if you've applied an additive style, such as Red, to the paragraph or a selection, or if you've added other attributes using the Properties inspector, those will also be removed. Instead of clearing a style, you may just want to change its attributes using the Properties inspector, so that you can preserve any additional text formatting.

Creating New Styles

There are several ways to create your own HTML style. One way is to format text as you like, and then save that formatting in a style. Another way is to make a copy of an existing style in the HTML Styles palette, and then edit that style. A third way is to create a style from scratch.

To save formatting as a style:

1. In the Document window, make some changes to a paragraph or a selected piece of text using the Properties inspector. For example, in **Figure 7.11**, I made the first paragraph into Heading 2 format, centered it, used the Arial font face, and changed the color to Corporate Blue.

2. With the text or paragraph selected, click on the New Style button on the bottom of the HTML Styles palette (**Figure 7.12**). The Define HTML Style dialog box will appear (**Figure 7.13**).

3. In the Define HTML Style dialog box, the formatting you applied to the text will be indicated. For example, if you made the text blue, the Color button will be blue. Type a name for your style in the Name text box.

4. Click the radio button for Selection or Paragraph, depending whether you want to create a paragraph or a character style.

5. Examine the other attributes, and change any that you like. For details, see the side-bar, *Font and Paragraph Attributes*, later in this chapter. When you're satisfied, click on OK to close the Define HTML Styles dialog box and return to the Document window.

The name of your style will appear in the HTML Styles palette (**Figure 7.14**). Now you can apply it to other pieces of text.

Figure 7.11 I modified this paragraph, and now I want to save the attributes as a style so I can apply them again and again.

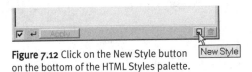

Figure 7.12 Click on the New Style button on the bottom of the HTML Styles palette.

Figure 7.13 All my formatting appears in the Define HTML Style dialog box.

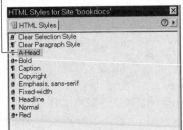

Figure 7.14 Now my new style, which I named A-Head, appears in the HTML Styles palette.

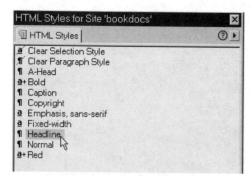

Figure 7.15 Click on the name of the style you want to copy. It's helpful to click on an instance of the style that occurs on the page; if there isn't one, or if you forget, you may accidentally format the paragraph the insertion point happens to be sitting in.

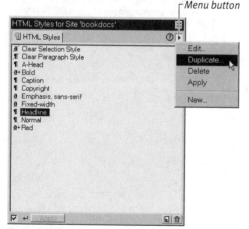

Figure 7.16 Click on the menu button, and select Duplicate from the menu that appears.

Figure 7.17 In the Define HTML Style dialog box, notice that the style is named HeadlineCopy. You might want to rename your copied style.

Another way to create an HTML style is to copy an existing style and then modify the style's attributes. For example, the preset Headline style uses the +5 font size. To create a smaller version of this style, you can copy the Headline style and then decrease the size.

To copy an HTML style:

1. In the Document window, click on some text already in the style you want to copy.

2. In the HTML Styles palette, select the style you want to copy.

3. Click the menu button at the top of the palette, and from the menu that appears, select Duplicate. The Define HTML Style dialog box will appear.

4. Type a new name for the new style in the Name text box.

5. Make any changes you wish to the properties of the style. For help, refer to *Editing Styles*, later in this chapter.

6. When you're all set, click on OK. The dialog box will close, and the new style will appear in the HTML Styles palette.

If you create or copy a style that's no longer useful, or if you decide to get rid of one of the preset styles, you can easily delete it.

CREATING NEW STYLES

To delete an HTML style:

1. In the HTML Styles palette, click on the style you want to delete.

2. Click on the Delete Style button

   or

   Click the menu button on the top of the HTML Styles palette, and from the menu that appears, select Delete (**Figure 7.18**). Either way, the style will be removed.

✔ Tip

■ There's no warning or confirmation dialog box, so try not to delete a style accidentally.

Menu button

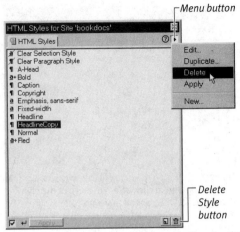

*Delete
Style
button*

Figure 7.18 To remove a style permanently from the HTML Styles palette, click on the menu button and select Delete from the menu; or click on the Delete Style button.

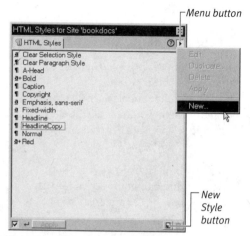

Menu button

New Style button

Figure 7.19 Click the menu button, and select New from the menu; or click on the New Style button.

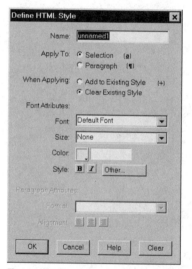

Figure 7.20 If you select unformatted text before you create a new style, the Define HTML Style dialog box is a blank slate.

The last way to create a new style is to build it from scratch using the Define HTML Style dialog box. Here, you choose the attributes you want directly in the dialog box.

To create an HTML style from scratch:

1. On the HTML Styles palette, click the New Style button

   or

   Click the menu button and, from the menu that appears, select New (**Figure 7.19**).

   Either way, the Define HTML Style dialog box will appear (**Figure 7.20**).

2. Type a name for your new style in the Name text box. Try to name it something memorable; Blue Centered Arial is more descriptive than Style 4.

3. To create a paragraph style, click the Paragraph radio button. To create a character or selection style, click the Selection radio button.

4. To create a style that supercedes any existing text formatting, click the Clear Existing Style radio button. To create a style that adds its attributes to existing formatting, click Add to Existing Style.

5. Select any attributes you like for the style. For help with Font attributes, see Chapter 5. For help with Paragraph attributes, see Chapter 6.

6. When you're finished, click on OK to save your changes and close the Define HTML Style dialog box. Your new style will appear in the HTML Styles palette.

CREATING NEW STYLES

Editing Styles

You can edit a style that preexists in Dreamweaver. You will also want to edit styles that you create. The following sections describe how to create styles, but first we'll examine all the attributes you can edit.

To edit an HTML style:

1. In the HTML Styles palette, click on the style whose attributes you wish to change.

2. Click on the menu button in the upper-right corner of the palette, and from the menu that appears, choose Edit. The Define HTML Styles dialog box will appear (as seen in **Figure 7.20**).

3. To rename the style, type the new name in the Name text box.

4. In the Apply To area of the dialog box, you can change the style from Paragraph to Selection, or vice versa, if you wish. Click the Paragraph or Selection radio button.

5. In the When Applying area of the dialog box, you can choose to override existing formatting (click the Clear Existing Style radio button) or to add the style's attributes to already-formatted text (click the Add to Existing Style radio button).

6. Select any attributes you like for the style. See the sidebar on this page for details about these attributes.

7. When you're finished, click on OK to save your changes and close the Define HTML Style dialog box. The edited style will be stored in the HTML Styles palette, and its changes will be active the next time you apply the style.

✔ Tip

- HTML styles are not automatically updated. To add new aspects of an edited style to text formatted by that style, you must select the text and reapply the style.

Font and Paragraph Attributes

In the Define HTML Style dialog box, many of the basic text attributes that are available in the Properties inspector or from the menu bar are available as style attributes. These are described fully in Chapters 5 and 6.

Font attributes are available for both selection and paragraph styles. You can set the following characteristics:

- The Font drop-down menu allows you to choose from sets of fonts. You can also add fonts to the list. See *Changing Font Face* in Chapter 5.

- The Size drop-down menu offers both physical and relative font sizes. See *Changing Font Size* in Chapter 5.

- The Color button lets you change the color of text. See *Changing Font Color* in Chapter 5 and *Colors and Web Pages* in Chapter 2.

- The Style area of the dialog box allows you to choose from Bold, Italic, and other text styles. See *Using Text Styles, Physical Text Styles,* and *Logical Text Styles* in Chapter 5.

Paragraph attributes are available only to paragraph styles. You can change the following options:

- The Format drop-down menu lets you choose whether the text block is a paragraph, a heading, or preformatted text. See *Paragraph Properties, Headings,* and *Preformatted Text* in Chapter 6.

- The alignment buttons let you align text to the left, right, or center of the page. See *Text Alignment* in Chapter 6.

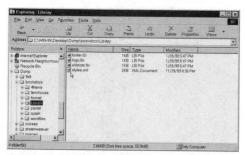

Figure 7.21 In Windows Explorer, I opened my Local Site root folder (called bookdocs) for one site, and then opened the Library folder within that folder.

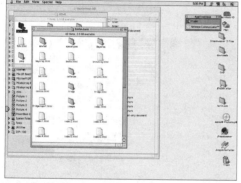

Figure 7.22 On my Mac, I clicked open each window in turn in order to get to to the folder containing my Local Site and its library folder.

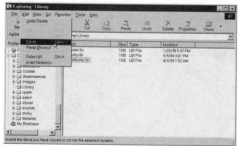

Figure 7.23 Then, I opened up the other Library folder in a different local site, and here I am pasting the styles.xml file into it.

✔ Tip

■ You can make a back-up copy of the Styles file the same way.

Using the Styles File

You may want to copy your styles for use in different sites or by different users. The HTML Styles file is called styles.xml, and it's stored in the Library folder of your local site.

The styles.xml file will not exist until you create at least one style other than those pre-set by Dreamweaver. And if you have more than one local site, remember that each site has a unique Library folder, and therefore, a unique styles.xml file. To share styles, you must copy the file into the Library of each local site.

For more about using local sites, see Chapter 3. For more about the Library, see Chapter 17.

To use the Styles file in more than one local site:

1. On your computer, locate the local site folder for the site containing the Styles file that you want to copy. This will vary based on where you set up your local site in Chapter 3.

   W Open Windows Explorer, and locate the local site folder (**Figure 7.21**).

   M Open your hard drive window, and locate the local site folder (**Figure 7.22**).

2. In the Local Site folder, open the Library folder and single-click on styles.xml.

   W From the Windows Explorer menu bar, select Edit > Copy.

   M From the Finder menu bar, select Edit > Duplicate.

3. Open the Library folder for the second site, or choose a temporary location to store your copied file, such as the Desktop.

4. Paste (Ctrl+V) or drag (on a Mac) the copy of the file into its new location (**Figure 7.23**).

If you want to share HTML styles with another computer or with a workgroup, you can do one of several things. You can e-mail the file to another user or you can put it on a disk; either way, you should instruct them to put it in the Library folder. Or, you can use the Site window to upload the file to a shared remote site.

To share an HTML style with other users on a remote site:

1. In the Site window, click on the Connect button to connect to your remote site (**Figure 7.24**).

2. In the right pane, open the Library folder and single-click on the styles.xml file (**Figure 7.25**).

3. Click on Put to upload the file

   or

   Click on Check In to upload the file and check it in with your username.

   Either way, the file will be uploaded to the remote site. If there is not yet a Library folder on the remote site, it will be created when the file is uploaded (**Figure 7.26**).

✔ Tips

- If you use Check In to upload the file, your copy of the file will become read-only. You can check out the styles.xml file again from the remote site to regain write access (so you can add and change styles), however, others won't be able to download the file.

- To find out how to set up a remote site if you haven't done so yet, see Chapter 3. For more about uploading and checking in, see Chapter 20. Chapter 20 also covers design notes, which you can use with the styles.xml file.

Figure 7.24 In the Site window, click on Connect to connect to the remote site. (You can open this window if it isn't already open by selecting Window > Site Files from the Document window menu bar.)

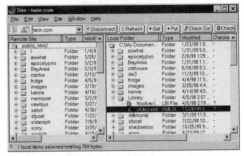

Figure 7.25 Open the Library folder and select the styles.xml file.

Figure 7.26 The styles.xml file was uploaded to the site, and the Library folder was created on the remote site.

USING THE STYLES FILE

WORKING WITH IMAGES

Figure 8.1 The splash page for Christian Cosas's personal home page uses a simple image against a plain background. Both the image and the text link point to the site's table of contents, shown in Figure 8.2.

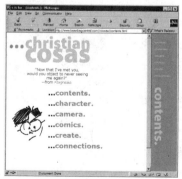

Figure 8.2 The site includes linked images—the words are all image files. With 11 images on the page including the background, the whole page weighs in at only 27K.

Chances are, if Mosaic hadn't introduced the prospect of inline image viewing in its Web browser in 1994, the Web still wouldn't be a big deal. Other Internet tools, such as WAIS and gopher, don't match the Web in popularity—not because the systems themselves aren't as versatile, but because the browsing software doesn't support inline media other than text.

Used to be, if you found an image online, you had to download it, get offline, and then open the image in a viewing program. That all seems like ancient history these days.

When used well, images can add not just visual interest but information and versatility to a Web page. **Figures 8.1** and **8.2** show Christian Cosas's site, which makes excellent use of images.

✔ Tips

- To find out about using background images, refer to Chapter 2.

- For instructions on making an image map, see Appendix A on the Web site.

Placing an Image

There are several ways to place images using Dreamweaver.

To place an image:

1. With the desired page open in the Document window, click at the place on the page where you'd like the image to appear.

2. From the Document window menu bar, select Insert > Image (**Figure 8.3**).

   or

   Click on the Image button in the Objects palette (**Figure 8.4**).

   or

   Press Ctrl+Alt+I (Command+Option+I).

   Regardless of the method, the Select Image Source dialog box will appear (**Figures 8.5** and **8.6**).

3. If you know the location of the image on the Web or on your computer, type it in the URL text box.

   or

   Browse through the files and folders on your computer until you find the image file. Click on the image file's icon, so that its name appears in the File name text box.

4. Click on OK to close the Insert Image dialog box. The image will appear at the insertion point in the Document window.

✔ Tip

■ If you haven't yet saved your page, a dialog box will appear telling you about file pathnames. Click on OK to close this dialog box. Ideally, you should select images that are stored on your local site. If you haven't yet set up a local site, see Chapter 3. Pathnames are described further in Chapter 9.

Figure 8.3 Select Insert > Image from the Document window menu bar.

Figure 8.4 Click on the Image button in the Objects palette.

Figure 8.5 The Select Image Source dialog box is similar to the familiar Open dialog box. If you click on a filename, a preview of the image is displayed.

Figure 8.6 The Select Image Source dialog box on the Mac. Click the Show/Hide Preview button to show or hide the image preview.

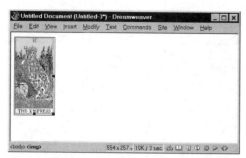

Figure 8.7 When you select an image, boxes called *handles* will appear in the lower-right corner of the image.

Figure 8.8 The Properties inspector, displaying properties for the currently selected image. Note that the Apply button is a tiny thumbnail of the selected image.

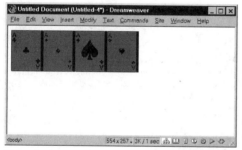

Figure 8.9 When multiple images are selected, they appear highlighted in gray, and handles are not visible.

Definitions

A *splash page* (**Figure 8.1**) is what you call an opening screen that leads in to the rest of a site. Not essential, the splash page should be simple, load quickly, and show you what the point of a site is. A *home page*, on the other hand (**Figure 8.2**), generally serves as a table of contents for the main sections of a site.

Selecting an Image

When you insert an image using Dreamweaver, it will remain selected, but you'll select an image any time you want to work with it.

When you select an image with Dreamweaver, boxes called *handles* will appear in the lower-right corner of the image (**Figure 8.7**), and a preview of the image will appear in the Properties inspector (**Figure 8.8**). This image preview acts as the Apply button for the image properties.

To select/deselect an image:

◆ To select an image, just click on it.

◆ To deselect an image, click on any other part of the Document window.

◆ To select multiple images, hold down the Shift key while you click on each image (**Figure 8.9**).

✔ Tips

■ When an image is selected, you can copy, cut, delete, or paste over it, just as you do with text in a word processor. All of these commands are available from the Document window's Edit menu.

■ Click once on an image to make the Properties inspector appear.

■ Double-click on an image to make the Select Image Source dialog box appear.

■ If you want to replace the file path for an image, drag the Src Point to File icon to a file in the Site window. See Chapter 20 for more about linking in the Site window.

The Properties Inspector

As with most HTML entities in Dreamweaver, the Properties inspector (**Figure 8.10**) displays properties specific to images when an image is selected.

To use the Properties inspector:

1. Display the Properties inspector, if necessary, by selecting Modify > Selection Properties from the Document window menu bar.

2. Select the image whose properties you'd like to investigate. The Properties inspector will display properties for that image with a thumbnail of the image appearing as the Apply button.

3. To display all the image properties that the inspector has to offer, click on the expander arrow in the bottom-right corner of the inspector (**Figure 8.11**).

✔ Tip

- You can also display the Properties inspector by clicking the image.

Expander arrow ⌐

Figure 8.10 When an image is selected, the Properties inspector will display the image properties. A thumbnail of the image will appear as the Apply button.

Figure 8.11 Click on the Expander arrow in the bottom-right corner of the Properties inspector (look at the pointer in Figure 8.10) to display the full set of Image properties.

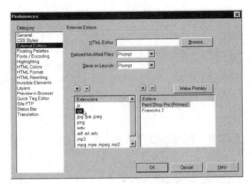

Figure 8.12 You can select an image editor in your preferences so that you can edit images while you're using them in Dreamweaver.

Image Editor Integration

If you want to edit an image while you're working with it in Dreamweaver, it's a snap. Dreamweaver 3 has full image editor integration, and you can set Dreamweaver to work with your favorite editor, whether it's Fireworks, Paint Shop Pro, or Photoshop.

To select an image editor, open the Preferences dialog box by pressing Ctrl+U (Command+U). Click on External Editors to bring that panel to the front of the dialog box (**Figure 8.12**). Click on Browse, and use the Select External Editor for Images dialog box to locate the program file for the image editor (on Windows, it will end in .exe). Click on Open to select the file, and OK to close the Preferences dialog box.

When you want to edit an image, just select it in the Document window and then click on Edit in the expanded Properties inspector (shown in **Figure 8.11**). The image will be updated when you return to Dreamweaver. If it isn't, click the Refresh button in the Properties inspector to reload the freshest copy of the image.

Figure 8.13 This image illustrates the best use of the JPEG format. It's a color photograph with lots of different colors, varying levels of contrast, and high-resolution details.

Figure 8.14 The images in this little collage are all GIFs. They have in common a limited palette, large areas that are the same color, and very little fine detail. The lower-right image is an animated gif.

How Do You Say CHEEZ?

Like a lot of computer lingo, there's some question as to the pronunciation of image file names. While *no one* says *gee-eye-eff*, people can't agree on whether it's pronounced *gif*, like gift, or *Jif*, like the peanut butter. (I personally prefer the *gif(t)* pronunciation.) The other terms are easier. JPEG is pronounced *jay-peg*, like a hyphenated name. And PNG is pronounced *ping*, as in pong.

Image Formats

Most Web browsers display two image formats: CompuServe GIF (known as simply GIF) and JPEG (also called JPG). Dreamweaver also supports an image format that is newly supported by generation 4 Web browsers: PNG.

If you've got digitized images that you want to use in your pages, but they're in a format other than GIF or JPEG, you need to use an image editing program to convert them to one of these formats before you can put them on the Web. (Generally, you can do this by selecting File > Save As or File > Export from the image editor's menu bar.)

JPEG & GIF: What's the Diff?

The JPEG format (**Figure 8.13**) was designed for digitized color photographs. JPEGs can support millions of colors, and they're best used when that's what you need. JPEGs are what's called a "lossy" format: the more you compress them, the more information they lose (information in the sense of number of colors, which can lead to decreases in sharpness of the image).

The GIF format (**Figure 8.14**) was invented by CompuServe so that folks on their online service could exchange graphics quickly and easily. GIFs support up to 256 colors (any 256, not a predetermined set). GIFs are the best choice for most nonphotographic images, as well as black-and-white or grayscale photographs and graphics.

✔ Tip

- Animated GIFs in the GIF89a format will display in Dreamweaver although the animation won't play in the Document window. For information about creating animated GIFs, see the book's Web site.

Image Properties

Once the image is on the page, there are several properties you can adjust. These include appearance properties (dimensions and border), layout properties (alignment, Vspace, and Hspace), and page loading properties (Alt tags and low source).

You can also provide a name for your images. This name doesn't show up on screen, but it can be useful if you're planning on working directly with the code, and it's essential for using images in JavaScript or VBscript code.

To name an image:

1. Select the image by clicking on it.

2. In the Properties inspector, type a name for your image (all lowercase, no spaces or funky characters) in the Image text box (**Figure 8.15**).

3. Press Enter (Return) or click on the Apply button.

The image will now be named in the code.

Apply button

Figure 8.15 Name your image by typing a name in the image text box and clicking on the Apply button.

PNG Pong

PNG is a new image format developed by some designers who were frustrated by the limitations of the GIF format and the lossiness of JPEG. Additionally, the GIF format is owned by CompuServe, who requires software that produces GIFs to license the GIF patent.

The PNG development group would like PNG eventually to replace the GIF as a patent-free, lossless image format with dozens of new features. But right now, only a handful of browsers can display it at all. Versions of Navigator or Explorer later than 4 should be able to display the PNG format. Additionally, users of Navigator 2 or later can download a plug-in to enable PNG viewing. You can find out all about PNG at http://www.cdrom.com/pub/png/.

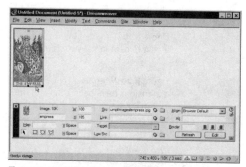

Figure 8.16 Select the image to display image properties in the Properties inspector.

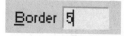

Figure 8.17 Type a number, in pixels, in the Border text box.

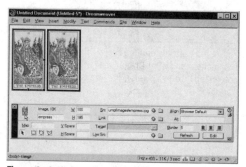

Figure 8.18 Click on the Apply button, and the border will appear around the image. I used a five-pixel border here.

Appearance Properties

In Dreamweaver, the default for displaying images is to display them without any border, but you can add a border if you'd like.

To add an image border:

1. Select the image to which you'd like to add a border (**Figure 8.16**). The Properties inspector will display the image properties.

2. If necessary, expand the Properties inspector by clicking on the Expander arrow in the lower-right corner.

3. In the Properties inspector, type a number in pixels in the Border text box (**Figure 8.17**).

4. Press Enter (Return), or click on the Apply button. The border will be displayed around the image in the Document window (**Figure 8.18**).

The default border color is black, unless you link the image, in which case the image border will take on the link color (see Chapter 9).

When you first place an image with Dreamweaver, it will have the original dimensions it was given when it was created. It's easy to reassign a new height and width to an image to make it fit into the layout of your page.

Transparent GIFs

All GIFs are rectangular, but some are more rectangular than others. You can use an image editing program to create a GIF89 or GIF89a, which support transparency and interlacing (see the sidebar, *Image Size*, later in this chapter). Everything that's a certain color (or colors) in the image will disappear. The trick to making this work to your advantage on a Web page is making the transparency color the same color as your page's background (or vice versa). For obvious reasons, the easiest colors to match are white and black. (To find out how to match the page's background color to an image's RGB color, see Chapter 2.)

To change image dimensions:

1. Select the image you'd like to resize. The Properties inspector will display the Image dimensions in pixels in the W(idth) and H(eight) text boxes.

2. In either text box, you can type a new measurement in any of the following units: pixels, centimeters (cm), inches (in), millimeters (mm), picas (pc), or points (pt).

   For instance, to change the image width to 2 inches, you'd type **2in** (no space between measurement and unit) in the W text box (**Figure 8.19**).

3. Press Enter (Return), or click on the Apply button. The Properties inspector will convert your measurements to pixels, if necessary, and the new measurement will be displayed in boldface in the text box (**Figure 8.20**).

The Document window will display the image's new measurement(s) (**Figure 8.21**).

✔ Tips

- To return the image to its original dimensions, click on the text box label (the letter W or H).

- If the browser knows the image dimensions when it loads the page, the page will finish loading faster, because the browser will pre-draw a space of the right size for the image.

- Changing an image's dimensions with Dreamweaver does not change the file size of the image.

- While Dreamweaver may re-render the image beautifully, the user's browser may not, and image quality could suffer.

Figure 8.19 Type the new measurement in the W or H text box.

Figure 8.20 When the original image dimensions have been changed, the new measurements are displayed in boldface.

Figure 8.21 After I changed the width to two inches (and after Dreamweaver converted it to 192 pixels), the image appeared as shown.

Drag to Resize

Images used to be a drag to resize using Dreamweaver, because it wouldn't automatically scale an image based on the values you typed in the Properties inspector. Now you can drag to resize an image, using the three selection handles shown in **Figure 8.21**, and Dreamweaver will enter the new H and W values in the Properties inspector. To constrain the image to its original scale, hold down the Shift key while you drag.

APPEARANCE PROPERTIES

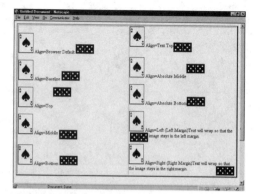

Figure 8.22 Here you can see the various alignment options demonstrated. Each option was applied to the domino graphic. Depending on the option, the domino is either aligned with the largest object in the same paragraph (the ace) or with the text.

Layout Properties

Image alignment is slightly more complicated than text alignment. There are 10 options for image alignment; those options are detailed in the sidebar on this page and demonstrated in **Figure 8.22**.

To adjust image alignment:

1. Select the image whose alignment you want to adjust.

2. In the Properties inspector, click on the Alignment drop-down box and select one of the alignment options displayed in **Figure 8.22**.

As soon as you select an option, the image will move. Some options visibly differ from others only when combined with other objects.

✔ Tip

- To align an image with the horizontal center of the page, select the image and select Modify > Alignment > Center from the Document window menu bar.

Notes on Alignment Options

- The Browser Default alignment is usually *Baseline*.

- The Baseline option aligns the bottom of the image with the baseline of the text or the nearest object. A text baseline is the imaginary line the text sits on.

- The Bottom option aligns the image's bottom with the bottom of the largest nearby object, and Top aligns the top of the image with the top of the object.

- Middle aligns the middle of the image with the text baseline.

- Text Top aligns the image's top with the tallest character in the nearest line of text.

- Absolute Bottom aligns the bottom of the image with the lowest descender in the nearest line of text (the letter *g*, in **Figure 8.22**).

- Absolute Middle aligns the middle of the image with the middle of the text.

- The Left and Right options align the image with the respective margin, wrapping the nearby text so that the image stays at the margin.

An image can bump right up against text or other images, as seen in **Figure 8.23**. (By default, Dreamweaver places a space between each image.) If you want your image to have some breathing room, you can put some invisible space around the image. Vspace is vertical space, above and below the image. Hspace is horizontal space, to the left and right of the image.

To adjust Vspace & Hspace:

1. Click on the image to which you want to add some space.

2. In the Properties inspector, type a number, in pixels, in the Vspace or Hspace text box (**Figure 8.24**).

3. Press Enter (Return) or click on the Apply button. You'll see the rectangle of highlighting around the image increase in size (**Figure 8.25**).

Most likely, you'll want to experiment with the amount of Vspace and Hspace you need on your pages. In **Figure 8.26**, the image at the center has 10 pixels of Vspace and Hspace surrounding it.

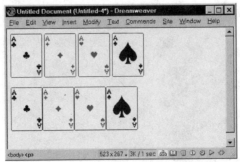

Figure 8.23 By default, Dreamweaver places a space between each image placed in a row. In the second row of images, I removed the spaces to place the images even closer together.

Figure 8.24 In the Vspace and/or Hspace text box, type the amount of space, in pixels, that you want to surround your image.

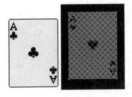

Figure 8.25 I added 10 pixels of both Vspace and Hspace to the image on the right. I dragged to highlight both the image and the space around it.

Figure 8.26 The center image, the ace of hearts, has 10 pixels of Vspace and Hspace surrounding it. Notice how the Vspace affects the entire paragraph (or row): the images above and below the ace of hearts are the same distance from the entire row, even though only one of the images has Vspace added to it.

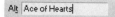

Figure 8.27 Type the alternate text description in the Alt text box.

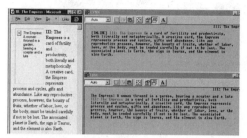

Figure 8.28 In the browser window at the left, IE4 has auto-image loading turned off. Instead of the broken image icon, the user sees the text description, and can decide whether to load the image. At the right are two windows from Lynx, the most popular text-only browser. The upper window shows the page without an Alt tag—all you see is [INLINE] to indicate an image. The other Lynx window displays the Alt tag.

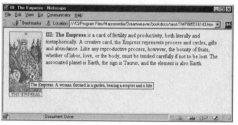

Figure 8.29 Alt tags come in handy even when browsing with images; when you mouse over the image in Navigator 4, you can read the Alt tag.

Beyond the Alt Tag

If you're using an image map (see Appendix A), a button bar, or some other navigational tool that relies on images as links, make sure you supply a text equivalent so that users who aren't loading images can still browse your site. Appendix C on the Web site discusses making a plain-text version of your site and other ways to accommodate users who don't or can't see images when browsing the Web.

Page Loading Properties

Not everyone who surfs the Web does so with image capabilities. Some users who have graphical browsers turn off image auto-loading, while others browse with a text-only browser. Visually impaired users may use text-to-speech browsers that read the page to them; and finally, cell phone users may access the Web on a tiny, text-only screen, or by having their phone service read the page aloud. The only way these users will know the content of your images is if you provide a text alternative, called an Alt tag.

To use an image Alt tag:

1. Select the image for which you want to provide an Alt tag.

2. In the Properties inspector, type a description in the Alt text box (**Figure 8.27**).

3. Press Enter (Return), or click on the Apply button.

Users who view your page without image-viewing capability will be able to read the text description to find out whether they want to view or download the image (**Figure 8.28**).

✔ Tips

- Users of many graphical browsers will see the Alt text displayed as a tool tip when they mouse over the image (**Figure 8.29**).

- Unlike a regular HTML entity, the Alt tag can be in plain English with capital and lowercase letters, spaces, and punctuation; and it can be much longer than the tiny box on the Properties inspector.

If your image is larger than 30K, it will take more than a few seconds to load. One option to take the pain out of waiting for this image to load is to provide a *low-source,* or *low-res,* image that will load more quickly. The low-res image will be replaced by the regular image once it finishes loading. **Figure 8.30** demonstrates this effect.

To use a low-source image:

1. Use your image editor to create a smaller, faster-loading image, such as a black-and-white or grayscale version of the image.

2. Select the image for which you created the low-source version.

3. In the Properties inspector's Low Source text box (**Figure 8.31**), type the location of the image, and press Enter (Return).

   or

   Click on the Browse icon, and use the Select Image Source dialog box to browse through the files and folders on your computer. When you locate the image, click on its name, and then click on Open to close the dialog box and return to the Dreamweaver window.

Your selection will not be visible in the Document window. You can try the effect if you preview the page in your browser, although it will be much faster on your desktop than if you had to download the image from the internet.

✔ Tips

- When you upload your page to the Web server, be sure to send both versions of the image with the page.

- You can drag the Low Src Point to File icon to the low-source image in the Site window. See Chapter 20 for details.

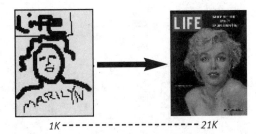

1K - 21K

Figure 8.30 The image on the right, which is the image I want to use on my page, is a 21K full-color JPEG. The image on the left, which took me about 10 seconds to make in a paint program, is a 1K black-and-white GIF. The low-source image will load immediately while the browser downloads the larger image. That way, no one has to feel like they're waiting.

Figure 8.31 Type the location of the image in the Low Src text box; click on the Browse icon to open the Select Image Source dialog box; or drag the Point to File icon to an image in the Sites window.

Figure 8.32 One common use of image rollovers is a set of buttons that "light up" when they're moused over. Dreamweaver's Launcher, mini-Launcher, and Objects palette use image rollovers to make buttons appear "pushed in" or "lit up."

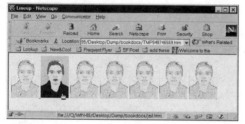

Figure 8.33 You can use any sort of images in a rollover, as long as they're the same size.

Image Rollovers

An *image rollover* is a JavaScript action that lets you swap the source of one image with another image file, so that when you mouse over an image, another image will appear (**Figures 8.32** and **8.33**).

The Rollover Image object sets up a simple behavior that accomplishes three things: Images preload when the page loads; when the user mouses over the specified image, a different image file is displayed; and when the user mouses away from the image, the original image is restored.

The two images need to be the same size, or the second image will be smooshed into the first one's shape.

For the best results, you must save your page before you begin.

Image Size

When you look at image properties in the Properties inspector, one thing you'll see is the image's size. This is a handy shortcut—otherwise, you'd have to use your operating system's file management system to see the file size of the image.

Why do you want to know the file size of your images? Because the smaller your image is—in kilobytes (K), not screen size—the faster it will load. Nothing kills interest in a Web site faster than a horrendous download time, and each image on your page increases that time, so it's wise to keep image size low.

You can see the total file size for your entire page, as well as an estimate of how long it will take to load, in the document window status bar.

What can you do to make images load faster?

◆ Always specify the dimensions of your image. Browsers will read this information and draw a space for the image, so that the rest of the page can load while it's waiting for the image data to come through.

◆ Provide a low-res version of high-resolution and other fat images. (See *To use a low-source image,* earlier in this chapter.)

◆ Use fewer colors. There are few good reasons to use millions of colors in run-of-the-mill graphics.

◆ Use GIFs for everything but color photographs and extremely high-color graphics.

◆ Provide thumbnails. If you're putting art or photographs on the Web, and you really need to use million-color JPEGs, put each large image on a separate page, and provide links to them through tiny, linked thumbnail images (image linking is described in Chapter 9).

◆ Use interlaced GIFs. This image format will load in chunks. Once all the chunks are loaded, the image will come together.

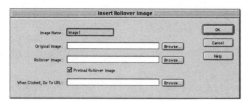

Figure 8.34 The Rollover Image dialog box lets you change the source of an image without even learning Behaviors.

Holy Rollovers

In Dreamweaver 1.0, you needed to create three JavaScript Behaviors in order to make a successful image rollover. In Dreamweaver 3, you can use a single dialog box. That's great.

To find out how to make more complicated image rollovers, see Chapter 15. You can use Behaviors to have user events other than mouseovers (such as clicks or keypresses) make the images change source; you can have an event for one image trigger a source change for a different image; you can make it so that mousing out doesn't require the source to swap back; or you can have the mouseout cause an entirely different image to appear.

To set up a Rollover Image:

1. From the Document window menu bar, select Insert > Rollover Image. The Insert Rollover Image dialog box will appear (**Figure 8.34**).

2. Select the source of the Original Image and the Rollover Image by typing the filenames in the respective text boxes, or by clicking Browse to use the Select Image source dialog box to select a local image.

3. Change the Name of the image if you like, by typing it in the Image Name text box.

4. Will your image link to another Web page? If so, type the URL in the When Clicked, Go To URL text box. Or click on Browse to select a page from your local site.

5. Click on OK to close the Insert Image Rollover dialog box and return to the Dreamweaver window.

6. Preview your page in a JavaScript-capable browser to test the rollover effect.

✔ Tips

- The Preload Images option will be checked by default—leave it checked. There's no good reason *not* to preload images, because it eliminates wait time that would otherwise be caused by having to download the replacement image only when it's requested.

- For more about links, see Chapter 9. For more about how rollovers work, see Chapter 15.

Working with
Links and URLs

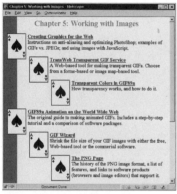

Figure 9.1 This page uses images, a background image, tables, and style sheets, but the real content is in the links. Even if I added background music, Shockwave, files, frames, and a flaming logo, the links would still be the meat here.

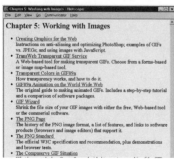

Figure 9.2 This is the same page as shown in Figure 9.1, with all the extras removed. The content remains the same—you can get there from here with nothing but links.

One could easily argue that links, more than fancy typographical or image capabilities, make the Web the Web (**Figures 9.1** and **9.2**). While the bells and whistles of the showier pages are what impress the easily impressed and cause the browser market to boom, the fact is that the most important element in the Hypertext Transfer Protocol—that http at the beginning of Web URLs—is the word hypertext. The transfer protocol part had been around in different forms, from FTP (File Transfer Protocol) to e-mail to Veronica and Archie, for years before the Web was much more than a concept.

The combination of clickable links to documents anywhere on the Internet and the ability to display in-line images is what made the first graphical Web browser, Mosaic, overshadow other hypertext efforts like gopher and WAIS.

With regular old HTML, you can link your pages to other documents within your own site or anywhere in the world. I say "documents" because you can link to images, multimedia files, and downloadable programs as well as other Web pages. You can make text or images into links, as well as linking on text entities that are part of headings, lists, tables, and frames.

Because making links is so impossibly easy with Dreamweaver, this chapter also explores some of the details of how to use links effectively and what makes up a URL.

In this chapter

I'll discuss what the difference is between absolute links, site-root relative links, and document-relative links, and then we'll find out how to make all three. We'll make image links and e-mail links, too. I'll also describe how to link from one part of a page to another using named anchors. You'll get a preview of targets, which are covered extensively in Chapter 11. Then we'll delve into link management, including changing a link sitewide, checking links, and fixing broken links. We'll also find out how to set link colors for a page. And throughout the chapter, I'll discuss URLs, pathnames, and smart linking strategies.

✔Definitions

- A *hyperlink*, or simply *link*, is a pointer from one page to another. The page that contains the link that you click on is called the *referring page*, and the destination of the click is called the *target* of the link (although there are some other definitions of target, too). The code for a link looks like this: `<A HREF="file.html">` linked text `</a>`. `A` stands for *anchor*, the original name for a link. HREF means Hypertext Reference.

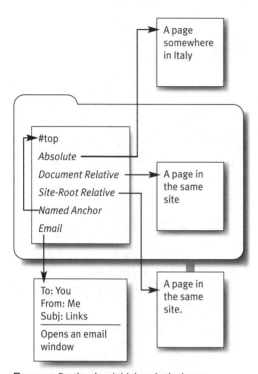

Figure 9.3 For the visual thinkers in the house, a representation of where links go.

Relative Links

Before you start putting links on your Web pages, you should be aware of the different kinds of pathnames you can use to link to another document on the Internet (**Figure 9.3**). There are four different kinds of pathnames you can use:

- **Absolute pathnames (http://www.tarin.com/BayArea/baynav.html)** point to a location on the Internet outside the site where the current page is located. In the pathname http://www.tarin.com/BayArea/baynav.html, the document baynav.html is located within the BayArea/ directory, which is within the root site www.tarin.com/.

- **Document-relative pathnames (../baynav.html)** point from the current document to another document within the same site, using "../" to denote when the browser needs to move up to another directory to retrieve the file. You can link from one document to another without using the full URL. The browser looks from the current page, but within the site, to locate the file.

- **Site-root-relative pathnames (/baynav.html)** also point from the current document to another document that's within the same site, but uses the server's directory as its base, and not the current page. This linking method is best used for large sites because it's useful for sites in which pages might be moved around.

- **Named anchors** link to a point within a page; either from point to point on a single page, or from one page to a specific location on another page.

Document vs. Site-Root?

If you're having trouble understanding the differences between Document-relative and Site-root-relative links, use Document-relative pathnames for your site.

Different Links
for Different Things

Except in those cases where you're using a relative link to a document in the same site as the referring page, you always need to specify the protocol type for the link. Even though some browsers can locate sites that lack the `http://` when typed into the browser's location field, most browsers won't recognize links without a protocol type being specified.

Besides http, there are several other kinds of protocols you may use; mailto and ftp are the two most common after `http`.

`gopher://`   Gopher hypertext index

`shttp://`   Secure Hypertext Transfer Protocol, used by secure commerce servers supporting the protocol

`ftp://`   File Transfer Protocol

`mailto:`   An Internet e-mail address; launches a mail composition window in some browsers

`news:`   A Usenet or other network news resource group or discussion group; often launches a newsgroup browser

`telnet:`   Remote access to a Telnet server; often launches a Telnet client

`wais://`   Wide Area Internet Search

In general, if the protocol type is left off a coded URL, the browser will look for a local file rather than an Internet URL.

Link text box   *Browse button*

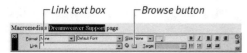

Figure 9.4 Highlight the text you want to make into a link.

Figure 9.5 In the Properties inspector's Link text box, type or paste the URL of the document you're linking to.

Figure 9.6 Press Enter (Return), and the text you selected will become a link.

Making Links

Making links with Dreamweaver is easier than eating pie. You don't even have to remember any keystrokes or use any dialog boxes—just use the ever-handy Properties inspector to put your links in there.

To make text links:

1. With your page open in the Document window, highlight the text you want to make into a link (**Figure 9.4**).

2. If necessary, display the Properties inspector (**Figure 9.4**) by selecting Modify > Selection Properties from the Document window menu bar.

3. In the Link text box, type (or paste) the location of the document to which you want to link (**Figure 9.5**).

4. Press Enter (Return).

Your text will now be linked, as indicated by underlining and a change of color of the text you selected (**Figure 9.6**).

✔ Tips

■ To unlink, delink, or remove a link, highlight the text or image that's currently linked. Then, in the Properties inspector, highlight the URL in the Link text box, and delete it. Press Enter (Return), and poof! No more link.

■ The Link text box is also a drop-down menu. Click on it to choose from a list of recently used links.

■ In Dreamweaver 3, you can link to a file on your local site by dragging the Point to File icon onto a file in the Site window. Read Chapter 20 to find out more about using the Site window for links.

Making Relative Links

An easy way to have Dreamweaver manage relative links is to create a local site on your hard drive (explained in Chapter 3).

To make a relative text link:

1. Save the page you're working on by selecting File > Save from the Document window menu bar. If this is the first time you're saving the page, the Save As dialog box will appear. Make sure you're saving the file in the directory (folder) of your choice, and type a filename in the File name text box. Click on Save to close the Save As dialog box and save the file.

2. Select the text you want to make into a link (as shown back in **Figure 9.4**).

3. In the Properties inspector, click on the Browse button 🗀. The Select HTML File dialog box will appear (**Figures 9.7** and **9.8**).

4. From the Relative To pull-down menu, select either Document or Site Root (**Figure 9.9**).

5. Browse through the files and folders on your computer until you locate the document to which you want to link. Click on the file's icon so that its name shows up in the File Name text box. The URL text box will display the link path (**Figure 9.10**).

6. Click on Open to choose the file. The Select HTML File dialog box will close, returning you to the Document window. You'll see your link underlined and the path displayed in the Properties inspector.

✔ Tip

■ If you're making a document-relative path for a file in the same directory, you can simply type the filename of the page in the Properties inspector's Link text box.

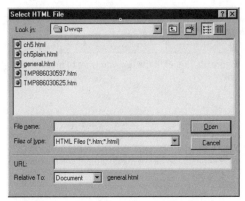

Figure 9.7 The Select HTML File dialog box functions like the Open dialog boxes you're used to by now.

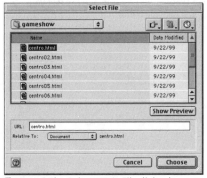

Figure 9.8 The Select HTML File dialog box on the Macintosh.

Figure 9.9 From the pull-down menu, select either Document, to make the link relative to the current page, or Site Root, to make the link relative to a central location on your Web site.

Figure 9.10 When you're all done, you should see a filename in the File Name text box and the path to that file in the URL text box.

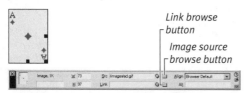

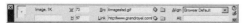

Figure 9.11 Select the image you want to make into a link.

Figure 9.12 Type or paste the URL in the Properties inspector, or click on the Browse button to choose a file.

Figure 9.13 After you specify the link in your Properties inspector, you can add a border to your image, if you like.

To make an image link:

1. With your page open in the Document window, select the image you want to make into a link by clicking on it (**Figure 9.11**).

2. If necessary, display the Properties inspector by double-clicking the image.

3. In the Link text box, type (or paste) the location of the document to which you want to link (**Figure 9.12**).

4. Press Enter (Return), or click on the Apply button.

Your image will be linked, and you can add a link border to it (**Figure 9.13**). To learn about how to add a border to your linked image, see the next page.

✔ Tip

■ To make a relative link, follow the steps on the preceding page in *Making Relative Links*. Make sure you click on the Link browse button, instead of the similar button next to the Image Src text box.

Auto-Fixing Relative Links

If you want Dreamweaver to fix relative links automatically when you perform a Save As (that is, save the file to a new location), you can set this option in the Preferences. Press Ctrl+U (Command+U) to view the Preferences dialog box, and click on General to bring that panel to the front. From the Update Links drop-down menu, select Always, Never, or Prompt. The Prompt option will ask you before updating link paths. When you're done, click on OK to close the Preferences dialog box.

To turn on a border:

1. Select the image by clicking on it.

2. If necessary, expand the Properties inspector by clicking on the expander arrow in the lower-right corner.

3. In the Properties inspector, type a number in the Border text box. In this case, I'll add a border value of "1".

4. Press Enter (Return), or click on the Apply button and the border will appear (**Figure 9.14**).

✔ Tip

■ You can also make a heavier border by typing a number other than 1 in the border text box.

Border width

Figure 9.14 To add a border to the image's link, specify a border width of 1 or higher in the Properties inspector.

Figure 9.15 Highlight the text you want to become an e-mail link.

Figure 9.16 Use the Insert E-mail Link text box to enter your text and your e-mail address.

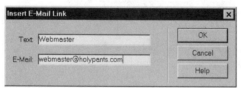

Figure 9.17 Include the full address in the format name@domain.suffix. Do not include the "mailto" protocol or any HTML.

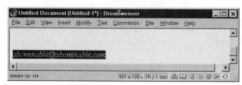

Figure 9.18 Highlight the text you want to turn into an e-mail link.

Figure 9.19 Type the full address, and type mailto: in front of it, without a space.

Figure 9.20 E-mail links look just like any other links: They're underlined and link-colored. I also used italics here.

Links to e-mail addresses look like this:

```
<A HREF="mailto:dreamweaver@tarin.com">
send mail</A>
```

You can insert them using a dialog box or the Properties inspector.

To insert an e-mail link (auto):

1. Highlight the text or image you want to make into an e-mail link, or just click the insertion point at the place where you want the link to appear (**Figure 9.15**).

2. From the Document window menu bar, select Insert > E-mail Link. The Insert E-mail Link dialog box will appear (**Figure 9.16**).

3. If you highlighted text to serve as a link in step 1, that text will appear in the Text text box. You may edit it or leave it as is, or you can type new text.

4. Type the full e-mail address in the E-mail text box (**Figure 9.17**).

5. Click on OK to close the Insert E-mail Link dialog box and insert your e-mail link.

To make an e-mail link (manual):

1. Highlight the text or image you want to make into an e-mail link (**Figure 9.18**).

2. In the Properties inspector Link text box, type mailto:address@domain.com, substituting the proper, full e-mail address for address@domain.com (**Figure 9.19**).

3. Press Enter (Return). Your text or image will become an e-mail link (**Figure 9.20**).

✔ Tip

- When your visitor clicks on an e-mail link in the browser window, the browser will generally pop open a mail window. You may also want to provide the address in plain text so that people using different software can get the e-mail address easily.

What's in a URL?

Your typical Web URL might look like this: `http://www.peachpit.com/`, but then again, it might look like this:

`http://www.macromedia.com/support/dreamweaver/whatsnew/`

or like this:

`http://husky.northern-hs.ga.k12.md.us/`

What's all that stuff mean, anyway?

The `http:` is the name of the protocol, which in the case of a Web site, is the Hypertext Transfer Protocol. (See the sidebar *Different Links for Different Things,* earlier in this chapter, for a description of each kind.)

The slashes (and those are forward slashes, *not* backslashes) indicate something else.

Everything between the first two slashes and the next slash is called the *domain name*.

The `www`, or whatever is the first "word" in a URL following the slashes, is the name of the Web server. Most folks these days use `www` because it's easy to remember.

The `.com` or `.gov` is called the *top-level domain,* which is administrated by InterNIC.

In the three-part URLs you see most often, such as `www.peachpit.com`, or `thomas.loc.gov`, the word between the `www.` and the `.com` is commonly called the *domain name*; it is referred to as the *second level domain* by administrators and the InterNIC. It's the part you buy, if you want to register, say, `macromedia.com`.

In the third example above, there is a several-level hierarchy to the domain name. If you read the URL from back to front, the `.us` is the US domain used by state governments and such. The `.md` is the Maryland subdomain; the `.k12` is the educational subdomain of Maryland; and the `.garrett` is the county subdomain of the educational system. The `.northern-hs` is the individual high school, and `husky` is the name of the Web server itself.

In the second example, the domain name itself is uncomplicated, and the rest of the URL, `support/dreamweaver/whatsnew/`, indicates three levels of directories within the Web server—which after all is just a computer like any other. Think of it like subfolders on your computer: `C:\Program Files\Macromedia\Dreamweaver`, for instance.

If the URL ends in a filename, as in `http://www.tarin.com/fridge.html`, that means that the `fridge.html` is the document itself that you're requesting. If the URL ends in a slash, it means that you're getting the *default file* for that directory. In most cases, `http://www.dhtmlzone.com/index.html` and `http://www.dhtmlzone.com/` are the same file.

MAKING LINKS

Common Top-Level Domains

.com	Commercial entity
.edu	Educational entity
.gov	U.S. Government
.mil	U.S. Military
.net	Network provider
.org	Nonprofit organization
.au	Australia
.ca	Canada
.ch	Switzerland
.cn	China
.de	Germany
.dk	Denmark
.es	Spain
.fi	Finland
.fr	France
.ie	Ireland
.in	India
.it	Italy
.jp	Japan
.kr	South Korea
.mx	Mexico
.my	Malaysia
.nl	Netherlands
.nz	New Zealand
.se	Sweden
.sg	Singapore
.tw	Taiwan
.uk	United Kingdom
.us	United States
.za	South Africa

Using Named Anchors

A named anchor consists of two parts: a named entity at a point on an HTML page, and a link to that anchor. While regular old links point to an entire document, named anchors link to part of a document. Very long documents should be broken into separate pages, but there can be cases where you want a clickable table of contents (or something similar) that will direct visitors to an area of a page instead of the top of it. You can also place a link to take users from the bottom of a page to the top (see **Figure 9.27**, next page.

First, you need to name the part of the page you want to link to. You can name a piece of text, an image, or a headline, for instance.

To name an entity:

1. With the page on which you want to insert a named anchor open in the Document window, click to place the insertion point at the place where you want the anchor, or highlight an entity to name (such as a piece of text or an image).

continues on next page

2. From the Document window menu bar, select Insert > Named Anchor. The Insert Named Anchor dialog box will appear (**Figure 9.21**).

3. Type a name for your anchor in the Anchor Name text box. This name should be a single lowercase word or number.

4. Click on OK to close the Insert Named Anchor dialog box and return to the Document window.

A dialog box may appear (**Figure 9.22**) that tells you what I'm about to tell you right now: You won't see any visible evidence of your anchor unless invisible element viewing is turned on.

To view invisible elements:

1. From the Document window menu bar, select View > Invisible Elements.

2. Any invisible elements on your pages will appear, in the form of icons (**Figure 9.23**). To figure out what an invisible element is or does, click on its icon, and the Properties inspector will display properties for that element (**Figure 9.24**).

Linking to Named Anchors

1. In the Document window, select the text or image you want to use as a link (**Figure 9.25**).

2. In the Properties inspector, type the pound sign (#) in the Link text box.

3. With no space between the pound sign and the name of the anchor, type the anchor name in the Link text box. For instance, if your anchor name is top, you'd type #top in the Link text box (**Figure 9.26**).

4. Press Enter (Return), and your text or image will become linked to the named anchor.

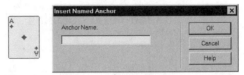

Figure 9.21 Name your anchor with the Insert Named Anchor dialog box. I'd rather name an anchor at this location "aced" than "ace_of_diamonds."

Figure 9.22 This dialog box appears when you insert an invisible element with invisible element viewing turned off.

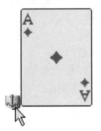

Figure 9.23 The little blip next to the image is the Anchor icon (it has a little anchor on it). You can view or hide these invisible element icons as needed by selecting View > Invisible Elements From the Document window menu bar.

Anchor element marker

Figure 9.24 Click on an invisible element icon, and the Properties inspector will display information about it.

Perhaps the deadliest candidate for biological weaponry is smallpox. American soldiers used it successfully against Indians by selling or giving them infected blankets. Purportedly, the disease is contained only in two laboratories, one in the United States and one in Russia. The smallpox story, however, does not end with the amazing, audacious eradication from nature of the virus.

Figure 9.25 Select the text or image you want to link to the named anchor.

Figure 9.26 Type the name of the anchor in the Link text box, preceded by the # sign.

✔ Tips

■ The page in **Figure 9.27** includes a table of contents at the top of the page. Even though the document is broken up into separate files, each link points to a specific part of each page (right above the section head). A link to the table of contents is included at the end of each section.

■ To link to an anchor on the same page, the Link text box only needs to include the # and the name of the link, as in #fred.

■ To link to an anchor on a page in the same directory, the link would be something like people.html#fred.

■ To link to an anchor on a page elsewhere on the Web, the link would be something like http://www.homer.com/donut.htm#mmm.

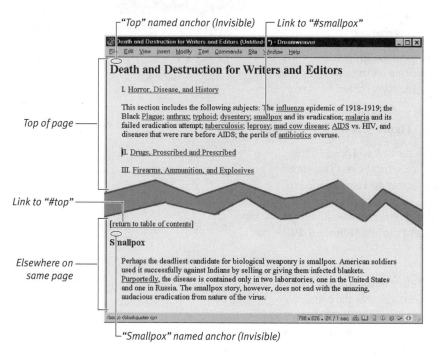

"Top" named anchor (Invisible) ⌐ *Link to "#smallpox"*

Top of page —

Link to "#top" —

Elsewhere on same page —

⌐*"Smallpox" named anchor (Invisible)*

Figure 9.27 This page is an example of a document that uses named anchors.

Aiming Targets

A *target* is an attribute of links that tells the link where to open the link in question. The main use of targets is in frames-based sites, which use targets to determine in which frame a link will open. This aspect of targets is thoroughly explained in Chapter 8. There are two kinds of targets that you might want to use in non-frames pages, however.

♦ `target=_blank` makes the link open in a new, blank browser window.

♦ `target=_top` makes the link replace the content of the current window

The other kinds of targets apply only to frames. If you're making a page that you plan on using in a frames-based site, refer to Chapter 12, which also includes instructions on how to set a base target for an entire page. To set a target in the current page, follow these steps:

1. Create a link as explained in *Making Links*, earlier in this chapter.

2. If necessary, expand the Properties inspector by clicking on the expander arrow in the lower-right corner.

3. From the Target pull-down menu, choose `_blank` or `_top` (**Figure 9.28**).

If you choose `_top`, the link will open in the same window as the current page. (This target is more useful for frames and isn't needed to make links behave.) Choosing `_blank` will make a brand-new browser window open and load the target of the link (**Figure 9.29**).

✔ Tip

■ Some HTML editors automatically insert the `target=""` attribute into the code. This is harmless; it simply reiterates that the link will open in the default or base target location. You can also remove this code with impunity in the HTML inspector.

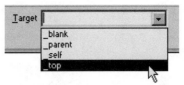

Figure 9.28 I used a `target=_blank` setting to make a link in the first browser window (back) open in a second browser window. Use this setting sparingly; it can get annoying if over-applied.

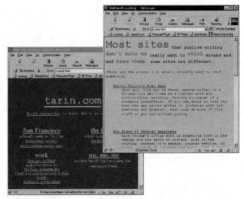

Figure 9.29 Clicking on a link on one page spawns a new browser window that then loads the link.

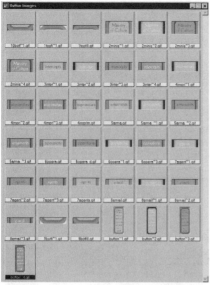

Figure 9.30 This is my collection of future button images, displayed in an image catalog program.

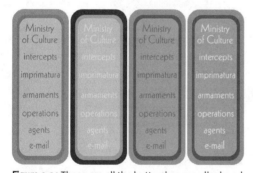

Figure 9.31 These are all the button images, displayed as navbars.

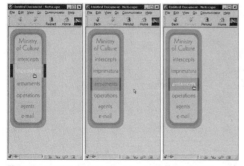

Figure 9.32 The three browser windows depict the three actions: Over, Down, Over While Down.

Using Navigation Bars

If you want to create a navigation bar, (also called *navbar* or *button bar*), to guide people through your site, Dreamweaver can simplify the process. Otherwise, you'd have to write a complex rollover for each button in the navigation bar. Using Dreamweaver, you just fill in the blanks.

A button can have as many as four looks in a Dreamweaver navigation bar: Up, or initial; Over, or "lit up" (when the user mouses over the button); Down, or "pushed in" (when the user clicks on the button); and Over While Down (when the user mouses over the button while it's "pushed in"). You need have only one set of images to create a navigation bar, but you must create a seperate image file for each state of each button on the bar. **Figures 9.30** and **9.31** show the four sets of images that will be used as buttons in the four different states. **Figure 9.32** shows the buttons in action.

✔ Tips

- This chapter assumes you're starting from scratch with a batch of images, but you can expedite things if you use Macromedia Fireworks to create your buttons. You can use the Button Editor to export the buttons along with prewritten HTML and JavaScript. Then you can edit the pages in Dreamweaver. In the Save As or Export dialog box of Fireworks, select Dreamweaver 3 from the Style drop-down menu in the HTML area of the dialog box.

- See Chapter 15 for tips on editing navbars with behaviors.

To make sure your links work properly, all your images should be stored in your local site (see Chapters 3 and 8), and the page should be saved before you begin.

To insert a navigation bar:

1. From the Document window menu bar, select Insert > Navigation bar. The Insert Navigation Bar dialog box will appear (**Figure 9.33**).

2. In the Up Image text box, type the filename of the image you wish to use; or, click on Browse, and use the Select Image Source dialog box (**Figure 9.34** and **9.35**) to select the image from a folder in your local site.

3. After you select the first image, Dreamweaver will insert a name for the button in the Element Name text box (**Figure 9.36**). You may edit this name if you wish.

4. Repeat step 2 for any additional positions for your button: Up, Down, and Over While Down.

5. If this button should be in the down state when the page loads (**Figure 9.37**), check the Show "Down Image" Initially checkbox. An asterisk will appear by the name of the selected over-while-down image. Usage example: You're putting a button bar on the Archive page; one of your buttons says "Archive," and you want the button to be pushed in when the user visits this page. You'd then change this option to highlight each section.

6. In the When Clicked, Go To URL text box, type the URL for your link; or, if the link is a page on your site, click Browse and use the Select HTML File dialog box to select the page and set the local path.

7. To insert another button, click on the + button. Then, follow steps 1-6 to specify images and links.

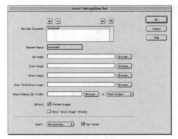

Figure 9.33 The Insert Navigation Bar dialog box.

Figure 9.34 The Select Image Source dialog box. With the preview turned on, you can make sure your button states look as they're supposed to.

Figure 9.35 The Select Image Source dialog box for the Mac. Click Show Preview to see a thumbnail of the selected image.

Figure 9.36 After you select the Up image, Dreamweaver inserts the button name in the Name text box.

Figure 9.37 On this navigation bar, the Ministry of Culture page will load with the Ministry button already selected, or down.

Figure 9.38 Navigation bars can be horizontal, too.

Figure 9.39 The navigation bar appears in the Document window. You can see the table border, barely, around the buttons.

Figure 9.40 Previewing the page in a browser lets you test all the rollover effects.

8. The navigation bar can display across the page or down the page. Select Vertically (**Figure 9.37**) or Horizontally (**Figure 9.38**) from the Insert drop-down menu.

9. To use tables to make your navigation bar stay in shape, select that checkbox.

10. To rearrange the order of the buttons, select a button name and then use the up and down arrow buttons to move the button through the list.

11. If you're not using dynamically served images, leave the Preload Images checkbox checked, so that the Web browser can fetch all the images for all the button states while the page is loading (instead of having to get them when the user mouses over them).

12. When you're finished, click on OK to close the Insert Navigation Bar dialog box and return to the Document window. Your navigation bar will be displayed (**Figure 9.39**).

13. After the button is on your page, you must preview it in a browser to test it (**Figure 9.40**). From the Document window menu bar, select File. Preview in Browser > [Browser Name], or Press F12.

✔ Tips

- See Chapter 2 for more about previewing.

- To find out how to modify the table Dreamweaver inserts with your navbar, see Chapter 10; in particular, the section *Row Heights and Column Widths* may help.

- To find out about adding the navbar to the Library for reuse, see Chapter 17.

- Make sure, when you put this page on the Web, that you upload all the images along with the page (see *About Dependent Files*, in Chapter 20). I'd recommend uploading a test page with the navbar on it, so you can check all the image locations, before you try to use it on a live page.

To modify your navbar:

1. From the Document window menu bar, select Modify > Navigation bar. The Modify Navigation bar dialog box will appear (**Figure 9.41**).

2. Make any necessary changes as described in the preceding section.

3. When you're done, click on OK to close the Modify Navigation Bar dialog box and insert your updated navigation bar.

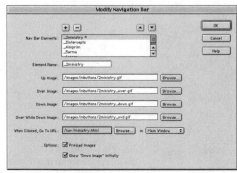

Figure 9.41 Modifying a navigation bar uses practically the same dialog box as the one for adding it.

Managing Links

Dreamweaver can help you keep track of links, check them, and update them. In this section, we'll discuss how to check links, how to fix links, and how to change a link sitewide.

✔ Tip

■ Chapter 20 describes more link management tips, including the Point to File option in the Site window, and visual linking with the Site Map (**Figure 9.42**).

Site Map ┐   ┌─Home page   ┌─Linking between pages

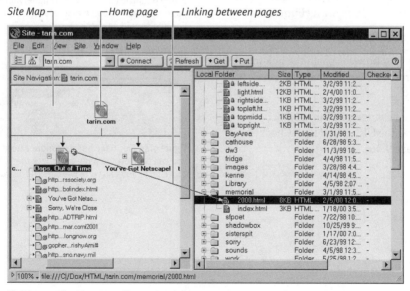

Figure 9.42 The Site Map offers a visual depiction of the site you can use to assess link relationships.

Checking Links

Dreamweaver can check all the relative links on a page or in a local site and see if any are broken. This does not check external links.

To check links on one page:

1. Open the page you want to check in the Document window.

2. From the Document window menu bar, select File > Check Links.

3. The Link Checker dialog box will appear (**Figure 9.43**). The Broken Links panel displays any links on your page that are not intact. This may include links to pages that exist but for which there is no copy on your local site.

To check external links:

1. Follow steps 1 and 2, above.

2. To see a list of external links on the current page, select External Links from the Show drop-down menu (**Figure 9.44**).

3. In the Link Checker, double-click on an external URL to select it (**Figure 9.45**).

4. Copy the URL (Ctrl+C or Command+C).

5. Open your browser, paste the link into the browser's location bar, and check the page.

6. You can change an external link by pasting the URL in the Link Checker (**Figure 9.46**).

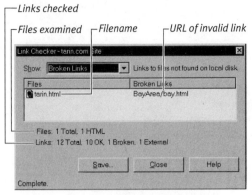

Figure 9.43 The Broken Links panel of the Link Checker dialog box displays relative links that do not exist on your local site.

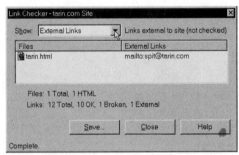

Figure 9.44 The external links summary for the same page indicates that an e-mail address is an external link and should be checked.

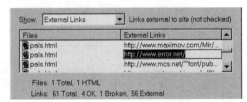

Figure 9.45 This page has a lot more external links. You can preview the page and check the links in the browser, or you can work with the URL list directly.

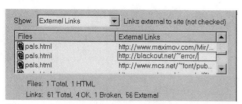

Figure 9.46 Here, I'm pasting in a new URL for a page that moved. Changes I make in this dialog box are saved even if I don't open the page in the Document window.

Figure 9.47 The Site window, displaying local files in the site I want to check.

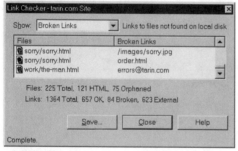

Figure 9.48 If I connect to my remote site (see Chapter 20), I'll be able to find out which of these pages are truly missing and which aren't copied to my local site.

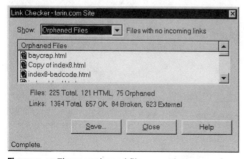

Figure 9.49 These orphaned files, mostly tests and backups, can be safely moved to a folder outside my local site, or they can be deleted.

To check links over a local site:

1. From the Document window menu bar, select Site > Open Site > Site name. The Site window will appear and display the contents of the selected site (**Figure 9.47**).

2. From the Site window menu bar, select Site > Check Links Sitewide. The Link Checker dialog box will appear (**Figure 9.48**) and begin scanning your local site.

3. This'll take a few seconds or so, depending on the size of your site. When it's done, the summary will display how many files were checked, how many links were checked, how many links are broken, and how many external links it found.

4. The Link Checker will also count any orphaned files; that is, files that are present in your local site, but are not linked to from any other page. To view a list of orphaned files, select Orphaned Files from the Show drop-down menu (**Figure 9.49**).

✔ Tip

- You can check links within a folder or a few files, too. Select the group of files in the Site window. Then select File > Check links from the Site window menu bar.

To save the results as a file:

1. In the Link Checker dialog box, click on Save. The Save As dialog box will appear.

2. Select the correct folder, type a name for your file, and click Save. Use the extension .txt; the file format is tab-delimited text.

✔ Tip

- You can insert the results onto a Web page as a table (**Figure 9.50**). From the Document window menu bar, select File > Import > Import Table Data, and in the dialog box (**Figure 9.51**), set the Delimiter to Tab, click the Browse button, and select the file you just saved. See Chapter 10 for explicit instructions on using this dialog box.

Fixing Links

You can use the Link Checker to help you fix links on a single page or over an entire site.

✔ Tip

- If File Check In/Check Out is enabled, Dreamweaver will check out any file you need to fix. See Chapter 20 for more on checking in and checking out, including how to turn it on and off (**Figure 9.52**).

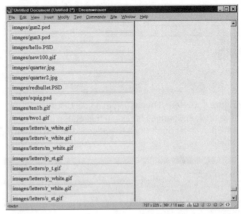

Figure 9.50 You can view the saved link data as a table.

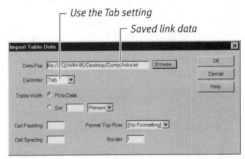

Figure 9.51 Chapter 10 explains what all this stuff means, but you can use this dialog box now to import your saved link data file.

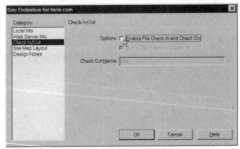

Figure 9.52 Chapter 20 describes how you can use file Check In and Check Out to keep track of group projects.

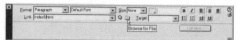

Figure 9.53 When I double-click on the broken link, the page opens in the Document window with the link conveniently highlighted.

Figure 9.54 I can fix the link in the Properties inspector. This was a simple typo.

Browse button

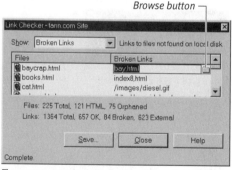

Figure 9.55 I can look for the file, in case I moved it or renamed it, using the Link Checker's Browse button.

Let the Circle Be Unbroken

When a link is fixed, it will disappear from the Link Checker's list of broken links. On the other hand, if the page doesn't exist on your local site, the Link Checker will still consider it broken.

The Link Checker checks image paths, and it also will mark an image path as broken if the image isn't on the local site.

To open a listed page:

1. Double-click on any page in the list to open it. The link or image reference you clicked on will be highlighted automatically in the Document window (**Figure 9.53**).

2. You can fix the highlighted link in the Properties inspector (**Figure 9.54**). Type the new link, or use the Browse For File button.

To fix broken links:

1. Use the Link Checker on a page, a group of pages, or a local site, as described earlier in *To check links on one page* or *To check links over a local site*.

2. In the Link Checker dialog box, click on the URL of a broken link. A file button will appear (**Figure 9.55**).

3. Type the correct URL (external or relative) over the old URL.

   or

   Click on the File button to open the Select HTML File dialog box. Choose the correct file from your local site and click on Select.

4. If the link occurs more than once, Dreamweaver will ask you if you want to fix all occurrences. Click on Yes to fix all links to that URL or click on No to change just this one link.

MANAGING LINKS

Changing a Link Sitewide

If you know the location of a file to which you link often has changed, you can edit all occurrences of that link easily.

To change a link sitewide:

1. From the Site window menu bar, select Site > Change Link Sitewide. The Change Link Sitewide dialog box will appear (**Figure 9.56**).

2. Type the old URL in the Change All Links To text box, or click Browse to choose the file.

3. Type the new URL in the Into Links To text box, or click Browse to choose the file.

4. Click on OK to start scanning for links to that file.

5. If any links are found, the Update Files dialog box will appear and list them (**Figure 9.57**).

6. To proceed with the changes, click Update.

7. If File Check In/Check Out is enabled, Dreamweaver will attempt to check out the files. See Chapter 20 for details. You can Cancel the FTP dialog box (**Figure 9.58**) and the files will still be updated.

✔ Tip

- Dreamweaver can automatically check links and change them over an entire site when you move a file or rename it. You can use the Site window as a file management tool, and it'll even warn you if you're about to delete a file that other pages link to. See Chapter 20 for details on moving and renaming files in the Site window.

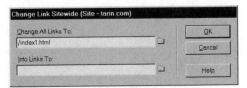

Figure 9.56 Find all links to any address, including an e-mail address or image path, and change them in a snap.

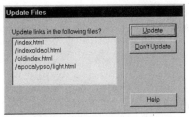

Figure 9.57 The Update Files dialog box lists everything that links to the given URL.

Figure 9.58 If you don't want to check out the files, click Cancel.

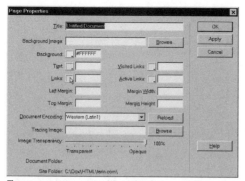

Figure 9.59 You can modify Link, Alink, and Vlink colors with the Page Properties dialog box.

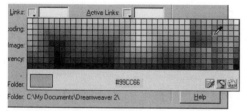

Figure 9.60 Click on the Colors button, and when the Colors palette appears, click on a color to select it.

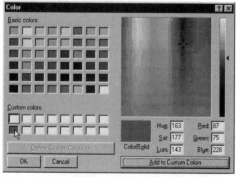

Figure 9.61 For tips on using this dialog box and the equivalent Color dialog box for the Mac, see Chapter 2.

Changing Link Colors

Link colors are part of what's known as *page properties*—the set of options that are applied to an entire page, rather than to an object on that page. The other page properties are covered in Chapter 2.

To change the link colors of a given page:

1. With the page open in the Document window, select Modify > Page Properties from the menu bar. The Page Properties dialog box will appear (**Figure 9.59**).

2. The text boxes marked Links, Visited Links, and Active Links control those colors for the current page. Type (or paste) the hex code for the desired color in the appropriate text box.

   or

   Click on the Color button beside the appropriate text box. The Colors palette will appear (**Figure 9.60**). Click on a color to select it.

   or

   Click on the Colors button in the Colors palette 🎨. The Color dialog box will appear (**Figure 9.61**). Click on a hue and shade to choose a color, and click on OK to close the Color dialog box and return to the Page Properties dialog box. (For details on using the Color dialog box for both platforms, refer to Chapter 2.)

3. In any case, when the hex code for the chosen color appears in the Page Properties dialog box, you can click on OK to close the dialog box and return to the Dreamweaver window, or you can modify the other link color options. The link color will be the only immediately apparent change.

Smart Linking Strategies

Links exist so visitors will click on them. While there's no single right way to make a link, keep these tips in mind so that your links will make people want to click.

- Link on a meaningful word or phrase that gives the user some idea of where they're headed.

  Right: Visit our renewable energy resource page to find out more.

  Wrong: Click here to find out more about renewable energy.

- When you link to something other than an HTML page, such as a sound or multimedia file, warn the user what's coming, and how big the file is.

  Right: Combustion (AU File, 153K)

  Wrong: My Friend Larry (This is wrong if it points to a 500K MIDI file with no warning.)

- If you're linking words within a sentence, stop the link before the punctuation, and don't underline spaces unnecessarily.

  Right: I grew up in Texas, Michigan, and Sri Lanka.

  Wrong: The best red wines come from France, Italy, Germany, and California, in that order.

- Making links into *non sequiturs* (such as the word cheese pointing to a Kung Fu movie site) can work well for irreverent sites, but isn't as effective when you want someone to visit a particular page on purpose.

- If you rely on images (particularly on button bars or image maps) as navigational tools, be sure to provide text equivalents of the same links.

- Come up with house rules about link length and structure, and stick to them.

Link, Alink, and Vlink

There are three kinds of Link colors: Link, Alink (Active Link), and Vlink (Visited Link). The link color is what users see when they haven't yet visited the target of the link. The Alink color is what they see while they're in the act of clicking on a link, and the Vlink color is the color the link assumes when the user has already visited the target page. (The last several days, weeks, or months of visits are recorded in the browser's History file, which is how the browser knows which links to assign the Vlink color.) If you don't choose colors for these options, the browser default colors will be used instead. In most cases, make sure that you have two different colors for Link and Vlink, so that users can tell what parts of your site they've already visited.

WORKING WITH TABLES

Club Luxe February Schedule		
Date & Time	Band Name	Booking Contact
02/12 9 p.m.	Inspired	Karen
02/13 10 p.m.	Long Walk Home	Karen
02/14 8:30 p.m.	Poetry Night	Leonard
02/16 10 p.m.	The Hangnails	LuAnn
02/17 9 p.m.	Little Lost Dog	Karen
02/18 9 p.m.	Bonewart	LuAnn
02/20 TBA	Rumpled Stilt Walker	Karen
02/21 8:30 p.m.	Poetry Night	Leonard
02/23 9 p.m.	Cardboard Milk Truck	LuAnn
02/25 10 p.m.	Alonzo & the Rats	Karen
02/26 9 p.m.	Lesson Plan	Karen
02/27 10 p.m.	Karaoke From Mars	Karen
02/28 9 p.m.	Poetry Night	Leonard

Figure 10.1 HTML tables can be used to create all kinds of data tables.

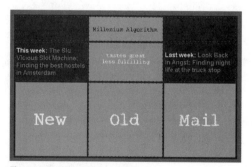

Figure 10.2 With a little imagination, you can use tables to replicate nearly any layout you can make with page layout programs such as Quark or PageMaker.

Table functionality was added to HTML to simplify presenting tabular data, such as scientific reports. While tables are still great for making, well, *tables* (**Figure 10.1**), clever designers quickly realized that tables could be used to vastly improve design options (**Figure 10.2**).

Like the mailboxes that line the wall at the post office, each individual cubbyhole, called a *cell,* holds discrete information that doesn't ooze over into the other boxes. As you can see in **Figure 10.3** on the next page, tables are divided into *rows,* which cross the table horizontally, and *columns,* which span the table vertically.

Hand-coding a table is tiresome at best. In fact, tables are probably the most convenient feature of most WYSIWYG Web page creation programs, although many of these tools code tables rather sloppily—not so with Dreamweaver.

Setting Up Tables

Creating a table is a three-part process, although the second and third steps often take place simultaneously.

1. First, you insert the table onto your page.

2. Then, you modify the properties of the table and its cells.

3. Finally, you insert content, such as text and images, into the table.

✔ Tips

- You can plan your table beforehand, if you know how many cells you want; or you can make it up as you go along, and add cells, rows, and columns as needed.

- While virtually every current Web browser handles tables correctly, many older browsers, and most nongraphic browsers, don't. See Appendix A on the Web site for tips on working with different kinds of browsers.

- If you're planning on working with dynamic content using layers, you can automatically convert tables to layers. From the document window menu bar, select Convert > Tables to Layers. See Chapter 14 for more on layers and instructions on how to convert tables to layers and vice-versa.

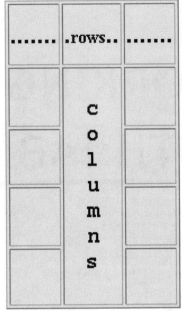

Figure 10.3 This table consists of three columns and five rows. The center column consists of only two cells, the larger of which was created by merging together four cells.

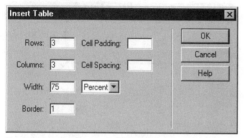

Figure 10.4 Choose Table from the Insert menu.

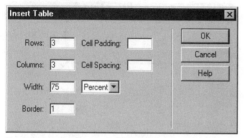

Figure 10.5 Click on the Table button on the Objects palette to open the Insert Table dialog box.

Figure 10.6 Click on the Width drop-down menu to make the width unit either pixels or percent of the browser window.

Figure 10.7 I inserted a new table with five rows and two columns.

To insert a table:

1. Click to place the insertion point where you'd like the table to appear.

2. You can insert a table in one of two ways:
   - From the Document Window menu bar, select Insert > Table (**Figure 10.4**).

   or

   Click on the Table button on the Objects palette: 田.

   Either way, the Insert Table dialog box will appear (**Figure 10.5**).

3. In the Rows text box, type the number of rows you want in your table.

4. In the Columns text box, type the number of columns you want your table to have.

5. Choose a width for your table.
   - You can choose to have your table occupy a certain percentage of the page.

   or

   You can choose the number of pixels your table will occupy.

   Type a number, either pixels or percent, in the Width text box.

6. Click on the Width drop-down menu to choose either pixels or percent (**Figure 10.6**).

   I'll discuss the other table options later in this chapter.

7. Click on OK to close the Insert Table dialog box. Your new table will appear (**Figure 10.7**).

✔ Tip

- Even if you specify an exact width in pixels, your table may resize itself—it will stretch to fit the content you put in it. If you set a percentage width, the table will resize based on the size of the user's browser window.

SETTING UP TABLES

171

Adding Content to a Table

Now that you've got your table right where you want it, you need to put stuff in it.

To add text to your table, just click in the cell where you want your text to go, and start typing and formatting (**Figure 10.8**).

Adding images to a table is just like adding images to any other part of a page. Just click in the table cell you want your image to live in, and then place the image as usual.

For more detailed instructions on working with images, refer to Chapter 8.

✔ Tips

- You can move from cell to cell in a table by pressing the tab key. Shift + Tab moves the cursor backwards.

- You can drag images and text into table cells from elsewhere on the page. Highlight the text or image, and then click on it and drag it into its new home.

- You may want to select an entire table in order to move it or copy it to another page. You can click and drag to highlight a table, but you can accidentally drag table borders that way. Here's a foolproof way to do it.

To select a table:

1. Click on the table that you want to select.

2. From the Document window menu bar, select Modify > Table > Select Table

   or

   Right-click (Ctrl+click) on the table, and from the pop-up menu that appears, select Table > Select Table.

Either way, your table will be selected (**Figure 10.9**) and you can copy, cut, drag, or delete it.

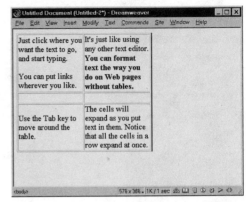

Figure 10.8 You can type and format text in a table just as you would text on a blank page.

Figure 10.9 The entire table will be selected. A dark outline will appear around the table, and handles will appear in the lower-right corner of the table.

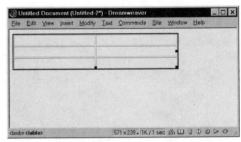

Figure 10.10 When the table is selected, the Properties inspector will display Table properties.

✔ Tip

- Selecting a table makes the Properties inspector display the table's properties automatically (**Figure 10.10**). This is the only way to display table properties.

Number of Days in Each Month	
January	31
February	28 (29)
March	31
April	30
May	31
June	30
July	31
August	31
September	30
October	31
November	30
December	31

Figure 10.11 Click to place the insertion point in your future table header cell.

Apply button   *Selected object's name (cell)*

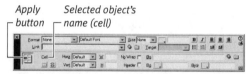

Figure 10.12 The Properties inspector, displaying Table Cell properties. You can tell which part of the table you've selected by the appearance of the Apply button and the displayed name of the selected object.

Number of Days in Each Month	
January	31
February	28 (29)
March	31
April	30
May	31
June	30
July	31
August	31
September	30
October	31
November	30
December	31

Figure 10.13 The text in the new table header cell is now bold and centered in the cell.

Using a header cell

A header cell can be used to indicate the purpose of your table. In most browsers, table header cells appear with their text boldfaced and centered in the cell.

To use a header cell:

1. Click in the cell (usually at the top of the table) that you'd like to designate as the header cell (**Figure 10.11**).

2. In the Expanded Properties inspector (**Figure 10.12**) click on the checkbox marked *Header*.

3. The text in the selected cell will be centered and boldfaced. (**Figure 10.13**).

✔ Tips

- The appearance of table header cells may vary slightly from browser to browser, but the concept is the same: they stand out from the rest of the table.

- You can make an entire row or column of cells into table header cells.

Using the no-wrap option

Text in table cells usually wraps to fit the width of the cell. If you turn off text wrapping, the cell will expand to fit the text.

To use the no-wrap option:

1. Select the column, row, or cell to which you want to apply the no-wrap option.

   ◆ To select a cell, just click in it.

   ◆ To select a column or row, you can click and drag to select the entire row or column; see To select a column or row, later in this chapter.

2. Click the No Wrap checkbox.

If there is already text in any of the cells to which the no-wrap option is applied, the cells may expand to fit the text within them (**Figure 10.14**).

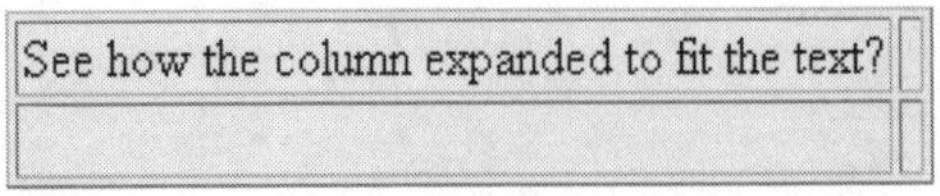

Figure 10.14 The cell expanded to fit the text that was suddenly no longer wrapped to fit the column.

Stupid No-Wrap Tricks

To break a line in non-wrapped text, press Enter (Return) to start a new paragraph, or Shift+Enter (Shift+Return) for a line break. If you change the cell's contents so there is extra blank space in the unused cell, you can clear column widths to close up empty space. See *To clear column widths,* later in this chapter.

Figure 10.15 Use the Align drop-down menu to choose the alignment setting.

Figure 10.16 Type a new number in the Rows and Cols text boxes and then click on the Apply button to add the new items.

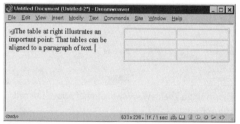

Figure 10.17 A right-aligned table, complete with placeholder icon.

Changing Table Size and Layout

You can adjust the appearance of your table by resizing or adjusting the number of elements in the table (by adding and removing columns and rows). You can also split or merge existing elements to adjust the layout.

To set table alignment:

1. Display the Properties inspector, if necessary, by selecting Window > Properties from the Document window menu bar. Select the entire table. The Properties inspector will display Table properties.

2. In the Properties inspector, click on the Align drop-down menu, and select Default, Left, Center, or Right (**Figure 10.15**).

Your table will change alignment (hopefully for the forces of good).

Adding cells to a table

There are several ways to add cells to a table. One quick way to change the dimensions of your table is by using the Properties inspector.

To change the number of cells:

1. Select the entire table to display Table properties in the Properties inspector, as seen previously in **Figure 10.10**.

2. To change the number of rows, type a new number in the Rows text box.

3. To adjust the number of columns, type a number in the Cols text box and click on the Apply button (**Figure 10.16**).

Terms of Alignment

If you align a table to the right, a small placeholder icon will appear in the left margin to mark the beginning of the table on the page. This icon may disappear if you change the alignment back to left. You can place the insertion point near this icon to put text to the left of the table, as seen in **Figure 10.17**.

Choosing the default setting will make the table follow the default browser settings.

Adding Rows and Columns

To add a single row:

1. Click in the table to place the insertion point in a table cell below where you want the new row to appear (**Figure 10.18**).

2. From the Document window menu bar, select Modify > Table > Insert Row, or press Ctrl+M (Command+M) (**Figure 10.19**). The new row will appear above the insertion point (**Figure 10.20**).

To add a single column:

1. Right-click (Ctrl+click) on the column directly to the left of where you want the new column to appear (as in **Figure 10.18**).

2. From the pop-up menu that appears, select Table > Insert Column (**Figure 10.21**).

A new column will appear to the left of the column you selected (**Figure 10.22**).

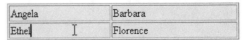

Figure 10.18 Place the insertion point below where you want the new row to appear.

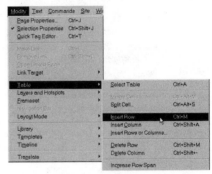

Figure 10.19 From the Document window menu bar, select Modify > Table > Insert Row.

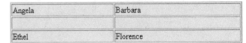

Figure 10.20 The new row will appear above the cell you selected.

Figure 10.21 Right-click (Ctrl+click) on the table, and choose Table > Insert Column from the pop-up menu. You can also add a single row above the insertion point this way.

Figure 10.22 A new column will appear to the left of the column you selected.

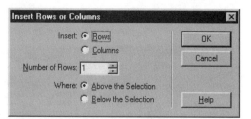

Figure 10.23 Use the Insert Rows or Columns dialog box to add more than one row to your table.

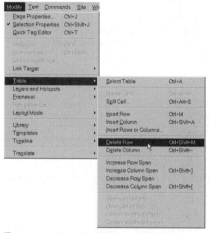

Figure 10.24 From the Document window menu bar, select Modify > Table > Delete Row, and the row will disappear. (You can select Delete Column, too.)

To add more than one column or row:

1. Click in the table to place the insertion point adjacent to where you want the new rows to appear.

2. From the Document window menu bar, select Modify > Table > Insert Rows or Columns. The Insert Rows or Columns dialog box will appear (**Figure 10.23**).

3. Click on the Rows radio button to add rows, or the Columns radio button to add columns.

4. In the Number of Rows text box, type the number of rows you want to add.

5. Select the position of the new elements.

   Rows: To place the new rows above the selected cell, click on the Above the Selection radio button. To place the new rows below the selected cell, click on the Below the Selection radio button.

   Columns: To place the new columns to the left of the selected cell, click on the Before current Column radio button. To place the new columns to the right of the selected cell, click on the After current Column radio button.

6. Click on OK to close the dialog box and add the new rows or columns to your table.

To delete a row:

1. Click to place the insertion point within the row you want to delete.

2. From the Document window menu bar, select Modify > Table > Delete Row (**Figure 10.24**), or press Ctrl+Shift+M (Command+Shift+M). The row and all its contents will disappear.

To delete a column:

1. Right-click on some empty space in the column you want to delete.

2. From the pop-up menu that appears, select Table > Delete Column (**Figure 10.25**). The column and all its contents will disappear.

To select a column or row:

1. Click inside a cell that's on the end of the column or row you wish to select.

2. Hold down the mouse button and drag up to select a column or across to select a row (**Figure 10.26**).

   or

   When you mouse over the top or left table border, the cursor will turn into a black arrow (**Figure 10.27**). When this happens, you can single-click to select the entire column or row.

✔ Tip

■ After you select two or more cells by clicking and dragging, you can hold down the shift key while clicking to select or deselect blocks of cells (**Figure 10.28**).

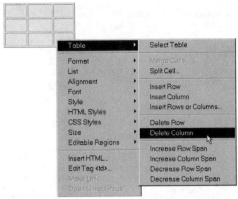

Figure 10.25 Choose Table > Delete Column from the pop-up menu, and the column will disappear. (You can select Delete Row, too.)

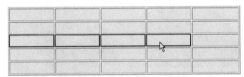

Figure 10.26 Click and drag to select all or part of a row.

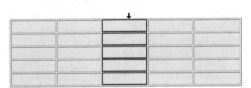

Figure 10.27 When you mouse over the top table border, the mouse pointer turns into an arrow that you can click to select a column. Use the left table border to select a row.

Figure 10.28 By shift-clicking and dragging, you can select blocks of cells.

Figure 10.29
Select the cells you
want to combine.

Figure 10.30 Cells in two
rows merge to create one
large cell that spans two
rows.

Figure 10.31 Select the
cell you want to split. It
may already span more
than one row or it may
be a single,
unadulterated cell.

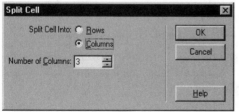

Figure 10.32 In the Split Cell dialog box, you can
specify whether to split a cell into columns or rows,
and how many.

Merging cells

Each cell generally occupies, or *spans,* a single
row or column. If you'd like a cell to be taller
than one row high, or wider than a single
column, you can increase the row span by
combining two or more cells to make, for
example, one cell that's twice as tall.

To merge cells:

1. Select the two or more cells you want to
   combine (**Figure 10.29**).

2. On the Properties inspector, click on the
   Merge Cells button: 🔲.

   or

   From the Document window menu bar,
   select Modify > Table > Merge Cells.

Either way, the cells will merge (**Figure 10.30**).

✔ Tips

- You can select an entire column or row
  to make a cell that spans the entire height
  or width of a table.

- If you change your mind, just follow the
  steps in the sidebar, *Mom & Pops's Row &
  Column Span,* on the next page.

Splitting a cell

You can split any cell by decreasing its row
span.

To split a cell:

1. Click to place the insertion point in the
   cell you wish to split (**Figure 10.31**).

2. On the Properties inspector, click on the
   Split Cell button: ⽥.

   or

   From the Document window menu bar,
   select Modify > Table > Split Cell.

   Either way, the Split Cell dialog box will
   appear (**Figure 10.32**).

continues on next page

CHANGING TABLE SIZE AND LAYOUT

3. In the Split Cell Into area of the dialog box, choose whether to split the cell into rows or columns by clicking on the appropriate radio button.

4. Type a Number of Rows (or Number of Columns) in the text box.

5. Click on OK to close the Split Cell dialog box and add the cells to the table (**Figure 10.33**).

Figure 10.33 This cell splits and three rows are created.

CHANGING TABLE SIZE AND LAYOUT

Mom & Pop's Row & Column Span

Selecting cells and then merging them or splitting them is the easiest way to change column span or row span. However, if you want to do it the old-fashioned way using old-fashioned terminology, you're welcome to. Note that you cannot split a single-span cell using this method.

To increase (or decrease) row span:

1. Click to place the insertion point in the upper of the two cells you want to combine (or in the cell you want to split).

2. From the Document window menu bar, select Modify > Table > Increase Row Span (Decrease Row Span). The table cell will combine with the cell directly below it (split from the table cell it was previously combined with).

To increase (or decrease) column span:

1. Click to place the insertion point in the leftmost of the two cells you want to combine (or in the cell you want to split).

2. From the Document window menu bar, select Modify > Table > Increase Column Span (Decrease Column Span). The table cell will combine with the cell directly to the right of it (split from the table cell it was previously combined with).

Figure 10.34 Type the width of the table in the W (Width) text box. Or, grab it by the handles and drag it to resize.

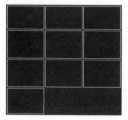

Figure 10.35 A single cell was added to this table. Note the blank space in the rest of the row.

Adding a Single Cell to a Table

While Dreamweaver doesn't directly support the addition of a single cell to a table, you can do it by adding a single line of code.

1. From the Document window menu bar, select Window > HTML. The HTML inspector will appear.

2. To add a cell at the end of a table, locate the closing table tag, `</TABLE>`, and type the following line of code just before it: `<tr><td> </td></tr>`

   This adds a new row `<tr>` with only one cell in it `<td>`. The ` ` gives the cell some content so it will show up.

3. Press Ctrl+S (Command+S) to save the changes to the HTML and the new cell will appear in the table (**Figure 10.35**).

You can experiment with placing this code at other places in the table.

Adjusting the Table Size

Besides adding and removing elements from the table, you can adjust the table's size and appearance by increasing or decreasing the height and width of the entire table, as well as the size of the columns and rows within it.

You may have set a width for your table when you created it, but you can easily adjust the width of the table at any point after that. The width of your table will be in either pixels or percent of screen width.

To set the table width:

1. Select the entire table to display the Table Properties in the Properties inspector (**Figure 10.34**). From the drop-down menu to the right of the W (Width) text box, choose either Pixels or Percent (%).

2. Type a number in the W (Width) text box.

3. Click on the Apply button, and the width of your table will change.

To resize a table:

1. Select the table. Three handles will appear in the lower-right corner of the table (**Figure 10.34**).

2. To make the table larger, click on one of the handles and drag the corner to the right and/or down.

   To make the table smaller, click on one of the handles and drag the corner to the left and/or up.

✔ Tip

■ You can use Dreamweaver's grid for exact measurements when resizing your table and its cells. To turn on the grid, select View > Grid > Show from the Document window menu bar. For more about the grid, see Chapter 1.

Dragging columns and rows

You can adjust column width or row height by simply clicking and dragging.

To drag columns and rows:

1. When you move the mouse over a border between cells, the pointer will turn into a double-headed arrow (**Figure 10.36**).

2. Click on the border and drag it to a new location (**Figure 10.37**). This will set the specifications for the dimensions of the table elements involved.

✔ Tips

■ While you can set row height, a row's height will expand to fit the content.

■ You can also set the height and width for an individual cell by selecting that cell. As with column and row dimensions, this is not as much an exact science as it purports to be; the size of the content and the quirks of the browser will vary your mileage.

Clearing row heights

If you have previously inserted some tall content, and the table's row heights have not contracted to fit the current content, you can clear row heights to shrink the table.

To clear row heights:

1. Select the entire table and the Properties inspector will display Table Properties (as shown in **Figure 10.34**).

2. In the Properties inspector, click on the Clear Row Heights button: ▦.

   or

   From the Document window menu bar, select Modify > Table > Clear Row Heights.

Any row heights previously set will be cleared (**Figure 10.39**).

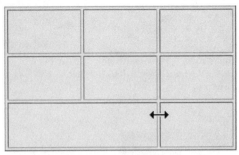

Figure 10.36 Mouse over the table border and the pointer will turn into a double-headed arrow.

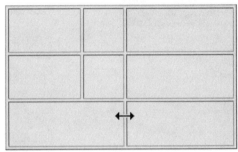

Figure 10.37 Use the double-headed arrow to drag the border to a new location.

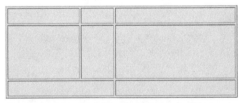

Figure 10.38 I put an image in this table and then cut it. Now, I'm left with all this space I don't need!

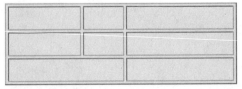

Figure 10.39 After you reset the row heights, the table will resize itself. We saw this table in **Figure 10.38**; notice how the column widths remain the same.

Figure 10.40 This column was set to occupy half the table width.

Figure 10.41 After column widths are cleared, the table will resize itself.

You Ought to Be in Pixels

If you set a column's width in pixels, the text you type or paste into the cells in that column will wrap to fit in the column. However, if you place an image wider than the column in one of those cells, the column will still expand to fit the image.

To set column and row dimensions:

1. Select the column or row whose width or height you'd like to specify. The Properties inspector will display properties of the selected column or row.

2. If the Properties inspector is collapsed, expand it by clicking on the Expander arrow in the lower-right corner.

3. Type a number in the W (Width) text box. To set a percentage rather than a pixel width, type the % character directly after the number (no space).

4. Type a number in the H (Height) text box. To set a percentage rather than a pixel height, type the % character directly after the number (no space).

5. If necessary, click the Apply button to apply the changes to the table. **Figure 10.40** shows a column set to occupy 50 percent of the table width.

✔ Tip

■ While most of the images in this chapter show little bitty tables, they can be translated easily into full-page layouts by setting the table width to 100 percent.

To clear column widths:

1. Select the entire table and the Properties inspector will display Table Properties.

2. In the Properties inspector, click on the Clear Column Widths button: 🔳.

   or

   From the Document window menu bar, select Modify > Table > Column Widths.

Any column widths set by you (either in the Properties inspector or by dragging a cell's border) or by Dreamweaver when the table was created will be reset to no value (**Figure 10.41**).

ADJUSTING THE TABLE SIZE

Converting Percentages and Pixels

You can convert any width or height measurements in your table from percentages to pixels. This is especially useful if you're working with tables created in another environment.

To convert from percentages to pixels:

1. Select the entire table and the Properties inspector will display Table Properties.

2. In the Properties inspector, click on the Convert Table Widths to Pixels button: ▦.

   or

   From the Document window menu bar, select Modify > Table > Convert Widths to Pixels (**Figure 10.42**).

To convert from pixels to percentages:

1. Select the entire table and the Properties inspector will display table properties.

2. In the Properties inspector, click on the Convert Table Widths to Percent button: ▦.

   or

   From the Document window menu bar, select Modify > Table > Convert Widths to Percent.

✔ Tip

■ While the changes won't be visible in the Document window, you can look at the changes in the HTML inspector by selecting Window > HTML from the Document window's menu bar, or by pressing F10.

Figure 10.42 With the table selected, choose Modify > Table > Convert Widths to Pixels from the Document window menu bar.

Figure 10.43 Type a name for your table in the Table Name text box.

Name That Table

If you're planning on working with table code directly, it may help to know which table you're working on, particularly if you've inserted a table within a table. You can name your table, in which case the table code will say something like

```
<table name="main">
```

To name your table, first select it. Then, in the Properties inspector, type a name in the Table Name text box to the right of the Apply button (**Figure 10.43**), and click on the Apply button. The table name will be inserted into the code.

Figure 10.44 Select the table cell you want to hold the new table.

Figure 10.45 Your new table appears inside the old table.

Creating a Table within a Table

When you have some complex design ideas to accomplish, you can insert a table within a larger (full-page size, for example) table.

To insert a table within a table:

1. Click in the table cell where you'd like to insert a new table (**Figure 10.44**).

2. Click on the Table button on the Objects palette and the Insert Table dialog box will appear.

3. Type a number of columns and a number of rows in the appropriate text boxes.

4. Click on OK to close the dialog box.

You'll see your new table inside the old table (**Figure 10.45**).

Saving Excel Spreadsheets and Word Tables as HTML Tables

Although you can't paste spreadsheet data into Dreamweaver as you can into FrontPage, you can still convert your Excel spreadsheets into tables. Dreamweaver 3's new features can also help. For Word, see *Cleaning Up Word HTML* in Chapter 3. For Excel, see *Inserting Tabular Data,* later in this chapter. For basic advice on converting tables into HTML, read on.

Excel 95, Excel 97, and 98 have utilities to save a spreadsheet as HTML. In Excel 95, choose Tools > Internet Assistant Wizard from the menu. For Excel 97 and 98, the command is File > Save as HTML. Both of these programs use Wizards to guide you.

You can also save Microsoft Word table data as HTML. In Word 95, you select File > Save As from the menu bar, and choose HTML (*.htm) as the file type. In Word 97 and 98, the command is File > Save as HTML.

Once you have one of these Office-created documents saved, you can open it in Dreamweaver and edit the page or cut and paste the table onto an existing page.

Working with Table Borders

By default, when you insert a table with Dreamweaver, a 1-pixel line, called a *border*, will delineate the cells and the edges of the table, but you can easily change the width of this border. (See the sections on cell padding and cell spacing later in this chapter for more about table spacing.)

To adjust border size:

1. Select the table to display table properties in the Property inspector.

2. In the Border text box, type a number and press Enter (Return), or click on the Apply button.

You'll see your border adjustments immediately (**Figure 10.46**); if you set the border width to 0, you'll see a light, dashed line (**Figure 10.47**). No worries: it won't show up in your browser (**Figure 10.48**).

✔ Tips

- You can change the border width to whatever you want, including 0.

- Setting the border width to 0 is also known as turning off table borders. You'll want to do this if you're using tables to lay out pages rather than display tabular information.

- It's useful to work with borders turned on (set to at least 1) while you're designing pages, so you can see what's going on. You can toggle off the dashed lines, too, for a quick preview. With table borders set to 0, select View > Table Borders from the Document window menu bar and they'll disappear.

- To find out about coloring table borders, skip ahead to *Coloring Tables*.

Figure 10.46 I gave my table a border width of 10. Borders larger than 1 affect only the outside edge of the table, while border widths of zero render all borders invisible.

Month	Birthstone
January	Garnet
February	Amethyst
March	Aquamarine
April	Diamond
May	Emerald
June	Pearl
July	Ruby
August	Peridot
September	Sapphire
October	Opal
November	Yellow Topaz
December	Blue Topaz

Figure 10.47 A table with a border width of zero is shown in Dreamweaver with light, dashed lines.

Month	Birthstone
January	Garnet
February	Amethyst
March	Aquamarine
April	Diamond
May	Emerald
June	Pearl
July	Ruby
August	Peridot
September	Sapphire
October	Opal
November	Yellow Topaz
December	Blue Topaz

Figure 10.48 This is the same table we saw in Figure 10.47. You can also see your table without dashed lines by toggling off the table borders. From the Document window menu bar, select View > Table Borders to uncheck that option. In the browser window, the borders are invisible.

Figure 10.49 Type values for cell padding and cell spacing in the Properties inspector.

Figure 10.50 We made the cell spacing 10 pixels wide. If we make the border width 0, the cell spacing will be invisible.

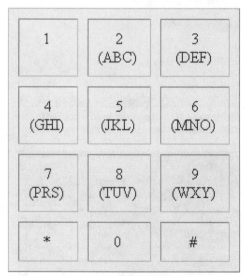

Figure 10.51 This is the same table shown in Figure 10.50, but we added 10 pixels of cell padding. Notice the space between the characters and the walls of the cells.

Adjusting Table Spacing

When you're using a table as a page layout tool, it's important to be able to control the space between elements in a table. We've already talked about table borders, which in part control the space between the table and the rest of the page.

Cell spacing is the amount of space between cells—sort of like table borders, but between the cells in a table rather than around the outside of the table. *Cell padding* is the amount of space between the walls of the cells and the content within them.

To adjust cell spacing:

1. Select the table to display table properties in the Properties inspector.

2. In the CellSpace text box, type a number (in pixels) (**Figure 10.49**).

3. Click on the Apply button.

Your changes will be visible in the width of the table's borders (**Figure 10.50**).

✔ Tip

■ Cell spacing changes may not be immediately visible on pages with table borders set to 0.

To adjust cell padding:

1. Select the table to display table properties in the Properties inspector.

2. In the CellPad text box, type a number (in pixels).

3. Click on the Apply button.

You'll notice a difference in the spacing between the content and the borders (**Figure 10.51**). If there is no content in your table at this point, you can see the changes by clicking within the cells and examining the distance between the cursor and the walls of the cell.

Adjusting Vspace and Hspace

If you want a certain amount of space around the edges of your table, you can adjust the *Vspace* (vertical spacing) and *Hspace* (horizontal spacing). Vspace inserts blank space above and below your table, and Hspace inserts space to the left and right of it.

To adjust Vspace and Hspace:

1. Select the entire table so that the Properties inspector displays table properties.

2. Expand the inspector to display the lower half, if necessary.

3. Type a number, in pixels, in the V Space text box to add space above and below your table (**Figure 10.52**).

4. Type a number, in pixels, in the H Space text box to add space to the left and right of your table.

5. Click on the Apply button to add the spacing to your page.

If you drag to select the table and some surrounding space (**Figure 10.53**), you can see the Vspace and Hspace surrounding the table. Without dragging, you can see the Vspace in **Figure 10.54**, indicated by the size of the cursor (it's taller than the table).

✔ Tip

■ Using cell padding and cell spacing is particularly useful if you're going to use tables in close proximity to other elements on your page, as shown in **Figure 10.55**.

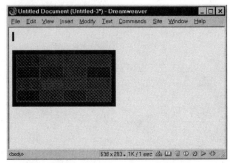

Figure 10.52 Type a number, in pixels, in the V Space and H Space text boxes on the Properties inspector.

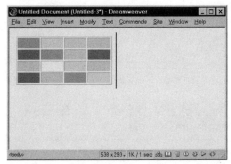

Figure 10.53 If you drag to select the table and some surrounding space, the table becomes reversed out, and you can see the Vspace and Hspace outlined around the table. I used 10 pixels of each.

Figure 10.54 With 10 pixels of Vspace applied to this table, the cursor becomes taller than the table is.

Figure 10.55 These tables have 10 pixels of space on each side to give them natural, borderless spacing from the rest of the page.

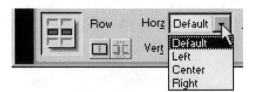

Figure 10.56 Horizontal alignment (Horz) options include Default, Left, Center, and Right.

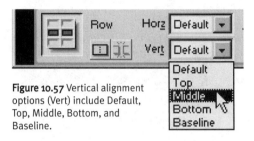

Figure 10.57 Vertical alignment options (Vert) include Default, Top, Middle, Bottom, and Baseline.

H=Default, V=Default	H=Left, V=Top	H=Center, V=Middle
H=Right, V=Bottom	H=Right, V=Top	H=Right, V=Middle
H=Default, V=Baseline	H=Center, V=Baseline	H=Right, V=Baseline

Figure 10.58 This table runs the gamut of content alignment options. The position of the Baseline vertical alignment is based on the imaginary lines that the characters rest on, and it generally follows the baseline of the bordering cells.

Adjusting Content Spacing

In addition to table spacing, you can adjust where the content in your table's cells is placed:

♦ In both horizontal and vertical alignment, choosing Default sets the alignment to the browser's default—usually left (horizontal) and middle (vertical).

♦ In most cases, then, you won't need to set alignment specifications for left or middle unless you're "changing it back" from a previous adjustment.

♦ Cell alignment properties override row and column specs, and column specs override row specs.

Changing Content alignment

Horizontal alignment within a cell is the same as regular alignment on a page: the text is aligned with the left, right, or center of the cell. Vertical alignment controls the position of the text between the top and bottom of a cell.

To change content alignment:

1. Click to place the insertion point in the column, row, or cell whose horizontal alignment you want to adjust. The Properties inspector will display properties for your selection. Verify that you selected the correct area by checking the Apply button on the Properties inspector.

2. Click on the Horz drop-down menu, and select an alignment option: Default, Left, Center, or Right (**Figure 10.56**).

3. Click on the Vert drop-down menu and select an option: Default, Top, Middle, Bottom, or Baseline (**Figure 10.57**).

4. Click on OK to close the dialog box.

Your changes will be apparent when you place content in that area of the table (**Figure 10.58**).

Coloring Tables

You can give a table a background color or background image that differs from the background of the overall page. You can also use different backgrounds in individual table cells.

To choose a table background color:

1. Select the table and the Properties inspector will display Table properties.

2. If the Table Properties inspector is collapsed, expand it by clicking on the Expander arrow.

3. In the Bg Color text box:
   ◆ Type or paste a hex value for the background color.

      or

      Click on the gray Color selector button to pop up the Colors palette (**Figure 10.59**). Hold down the mouse button and drag the pointer to select a color (**Figure 10.60**).

      or

      On the Colors palette, click on the Colors button 🎨 to open up the Color dialog box (**Figure 10.61**). For more on using the Color dialog box, see Chapter 2.

When you're finished making your selection, click on your color choice, and click on OK to close the Color dialog box, if necessary. The color change should be apparent immediately.

✔ Tips

■ You can follow these steps for a single cell, a selection of cells, a column (**Figure 10.62**), or a row or entire table.

■ To escape without choosing a color, press the Esc key (Windows only), or click on the space below the Colors palette. More color shortcuts are discussed in Chapter 2.

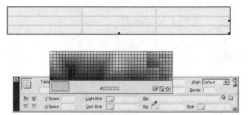

Figure 10.59 Click on the Color Selector button to pop up the Colors palette.

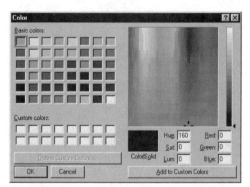

Figure 10.60 Choose a color from the Colors palette by clicking on it.

Figure 10.61 The Color dialog box offers additional color selection options. The Color dialog box for the Macintosh is substantively different, as discussed in Chapter 2.

Figure 10.62 I colored one column in this table. Notice that the table, the page, and the column use three different colors.

COLORING TABLES

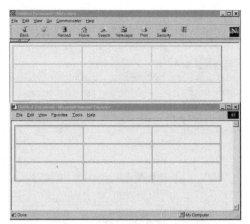

Figure 10.63 This table, seen in Navigator 4.5 on top and IE 5 below, has colored borders. In Navigator, the color appears only on the table's outer edges.

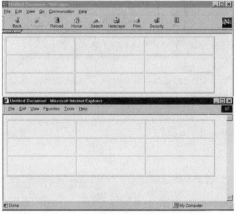

Figure 10.64 I used yellow for the light border color and dark gray for the dark border colors. Navigator doesn't display light or dark border colors, and IE displays both.

Adjusting border colors

There are three possible border color selections you can make: Border, Light Border, and Dark Border.

To adjust border colors:

1. Select your table to view table properties in the Properties inspector.

2. For one (or all) of the color choices, Border, Light Border, and Dark Border, follow step 3 in *To choose a table background color* on the previous page.

Figure 10.63 shows a table with colored borders, and **Figure 10.64** shows a table with light and dark border colors.

✔ Tips

■ You can adjust the color of the border, the light border, or the dark border for a row, a column, or a single cell as well.

■ Netscape shows border colors as shades of the selected colors. A lighter tint appears on the upper and left borders of the table, and a darker shade appears on the lower and right borders of the table.

■ Internet Explorer shows border colors as a solid outline around each cell in the table, unless light and dark border colors are selected, in which case the regular border color is not shown at all.

■ Navigator will display the Border color, but not the Light and Dark Border colors. Those are conventions of Internet Explorer.

■ You can set the Border, Light Border, *and* the Dark Border, but all three of them will not show up at once. However, this is the only way to get shaded borders in both Navigator and IE.

COLORING TABLES

191

Setting a background image

You can set a background image for an entire table, a table cell, a column, or a row.

To use a table background image:

1. In the Document window, select the table or table element you want to supply with a background image.

2. In the Properties inspector, type the URL of the image you want to use in the Bg text box (the larger of the two identically named text boxes) (**Figure 10.65**).

   or

   Click on the Browse button to open the Select Image Source dialog box and select the image from your local machine.

   or

   If you're using a local Site, drag the Point to File icon onto the image file in the Sites window.

   Either way, the image path will appear in the Bg text box, and the image will load in the table in the Document window

Figure 10.66 shows a table that uses a background image.

✔ Tip

- A convenient shortcut for coloring tables is the Format Table dialog box (**Figure 10.67**), which allows you to choose from predetermined background color schemes. To use the dialog box, select Commands > Format Table from the Document window menu bar.

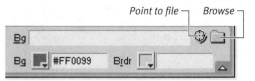

Point to file   *Browse*

Figure 10.65 Type the pathname of the background image in the Bg text box on the Properties inspector, or click on the Browse or Point to File buttons to use those options.

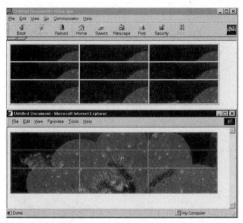

Figure 10.66 I used a table background image in this table. Navigator (top) tiles the image in each cell, while IE (bottom) uses the image as a background for the entire table.

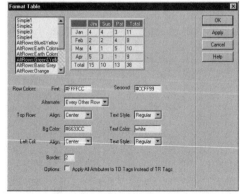

Figure 10.67 Use the Format Table dialog box to choose from predetermined color schemes. Any color choices you make for columns or individual cells will override these default schemes.

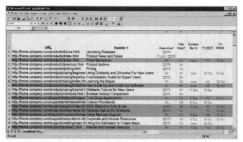

Figure 10.68 I want to put this Excel production worksheet on the corporate intranet. I convert it to HTML so that anyone in the office can access it without needing Excel in order to open it. Before I can import this file into Dreamweaver, I will need to save it as a CSV file.

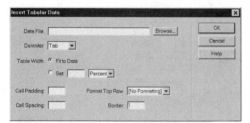

Figure 10.69 The Insert Tabular Data (or Import Table Data) dialog box allows you to choose a database or spreadsheet file to import as an HTML table, and to set parameters for how that table will look.

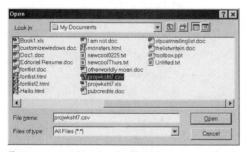

Figure 10.70 In choosing the file to import, note that I chose the CSV file (comma-separated values, in Microsoft terms) rather than the XLS (Excel Spreadsheet file) just below it.

Inserting Tabular Data

Using Dreamweaver 3, you can import complex sets of data from database or spreadsheet files into an HTML table. Theoretically, any program that can save content as a delimited data file (particularly comma- and tab-delimited) can be imported. Specific examples are Microsoft Excel, Microsoft Access, 4D, Emacs, and Oracle (**Figure 10.68**).

Before beginning, you (or your database expert) need to export the information from the database or spreadsheet program into a data file. You must know what character the file uses as a delimiter. If you don't know, get it from your database engineer.

✔ Tip

- Nearly any database, spreadsheet, or even address book program can save data as comma-delimited or tab-delimited data files. Two notable exceptions are Lotus Notes and Filemaker. You may need to save out data and format it in another application to use data from these applications in a Dreamweaver table.

To import table data:

1. You can use either of two menu commands that work exactly the same. From the Document window menu bar, select Insert > Tabular Data.

   or

   From the Document window menu bar, select File > Import > Import Table Data. Either way, the Insert Tabular Data (or Import Table Data) dialog box will appear (**Figure 10.69**). The dialog boxes are identical aside from their names.

2. To select the data file containing the data to be inserted into your table, click Browse. The Open dialog box will appear (**Figure 10.70**).

continues on next page

3. Select the file and click on Open. You will return to the Insert Tabular Data (or Import Table Data) dialog box (**Figure 10.71**).

4. Your data file uses punctuation to mark the spaces between table cells. Usually, the file is comma-delimited or tab-delimited; it may also use semicolons or colons. Choose the proper mark from the Delimiter drop-down menu.

or

If the file uses another delimiter, select Other, and then type the name of the delimiter in the text box that appears.

5. You and Dreamweaver will allocate the width of the table in the Table Width area of the dialog box (**Figure 10.71**).

To base the table width on whatever space the data takes up, click the Fit to Data radio button. (You can reformat the table later.)

or

To set the width, at 100 percent, for example, type an amount in the Set text box, and then choose Pixels or Percent from the Set drop-down menu.

6. To preset Cell Padding and Cell Spacing, type a number in those text boxes. (See the previous section, *Adjusting Table Spacing*, to find out how this works.)

7. Presumably, the top row will consist of column headings; *Mailing Address*, for example. To format the top row, select Bold, Italic, or Bold Italic from the Format Top Row drop-down menu (**Figure 10.71**).

8. To set a border (1, 0, or other), type a number in the Border text box.

9. When you're done, click on OK, and Dreamweaver will import the data and create the table in the Document window (**Figure 10.72**).

Format Top Row drop-down menu

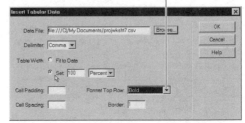

Figure 10.71 I have selected a file to import (the path is shown in the Data File text box); I have selected Comma as the delimiter; I have set the width of the table to 100 Percent of the page; and I have chosen Bold as the top-row formatting.

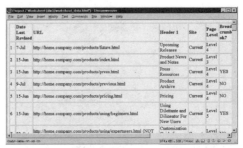

Figure 10.72 After importing the file, Dreamweaver drew this (rather plain) table. I will need to make some changes to make it look better. Also, any columns or fields that were hidden in the Excel file are still imported into the Dreamweaver table.

Figure 10.73 You can use the Export Table dialog box to save an HTML table as a data file.

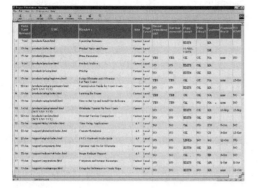

Figure 10.74 I applied Dreamweaver's autoformatting (Commands > Format Table). I also shortened the URLs to site-root relative paths to make the table easier to navigate, and applied some font formatting to the header cell.

Exporting Tables

You can also export table data from Dreamweaver into a data file. For instance, if you import data into Dreamweaver and then update the information in Dreamweaver, you may want to open the updated data in your database or spreadsheet program.

Before you begin, you need to have a page containing a table with data in it open in Dreamweaver.

To export table data:

1. From the Document window menu bar, select File > Export > Export Table. The Export Table dialog box will appear (**Figure 10.73**).

2. From the Delimiter drop-down menu, select the delimiter you wish to use. This should be the default delimiter of the program you'll be importing the data into. If you're not sure, Comma and Tab are safe bets.

3. In data files, line breaks are actually characters. From the Line Breaks drop-down menu, select the platform your data file will be opened on. If you're not sure, check with your database guru; if you have to guess, pick Windows.

4. Click on Export and the Export Table As dialog box will appear. You will need to supply a file extension with your filename. If you're not sure what extension to use, you can add it later by changing the name of the file.

5. Click on Save. The Export Table As dialog box will close and the file will be saved on your computer.

Sorting Table Contents

Typing stuff into a table can be a pain in the butt if you need the contents to be in order. In Microsoft Word and Microsoft Excel, you can type the stuff in any order you like and then sort table contents alphabetically or numerically. In Dreamweaver, you can do the same thing. No, really!

To sort table contents:

1. Click within the table you want to sort.

2. From the Document window menu bar, select Commands > Sort Table.
   The Sort Table dialog box will appear (**Figure 10.75**).

3. From the Sort By drop-down menu, select the column (by number) to sort by first.

4. From the Order drop-down menu, select Alphabetically or Numerically.

5. From the next drop-down menu, select Ascending (A-Z, 1-9) or Descending (Z-A, 9-1).

6. To sort by a secondary column next, repeat steps 3-5 for the Then By section of the dialog box.

7. To include the first row in your sort, check the Sort Includes First Row checkbox.

8. To have any row formatting travel with the sort, check the Keep TR Attributes With Sorted Row checkbox.

9. Click on OK to close the Sort Table dialog box. The table will be sorted according to the criteria you specified.

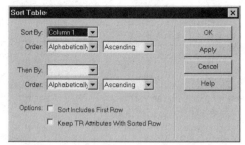

Figure 10.75 Use the Sort Table dialog box to specify criteria by which to sort the contents of a table.

USING FRAMES

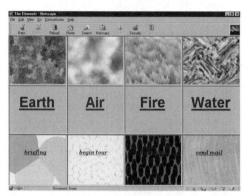

Figure 11.1 Each frame is a distinct document with its own content—including different link and background colors and background images.

Web pages that use frames can be extremely versatile. A frames-based page is divided into several windows-within-windows, like the panes in an old-fashioned window (**Figure 11.1**).

While a frames-based page acts like a single Web page, each frame contains a single HTML document that can include completely separate contents and independent scrollbars.

The glue that holds together these documents is called the *frameset definition document,* or the *frameset page;* a frameset is a set of frames, and the frameset page is what defines them as a set.

Frames and Navigation

You can use frames to create some nifty layouts. Because each page is a discrete HTML document, it can contain any HTML element except the <FRAMESET> tag—although we'll find out how to embed frames within frames in the section called *Nested Framesets*.

Frames are best used when you want part of your page, such as a toolbar or a table of contents, to be visible the entire time the page is in the window—regardless of what kind of scrolling your visitors do.

Each document in a frameset is an individual HTML document. In the background, the frameset page acts as mission control, holding together all the documents. Each frame has a default document anchored to it so that something will load when the frames page is loaded. You can see the code for a frameset page in **Figure 11.2**. **Figure 11.3** presents a diagram of the frame structure.

✔ Tip

■ The frameset page is called that because it includes the <FRAMESET> tag, which defines the layout of the frames-based page, the location and names of the initial pages that occupy each frame, and details about the appearance and actions of the frames.

Figure 11.2 A frames-based page is held together behind the scenes by a frameset page, which keeps track of what belongs where. This is the frameset page code for the page in Figure 11.1.

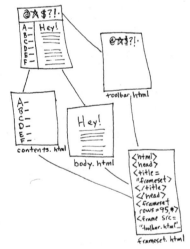

Figure 11.3 An infinite number of pages can be associated with a frames page via links.

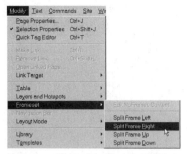

Figure 11.4 Choose Modify > Frameset from the Document window menu bar.

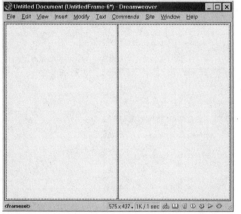

Figure 11.5 The Split Frame Left and Split Frame Right commands both split the current frame in half with a vertical frame border.

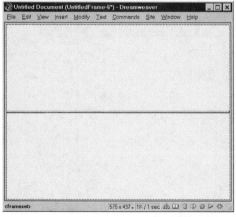

Figure 11.6 The Split Frame Up and Split Frame Down commands both split the current frame in half with a horizontal frame border.

Setting Up a Frames Page

Dreamweaver will automatically create a frameset when you divide a page into more than one frame.

To create frames by splitting the page:

1. Start Dreamweaver, and open a blank window, if necessary.

2. From the Document Window menu bar, select Modify > Frameset > (**Figure 11.4**). And then choose one of the following options:
   - Split Frame Left (**Figure 11.5**)
   - Split Frame Right (**Figure 11.5**)
   - Split Frame Up (**Figure 11.6**)
   - Split Frame Down (**Figure 11.6**)

3. The window will split to display two frames.

Creating Frames by Dragging

You can also create a frame border and drag it to create multiple frames on a page.

To create a frame by dragging:

1. From the Document window menu bar, select View > Frame Borders. A heavy outline will appear around the blank space in the window (**Figure 11.7**).

2. Hold down the Alt (Option) key and click on one of the borders.

3. Drag it to a new location (**Figure 11.8**), and release the mouse button when you've positioned the border where you choose (**Figure 11.9**).

You now have two frames in the window.

✔ Tip

- You can drag the corner where the borders intersect to create four new frames at once (**Figure 11.10**).

Figure 11.7
The heavy outline that appears should resemble the frame borders you've seen on pages around the Web.

Figure 11.8
Hold down the Alt (Option) key and click on the border, and you can create a new frame by splitting the original page.

Figure 11.9
Let go of the mouse button when the frame border is where you want. Ta-da! You now have two frames.

Figure 11.10
If you hold down the Alt (Option) key and click the corner of a frame border, you can drag it to split the page into four frames.

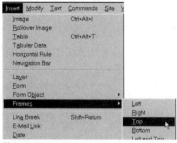

Insert Modify Text Commands Site

Figure 11.11 Select Insert > Frames from the Document window menu bar, and then choose a layout option.

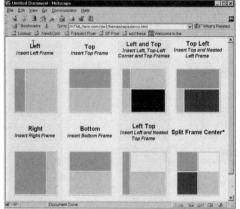

Figure 11.12 The heading over each layout is its name in the Insert > Frames menu, and the subhead is the name of the layout in the Frames panel of the Objects palette. Split Frame Center, is available only in the Objects palette.

Figure 11.13 I selected Left Top from the Insert > Frames menu, and the layout appeared in the Document window. Note that the frame borders are not heavy; they've been turned off in the preset attributes of the layout.

Quick and Dirty Frames

Two new features in Dreamweaver 3 are the command Insert > Frames and the Frames panel on the Objects palette, both of which allow you to choose a basic, preset frames page layout. Select a layout from the menu, and it will appear in the Document window.

If you create a frames page using one of these methods, you can skip the next couple of sections about how to add frames to a page, but even if you love the designs as they are, be sure to read the section called *Targeting Links*, later in this chapter.

To use the Insert Frames menu:

1. Create a new, blank page.

2. From the Document window menu bar, select Insert > Frames (**Figure 11.11**), and then choose one of the following options, as shown in **Figure 11.12**:
   ◆ Left
   ◆ Right
   ◆ Top
   ◆ Bottom
   ◆ Left and Top
   ◆ Left Top
   ◆ Top Left

   (The last item, Split Frame Center*, splits existing frames.)

   The Document window will create the frameset design you selected (**Figure 11.13**).

✔ Tip

■ Frames pages created using the Frames menu or Objects palette shortcuts do not have frame borders, and they may have preset resize and scrollbar settings. (See *Frameset Options*, later in this chapter for more about these features). The frames on these pages are also prenamed; see *Naming Frames*, later in this chapter, for more about this.

The Objects palette also offers similar options for adding frames-based layouts with the click of a button, as seen previously in **Figure 11.12**.

To create frames using the Objects palette:

1. Display the Objects palette, if necessary, by selecting Window > Objects from the Document window menu bar. The Objects palette will appear (**Figure 11.14**).

2. Click the menu button at the top of the Objects palette, and from the menu that appears, select Frames (**Figure 11.15**). The Objects palette will display Frame objects (**Figure 11.16**).

3. On Windows, if you mouse over the objects displayed, you'll see tool tips describing various options. Click on any button to draw that layout, or drag the button to an existing frame to split a single frame in the manner pictured.

✔ Tips

■ *Nested Framesets* are described in detail in the section with that name.

■ As with the Insert > Frames menu command, the frames created using the Object palette may have preset values for borders, the names of the frames, and other options such as scrollbars. These options, and how to change them, are described later in this chapter.

Figure 11.14 You can select the Objects palette by pressing Ctrl+F2 (Cmd+F2), or by selecting Window > Objects from the Document window menu bar.

Figure 11.15 Click on the menu button on top of the Objects palette to display various flavors of objects, including Frames.

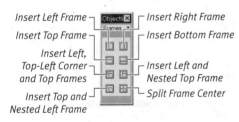

Insert Left Frame | Insert Right Frame
Insert Top Frame | Insert Bottom Frame
Insert Left, Top-Left Corner and Top Frames | Insert Left and Nested Top Frame
Insert Top and Nested Left Frame | Split Frame Center

Figure 11.16 Frames objects are actually layouts that you can apply to your page with the click of a button. I resized the palette (by dragging the lower-right corner) after selecting Frames objects.

QUICK AND DIRTY FRAMES

Figure 11.17
In this figure, the Frames inspector stands alone. In Figure 11.18, I've dragged it onto a set of stacked palettes, as described in Chapter 1.

The Frames Inspector

The Frames inspector is a useful tool for selecting individual frames or entire frame-sets. To view the Frames inspector, select Window > Frame from the Document window menu bar or press Ctrl+F10 (Command+F10). The Frames inspector will appear (**Figure 11.17**).

You will need to select individual frames when modifying properties.

To select a frame:

1. Hold down the Alt (Shift + Option) key and click on the frame in the Document window.

    or

    In the Frames inspector, click on the frame you want to select (**Figure 11.17**).

2. In either case, a dashed line will appear in the Document window around the frame you selected, and the Properties inspector will display properties for that frame (**Figure 11.18**).

Selecting a frameset

You can select an entire frameset in one of two ways:

◆ Click on any of the frame borders in the Document window.

    or

◆ In the Frames inspector, click on the border around the outside edge of the frames.

Either way, the Properties inspector will display properties for the frameset, and a dashed line will appear around all the frames in the frameset (**Figure 11.19**).

Note that the Properties inspector displays all the columns and rows in a frameset, but that all frames are shown as if they had the same dimensions.

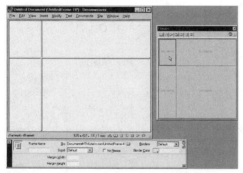

Figure 11.18 When you select a frame, a heavy line appears around the frame in the Frames inspector, and a dashed line appears around it in the Document window. Additionally, the Properties inspector displays Frame properties for the frame you selected.

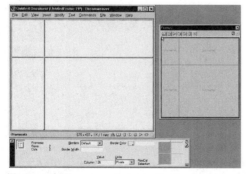

Figure 11.19 When you select an entire frameset by clicking on the frame border in the Document window or Properties inspector, the Properties inspector displays properties for the frameset.

Modifying the Frame Page Layout

You have limitless options when it comes to laying out pages with frames. You can divide frames the same way you created them initially: by splitting or by dragging. You'll probably do some experimenting before you achieve the layout you want.

To split frames:

1. In the Document window, click within the frame you want to split.

2. From the Document window menu bar, select Modify > Frameset > (as shown earlier in **Figure 11.4**), and then choose one of the following options: Split Frame Left, Split Frame Right, Split Frame Up, or Split Frame Down.

Splitting left or right, up or down may look exactly the same unless there is already content in the frame. For example, the left window in **Figure 11.20** shows a frame that was split left, and the right window shows the same frame split right instead.

To drag and reposition frame borders:

1. Mouse over the border between two frames, and the pointer will turn into a double-headed arrow (**Figure 11.21**).

2. Click on the border, and drag it to a new location. When the border appears where you want it to, release the mouse button.

✔ Tip

■ To split a frame while dragging it, hold down the Alt (Option) key while you click the mouse button (**Figure 11.22**).

Figure 11.20 These two frames pages are pretty much the same. In the one on the left, the top frame was split left, while in the right-hand window, the same frame was split right. Which option you choose depends on where you want any content in the frame to land.

Figure 11.21 When you mouse over a border between frames, the pointer becomes a double-headed arrow that you can use to drag the border.

Figure 11.22 If you hold down the Alt (Option) key while clicking on the frame border, you can split a frame by dragging the border.

Figure 11.23 Click on the border of the unwanted frame, and drag it off the page. You'll get rid of both the frame and the border.

Figure 11.24 You can also drag a frame border into another frame border to get rid of it.

Figure 11.25 Either way, you'll be free of the unwanted frame.

Deleting a Frame

You can keep splitting frames until you achieve the layout you want, but if you create a few frames too many, getting rid of them is easy.

To delete a frame:

1. Click on the frame border, and drag it off the page (**Figure 11.23**).

   or

   Click on the frame border, and drag it until it meets another border (**Figure 11.24**).

2. Let go of the mouse button. The frame will disappear (**Figure 11.25**).

Dragging Content Between Frames

Before you delete that frame, you can drag its content into another frame on the page. This works for all sorts of objects, including text, images, multimedia objects, and form fields. Click on the object to select it, or highlight the text you wish to move. Click and hold down the mouse button while you drag the object to a new frame. When the stuff is where you want it, let go of the mouse button, and it will reappear in the new location.

Nested Framesets

Once your initial frame page layout is created, you can divide the space within any individual frame by inserting another frameset that is *nested* within the original frameset. Dreamweaver creates nested framesets automatically when you split a frame. The original frameset is called the *parent,* and the frameset within the parent set is called the *child.* You can theoretically keep nesting framesets until the cows come home, and the hierarchy will always have the child frameset reporting to its immediate parent.

An original frameset is shown in **Figure 11.26**. In framesets with no nested framesets inside them, all frame borders go from one edge of the window to the other. In **Figure 11.27**, The first frameset includes one frame of its own (the left-hand frame), plus the nested frameset. The second, nested frameset includes the two frames in the right-hand column.

Creating a nested frameset involves the same tasks as any other frameset. You can watch how Dreamweaver modifies the code by keeping the HTML inspector open while you follow these steps.

To create a nested frameset:

1. Open (or create) a frameset page in the Dreamweaver window (**Figure 11.26**).

2. Click in one of the frames, and then split it by selecting, from the Document window menu bar, Modify > Frameset > and then Split Frame Left, Right, Up, or Down. In **Figure 11.27**, I selected Split Frame Up.

Dreamweaver has created a second frameset nested within the original frameset. You can examine the structure of the document by using the Frames inspector.

Figure 11.26 In the HTML inspector, you can see the highlighted code for the frameset, which includes the locations of the documents within it. Two frames, one frameset.

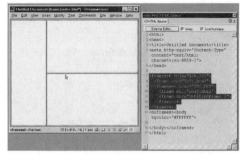

Figure 11.27 Now, in the HTML inspector, you can see a frameset tag nested within the frameset tag.

Nested frameset (child) code selected
Child frameset selected
Tag Selector with nested frameset tag selected

Figure 11.28 Dreamweaver automatically nests a new frameset inside the original, and you can select the child frameset with the Frames inspector. In the HTML inspector, you can see that only the nested frameset code is selected. And in the tag selector, you can see two <frameset> tags, the second of which is selected.

✔ Tips

■ Remember that you may have already created nested framesets by splitting frames or by using one of Dreamweaver's preset layouts.

■ The main reason you need to be aware of nested framesets is so that you can select and modify them separately. I bet you're glad you don't have to hand-code this stuff.

To view the structure of a document:

1. Display the Frames inspector, if necessary, by selecting Window > Frames from the Document window menu bar.

2. As you click on each frame in the Frames inspector, it becomes highlighted. Additionally, a dashed line appears around the frame in the Document window.

3. To select an embedded frameset, click on the heavy border around the frameset in the Frames inspector (**Figure 11.28**). A dashed line will appear around each frame in the embedded frameset.

NESTED FRAMESETS

Setting Column and Row Sizes

Frames, just like tables, are divided into columns and rows. You could think of the individual frames in a set as cells, each of which occupies a certain number of columns and rows. (See Chapter 10 for more on cells, columns, and rows).

When you split a frame or drag a frame border, Dreamweaver translates the information about the position of the frame border into a height or width amount for each frame, in pixels or percent of the window. To adjust the height or width of a frame, you can adjust the row height or column width.

The page in **Figure 11.29** is comprised of two framesets (look at the Frames inspector to see this more clearly). The first frameset is made up of two rows. The top frame, or row, is 112 pixels high. The bottom row is set relative to that height; it will take up the rest of the browser window, however small or large (**Figure 11.30**).

The embedded frameset is made up of two columns. The left column occupies 25 percent of the available space—in this case, it's both 25 percent of the parent frame and 25 percent of the window. The right column, then, can be set to either 75 percent or to relative to the parent frameset's width.

✔ Tips

■ Since the dimensions of any column or row affect the dimensions of the entire frameset, row height and column width are frameset properties, rather than frame properties.

■ It makes sense to set the height and width for one column or row in particular, and to set all other heights and widths as relative to that area of the page.

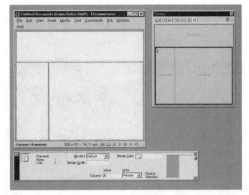

Figure 11.29 The frameset is made up of two rows (across the window), and a nested frameset that has two columns (vertical divisions of the lower frame). In this figure, the Properties inspector is displaying Frameset properties for the child (nested) frameset.

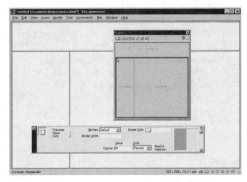

Figure 11.30 Here, you see the same frameset, in a resized (larger) window. Notice how the top frame retains the same, exact size (112 pixels) while the bottom frames retain their proportional settings. The left frame still occupies 25 percent of the window.

■ You must set a height or width for each frame in a document in order to guarantee that pixel or percentage widths will be followed when the window is resized.

Drop-down menu for pixels, percentage, or relative

Tabs for selecting columns and rows

Apply button

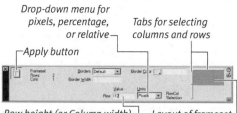

Row height (or Column width) ⌐ *Layout of frameset* ⌐

Figure 11.31 The Properties inspector displays frameset options when you click on a frame border in the Document window.

Figure 11.32 Click on a tab in the frameset preview of the Properties inspector to adjust settings for that column or row.

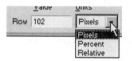

Figure 11.33 Select either Pixels, Percent, or Relative as the units for the height or width measurement.

To adjust row height and column width:

1. Select the frameset by clicking on a frame border. The frameset properties will appear in the Properties inspector (**Figure 11.31**).

2. Click on the Expander arrow in the bottom-right corner of the inspector to display column or row values, depending on your selection.

3. Select the column or row whose area you wish to define by clicking on the associated tab, above the column or to the left of the row, in the Properties inspector (**Figure 11.32**).

4. Type a value for the column or row in the associated text box and select one of the following units from the drop-down menu (**Figure 11.33**):

   - Pixels sets an exact height or width. When the frameset is loaded in the browser, pixel measurements are followed exactly.

   - Percent refers to a percentage of window (or frameset) size.

   - Relative means that the height or width will be flexible in the frameset, compared to other elements that were given specific pixel or percent measurements.

5. Click on the Apply button to apply the height or width changes to the frameset.

6. Repeat these steps for the remainder of the elements in the frameset.

✔ Tip

- When a browser is loading a frameset page, it draws the layout in the following order:

   - Pixel measurements are given their space allotment first.

   - Columns or rows with Percentage measurements are drawn next.

   - Frames with Relative settings are drawn to fill the rest of the available space.

SETTING COLUMN AND ROW SIZES

Setting Content Pages

There are two ways you can go about putting content into those pretty, blank frames. One way is to open an existing page in the framework of the frameset; the other way is to create your new page right now in the Dreamweaver Document window.

In either case, to determine what your frames page will display when it's loaded into a Web browser, you'll attach a URL to each of the frames in the set.

To attach a page to a frame:

1. Select the frame you want to put some content in. The Properties inspector will display the properties of that frame (**Figure 11.34**).

2. The SRC text box currently displays the pathname of the blank, untitled, unsaved page that's in it currently. You can:

   ◆ Type (or paste) a location of an existing page—on the Web or on your computer—into the text box.

   ◆ Click on the Properties inspector's Browse icon 🗀 to open up the Select HTML File dialog box (**Figure 11.35**).

   ◆ From the Document window menu bar, select File > Open in Frame to display the Select HTML File dialog box.

If you use one of the two latter options, locate the file on your computer, and then click on Open (Choose) to attach the file to the frame you selected. (See Chapter 2 if you need more information on using the Select HTML File dialog box.)

If the file you selected is on your local machine, it will appear in the frame within the Document window.

If you type a full Internet URL in the Frame Properties SRC text box, the Document window will display the "Remote File" message (**Figure 11.36**).

Figure 11.34 When the Properties inspector displays frame properties, you can set the location for the default frame document in the SRC text box.

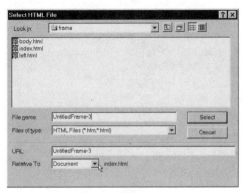

Figure 11.35 Use the Select HTML File dialog box to choose a file to load in the frame.

Figure 11.36 If you're connected to the Internet when you preview this page in your browser, the browser should load the remote file in the frame.

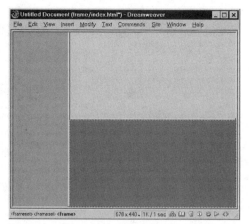

Figure 11.37 This page has three frames, each of which uses a different background color. Back in Figure 11.1, eight of the 12 frames used different background images.

Relativity Theory

In my experience, in most browsers, frames documents should be linked to one another using *document relative links* rather than site root relative links. The frameset document contains the links, and the initial frames pages within the frameset should be given paths relative to that page.

As you can see in **Figure 11.35** on the previous page, when you select a file to use in a frame, you have the option, in the drop-down menu at the bottom of the Select HTML File dialog box, to choose that the files be Relative To the Document or to the Site Root. Choose Document, and Dreamweaver will automatically choose the Frameset page as the relative one.

After you save a page as described in the next section, you can check to see if it has a Document Relative relationship by following steps 1 and 2 in *Setting Content Pages,* earlier in this chapter, and then confirming that the Relative To drop-down menu indicates Document.

Creating Content within a Frame

Creating and editing content within one of the frames in a frameset is the same as doing so in a blank Dreamweaver window, only with less screen real estate.

On frames pages you can put text, images, multimedia objects, and tables—anything that you can use on a non-frames page.

✔ Tip

- Of course, you can create a page in Dreamweaver, save it, and then attach it to a frameset (as described in the preceding section), but if you're creating simple content, you can work easily in the frameset.

Setting the background color for a frame is just like setting the background color for a stand-alone page. Each frame, remember, is a single HTML document, or page, and each page in the frameset has its own page properties. **Figure 11.37** shows a frames page in which every frame has a different background.

To set a frame background:

1. Display the page properties for the frame in one of two ways:
   - ◆ Right-click (Ctrl+Click) on the frame and select Page Properties from the pop-up menu.
   - ◆ From the Document window menu bar, select Modify > Page Properties.
   Either way, the Page Properties dialog box will appear.

2. From here, you can adjust page properties for that frame, including background color, background image, text colors, and link colors.

For more on working with Page Properties, see Chapter 2.

Saving Your Work

Because frames pages are made up of multiple documents, saving them is a multistep process. If you just press Ctrl+S (Command+S), you might not be quite sure of which page you're saving, because Dreamweaver's Save dialog box doesn't offer any distinguishing marks. You need to save each frame separately because they are distinct documents.

You can skip these steps for any previously completed pages you attached to the frameset, as described in *Setting Content Pages*, earlier in this chapter.

Figure 11.38 This Save As dialog box is no different from any other one in Dreamweaver. Some other Web page programs, such as Microsoft FrontPage, have distinct Save As dialog boxes for the different parts of a frameset.

To save each frame:

1. Select the frame that you want to save by clicking on it in the Frames inspector.

2. From the Document window menu bar, select File > Save, or press Ctrl+S (Command+S). The Save As dialog box will appear (**Figure 11.38**, **Figure 11. 39**).

3. Type a meaningful filename in the File Name text box. You'll want to be able to distinguish one frame file from another when dealing with these documents later, so choose a name such as left.html or main_body.html rather than frame1.html.

4. Make sure that the Save In list box displays the folder you want to save the files in; otherwise, browse through the folders on your computer and select one.

5. Click on Save to close the Save As dialog box and return to the Document window.

6. Repeat these steps for each frame.

✔ Tip

- If you create work within a frame in the Document window, you can save your work, and Dreamweaver will automatically set the URL for that page as the default page for that frame.

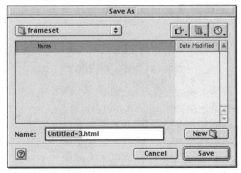

Figure 11.39 The Save As dialog box on the Mac.

Saving All Your Work at Once

After you've saved all the pages in your frameset once, you can periodically save all of them at the same time.

From the Document window menu bar, select File > Save All. Changes to documents currently open in any Dreamweaver window will be saved. A Save As dialog box will appear for any previously unsaved documents open in Dreamweaver.

SAVING YOUR WORK

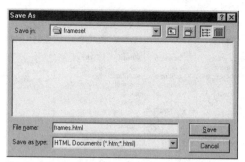

Figure 11.40 The URL for this page will end up being something like http://www.yoursite.com/frameset/frames.html. If you want your frameset to appear as the default page in a directory, name the frameset document index.html, or whatever your house convention is for a default page.

Titling the Frameset Page

Because the frameset page is the one whose URL you'll point to, and because it's the page-in-charge, you need to give it a title:

1. Select the frameset by clicking on the outermost frame border in the Document window or in the Frames inspector.

2. From the Document window menu bar, select Modify > Page Properties. The Page Properties dialog box will appear.

3. Type the title for your page in the Title text box.

4. Click on OK to close the Page Properties dialog box.

You'll see the title in the title bar when you preview the page in the browser window.

Saving the Frameset Page

The frameset page, which contains all the behind-the-scenes data that makes the page function as a frames page, needs to be saved separately as well.

To save the frameset page:

1. With your frames page visible in the Document window, choose File > Save Frameset from the Document window menu bar. The Save As dialog box will appear.

2. Type a meaningful filename in the File Name text box. This filename will be part of the URL, or pathname, for the entire frames-based page (**Figure 11.40**).

3. Make sure that the Save In list box displays the folder you want to save the files in; otherwise, browse through the folders on your computer until you find the one you want.

4. Click on Save to close the Save As dialog box and return to the Document window.

✔ Tips

- It's helpful to save all the files in a frameset in the same folder in order to keep those files separate from the rest of the HTML files on your computer. That way, not only will you be able to locate the files easily and distinguish them from your other projects, you'll have them tidily in their own folder when you get ready to upload them all to the Web.

- Of course, if you also place frameset files in their own directory on your Web site, you should use document relative filenames, which will keep everything tidy.

- When you open your site in the browser window, it's the frameset document that you will be using as the URL.

Frameset Options

There are several options you can set for the frames in your page, including options for scrollbars and borders, whether the frames can be resized, and margin settings for each frame.

You can set scrollbar options for each frame on a page. **Figure 11.41** demonstrates these options.

To set scrollbar options:

1. Select the frame whose scrollbar settings you want to change.

2. In the Properties inspector, choose a scrollbar option from the Scroll drop-down menu (**Figure 11.42**):
   - ◆ *Yes* (the frame will always have scrollbars, whether they're needed or not)
   - ◆ *No* (the frame will never have scrollbars, whether they're needed or not)
   - ◆ *Auto* (the frame will display scrollbars when they are needed)
   - ◆ *Default* (uses browser default settings, which are usually Auto)

Note that these scrollbar settings affect both horizontal and vertical scrollbars. The Yes and No settings should be used with discretion.

Generally, when a frames page is loaded into a browser window, the user can resize the frames to personal taste or viewing convenience. If you want some or all of the frames in your page not to be resized, you can set the No Resize option.

To use the No Resize option:

1. Select the frame whose scrollbar settings you want to change. The Properties inspector will display settings for that frame.

2. Place a check mark in the No Resize checkbox.

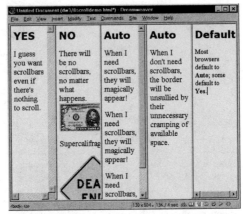

Figure 11.41 Scrollbar options demonstrated here are, from left to right, Yes, No, Auto (with scrollbars), Auto (without scrollbars), and Default. Obviously, Auto makes the most sense most of the time.

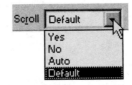

Figure 11.42 Choose one of the scrollbar options from the drop-down menu on the Properties inspector.

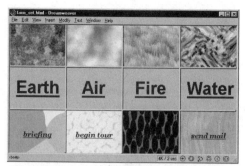

Figure 11.43 Here's the same page we saw in Figure 11.1, with a normal, default frame border. To change back to this setting after a departure, use a frame border of 5.

Figure 11.44 Here's the same page with a border width of zero.

Figure 11.45 Same thing, with a rather thick border of 10. Play around with it; the most interesting effects are between 0 and 10.

Obviously, all frames adjacent to frames with the No Resize option selected will not be able to be resized on that border. In **Figure 11.41**, it sure would be nice to be able to resize some of those frames.

You can turn off borders for the frames on a page, and you can set the width of all the borders on a page. These are frameset options rather than a single-frame option.

Figures 11.43–45 show the same page, with frame borders turned off in **Figure 11.44**, and a border width of 10 in **Figure 11.45**.

To set border options:

1. Select the frameset. The Properties inspector will display frameset options (as shown earlier in **Figure 11.19**).

2. From the Properties inspector's Borders drop-down menu, choose one of the following options:
   - *Yes* (displays all frame borders)
   - *No* (hides all frame borders)
   - *Default* (uses browser default settings, usually displaying borders)

3. If you want to change the border width, type a number, in pixels, in the Border Width text box.

4. Press Enter (Return), or click on the Apply button to apply your changes to the page.

✔ Tips

- In case you change your mind and want to go back to "normal" frame borders, the default border width is 5.

- You can display or hide borders while you're working in Dreamweaver, regardless of what your final browser settings are. Just select View > Frame Borders to toggle the borders on and off.

- Border width affects the spacing between the frames on a page whether or not the borders themselves are displayed.

To choose a border color:

1. Select the frameset, and the frameset properties will appear in the Properties inspector.

2. Choose a border color by:
   - Typing or pasting a hex code in the Border Color text box ![Border Color].
   - Clicking on the Border Color button to display the Colors palette, and then clicking on a color in the Colors palette ![icon].

     or

   - Displaying the Colors palette, clicking on the Colors button, and using the Colors dialog box to select a specific color (see Chapter 2).

The color you selected will be displayed on the frame borders (**Figure 11.46**); the appearance will differ depending on border width.

✔ Tips

- You can set border colors for individual frames, which will override any border color settings you made for the entire frameset, although your mileage may vary (**Figure 11.47**).

- Border colors will not display if the borders are turned off or set to 0 width.

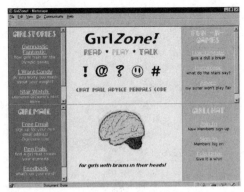

Figure 11.46 This frameset has colored borders and a border width of 3.

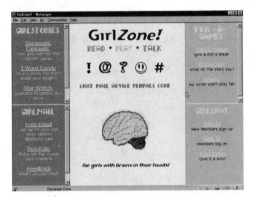

Figure 11.47 I changed the border color setting *only* for the top-left frame, and all the borders were affected except the border between the middle and right frames.

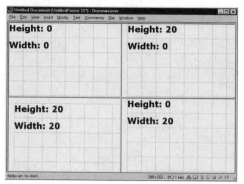

Figure 11.48 I turned on the grid in this view (View > Grid > Show) so that you could see the difference that margin settings make. Each of these four frames has different margin settings. Experiment with different settings for pages that use images or different sizes of text.

Setting Margins

Before Dynamic HTML, the only way to set page margins was by using frames. You can set two border values for each frame in a set: Margin Width (left and right margins) and Margin Height (top and bottom margins).

To set margins:

1. In the Frames inspector, select the frame whose margins you'd like to set.

2. In the Properties inspector, type a number (in pixels) in the Margin Width and/or Margin Height text boxes.

3. Press Enter (Return), or click on the Apply button to see your changes take effect.

Figure 11.48 demonstrates the effect that margins can have. In Dreamweaver 3, the upper-left corner of the grid, also called the *zero point,* actually moves in relation to the upper-left corner of the frame. This is a more accurate and useful depiction of the placement of the content of a frame than in earlier editions of the program. For more about the grid, see Chapter 1. See Chapter 10 to use style sheets to set other kinds of margins.

SETTING MARGINS

Targeting Links

Now you have a frames page that looks exactly like you want it to, and you have a default document attached to all the frames in your page. Before you can call your page finished, you need to set targets for the links in your pages.

When you click on a link in a regular Web page, it generally opens in the same window as the last document you were viewing. In a frames page, however, in which several documents occupy the same window, you don't always want the result of the user's next click—the *target* page—to appear in the same frame as the link they clicked on. A target tells the link in which frame it should open.

You can set targets so that when you click on a link in a frame, the link opens either in a particular frame in the frameset, or in a specialized target option such as a new window.

- If you don't declare any targets for a particular frame, the target page will open in the same frame as the link.

- You can set targets so that clicking on a link in one frame opens the page in another frame. Or, you can use one of the special targets (see the sidebar on this page) to control where a document opens.

- You can set a default, or base target, for all your frames; you only need to set individual targets for links that differ from the frame's default target.

Specialized Targets

In addition to targeting links to open in a specific frame, you can set targets that will control which window the pages will appear in.

- `target=_blank` makes the link open in a new, blank browser window.

- `target=_top` makes the link replace the content of the current window.

- `target=_parent` makes the link open in the parent frame, in cases where you're using nested framesets.

- `target=_self` makes the link open in the same frame as the link.

Figure 11.49 Name each frame by selecting it and then typing a meaningful word in the Frame Name text box.

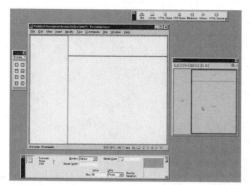

Figure 11.50 After you've named your frames, the Frames inspector will display the name of each frame.

- As is the case with most HTML entities, no spaces are allowed in frame names. Underscores are okay, but hyphens are not. Try to restrict yourself to lowercase letters and numbers.

- Another great Dreamweaver advantage: you don't have to remember, memorize, write down, or tattoo the names of your frames on your forehead; just refer to the Frames inspector.

Naming Frames

Before you can set targets, you need to name each frame. A frame name is different from a filename or a page title. The frameset page needs to know both the filename and the frame name of each page in order to be able to load the pages in the proper position and order.

✔ Tip

- The page title, in cases of frames pages, is unnecessary for all but the frameset page. The page title, as you'll recall, appears in the title bar of the Web browser; it's the frameset page's title that shows up when the frameset page is loaded. See *Titling the Frameset Page*, earlier in this chapter.

To name a frame:

1. Select the frame you want to name by clicking on it in the Frames inspector. The Frame properties will appear in the Properties inspector.

2. Type a meaningful name in the Frame Name text box (**Figure 11.49**). You should be able to distinguish one frame from another by their names; for example, upper_left, main, or toolbar.

3. Press Enter (Return), or click on the Apply button. The name will remain in the Frame text box.

4. Repeat these steps for all the frames in the window.

When you open the Frames inspector, the names of the frames will be displayed there (**Figure 11.50**).

✔ Tips

- After you name your frames, their names will appear in the Properties inspector's Target drop-down menu. In the upcoming section, Setting Targets for Individual Links, you'll choose a target from that menu.

Setting Targets

Once you name your frames, you can set a target for an entire frame or for individual links.

Setting a base target for a frame

By default, the target for each frame is the frame itself. To set a different default target, also known as a *base target*, you need to specify the name of the target in the code.

To set a base target:

1. Click in the frame whose base target you want to set.

2. Open the HTML inspector for that frame by pressing F10, or by selecting Window > HTML from the Document window menu bar.

3. Locate the <HEAD> tag, near the top of the HTML window. It should look something like this: ──────────────→

4. Within the <HEAD> tag, but after the <TITLE> tag, type the following line of code

   `<base target="name">`

   where name is replaced by the name of the frame you want to make the default target, or one of the special targeting instructions, such as "_top" (quotation marks included).

5. Your code should now look something like this: ──────────────→

6. Press Ctrl+S (Command+S) to save the changes to your code. You can close the HTML inspector, if you like.

While behind-the-scenes changes like this one won't show up visibly in the Dreamweaver window, you can preview your frames page in the browser window and test them to make sure they work.

```
<head>
<title>Untitled Document</title>
<meta http-equiv="Content-Type"
content="text/html; charset=iso-
8859-1">
</head>
```

```
<head>
<title>Untitled Document</title>
<base target="main_frame">
<meta http-equiv="Content-Type"
content="text/html;
charset=iso-8859-1">
</head>
```

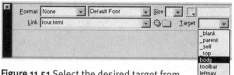

Figure 11.51 Select the desired target from the Target drop-down menu.

Figure 11.52 Here's what you'll see when you first visit numbers.html: two frames introducing you to the site.

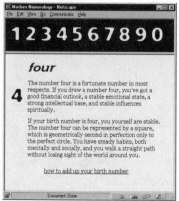

Figure 11.53 Click on one of the numbers in the top frame, and a new page opens in the bottom frame. The top frame has a base target of body, which is the name of the bottom frame.

When you want to set a target for a link that differs from the default, or base target, use the Properties inspector to select a target for the link.

To target individual links:

1. Select the text or image that you want to target. The Properties inspector will display properties for that object.

2. If there's not a link specified for that object as yet, type or paste the URL for the link in the Link text box.

3. From the Target drop-down menu (**Figure 11.51**), select a target. This can be either the name of one of the other frames on the page, or one of the special targets discussed in *Target Options,* earlier in this chapter.

You're all set.

Figures 11.52 and **53** demonstrate a simple, common use of targeting: click on a link in the top frame, and it opens in the bottom frame.

Testing Your Targets

It's vitally important, more so than with almost any other kind of Web page, that you test every link on your frames-based pages. You need to make sure that the links open where you think you told them to open. Targets can be tricky—they don't need to be difficult, but they absolutely must be done correctly if you don't want to drive your visitors away for good. **Figure 11.54** shows the evil recursive frame problem: a link to the entire frameset was accidentally targeted to open in one of the frames.

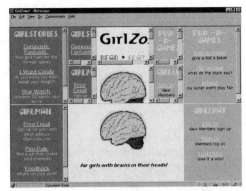

Figure 11.54 A misplaced target can be ugly, at best. Here, we see a recursive frameset—a link to the entire frameset was accidentally targeted to open in the top, center frame.

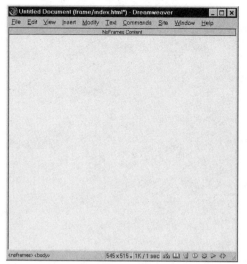

Figure 11.55 From the Document window menu bar, select Modify > Frameset > Edit No Frames Content, and the Document window will display the blank no-frames page.

Figure 11.56 With very little effort, I created a no-frames page that includes all the same links as the frameset page. To appease very old browsers, I also avoided frills like tables, background images, and image maps. See Appendix C on the book's Web site for more details.

Creating No-Frames Content

Not everyone who visits your site will have a frames-capable browser. While most people are using some version or other of Netscape Navigator or Internet Explorer, not everyone is. See Appendix C on the Web site for the details. The point is that if you don't offer your non-frames visitors something, they won't see anything at all.

At the very least, you need to leave a message that says something like, "This site requires a frames-capable browser, such as Netscape Navigator 2 or later, or Internet Explorer 3 or later." Providing links to a site where they can download this software is also a good idea.

But even that is shortchanging your guests, in a way. Without much work at all, you can give them a fully functional page that will connect them with much of the same information.

To create a no-frames page from scratch:

1. To view the no-frames page, from the Document window menu bar, select Modify > Frameset > Edit No Frames Content. The Document window will display the blank no-frames page (**Figure 11.55**).

2. You can edit this page, including page properties such as background color, the same way you would when creating a page from scratch.

   or

   You can select the contents of an existing page, copy them, and paste them into the no-frames page.

Figure 11.56 shows the no-frames page we created as the alternative to the frames-based page shown in **Figures 11.52** and **53**.

To return to the frames view, just select Modify > Frameset > Edit No Frames Content again.

To use existing code in a no-frames page:

1. In the HTML inspector or your favorite code editor, open the HTML or text for the page you want to use.

2. Select all the code between (and including) the <body> and </body> tags, and copy it to the clipboard.

3. In the Dreamweaver Document window, view the no-frames page by selecting Modify > Frameset > Edit No Frames Content from the menu bar. The Document window will display the no-frames page.

4. View the HTML for this page—which is really just part of the frameset document. The empty no-frames code should look like this:

   ```
   <noframes><body bgcolor="#FFFFFF">
   </body></noframes>
   ```

5. Select everything between the <noframes> and </noframes> tags, and delete it.

6. Paste in the HTML from the code you copied in step 2. You should get something like this:

   ```
   <noframes>
   <body bgcolor="#000000">
   This is all the neat content that's
   on my frames page, including
   <A HREF="links.html">links</A>
   and everything!
   </body>
   </noframes>
   ```

7. Save the changes to your HTML, and close the HTML inspector. The page you pasted in will show up in the No Frames Content window.

No-Frames Tips

Check to make sure that:

♦ You don't include any <html> or </html> tags within the <noframes> tags.

♦ You include one, and only one set of <body> and </body> tags between the <noframes> tags.

When you preview no-frames content in your regular browser, it won't show up. Why? Because your regular browser is probably frames-capable, and it will load the frames-based page instead—they are the same document, after all.

See Appendix C, on the Web site, for information about getting and using a non-frames browser for previewing your documents.

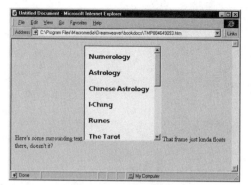

Figure 11.57 The inline frame is a particular feature of Internet Explorer—you'll need to experiment with the IFRAME attributes quite a bit to figure out how they work.

Inline Frames

Internet Explorer (IE) has introduced a proprietary tag called <IFRAME> to make frames appear within a page (**Figure 11.57**). This technique, called *inline frames* or *floating frames,* only works with Internet Explorer version 3 or later.

To use inline frames:

1. With the appropriate page open in the Document window, view the HTML code by selecting Window > HTML from the Document window menu bar.

2. Insert the following code

```
<IFRAME SRC="float.html">
</IFRAME>
```

where "float.html" is replaced by the URL for the content you want to appear in the floating frame.

3. Type or paste some no-iframes content between the two tags, such as "To view this page, you need MSIE 3 or later."

4. Press Ctrl+S (Command+S) to save the changes to the code.

You'll need to view this page in IE to see the iframe.

This is the code for the iframe in **Figure 11.57**:

```
<IFRAME name="toc" src="toctoc.html"
frameborder=1 height="80%" width=200
scrolling=yes align=center, bottom>
You must use Internet Explorer to view
the inline frames on this page, but you
can get the same content
<a href="toctoc.html">here</a>.
</IFRAME>
```

✔ Tip

■ You can create the same visual effect by using borderless frames in combination with scrollbar options, and the page will be viewable by many more visitors.

Other IFRAME Attributes

You can adjust the appearance and behavior of an IFRAME by using these other attributes within an IFRAME tag. You should recognize most of these attributes from this and other chapters. As always, the pipe (|) means "or."

```
name="name"
align=top|middle|bottom|left|right|
   center
```

(pick two, as in align="top, center")

This has more to do with the relationship between the frame and the other content than with the position of the frame.

```
frameborder=1|0   (1=yes, 0=no)
height=x|"x%"
width=x|"x%"
marginheight=x
marginwidth=x
scrolling=yes|no|auto
```

INLINE FRAMES

FILLING OUT FORMS

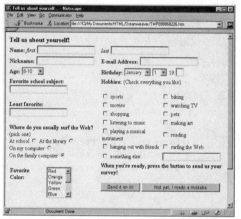

Figure 12.1 This feedback form includes most of the different kinds of fields that you can have in a form. I laid out the form using tables.

You fill out forms routinely when you apply for a driver's license or pay taxes or change addresses. Forms are getting to be more and more routine on the Web, too. Large sites nearly always make some sort of appeal for personal information.

You'll want your visitors to fill out forms because it's the most efficient way for them to give you feedback about your site or about their identities (**Figure 12.1**).

Online shopping sites, visitor surveys, and guestbooks use forms to collect data (called *input*) from your users. This data is then sent to a form handler—usually a CGI script, although other custom scripts can be used—which does something with this data. In some cases, such as surveys, the script simply saves the input for the site management to look at later. In other cases, such as search engines, the script takes the input and immediately uses it to provide some response or results for the user's edification. Some form of inter-action with the user—even a simple thank-you page—is essential to assure the user that the information wasn't sent into a vacuum.

Dreamweaver simplifies the process of creating forms for your site. In this chapter, you'll learn the basics of how to create and name form objects such as checkboxes, radio buttons, drop-down menus, and text fields.

Creating a Form

The first step in creating a form is to put the form itself, represented by the <FORM></FORM> tags, on your page. It will be delineated in the Document window by a dashed red line that will be invisible when the page is loaded in the browser window (**Figure 12.2**).

Dreamweaver's Objects palette is especially handy for automating the process.

To display form objects on the Objects palette:

1. Display the Objects palette by selecting Window > Objects from the Document window menu bar.

2. On the Objects palette, click on the menu button at the top.

3. From the pop-up menu that appears, choose Forms (**Figure 12.3**).

The Objects palette will display form objects (**Figure 12.4**).

To create a form:

1. You must have invisible element viewing turned on to view Form borders. To turn it on, select View > Invisible Elements from the Document window menu bar.

2. From the Document window menu bar, select Insert > Form.

   or

   On the Objects palette, click on the Insert Form button: ▢ .

The form will appear (**Figure 12.5**). By default, your form will occupy 100 percent of the page width. The height is determined by the content you place within the form borders. You cannot resize forms with Dreamweaver, although you can format their content using tables (see Chapter 10 to find out how to use tables).

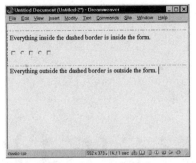

Figure 12.2 In the Document window, forms are outlined by a red, dashed border.

Figure 12.3 Click on the menu button on the Objects palette and choose Forms from the pop-up menu.

Figure 12.4 The Objects palette with form objects displayed. Note that I resized the palette—you can do that by clicking and dragging its lower-right corner.

Figure 12.5 A new, blank form.

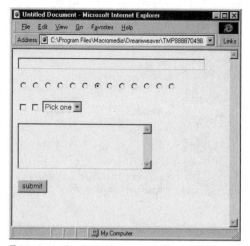

Figure 12.6 What is this form for? Without labels, it's impossible to tell.

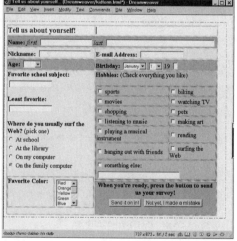

Figure 12.7 This is the same form we saw in Figure 12.1 with the table, form borders, and labels revealed in the Document window.

Formatting Forms

It's essential to label each field in a form; otherwise, the users won't know what the heck they're supposed to do (**Figure 12.6**). I don't specify this in the steps for adding each field because it's pretty unlikely that you're going to forget.

You can use line breaks, paragraph breaks, preformatted text, or tables to format the stuff in your forms (**Figure 12.7**). A form can include nearly any HTML entity—text, images, tables—except another form. You can put a form in a table, or a table in a form, but you can't put a form within a form. You can, however, include more than one form on a page—just don't try to overlap them.

✔ Tip

■ You can find out about working with tables in Chapter 10. I discussed text formatting in Chapters 5 and 6.

Adding Form Objects

Form objects, commonly referred to as form fields, are the nuts and bolts of a form. They're the boxes and buttons that people click on or type in to make their mark (technically called their *input*) on a form.

Figure 12.8 The Objects palette, displaying form objects.

There are five different common flavors of form objects, each of which has its own button on the Objects palette (**Figure 12.8**), as well as its own entry in the Insert > Form Object menu, as do some of the less common ones.

Text fields (also called text boxes) come in two flavors: single-line and multi-line. If a form was a test, a single-line field would be a short answer question (**Figure 12.9**), and a multi-line would be an essay question (**Figure 12.10**).

Figure 12.9 A single-line text box

Checkboxes can be used singly or in groups of two or more (**Figure 12.11**). Checkboxes allow the user to specify yes or no answers.

Radio buttons, named after the buttons on old-fashioned console radios, always come in groups of two or more (**Figure 12.12**). They allow you to choose only one of a set of options—when you push in one button on a radio, the other buttons pop out.

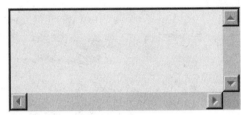

Figure 12.10 A multi-line text box

Lists and *menus* allow the user to choose from a long list of options that don't take up too much space on the page. What Dreamweaver calls a *menu,* is also called a *drop-down menu;* it drops down when you click on it to reveal the full set of options. A list box offers several choices at once; in some cases, the user can choose more than one item from a list box (**Figure 12.13**).

Figure 12.11 A flock of checkboxes

Buttons are what makes the form do something. A *submit button* sends the form off over the wires to its final destination. A *reset button* clears all the values entered in a form and resets the form to its default, or starting, values (**Figure 12.14**).

Figure 12.12 A gaggle of radio buttons

Figure 12.13 A drop-down menu and a list box

Figure 12.14 Submit and reset buttons

Figure 12.15 The Properties inspector

Name That Value

When you name a form field, you may never need to personally read the form input but if you did, you'd see results in this format:

```
name=value      name=value
name=value      name=value
name=value
```

The name is the name you give the field, and the value is the input the user fills the field with. One argument for recognizable names for form fields is so that if there's a problem, it's with "The address field," not with "field six."

In a text box, the value of the input is equal to what the user's type. Input for a text field might look like this:

```
address="675 Onionskin Road"
```

For a checkbox or a radio button, you really need to specify what value the field has by providing unique text that signifies what specific input means.

This is particularly important if you're using several checkboxes; a value of "checkbox5" won't tell you anything.

Checkbox input in form results could look like any of the four examples below:

```
carowner=yes      carowner=checked
carowner=carowner
```

I know, I said four examples—if it isn't checked, it doesn't get sent with the form results at all. I'll point out any eccentricities like this along the way.

Names and Values

Each gadget, or form field, in a form is also known as an *input item* (the HTML tag is often `<input>`). That means it's used to collect input from the people who use it.

Each input item is represented in the form results by a name and a value. The *name* is a unique signifier that tells you (or the script handling the form) which field is which. The *value* is the content of the field.

Names and values are required for form fields; if you forget them, Dreamweaver will provide sequential names and values, such as `radiobutton`, `radiobutton2`, `radiobutton3`, and so on. Those sorts of names aren't very useful; for more about choosing a name and where values come in, read the sidebar, this page.

It's always useful, but the Properties inspector will come in particularly handy for formatting just about everything—both the text of the labels and the form fields themselves. The Properties inspector will display unique properties for each form field—and it's what you'll use to specify names and values.

To display the Properties inspector:

◆ From the Document window menu bar, select Modify > Selection Properties.

or

From the Document window menu bar, select Window > Properties.

or

Press Ctrl + F3 (Command + F3)

Either way, the Properties inspector will appear (**Figure 12.15**).

Text fields are used to collect data that you can't predict. You can't offer a multiple choice menu for every possible name or e-mail address, for instance. For short answers, such as address information or favorite TV show, you'll use a single-line text field.

To create a single-line text field:

1. In the Document window, click within the form boundaries.

2. From the Document window menu bar, select Insert > Form Object > Text Field.

   or

   On the Objects palette, click on the Text Field button ▢ , or drag the button to the page.

   A single-line text field will appear:

   You can resize it, if you like.

3. To resize the text field, type a number, in characters, in the Char Width text box of thr Properties inspector (**Figure 12.16**).

4. Click on the Apply button or press Enter (Return), and your text field will resize.

You can use a single-line text box to collect password information, in which case the stuff they type in the box will become *** or ⋯.

To create a password box:

1. Click on the text field to select it, and make sure the Properties inspector is open (**Figure 12.16**).

2. In the Type area of the Properties inspector, click on the Password radio button.

There won't be any visible change, but when your page is on the Web, the stuff the user types in it will be replaced by asterisks or bullets to prevent accidents and deviousness (**Figure 12.17**).

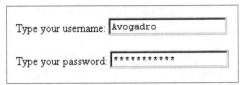

Figure 12.16 The Properties inspector, displaying properties for a single-line text field.

Figure 12.17 The first text box is a normal single-line text box, while the second one is a password box.

Displaying Properties

You can display properties for any form field by double-clicking it. The Properties inspector will appear, displaying form object properties.

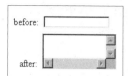

Figure 12.18 Change a single-line text field into a multi-line field by clicking on the Multi-line radio button in the Properties inspector.

Figure 12.19 To change the dimensions of a multi-line text box, type a character width and a line height in the Properties inspector.

A multi-line text field will create a "feedback box" that you can use to elicit longer responses from your users. Multi-line text boxes are commonly used for guestbooks, e-mail forms, and any other case in which you want more than a few words from your visitors.

To create a multi-line text field:

1. Create a single-line text field, as described on the previous page.

2. Double-click the text field, and the Properties inspector will appear if it isn't already showing.

3. In the Type area of the Properties inspector, click on the Multi-line radio button. The text field will change appearance (**Figure 12.18**).

To resize a multi-line text field:

1. Select the multi-line text field.

2. In the Properties inspector, type a number (in characters) in the Char Width text box.

3. Type a number of lines in the Num Lines text box.

4. Click on the Apply button. The text box will resize to your specifications (**Figure 12.19**).

✔ Tip

■ Unfortunately, you can't resize a multi- or single-line text field by clicking and dragging.

NAMES AND VALUES

You can set a character limit for a single-line text field.

To restrict the number of characters allowed:

1. Click on a single-line text field to select it, or double-click it to display the Properties inspector.

2. In the Max Chars text box, type the maximum number of characters you'll allow in this field, and click the Apply button.

In a Web browser, the user will not be able to type more than the number of characters you specified. (Generally, they'll hear beeping when they try to type past the limit.)

If you want to give your visitors an example of what kind of input you're expecting, you can set an initial value for either kind of text box.

To set an initial value:

1. Select the text box, (either single- or multi-line), and view the Properties inspector.

2. In the Init Val text box, type the text you want to have displayed in the text box, and click on the Apply button.

The text will show up in the text box in the Document window (**Figure 12.20**) and in the Web browser.

✔ Tip

■ Beware of using the initial value. While it might seem like a great idea at the time, a lot of wise guys (or dumb guys) won't bother to change something that's already filled in. It might be better, in some cases, to use example text outside the box, as shown in **Figure 12.21**.

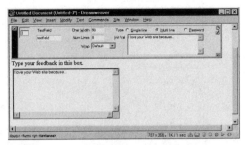

Figure 12.20 The text you type in the Properties inspector's Init Val text box will be included in the form field.

Figure 12.21 In the first text box, the user may neglect to replace the supplied text with his or her real e-mail address. In the second instance, the user is given a visual example, but the text box is left blank.

Figure 12.22 The Properties inspector for a File field allows you to set the character width, maximum number of characters, and initial value for the file's location.

File Fields

One kind of form field you may have reason to use, albeit rarely, is the *file field*. The file field consists of a text box and a button marked Browse. This field is used when you want your visitors to be able to upload files from their local computer to your remote server. The Browse button will open the Open File dialog box in their Web browser, which they will use to select the file; then they will use the form's submit button to send you the file.

To insert a file field, click on the Insert File Field button ![icon] on the Forms panel of the Objects palette, or select Insert > Form Object > File Field. The file field will appear: ![field]

You can set a maximum character width, a maximum number of characters, and an initial value for this field in the Properties inspector just as you can for normal text fields. See **Figure 12.22**.

When users type in a multi-line text field, scrollbars appear when the user types text that's longer than the field. However, the text won't wrap in a multi-line text field unless you turn that option on.

To wrap text in a multi-line text field:

1. Select the multi-line text field.

2. Display the full Properties inspector by clicking on the Expander arrow in the lower-right corner.

3. From the Wrap drop-down menu, select either Default (the browser default, sometimes wrap and sometimes not), Virtual (the text will wrap onscreen, but no line breaks will be inserted in the form input), or Physical (the browser will insert line breaks into the form input where they occur onscreen).

As with all form fields, it's a good idea to name your text fields so you can tell them apart.

To name a text field:

1. Select the text box and view the Properties inspector.

2. In the TextField text box, highlight the text field text and type over it, replacing it with a meaningful word that will indicate the purpose of the field.

3. Click on the Apply button.

Your text field will be named in the code, as well as in the form results that your users will submit.

NAMES AND VALUES

Checkboxes, which often appear in groups, allow users to make one or more selections from a set of options.

To create a checkbox:

1. Click to place the insertion point within the form in the Document window.

2. From the Document window menu bar, select Insert > Form Object > Check Box.

   or

   On the Objects palette, click on the Insert Checkbox button ⊠, or drag the button to the form in the Document window. The checkbox will appear: ⬚.

3. Repeat step 1 for each checkbox in the set.

Remember to give each checkbox a uniquely useful name and value.

To specify name and value:

1. Select the checkbox by clicking on it, and double-click if you need to display the Properties inspector (**Figure 12.23**).

2. In the Checked Value text box, type the text you want to see if the user checks the box. Good examples include send_info or owns_dog.

3. Name the checkbox by typing a name for it in the CheckBox text box. For example, the name could be mail or dog.

4. Click on the Apply button.

✔ Tips

■ If the user does not check off the checkbox, there will be no indication of the checkbox at all in the form results.

■ If you want the checkbox to appear checked when the page is loaded, click on the Checked radio button in the Initial State area of the Properties inspector.

— Apply button

Figure 12.23 The Properties inspector, displaying checkbox properties.

■ If the user does check off the checkbox, the results will say something like NAME=VALUE. In our example above, the results would be mail=send_info or dog=owns_dog.

■ Names and values are case-sensitive.

Figure 12.24 The Properties inspector, displaying radio button properties.

While checkboxes can appear either singly or in groups, radio buttons always appear in groups. You can use radio buttons for yes/no, true/false, or multiple-choice questions.

To insert a radio button:

1. Click to place the insertion point within the form in the Document window.

2. From the Document window menu bar, select Insert > Form Object > Radio Button

   or

   On the Objects palette, click on the Insert Radio button, 🔘 , or drag the radio button to the form in the Document window. A radio button will appear: 🔘

3. Repeat step 2 for each radio button in the set.

You must name each radio button in a group with the same name, and you must give each radio button in a group a different value.

To specify names and values:

1. Select a radio button, and display the Properties inspector, if necessary (**Figure 12.24**).

2. Type a name for the group of radio buttons in the RadioButton text box.

3. Type a value for that particular radio button in the Checked Value text box.

4. Repeat steps 1–3 for each radio button in the set. Be sure to spell the name exactly the same, and to give each button a different value, such as "very satisfied," "meets expectations," or "dissatisfied."

continues on next page

NAMES AND VALUES

5. Select one of the buttons to be initially selected when the page is loaded. Click on that button and, in the Properties inspector, click on the Checked radio button.

6. Click on the Apply button to apply your changes to the form.

✔ Tips

■ A group of radio buttons as described on this page is a set wherein only one button can be clicked at a time. The only way to create a group of radio buttons, and to give them group properties, is to give each button in the group the same exact name (in the Properties inspector).

■ You can check to make sure you've grouped your radio buttons properly by previewing the page in a browser and making sure that, when you click on each button in turn, the other buttons in the set become deselected.

■ If you use more than one group of radio buttons in a single form, be sure to give each group a unique name.

■ To ensure the name is exactly the same for a group of buttons, you can copy and paste the name for each button.

■ Names and values are case-sensitive.

Figure 12.25 The Properties inspector, displaying menu properties.

Figure 12.26 The Initial List Values dialog box is where you add menu items to your menus and lists.

Figure 12.27 Press the Tab key to move to the next column and type the value for the menu item.

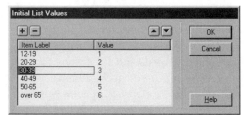

Figure 12.28 Use the + and – buttons to add and delete items—and the Up and Down arrow buttons to rearrange the order of the list.

You can offer a range of choices by using drop-down menus, also called pull-down menus or pop-up menus.

To create a menu:

1. Click to place the insertion point within the form in the Document window.

2. From the Document window menu bar, select Insert > Form Object > List/Menu.

   or

   On the Objects palette, click on the Insert List/Menu button 🖼, or drag the button to the form in the Document window.

An itty-bitty drop-down menu will appear:

To fill the menu with menu items:

1. Click on the list to select it, and display the Properties inspector (**Figure 12.25**).

2. Click on the List Values button. The Initial List Values dialog box will appear (**Figure 12.26**).

3. Click below the Item Label menu button, and a text field will appear beneath it.

4. Type a menu item (what you want to appear in the menu) in the Item Label text field.

   If you want the values (the information that will appear in the form results) to be the same as the item labels, you can skip steps 5 and 6.

5. Press the Tab key or click on the Value menu button, and a text field will become visible (**Figure 12.27**).

6. Type the value of the menu item in the Value text field.

7. Repeat steps 2–6 for each menu item you want to include. (Press the Tab key or click on the + button to create a field for each new menu item.)

NAMES AND VALUES

Editing menu items

You can edit this list before you close the dialog box (**Figure 12.28**).

To edit the menu items:

1. You can rearrange the menu items by moving them up and down through the list.

   ◆ To move an item up through the list, click on the Up arrow button.

   ◆ To move an item down through the list, click on the Down arrow button.

2. You can add or delete items as necessary.

   ◆ To delete an item, click on it, and then click on the – (minus) button.

   ◆ To add an item, click on the + button, and then move the item to a new location in the list, if desired.

3. And of course, you can edit the text of the menu items themselves. Just click on the item, and type your changes in the text field.

When you're all done with the Initial List Values dialog box, click on OK to close it. You'll return to the Document window. The menu will appear larger than it was before, which indicates that it contains multitudes, but Dreamweaver doesn't display the menu as active—you won't see the menu items themselves.

✔ Tips

■ To proofread your menu, you need to preview it in the browser window (**Figure 12.29**). Once there, you can click on it to drop-down the menu and scroll through the list of items.

■ Don't forget to name your menu by typing a name in the List/Menu text box on the Properties inspector.

Figure 12.29 When you load the page in the browser window, you can click on the menu to make sure it looks the way you desire.

Menu Design

Normally, form objects, when viewed in the browser window, are displayed in the system font: Arial size 2 for menus, (Chicago or Charcoal, on the Mac) and Courier size 3 for text boxes.

You can change the look of a drop-down menu or a text box by changing its font face and size. Be sure to test these effects in your favorite browser. The trick here is that if you select just the form field in the Dreamweaver window, you'll see menu object properties in the Properties inspector, rather than text properties. To select a form object and change its font face, follow these steps:

1. Select, by clicking and dragging or by shift-clicking, more than one form object (a menu and a checkbox, for instance), or a form object and some text. The Properties inspector will display text properties.

2. Change the font face of the selected items by selecting it from the Font Face drop-down menu.

3. Change the font size of the selected objects by selecting size from the Size drop-down menu.

4. Preview the form in the browser window to see what your changes look like.

Figure 12.30 The Properties inspector, displaying list properties

Figure 12.31 I gave the list a line height of 5. Because I have more than five items, scrollbars appear in the list box.

Figure 12.32 To specify a menu item other than the first as the initial selection, select the menu item from the Initially Selected list box in the expanded Properties inspector.

Creating a list box

The drop-down menu is one kind of list-type form field you can create; the other kind is the list box. List boxes can be several items high and can offer the possibility of multiple selections.

To create a list box:

1. Create a menu, as described in *To create a menu,* earlier in this chapter. (You can input the menu items at any point.)

2. Display the Properties inspector by double-clicking the menu object.

3. In the Properties inspector, click on the List radio button (**Figure 12.30**).

4. To adjust the height of the list, type a number of lines in the Height text box (**Figure 12.31**). The menu will change appearance in the Document window.

5. To allow multiple selections, make sure the Selections checkbox is checked. To disallow multiple selections, deselect the Selections checkbox.

6. Name your list by typing a name in the List/Menu text box and clicking on the Apply button.

✔ Tips

■ To add menu items to a list box, follow the steps in the section *To fill the menu with menu items,* earlier in this chapter. The dialog boxes are identical.

■ To specify the initial selection in a menu or list, select a menu item from the Initially Selected list box in the Properties inspector (**Figure 12.32**). If no selection is made, the first item in the list will be the initial selection.

NAMES AND VALUES

Jump Menus

A jump menu, new in Dreamweaver 3, is a specialized kind of list or menu; when a visitor selects an option from a jump menu, their browser takes them to a URL associated with that option. Dreamweaver jump menus use JavaScript to do their magic, but it's all written behind the scenes and affixed to a regular list or menu without your having to worry about it.

Keep in mind, though, that not all browsers support JavaScript. See Chapter 15 for more about JavaScript, and be sure to offer alternate options for visiting all the pages in the menu.

To create a jump menu:

1. Save your page, if you haven't done so, to make any relative URLs work properly.

2. Click within the form borders on the page.

3. On the Objects palette, click on the Insert Jump Menu button , or drag the button to the page. The Insert Jump Menu dialog box will appear (**Figure 12.33**).

4. First, we'll specify the URL. To select a page from your local site, click Browse, and locate the document on your computer.

   or

   Type (or paste) the URL (either a full path or a relative URL) of the page in the When Selected, Go to URL text box.

5. If you selected a document from your local site, the Text and Menu Items fields will be filled in (**Figure 12.34**).

   To edit or add the text that will appear in the menu, type the text in the Text text box. The Menu Items field will display both the text and the URL for your selection.

6. Repeat steps 4 and 5 for each additional menu item.

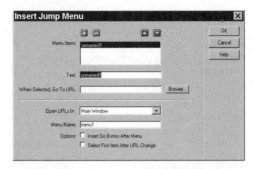

Figure 12.33 The Insert Jump Menu dialog box allows you to specify a list of pages the user can visit by choosing them from a menu or list.

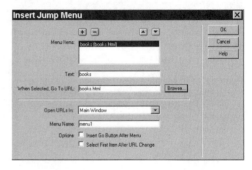

Figure 12.34 If you select a page from your local site as a list option, Dreamweaver will guess the text you want to use based on the filename of the page. You can edit this text later.

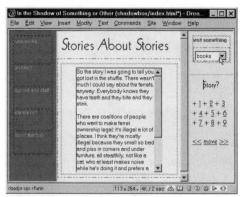

Figure 12.35 The only object in the form in the upper-right corner is a jump menu. The menu must appear in a form to work properly in the widest range of browsers, but you can make it the only object in the form.

Figure 12.36 The Properties inspector for a jump menu offers the same options as it does for a regular list or menu.

7. Type a name for the menu in the Menu Name text box.

8. When you're finished, click on OK to close the Insert Jump Menu text box.

Editing the jump menu

The jump menu uses the same form-field code as does a regular list or menu. After you close the Insert Jump Menu dialog box, you can edit your choices by selecting the menu and then clicking on the List Values button on the Properties inspector (**Figure 12.36**). To edit your jump menu, follow the instructions in the preceding sections, *To fill the menu with menu items* and *To edit the menu items*.

✔ Tip

■ More editing options for Jump Menus using behaviors are described in Chapter 15.

Changing the appearance

You can make your jump menu either a drop-down menu or a list box by selecting either the Menu or the List radio button on the Properties inspector (**Figure 12.36**). For details about additional options for list boxes, see the section *To create a list box,* earlier in this chapter.

You can also choose which item to select initially by choosing an item from the Initially Selected list box. To have the menu return to this initially selected item after the user has used the menu to visit a new page, check the Select First Item After URL Change checkbox in the Insert Jump Menu dialog box.

No Script Required

I've already mentioned that you don't have to worry about the JavaScript involved in creating a jump menu. Even better, the actions involved in this widget are all *client side*; that is, the action of selecting the page to visit is performed by the browser, not by a remote script. This means that you don't need to add a submit button or set up a form handler, as you do to make regular forms work.

I recommend creating a separate form for a jump or go menu. If you place this form inside a table, it can take up as little space as possible on your page (**Figure 12.35**).

You can make the selections in a jump menu open in a new window (**Figure 12.37**). First, you have to create the window. It's best if you create the code for the new window before you add the jump menu, so that the window name will appear in the Open URLs In drop-down menu in the Insert Jump Menu dialog box.

✔ Tips

■ To create an additional window for the jump menu URLs to open in, see *Open Browser Window* in Chapter 15.

■ To change the text on a Go button, see *To rename your button,* later in this chapter.

Hidden form fields

Besides the regular widgets you can use on a form, you can place hidden form fields in the code so that some fixed information is passed along with the rest of the data. This information might include the URL of the form, the version of the form, or any other information you want to receive with the form results.

To create a hidden form field:

1. Click to place the insertion point at the place on the form where you want the invisible field to be inserted.

2. From the Document window menu bar, select Insert > Form Object > Hidden Field

   or

   Click on the Insert Hidden Field button on the Forms panel of the Objects palette, or drag the button to the page.

   If you have Invisible Element viewing turned on, a Hidden Field icon will appear:

3. Type the value of the hidden field in the Value text box in the Properties inspector.

Figure 12.37 You can make selections from a jump menu appear in a new window, which may be a smaller, "remote" or "channel" style window, or a regular browser window whose size you specify.

Figure 12.38 You can add a Go button, pictured here, by checking the Go Button checkbox in the Insert Jump Menu dialog box, which we saw previously in Figure 12.33.

To Go Button or Not to Go Button?

In the Insert Jump Menu dialog box, there's a checkbox marked Go Button. If this box is unchecked *and* the jump menu is a drop-down menu, the browser will jump to the page as soon as the visitor has made a selection from the menu.

If you check the Go Button checkbox (which you *must* do if you're using a list box), the automatic action will be replaced by a button the user can click on when he or she is done choosing (**Figure 12.38**).

Unfortunately, you can't add a Go button after you close the Insert Jump Menu dialog box, but you can delete it if you don't want it anymore.

JUMP MENUS

Tweaking Your Menus and Boxes

Dreamweaver doesn't support the rather handy disabled attribute for menu items, but you can easily add the disabled attribute in the code. The disabled attribute allows you to prevent a user from selecting a particular menu item. If the first item in your drop-down menu is something like "Pick your favorite color," you want to make sure they can't submit that item.

To add this attribute to a list or menu item, follow these steps:

1. Click on the list or menu in the Document window.

2. View the code for your page by selecting Window > HTML from the Document window menu bar. The code for the list or menu will be highlighted in the HTML inspector.

   The code for the menu or list should look something like this:

   ```
   <select name="menu">
       <option value="">red</option>
       <option value="">white</option>
       <option value="">blue</option>
   </select>
   ```

   Each option is a list item.

3. To prevent users from submitting a particular selection, add the disabled attribute to the option tag:

   ```
   <option disabled value="">
   red</option>
   ```

   Save your changes to the HTML, and be sure to test the form to make sure these changes work the way you want them to.

4. Type a name for the hidden field in the Name (unlabeled) text box.

You won't see the hidden fields on the Web page (duh!), but the value will be sent with the rest of the data when the user submits the form.

✔ Tips

- If you use more than one hidden field, be sure to give each one a different name.

- To view invisible elements, select View > Invisible Elements from the Document window menu bar.

Submit and reset buttons

There are three kinds of buttons you can put at the bottom of a form for your visitors to make use of.

Submit buttons are what you push to send the form off to the form handler, which compiles all the input and then does something with it.

Reset buttons clear the form of any new input and reset the form to its initial state.

The last kind of button (a "nothing" button) has no action; that is, it will neither reset nor submit the form, but it can be used with JavaScript or other active content to do *something*.

JUMP MENUS

To create a button:

1. Click to place the insertion point within the form in the Document window.

2. From the Document window menu bar, select Insert > Form Object > Button

   or

   On the Objects palette, click on the Insert button button  , or drag the Insert button to the form in the Document window.

3. A submit button will appear: submit

4. Display the Properties inspector, if necessary, by choosing Modify > Selection Properties (**Figure 12.39**) from the Document window menu bar.

5. Choose the type of button you want:

   ◆ If you want a Submit button, click on the Submit radio button.

   ◆ If you want a Reset button, click on the Reset radio button.

   ◆ If you want a nothing button, click on the None radio button.

6. Click on the Apply button to apply your changes to the button.

✔ Tips

■ It's a convention on most Web pages that the Submit button appears to the left of the Reset button at the bottom of the form.

■ Dreamweaver displays push buttons with a smaller font face than either Navigator or MSIE uses.

■ You can change the size of the push button, too. See the instructions in the sidebar called Menu Design on page 240.

Figure 12.39 The Properties inspector, displaying button properties.

Covering Your Assets

Although most browsers these days support forms, some browsers can't deal with them—they display them improperly or not at all. Even some versions of Internet Explorer have bugs that prevent proper handling of forms, as well as of `mailto:` addresses. If getting input (or orders!) from your visitors is important to you, be sure to visibly include an e-mail address on your site—not just a hidden `mailto:` link.

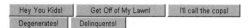

Figure 12.40 Your buttons can say anything you want.

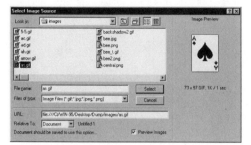

Figure 12.41 The dialog box for inserting an image field is exactly like the generic Select Image Source dialog box.

You can call your buttons whatever you want. By default, the submit buttons will say *Submit* and the reset buttons will say *Reset,* but that's an option, not an imperative. I've seen reset buttons named Gorilla and submit buttons named Fish.

To rename your button:

1. Click on the button to select it, and display the Properties inspector, if necessary.

2. In the Button Name text box, type the text you want to appear on the button, and click on the Apply button.

Your button will be renamed (**Figure 12.40**).

Instead of the standard gray push buttons that usually appear in forms, you can use images as buttons. This method only works for submit buttons.

To create an image field:

1. Click to place the insertion point at the place on the form where you want the image button to appear.

2. From the Document window menu bar, select Insert > Form Object > Image Field

   or

   Click on the Insert Image Field button on the Forms panel of the Objects palette, or drag the button to the page.

   The Select Image Source dialog box will appear (**Figure 12.41**).

3. This dialog box is just like the Insert Image dialog box. Type the pathname of the image in the Image File text box, or select the image from your hard drive.

4. Click on OK to close the Select Image Source dialog box. The image will appear in the Document window with a dashed line around it.

continues on next page

JUMP MENUS

5. Display the Properties inspector, if necessary (**Figure 12.42**). The Src text box will display the path and filename of the image.

6. Type a name in the Name text box.

7. Type the alternate text for the image in the Alt text box.

✔ Tips

■ Along with form object properties, Image field properties include image properties such as image height (H), image width (W), alt text (Alt), and image alignment (Align). If you need information on using these fields, consult Chapter 8.

■ Along with the results of your form, you'll get coordinates that say where on the image the user clicked, appended to the *name* text (name.x and name.y).

Figure 12.42 The Properties inspector, displaying Image Field properties. The dashed border around the image indicates that it's an image field rather than a plain old image.

JUMP MENUS

Figure 12.43 When the Properties inspector displays Form properties, you can choose the method and action of the form handler.

Making It Go

In order to make a form actually do something, you have to set it up to work with a CGI script or other custom script, called a form handler. Dreamweaver can't write the script for you—you have to take care of this part on the server end. Many Internet service providers make available standard scripts for common forms such as mail forms and guestbooks, and they may offer other scripts as well. If you're working on a larger project, you may need to consult with a programmer, your systems administrator, or both.

Forms are sent by one of two methods: GET, which sends the results of the form in the URL submitted to the script; and POST, which encodes the material sent to the script. Check with your sysadmin to see which method you should use.

Remember, you do not need to set up a form handler to run a Jump menu. Those use client-side JavaScript that Dreamweaver writes for you.

To set up the form handler:

1. In the Document window, select your form by clicking on the dashed border around it.

2. Choose the method and action of the form handler in the Properties inspector (**Figure 12.43**).

   ♦ Click on the Method drop-down menu, and choose either GET or POST.

   ♦ In the Action text box, type the URL of the CGI or other script that will be processing the form.

3. Click on the Apply button to apply these changes to the form.

You won't see any changes in the Document window, but you can examine the HTML to make sure they're there.

The Button Tag

Another way to use images as buttons is by using the button tag instead of the input tag. The button tag allows images to be used as reset and nothing buttons, too.

1. Follow steps 1–4, at right.

2. Select the image field in the Document window.

3. View the HTML inspector by pressing F10. The code for the button will be highlighted in the inspector.

4. Replace the button code with this code:

   ```
   <button type=submit name="name"
   → value="value">
   <img src="button.gif">
   </button>
   ```

   The button type can be submit, reset, or button (for forms that call a script—the "nothing button"). The name is the name of your button image; the value can reflect the value you want to be transmitted; and the src is the source of your image.

5. Save the changes to the code, and preview the page in a browser to make sure it works.

STYLIN' WITH STYLE SHEETS

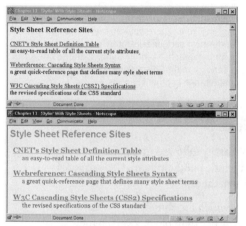

Figure 13.1 All I had to do was create four simple styles to completely redo the look of this page (top is pre-styles, bottom is with styles). Rather than applying color, font, and text style changes by hand, I created a style sheet. (You can't specify exacting indents without using styles.)

After years of grumbling about the design limitations of HTML, and despite the debate from the old-school digerati about how HTML is a markup language, not a layout language, Cascading Style Sheets (CSS) have become a standard.

A *style* is a group of attributes that are called by a single name, and a *style sheet* is a group of styles. Style sheets simplify the formatting of text, as well as extending the kinds of formatting you can apply (**Figure 13.1**). When you update a style, all instances of that style are automatically updated as well.

Style sheets are used primarily to format text, although some style attributes, such as positioning, can be used to format images and other objects as well.

✔ Notes

- One of the properties that style sheets add to HTML is the ability to better control positioning of elements on the page. Because style sheets cover so much territory, I cover positioning in Chapter 14.

- Style sheets work only in 4.x or later browsers such as Navigator 4 or 4.5 and MSIE 4 or 5. Some properties of style sheets are recognized by generation 3.x browsers, but most earlier browsers simply ignore them.

In This Chapter

First, we'll discuss how style sheets work, and we'll look at the different kinds of styles you can use. Then we'll go over the basics of creating and editing style sheets. After that, we'll learn how to apply style sheets to your Web pages. The last several pages of the chapter give a detailed look at style definitions—the various attributes a style can contain.

Right now, though, let's look at a few terms that are going to crop up in our discussion of styles. This chapter is a bit more code-heavy than previous chapters. You still don't have to write code—Dreamweaver takes care of that—but I will be discussing behavior of styles at the tag level (**Figure 13.2**), rather than just the way they look or act.

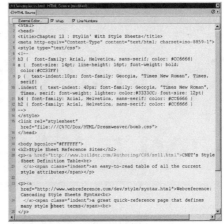

Figure 13.2 This is the code for the second example page in Figure 13.1. As you can see, styles operate, for the most part, on tags rather than on selections, (p for paragraph, h3 for heading, 3, and so on), so I spend more time discussing specific tags in this chapter than in other chapters.

Definitions

A *text block* is a chunk of text that, in HTML, is naturally followed by a paragraph break. Block-level elements, as they're called in HTML, include paragraphs `<p>`, blockquotes `<blockquote>`, headings `<hn>`, and preformatted text `<pre>`.

Block-like elements include lists, tables, and forms, which are somewhat self-contained structures that envelop a group of other line-level (rather than block-level) elements.

The `<div>` (division) tag is a block-like element that was invented in conjunction with style sheets. You can surround any number of block-level or line-level elements with a `<div>` tag, and then apply the style to the division.

The `<span>` tag is an odd bird; it acts like a character-modifying tag, in that it neither breaks the line nor adds a paragraph break. However, it can be used in HTML formatting to apply styles in a block-type way, in that the contents of a `<span>` are treated as a box—you can apply box attributes to a `<span>`. (See *Style Definitions* at the end of this chapter.)

Parent tags, simply put, are the tags that surround an element. On a Web page, all content tags are surrounded by the `<html>` and `<body>` tags. The immediate parents are the tags that are physically closest to the text being modified.

Inheritance is the process by which text blocks inherit properties from the various tags and styles that envelop them.

Not all properties can be inherited, and some overrule others. See *About Conflicting Styles*, later in this chapter.

Figure 13.3 Click on the CSS Styles button on the Launcher (or on the Launcher bar in the Document window status bar) to launch the CSS Styles palette.

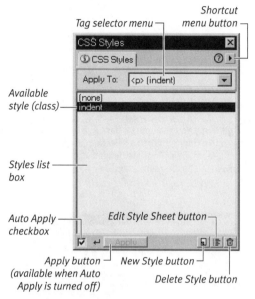

Figure 13.4 The CSS Styles palette will be blank when you first open it. I've included a style here for labeling purposes.

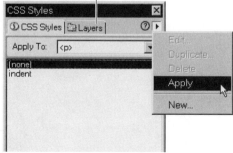

Figure 13.5 Note two things about the CSS Styles palette: It's stacked with another palette (the Layers palette), and the button on the side offers a pop-up menu. To stack or unstack a palette, drag its name tab onto or off of another palette.

How Style Sheets Work

With regular HTML, if you wanted all your links to appear italic, you had to apply italic formatting to each link separately:

`<i><a href="link.html">link</a></i>`

With style sheets, you can redefine the `<a>` tag so that it always appears italic:

`a {font-style: italic}`

Even better than that: if you later decide that you'd rather have all the links bold instead of italic, you simply change the style rather than changing all the instances:

`a {font-weight: bold}`

Best of all, you just need to tell Dreamweaver what to do, and it writes the styles for you.

Like other specialized tasks in Dreamweaver, writing style sheets is made easier by using a palette—in this case the CSS Styles inspector.

To display the CSS Styles inspector:

◆ From the Document window menu bar, select Window > CSS Styles.

or

Press the F7 key.

or

Click on the CSS Styles button on the Launcher (**Figure 13.3**).

The CSS Styles inspector will appear (**Figures 13.4** and **13.5**).

You'll use the CSS Styles inspector for three things:

◆ Clicking on the Edit button is the fastest way to open the Edit Style Sheet dialog box, which you'll use quite a bit in this chapter.

◆ Choosing a tag from the drop-down menu is the same as clicking on the tag selector in the Document window status bar.

◆ Once you write some styles, you can choose style classes from the inspector's list box.

253

Kinds of Style Sheets

There are four kinds of styles you can use, and Dreamweaver supports all of them.

The first kind, which we looked at on the previous page, involves *redefining an HTML tag* so that it includes new properties, as well as retaining its own. For example, you can redefine the <h2> tag so that it always appears red and it always uses the Arial font face (**Figure 13.6**).

```
h2 { color: red font-family: Arial}
```

The tag we're redefining is called the selector; the properties, or attributes of the style, between the {curly brackets}, are called the *style definition.*

The second kind of style is called a *class.* In this case, you name and define a style, which you then apply to blocks or spans of text (**Figure 13.7**). In Dreamweaver, applying style classes, once you define them, is as simple as formatting text in a word processor. Instead of applying bold, you apply the `.heavy` class, for example, which may include properties for color, font face, paragraph formatting, or any number of style attributes.

✔ Attention!

- CSS Styles, as a part of Dynamic HTML, are not supported by browsers earlier than 4.0. If you want to save text characteristics as an HTML style that uses regular, vanilla HTML tags, see Chapter 7, *Creating HTML Styles.*
- If you want to create CSS and non-CSS versions of a page, create the CSS one first, and clear that page of all HTML text formatting before you begin. You can do this with the HTML Styles inspector: Select the entire page, and then click on the Clear Character Styles button. See the sidebar on the next page for export tips.

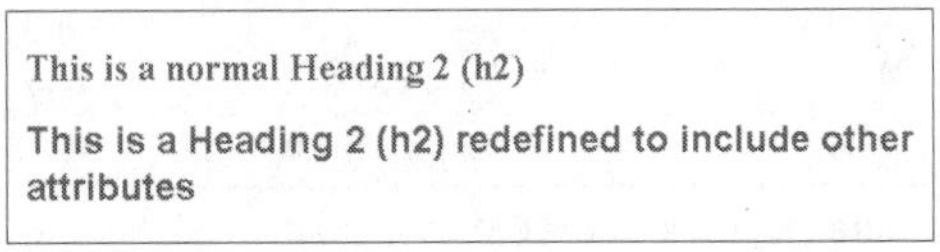

This is a normal Heading 2 (h2)
This is a Heading 2 (h2) redefined to include other attributes

Figure 13.6 When you redefine the h2 tag, it retains its original properties, such as its boldness, its size, and the paragraph breaks that surround it.

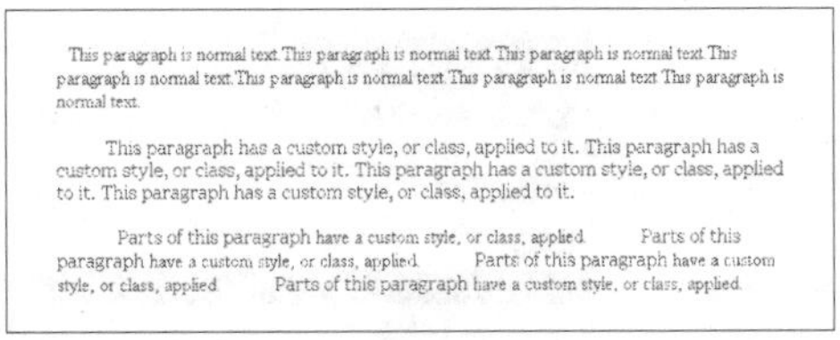

This paragraph is normal text This paragraph is normal text This paragraph is normal text This paragraph is normal text This paragraph is normal text This paragraph is normal text This paragraph is normal text.
This paragraph has a custom style, or class, applied to it. This paragraph has a custom style, or class, applied to it. This paragraph has a custom style, or class, applied to it. This paragraph has a custom style, or class, applied to it.
Parts of this paragraph have a custom style, or class, applied Parts of this paragraph have a custom style, or class, applied Parts of this paragraph have a custom style, or class, applied Parts of this paragraph have a custom style, or class, applied

Figure 13.7 You can apply a class to a text block (the second paragraph) or to a selection (the third paragraph). Selections are defined as spans and are enveloped by the <span> tag.

Convert to 3.0 Browser Compatible
Convert
Layers to Table
CSS Styles to HTML Markup
Both
OK
Cancel
Help

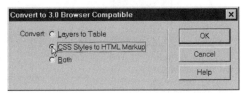

Figure 13.8 Choose CSS Styles to HTML Markup in the Convert to 3.0 Browser Compatible dialog box.

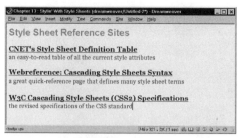

Figure 13.9 After backwards conversion, the text formatting looks like this.

Saving CSS as Plain HTML

After you create a CSS page, you may decide to create a plainer version of it for your technologically deficient visitors.

1. Open the CSS page in the Document window.

2. From the Document window menu bar, select File > Convert > 3.0 Browser Compatible. The Convert to 3.0 Browser Compatible dialog box will appear (**Figure 13.8**).

3. In the dialog box, click on the CSS Styles to HTML Markup radio button.

4. Click on OK. Dreamweaver will open the converted page in a new window.

5. Make any modifications you want, then save the page.

Figure 13.9 shows the converted page. It lost the indents, but the font formatting is mostly the same.

To find out about converting from layers to tables and vice versa, see Chapters 10 and 14.

To create a script that serves a CSS or non-CSS version of the page based on the browser version, see *Check Browser*, in Chapter 15.

In Dreamweaver, these first two styles—redefining an HTML tag and defining a class—are delineated in the <head> tag of the document (which comes before the <body>).

✔ Tip

■ In most cases, tag redefinitions and classes are located in the <head> tag of the document. You can define a style within a single tag, but that sort of preempts the entire reason for style sheets in the first place. In Chapter 14, you'll see instances of this in which each layer's style is given an ID attribute and defined within the <div> or <layer> tag.

The third and fourth kinds of styles involve creating a more literal *linked* or *imported* style sheet, which is a separate document that defines your styles. In your Web pages themselves, you link to or import the style sheet. (Linked and imported styles can include both the first two kinds.)

The implication, of course, is that once you create a style sheet document, you can link to it from any number of Web pages. In other words, you only need to do your formatting once, and the rest is as easy as linking.

In this chapter, I'll cover all four of these methods.

Creating a Style

Every move you make in creating and editing style sheets starts with one of two dialog boxes: the Edit Style Sheet dialog box or the New Style Sheet dialog box. After we look at these two dialog boxes, I'll discuss how to redefine an HTML tag and how to create a style class.

When you want to look at all your existing styles and edit, add, or delete a style, you can use the Edit Style Sheet dialog box.

To open the Edit Style Sheet dialog box:

◆ From the Document window menu bar, select Text > CSS Styles > Edit Style Sheet, or press Ctrl+Shift+E (Command+Shift+E).

or

On the CSS Styles inspector, click on the Open Style Sheet button.

Either way, the Edit Style Sheet dialog box will appear (**Figure 13.10**).

If you're creating a new style, you can jump ahead to the New Style dialog box.

To open the New Style dialog box:

◆ On the CSS Styles inspector, click on the New Style button (**Figure 13.11**).

or

Click the menu button on the CSS Styles inspector, and select New from the menu that appears (**Figure 13.12**).

or

On the Edit Style Sheet dialog box, click on New.

Either way, the New Style dialog box will appear (**Figure 13.13**).

Figure 13.10 The Edit Style Sheet dialog box is where you make your first move.

Figure 13.11 Click on the New Style button on the CSS Styles palette.

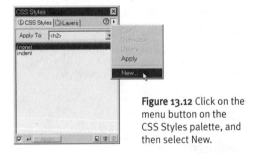

Figure 13.12 Click on the menu button on the CSS Styles palette, and then select New.

Figure 13.13 The New Style dialog box lets you choose which kind of style sheet you're going to create.

CREATING A STYLE

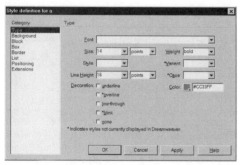

Figure 13.14 Choose an HTML tag, from *a* to *var*, from the drop-down menu. The menu doubles as a text box where you can type any HTML tag.

Figure 13.15 The Style Definition dialog box offers a kazillion choices, which I discuss in the second half of this chapter.

Tags that have been redefined

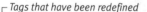

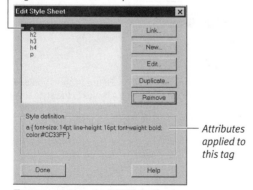

Attributes applied to this tag

Figure 13.16 Open the Edit Style Sheet dialog box to view the HTML tags you've redefined. Click on a tag to view a list of attributes.

To redefine an HTML tag:

1. Open the New Style dialog box.

2. Click on Redefine HTML tag (**Figure 13.13**).

3. Select a tag from the drop-down menu (**Figure 13.14**), or type a tag in the text box (without the <brackets>).

4. Click on OK. The New Style dialog box will close, and the Style Definition dialog box will open (see **Figure 13.15**).

5. Select the attributes you want to add to the tag, using the guidelines in the *Style Definitions* section of this chapter. To move from one panel of the dialog box to another, click on the name of the category in the list box at the left of the Style Definition dialog box.

   ◆ Don't worry—I'll explain what all those style attributes do in the second half of this chapter.

6. When you're finished making your selections, click on OK. The Style Definition dialog box will close, and you'll return to the Edit Style Sheet dialog box.

7. Click on Done to close the Edit Style Sheet dialog box and return to the Dreamweaver window.

Any changes you make to your selected tag will be visible as soon as you use the tag.

✔Tips

- The selected HTML tag will retain its intrinsic properties, as well as taking on the new attributes you define.

- For redefined HTML tags, use the tag in order to apply the style.

- Redefined HTML tags are displayed in the Edit Style Sheet dialog box, not the CSS Styles inspector (**Figure 13.16**).

CREATING A STYLE

To create a style class:

1. Open the Edit Style Sheet dialog box.

2. Click on New. The New Style dialog box will appear.

3. Click on the Make a Custom Style (class) radio button (**Figure 13.17**).

4. Type a name (one word, all lowercase) for the class in the text box. The name must start with a period (.), but if you leave it out, Dreamweaver will add it for you.

5. Click on OK. The New Style dialog box will close, and the Style Definition dialog box will appear (**Figure 13.18**).

6. Select the attributes you want to add to the tag, using the guidelines in the *Style Definitions* section of this chapter. To move from one panel of the dialog box to another, click on the name of the category in the list box at the left of the Style Definition dialog box.

7. When you're finished making your selections, click on OK. The Style Definition dialog box will close, and you'll return to the Edit Style Sheet dialog box.

8. Click on Done to close the Edit Style Sheet dialog box and return to the Document window.

The names of the classes you create will be added to the styles list box in the CSS Styles inspector (**Figure 13.19**).

✔ Tip

■ If you name a style but do not specify any attributes for it in the Style Definition dialog box, Dreamweaver will not save the style and it will not appear in the CSS Styles inspector.

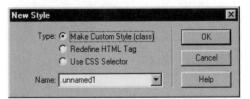

Figure 13.17 Click on the Custom Style (class) radio button to create a class, or custom style, to be applied to certain tags or selections on your page.

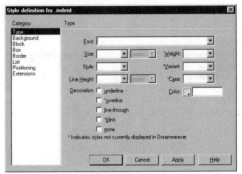

Figure 13.18 The Style Definition dialog box is where you choose the attributes of your style. Because there are so many attributes, I define them all in *Style Definitions* at the end of this chapter.

Figure 13.19 As you add classes to the style sheet, they will appear in the CSS Styles palette.

Figure 13.20 What does that third button do?

Defining New Selectors

You may have been wondering about that third option on the Create New Style dialog box: Use CSS Selector (**Figure 13.20**). As I've said previously, one way to create a style is to redefine an HTML tag, called a *selector* in that context.

You can also create a style for more than one selector at a time. There are three instances in which you would to this: The first is modifying a *group* of selectors; the second is naming an *ID* instead of creating a class; and the third is modifying a *contextual selector*, or modifying the behavior of nested tags. When you want to define a style that would apply to several different tags.

Anchor Color Pseudoclasses

The style sheet standard defines a class that is applied to entities other than HTML Specification Standard tags as a *pseudoclass*. The primary example of this is the three flavors of links: links, visited links, and active links (see Chapter 9 for more about these distinctions).

Pseudoclasses other than anchor are not supported by IE.

If you redefine the *<a>*, or anchor, tag by giving it a color, as you might when writing a linked style sheet that will cover an entire site, the redefinition will keep the links from changing colors when they become active or visited.

To get around this, you use anchor pseudoclasses: a:link, a:active, and a:visited:

1. Open the Edit Style Sheet dialog box.

2. Click on New. The New Style dialog box will appear.

3. Click on the Use CSS Selector radio button (as shown in **Figure 13.20**).

4. The text box is also a drop-down menu; click on it and select one of the anchor pseudoclasses.

5. Click on OK. The Style Definition dialog box will appear. To define a color for this pseudoclass, use the color option in the Text panel of the dialog box (see the section called *Type Attributes*, later in this chapter, for more information).

6. Click on OK to close the Style Definition dialog box.

7. Repeat steps 2–6 for the other two pseudoclasses, if you like.

Defining a group of tags

You can create a style that defines an entire group. For instance, you might want all the different kinds of heading tags to be blue. Instead of setting a style for each <hn> tag individually:

```
h1 { color: blue }
h2 { color: blue }
```

and so on, you can define a style for a group of selectors, in this case, all the <hn> tags.

```
h1, h2, h3, h4, h5, h6 { color: blue }
```

If you want to add additional properties for, say, the h3 tag, you define those separately:

```
h1, h2, h3, h4, h5, h6 { color: blue }
h3 { font-family: Courier, Courier New }
```

Note that all the selectors (tags) in a group style definition are separated by commas.

Unfortunately, Dreamweaver 3 no longer directly supports defining groups of selectors like this. You need to apply your group selector directly to the code.

To define a group of tags:

1. As a shortcut, define a single tag out of your group (for example, the h1 tag).

2. Open the HTML inspector (F10), and locate your new style inside the <head> tag at the top of the document (**Figure 13.21**).

3. Type the additional tags you want to modify, using commas to separate them (**Figure 13.22**).

When you use any of the tags in your group, the changes will appear (**Figure 13.23**).

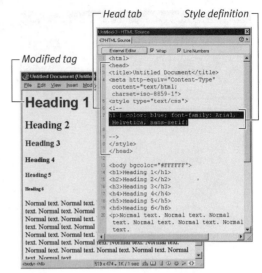

Head tab   Style definition

Modified tag

Figure 13.21 In the HTML inspector, locate the style you created in step 1. It's in the head tag; my example is the h1 tag.

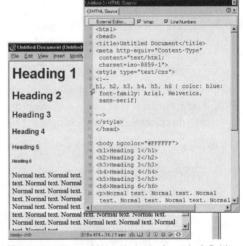

Figure 13.22 Type additional tags in the style definition, and separate them by commas.

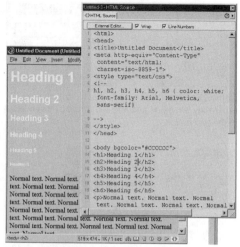

Figure 13.23 Here, I redefined all h tags to appear in Arial and in white (on a gray background). Normal text on the page is black and in Times New Roman (the default font face).

Figure 13.24 Type the name for your ID, preceded by the # sign.

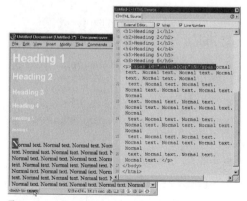

Figure 13.25 To apply an ID, add the attribute to a tag. Here I added the <span> tag around a letter and added the id attribute to it.

Defining an ID

As we've seen, most custom styles use the class attribute to modify a tag:

```
<p class="indent">indented text</p>
```

You can instead define an ID, although you'll have to use it manually. Why use an ID instead of a class? Some JavaScript functions rely on the ID attribute. The ID attribute is also commonly used in naming layers, which are discussed in Chapter 14. Style sheet formatting applied to a layer is generally applied by creating an ID.

1. Open the New Style Sheet dialog box.

2. Click on the CSS Selector radio button.

3. Type a name for your ID selector, using a # sign instead of a period (**Figure 3.24**):

   ```
   #initialCap
   ```

4. Click on OK, and create the style as usual.

Unfortunately, IDs don't show up in the CSS Styles inspector. To apply an ID, add the attribute to a tag, such as p, div, or span, as shown in **Figure 13.25**.

Contextual selectors

Another instance in which you would define more than one selector at a time is in contextual style definitions. These apply to nested HTML tags. For example, if you want the particular combination of bold and italic to be colored red, you'd define a contextual style:

```
b i {color: red}
```

In this case, text nested in both the bold and italic tags would turn red, but other bold or italicized text would not:

```
<b><i>this text is red</i></b>
<i>this text is not red</i>
<b>and neither is this</b>

<i><b>nor this</b></i>
```

Note that contextual selectors are separated by only a single space.

To define a style for a contextual selector:

1. Open the Edit Style Sheet dialog box.

2. Click on New. The New Style dialog box will appear.

3. Click on the CSS Selector radio button.

4. Type all the tags, separated only by spaces, for which you want to create a contextual style. For example: b i (**Figure 13.26**).

5. Click on OK, and create the style as usual.

I used white text on the page in **Figure 13.27** to illustrate words affected by the b i nesting.

✔ Tip

■ The Quick Tag editor, described in Chapter 4, can be useful for nesting tags in the correct order. Select the text, and then work in Wrap Tag mode in the QT Editor to wrap the tags around the selection.

Figure 13.26 Type the contextual selectors, in the order they will be nested and separated by a space, in the text box.

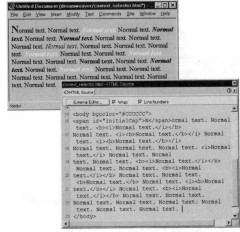

Figure 13.27 The words in the Document window that appear in white are surrounded by the contextual selector, which consists of the bold and italic tags in the proper order.

Examples of Contextual Styles

◆ ul li or ol li for items in an unordered or ordered list (your mileage may vary)

◆ td a for the first link that appears within a table cell

◆ td p for the first paragraph in a table cell (would not effect paragraphs not in a table)

◆ b a for bold links

◆ blockquote blockquote for nested indents

◆ center img for centered images

Figure 13.28 In the Edit Style Sheet dialog box, click on Link.

Figure 13.29 Type the pathname for your new style sheet in the Link External Style Sheet dialog box. Dreamweaver will create the file in the location you specify.

Figure 13.30 The name of the linked style sheet you created will appear in the Edit Style Sheet dialog box.

Linked and Imported Style Sheets

Style sheets for individual pages are versatile, but if you want to create a style sheet that can be used on more than one page (actually, on as many pages as you want), then you should create a linked or imported style sheet.

To create a new linked or imported style sheet:

1. Save the page you are working on. Dreamweaver prefers that you add linked style sheets only to saved pages.

2. Open the Edit Style Sheet dialog box (**Figure 13.28**)and click on Link. The Link External Style Sheet dialog box will appear (**Figure 13.29**).

3. Type a filename for your new file, ending in .CSS, in the File/URL text box. If your style sheet will not be located in the same directory as your page, include the directory information in the pathname (as in `/styles/master.css`).

4. Choose a linking method:

   ◆ To use the new file as a linked style sheet, click on the Link radio button.

   ◆ To use the new file as an imported style sheet, click on the Import radio button.

5. Click on OK to close the Link External Style Sheet dialog box. You'll return to the Edit Style Sheet dialog box, where you'll see the name of the style sheet you just created (**Figure 13.30**).

✔ Tip

■ The kinks aren't yet worked out of style sheet importing in either Navigator or Explorer, so linking to the style sheet is recommended rather than importing it.

Before you can save your style sheet, you need to add at least one style to it.

To add styles to a linked style sheet:

1. In the Edit Style Sheet dialog box, click on the name of your style sheet in the styles list box.

2. Click on Edit. The Style Sheet (name) dialog box will appear (**Figure 13.31**).

3. Click on New. The New Style dialog box will appear (**Figure 13.32**).

4. Now you can add styles to your style sheet in the same way you'd add them to an individual page:

    ◆ To redefine HTML tags, follow steps 3–7 in *To redefine an HTML tag*, earlier in this chapter.

    ◆ To create a class, follow steps 3-7 in *To create a style class*, earlier in this chapter.

    ◆ To create a new selector, refer *Defining New Selectors*, earlier in this chapter.

5. Follow steps 3 and 4 for every style you want to add to your style sheet.

6. When you have added some styles to your style sheet that you want to save, click on Save in the Style Sheet (name) dialog box (**Figure 13.31**). The styles will be added to the style sheet.

Now you have an external style sheet linked to the current page. Be sure to check the link URL when you upload the page to your Web site. It's in the code and looks something like this:

```
<link rel="stylesheet"
href="/styles/master.css">
```

For imported styles, the code will look something like this:

```
@import "import.css"
```

Figure 13.31 Use the Style Sheet dialog box to add styles to your linked style sheet.

Figure 13.32 The New Style dialog box. From here on out, adding stuff to a linked Style Sheet is the same as creating new styles for a single page.

What Little Style Sheets Are Made Of

An external style sheet, or .CSS document, is just made up of a few lines of style definition code. If you use only one style in an external style sheet, it will only contain one line of code. Try opening a .CSS document in your text editor to see how simple it is— that's why linked style sheets don't add much load time to Web pages.

Figure 13.33 In the Link External Style Sheet dialog box, click on Browse to select an existing Style Sheet from your hard drive.

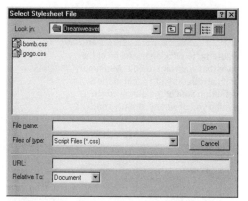

Figure 13.34 The Select Stylesheet File dialog box is just like the Open dialog boxes you're familiar with.

Figure 13.35 After you link to an existing Style Sheet, you'll see its filename displayed in the Edit Style Sheet dialog box. To apply an external style sheet, you simply link to it, as described in *Linked and Imported Style Sheets*.

After you initially create and link to an external style sheet, Dreamweaver will save it on your hard drive, and you can link to it over and over again.

To link to an existing style sheet:

1. Open the Edit Style Sheet dialog box.

2. Click on Link. The Link External Style Sheet dialog box will appear (**Figure 13.33**).

3. Click on Browse (Choose, on the Mac). The Select Stylesheet File dialog box will appear (**Figure 13.34**).

4. Browse through the files and folders on your computer until you locate the .CSS file you want to link to.

5. When you locate the file, click on it, and then click on Open. The dialog box will close, and you'll return to the Link External Style Sheet dialog box.

6. Choose a linking method:

   ◆ To link to the style sheet, click on the Link radio button.

   ◆ To import the style sheet, click on the Import radio button.

7. Click on OK. The Link External Style Sheet dialog box will close, and you'll return to the Edit Style Sheet dialog box, where you'll see the name of the style sheet you selected (**Figure 13.35**).

LINKED AND IMPORTED STYLE SHEETS

Editing Style Sheets

When you edit a style sheet, all instances of that style will automatically be updated on the pages to which it applies. Whether you change from brown to green, right-aligned to justified, Arial to Courier, or scrap a style entirely, your changes will be reflected instantly.

To edit a style sheet:

1. Open the Edit Style Sheet dialog box by selecting Text > CSS Styles > Edit Style Sheet from the Document window menu bar; by pressing Ctrl+Shift+E (Command+Shift+E); or by clicking on the Edit Style Sheet button on the CSS Styles inspector.

2. Click on the name of the style sheet you wish to edit in the styles list box (**Figure 13.36**), whether that style is an HTML tag you have redefined; a class; or a group of selectors. You can also open this dialog box simply by double-clicking the name of a style class in the CSS Styles inspector.

3. Click on the Edit button. The Style Definition dialog box will appear (**Figure 13.37**).

4. Make your changes to the style in the Style Definition dialog box. (See *Style Definitions* at the end of this chapter for details.)

5. When you're done, click on OK to close the Style Definition dialog box and return to the Edit Style Sheet dialog box.

6. Click on Done to close the Edit Style Sheet dialog box and return to the Document window. Your changes will take effect immediately.

   or

   You can click on another style sheet and click on Edit to edit that style sheet; or you can click on New to create a new style sheet.

Figure 13.36 Click on the name of the style that you want to edit. A summary of its attributes will appear in the Style definition area of the dialog box to remind you of what it already contains.

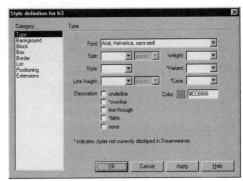

Figure 13.37 In the Style Definition dialog box, you make your changes to the style.

✔ Tips

- When you select a style in the Edit Style Sheet dialog box, a summary of the attributes it contains will appear in the Style definition area of the dialog box.

- To edit the styles in an external style sheet, follow steps 1 and 2. When you click on Edit, the Style Sheet (name) dialog box will appear, which lists the names of all the styles in the external style sheet. From there, follow steps 2-6 for the styles in the external style sheet that you wish to edit.

Figure 13.38 The Duplicate Style dialog box is pretty much the same as the New Style dialog box.

Figure 13.39 Deleting a style is easy.

Deleting a Style Sheet

If you define a style and then decide you don't need or want to use it anymore, it's a snap to delete it, and Dreamweaver will remove the offending code for you.

1. Open the Edit Style Sheet dialog box.

2. Click on the name of the style you want to delete (**Figure 13.39**).

3. Click on Remove.

4. Click on Done to close the Edit Style Sheet dialog box.

Deleting an external style sheet doesn't remove it from your hard drive; it simply removes the links to it from the current page.

You may want to create two styles that are very similar. You can make a copy of a style and then edit it. You can duplicate tag and selector styles as themselves or as classes, or vice versa.

To make a copy of a style:

1. Open the Edit Style Sheet dialog box.

2. Click on the name of the style in the list box. (You can't duplicate external style sheets this way).

3. Click on Duplicate. The Duplicate Style dialog box will appear (**Figure 13.38**); this is pretty much the same as the New Style dialog box.

4. You must rename the style before you can duplicate it.

   ◆ To save the duplicate style as a class, click on the Make Custom Style (Class) radio button, and type a name for the style in the text box.

   ◆ To apply the duplicate style to a different HTML tag, click on the Redefine HTML Tag radio button, and select a tag from the drop-down menu (or type a tag without the <brackets> in the text box).

   ◆ To apply the duplicate style to a set of tags, type the tags, either a pseudo-class, an ID, or a contextual set (such as b i) in the text box.

5. Click on OK. The Duplicate Style Sheet dialog box will close, and you'll return to the Edit Style Sheet dialog box, where you'll see the name of your new style selected in the list box.

Now you can edit your new style, if you wish, by clicking on the Edit button.

Applying Style Classes

Unlike redefined tags or linked style sheets, you must apply a class to a block of text.

To apply a class:

1. Select the text to which you want to apply the class.

   ◆ To select an entire paragraph (or other block-level element), simply click to place the insertion point within the paragraph (**Figure 13.40**).

   ◆ To select the text within a particular tag, click on the text and then on the tag selector in the status bar of the Document window. Or use the tag selection menu in the CSS Styles inspector (**Figure 13.41**).

   ◆ To select a span of text within a paragraph or other tag, select the text with the mouse or arrow keys (**Figure 13.42**).

2. From the Document window menu bar, select Text > CSS Styles, and then choose the class from the submenu.

   or

   In the CSS Styles inspector, click on the name of the class in the list of styles.

The style will be applied to your selection. You may need to view the page in Navigator 4 or later, or MSIE 4 or 5 to see all the attributes of the style sheet.

To remove class formatting:

1. Select the text or tag from which you want style formatting removed.

2. From the Document window menu bar, select Text > Custom Style > None.

   or

   In the CSS Styles palette, click on (none) in the class list box.

This paragraph is normal text. This paragraph is normal text. This paragraph is normal text. This paragraph is normal text. This paragraph is normal text. This paragraph is normal text. This paragraph is normal text.

Figure 13.40 To select a paragraph or other block-level element, simply click the insertion point within it.

Figure 13.41 To select a particular tag, click on the text within the tag, and then choose a tag from one of the tag selectors, either in the Document window's status bar or in the CSS Styles palette.

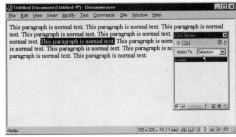

Figure 13.42 To select a span of text, simply select the text you want to modify—notice how the tag selection menu in the CSS Styles palette reads "selection." Dreamweaver will add a <span> tag automatically.

Spanning

Styles can be applied to any tag, but they must be applied to an existing tag—not just to freewheeling text. If the selection to which you apply a class is not confined by a parent tag, Dreamweaver will automatically insert a <span> tag to which the class will be applied—this is one of Dreamweaver's most profoundly convenient style editing features. The <span> entity is a nonbreaking, nonintrusive way to define a text block without creating a new paragraph.

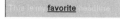

Figure 13.43 This is what the example code looks like in the Document window.

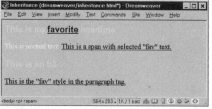

Figure 13.44 The various styles alone and mixed.

Figure 13.45 Here's the code for Figure 13.44.

Your Parents' Inheritance

Tags that surround a piece of text are called *parents*. Parent tags also have parent tags, the whole way up through the <body> and <html> tags that surround all the content in a document. While the cascading rule applies to these nested tags, what about nested styles? In other words, what happens when you have a style sheet that has a linked style sheet as well as style sheets located on that page?

Again, the closer the style is, the more influence it has. Modifications made to particular pieces of text win out over modifications made to an entire document (called *global styles*); and global styles win out over imported styles; and imported styles win out over linked styles.

About Conflicting Styles

What happens when you apply two conflicting styles to the same text?

Suppose you have defined the paragraph style with the following properties:

```
p { font-family: "Courier New,
Courier, mono; font-size: 14pt}
```

And then, suppose your link style is as follows:

```
a { font-family: "Arial, Helvetica,
sans-serif;}
```

Who would win? That's where the *cascading* in Cascading Style Sheets comes in. Styles, like tags, are nested around elements. The style that's closest, physically, to the text that it modifies has precedence over the other styles that might effect it. So in this example, the <a> tag would have precedence:

```
<p>All of this text is in the same
paragraph, but this <a href="piece.html">
piece</a> is also linked.</p>
```

In the following example, no matter what style modifications have been made to the <body> and <h3> selectors, the <span> tag will dominate them in the hierarchy for the word "favorite." (See **Figures 13.43-13.45**.)

```
<head>
<style type="text/css">

<!-
body { color: white; background-color:
gray}
h3 {color: yellow}
.fav {color: black; text-decoration:
underline}
->
</style>
</head>
<body>
<h3>This is my <span class="fav">
favorite</span> headline</h3>
</body>
```

269

Style Definitions

Now, at last, we come to the section of the chapter where I finally describe the style attributes you can use in your custom styles. There are eight different categories of custom styles in Dreamweaver, each of which contains several different single attributes you can apply to a block of text. The categories are:

◆ **Type** attributes (**Figure 13.46**) refer to font formatting, such as font face, font size and color, and weight and style.

◆ **Background** attributes (**Figure 13.47**), such as background color and image, can be applied either to a text block or to the <body> tag to control an entire page.

◆ **Block** attributes (**Figure 13.48**) control the spacing and shape of text. Alignment and indent are block attributes.

◆ **Box** attributes are applied to the box that surrounds a block element, and can also be applied to <span> selections. Box attributes include padding and margin controls to shape the space.

◆ **Border** attributes are a subset of box attributes. Border attributes can make the usually invisible box around a style box visible with borders and colors.

◆ **List** attributes affect the formatting of ordered and unordered lists, including the appearance of the numbers or bullets.

◆ **Positioning** controls allow you to determine the location of elements on the page. (Because there are so many, and because this chapter is quite long enough already, I discuss positioning in the next chapter.)

◆ **Extensions** to style sheets are generally unsupported by current browsers, although some visual effects are supported by MSIE 4 and 5.

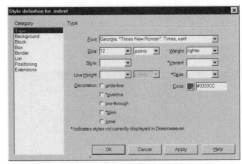

Figure 13.46 All the attributes you could ever want, eight categories high.

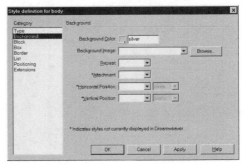

Figure 13.47 If you change text colors using style sheets, you can also modify the background. That way, users with 3.0 or earlier, non-CSS browsers will see one complete color scheme, and 4.0 or later browsers will display another.

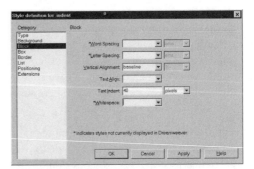

Figure 13.48 Block attributes allow for more typographic control, such as indents and line wrapping (white space).

Units

The following units are used to define various spatial relationships in style sheets:

pixels (px) are the little dots that makeup the picture on your computer monitor. **inches (in)**, **centimeters (cm)**, and **millimeters (mm)** are the same as their real-world equivalents.

picas and **points** are typographical measurements from the days of hand-set type. There are six picas in an inch, 12 points in a pica, and 72 points in an inch. (That's why most font sizes are based on the number 12.)

ems and **exs** are also handset-type measurements. An em, as in the letter *m*, is a square piece of type. The width of an em is one pica in a monospace font; in digital terms, this width may vary slightly from font to font and should be treated as a relative measurement. An ex, on the other hand, is the height of the letter *x*, which is shorthand for "average height of the lowercase alphabet in this font without any ascenders or descenders."

percent (%) , in the case of style sheets, refers to percentage of the parent tag. If the only parent tag is the <body> tag, then $ will apply to the width of the screen. If the parent tag is a table cell, then the style block will occupy x% of that cell. If the parent unit is a text block such as a paragraph or <span>, things might get funky. Experiment with percentages to see what happens.

To use the Style Definition dialog box:

1. To move from one panel of the dialog box to another, click on the category's name in the list box on the left side of the dialog box.

2. Select items from pull-down menus, check checkboxes, and type number values.

3. Some pull-down menus double as text boxes.

4. To select units for an attribute, first select *value* from the drop-down menu, then type a number (you can change it later) over the word *value* in the text box, and then choose a unit from the units pull-down menu.

5. Leave any items blank or unchanged that aren't needed.

Type Attributes

Type attributes are probably the styles you're going to use most often, and they include those previously defined by the `<font>` tag (now deprecated). The Type panel of the Style Definition dialog box is shown in **Figure 13.49**.

Type attributes include:

Font chooses a font face or a font family.

Size (**Figure 13.50**) sets a font size for the text. You can choose from a number of different units to set the size for the text.

The size attribute offers point sizes ranging from 9 (smallest) to 36 (largest), which roughly correspond to the 1–7 font size scale in basic HTML.

If point sizes don't do it for you, you can set a size in a number of other units, including pixels (px), inches (in), centimeters (cm), millimeters (mm), picas, ems, and exs.

Additionally, you can set relative sizes ranging from "largest" to "xx-small."

Style, as in regular text style, lets you set text as Normal, Italic, or Oblique (**Figure 13.51**).

☞ Normal, or "upright," italic, and oblique are three font styles; *oblique* means "slanted." Navigator follows the rule for font selection literally here: it looks for a font with "oblique" properties in the selected font family, and if it doesn't find one, it uses a normal font, whereas Explorer will display oblique text as italic.

✔Tip

■ To find out about adding fonts or font families to this dialog box, see *To Define a Font Combination,* in Chapter 3.

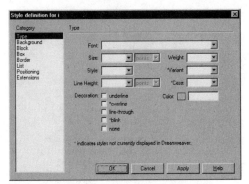

Figure 13.49 The Type panel of the Style Definition dialog box.

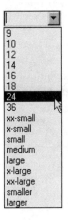

Figure 13.50 The whole family of font sizes.

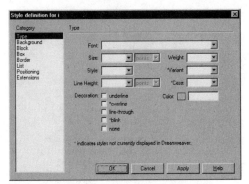

normal text *italic text oblique text*

Figure 13.51 Font styles in Internet Explorer: Normal, Italic, and Oblique.

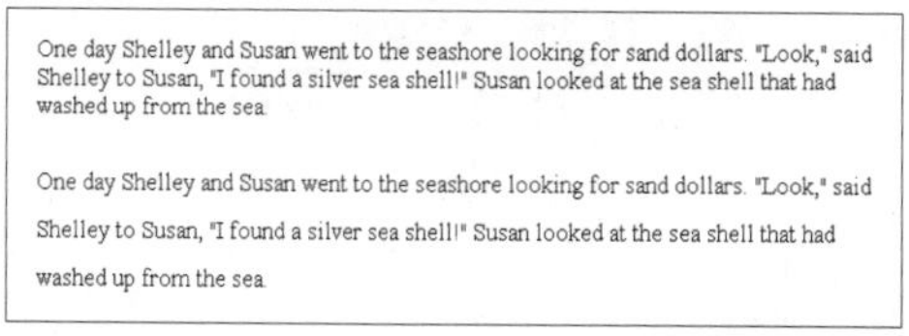

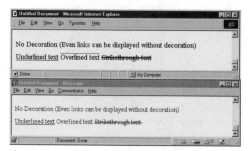

Figure 13.52 Line height as interpreted by Navigator. The top paragraph has no line height set. The second paragraph has a line height of 24 points (to a font size of 14 points).

Figure 13.53 Text decoration, as displayed by Internet Explorer (above) and Netscape Navigator (below). Note that Navigator does not display overline.

☞ **Line Height**, a typographical setting not available in regular HTML, determines the height of each line in the text block (**Figure 13.52**). If the font size is 12 points, and the line height is 16 points, you'll have a good bit of extra space between each line. (Normal line height provides an offset of approximately two points.) Browsers may interpret "normal" line height however they choose. This setting may cause problems with IE3.

Decoration (**Figure 13.53**) can apply underlining, overlining*, strikethrough (line-through), or blinking* to the text.

✔ Tip

- Because the default for regular text is no decoration, and the default for linked text is underlining, you can remove the default underlining from links by selecting None from the Decoration category and applying it to the <a> tag. (Text decoration is not inherited, so if you apply it simply as a paragraph style, links will still appear underlined.)

* Attributes with an asterisk (*) are not displayed in the Document window.

☞ Pointer items discuss how different browsers may treat an attribute.

Type Attributes

Weight (**Figure 13.54**) is the same as **boldness** `<b>`, or `<strong>`. You can apply a relative weight (lighter, normal, bold, bolder), or a numerical weight from 100–900 (**Figure 13.55**). The weight of normal text is generally 400, while boldface text has a weight of about 700.

The only font **Variant*** currently supported by Dreamweaver is SMALL CAPS.

Case* allows you to apply all-lowercase, all-uppercase, or title case (The First Letter In Each Word) to a text block. This would come in especially handy for setting headers or captions.

Color, of course, acts the same as `<font color=n>`.

✔Tip

- To find out about selecting colors, see *Colors and Web Pages* and *Modifying the Page Background* in Chapter 2.

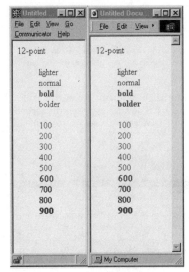

Figure 13.54 Weight variations, at 12 points. Neither browser does much with lighter weights, and Navigator also handles "bolder" unpredictably (sometimes it reads that attribute just fine, but sometimes, it doesn't).

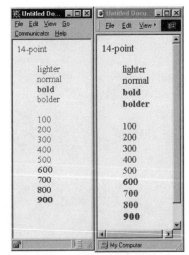

Figure 13.55 The differences between how Navigator and Explorer handle text are apparent in this figure. While the treatment of the fonts was practically the same at 12 points, at 14 points Explorer (on the right) gets decidedly heavier with its text weights.

Figure 13.56 You can define properties of a background color or image for either a text block or the page body using the Background panel of the Style Definition dialog box.

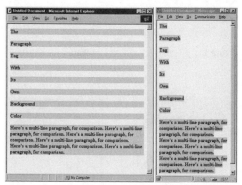

Figure 13.57 I redefined the paragraph tag to have its own background color. Explorer (on the left) makes paragraphs occupy 100 percent of the parent tag (the page body, in this case) by default, and colors in the entire width. Navigator (on the right) colors in only the part of the paragraph that contains content.

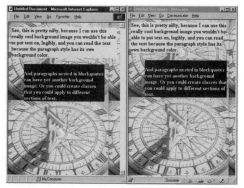

Figure 13.58 If you use a background color (first paragraph) or background image (second paragraph) for a text block, it will be superimposed over the page background. Note how the blockquote style (second paragraph) is rectangular in both Explorer and Navigator (right).

Background Attributes

Background attributes allow you to place a background color or image behind a text block. They will be superimposed over any other background color or image on the page. The Background panel of the Style Definition dialog box is shown in **Figure 13.56**.

✔Tips

- To set the background color or image for a page, see *Modifying the Page Background* in Chapter 2.

- To set the background color or image for a table, see *Coloring Tables* in Chapter 10.

- To use style sheets to apply a background color or image to an entire page, apply the style to the <body> tag.

Background attributes include:

Background color and **background image** can be applied to an entire page or to a text block (**Figure 13.57**). If both are used, the text block background will be superimposed over the page background (**Figure 13.58**).

The rest of the attributes all apply to a background image.

continues on next page

---

* Attributes with an asterisk (*) are not displayed in the Document window.

☞ Attributes with a ☞ are not supported by current browsers.

Repeat (**Figure 13.59**) determines whether the background image is tiled, and if so, how. If the image is displayed in an element that is smaller than the image dimensions, the image will be cropped to fit the element's dimensions.

*No-repeat** prevents the image from tiling.

Repeat tiles the image as it would be tiled in a page background image: from left to right in columns proceeding down the page.

*Repeat-x** displays a horizontal "band" of images; the image is tiled in one row across the page.

*Repeat-y** displays vertical "band" of images; the image is tiled in one column down the page.

Attachment means the relative attachment of the background image to the page, in particular for full-page background images. Normally, when you scroll through a page, the background image moves, and so does the content—this is both default and scroll. The fixed attachment attribute fixes the background image in place, so that when you scroll through a page, the content "moves," and the background image "stands still" (**Figure 13.60**). ☞ Currently, IE4 supports the fixed option, but Navigator 4.5 treats fixed as scroll.

Horizontal position and **vertical position** mark the position of the background image, relative to the element. I discuss positioning in Chapter 14.

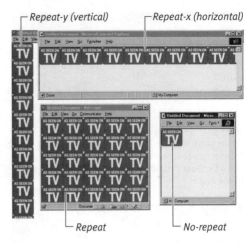

Repeat-y (vertical) — *Repeat-x (horizontal)*

Repeat — *No-repeat*

Figure 13.59 The four flavors of background repeat.

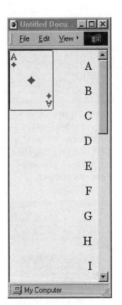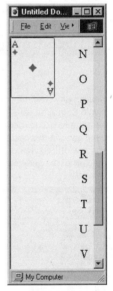

Figure 13.60 A demonstration of the fixed attachment background attribute (also called a *watermark*) in Internet Explorer. The image of the ace is set not to repeat. Normally, a tiny background image like this one would scroll off the screen. With fixed attachment set, the ace stays in place while you scroll through the text at right.

BACKGROUND ATTRIBUTES

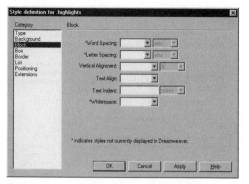

Figure 13.61 The Block attributes panel of the Style Definition dialog box.

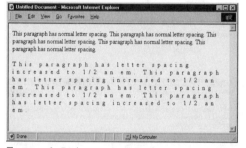

Figure 13.62 Explorer 5 processes letter spacing, but neither browser supports word spacing as of yet.

Block Attributes

Block attributes apply typographical constraints to the alignment and spacing of words and characters within the selected element. The Block panel of the Style Definition dialog box is shown in **Figure 13.61**.

Block attributes include:

Word spacing* is used to adjust the space between words, and **Letter spacing*** is used to adjust the space between characters.

Units available for using word and letter spacing include "normal" (no units), pixels, inches (in), centimeters (cm), millimeters (mm), picas, ems, and exs.

☞ I could not produce appreciable changes in word spacing in either Navigator or MSIE, which places this attribute in the "real soon now" category. Explorer deals with letter spacing (**Figure 13.62**), and Navigator does not.

☞ You can specify either positive or negative values, although not all browsers will support the latter.

☞ If property alignment is set to justify, this will most likely overrule word spacing, while letter spacing will override justification.

☞ The "normal" settings for word and letter spacing are left up to the individual browser.

Vertical alignment* controls the vertical position of the selection. Vertical alignment is related to positioning, which I discuss in Chapter 14.

continues on next page

---

* Attributes with an asterisk (*) are not displayed in the Document window.

☞ Attributes with a ☞ are not supported by current browsers.

Text align sets alignment for the text within the margins of the page or the block unit. As in regular HTML, alignment options are left, right, and center, with the additional justify option (**Figure 13.63**).

Text indent* applies a tab-like indent to the first line of a block-type element (**Figure 13.65**).

*Dreamweaver displays indents unpredictably.

Units available for using indents include "normal" (no units), pixels, inches (in), centimeters (cm), millimeters (mm), picas, ems, and exs.

☞ You can use negative values to create a hanging indent, but not all browsers will support this.

✔ Tip

■ Indents are not inherited, which means that line breaks used within paragraphs can cause unpredictable indent behavior. You might experiment with applying a class with indent properties to spans within paragraphs, which is what I did to get the indents in **Figure 13.65**.

Whitespace* controls the use of spacing within the selection. *Normal* ignores extra spaces and text-based breaks; *Pre* treats the text as if it were enclosed in `<pre>` tags, conserving the use of spaces and text-based breaks; *Nowrap,* similar to the nowrap setting for table cells, allows the line to break only when a `<br>` tag is used. This last setting is useful particularly for layers and block elements with dimensions smaller than 100 percent of the page.

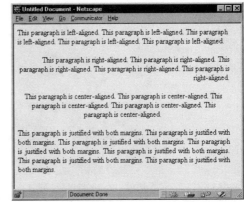

Figure 13.63 Text block alignment options, from top to bottom, are left, right, center, and justify. Note that the margin gutter is greater on the right than on the left; Navigator is leaving room for a scrollbar. (Explorer displays vertical scrollbars whether they're needed or not.)

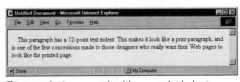

Figure 13.64 A paragraph with a 12-point indent.

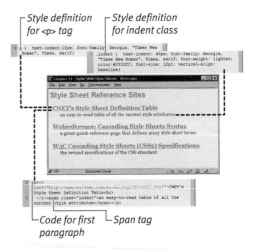

Figure 13.65 The indent property is not inherited, so tags within the block element—the `<p>` in this case—won't be indented unless you apply separate `<span>` formatting.

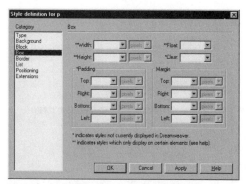

Figure 13.66 The Box attributes panel of the Style Definition dialog box allows you to define the dimensions of the imaginary box that surrounds text blocks.

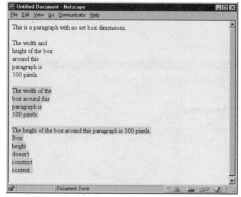

Figure 13.67 The box attributes of these paragraphs, from top to bottom: None, 100x100 pixels, 100 pixels across, and 100 pixels high. Horizontal measurements will break a line, but vertical measurements will not crop content. I used a background color on the bottom two paragraphs so you could see the dimensions more clearly.

* Attributes with an asterisk (*) are not displayed in the Document window.

☞ Pointer items discuss how different browsers may treat an attribute.

Box Attributes

You can imagine all style modifications to HTML elements as being rectangular, or box-shaped. Box attributes, then, are styles applied to the (generally invisible) box that surrounds a block (or span) of text. The Box panel of the Style Definition dialog box is shown in **Figure 13.66**.

Box attributes include:

Height* and **Width*** of the box can be expressed in a number of units, including pixels, inches (in), centimeters (cm), millimeters (mm), picas, ems, and exs, and percentage of the parent unit (%). To use the default dimensions of the box, leave these spaces blank, or choose *Auto*. Dreamweaver handles box dimensions correctly only for images and layers.

Box width will break a line, but box height will not crop the content of the box to fit within the box (**Figure 13.67**).

Navigator respects box dimensions, but Explorer does not. Navigator only displays boxes as true rectangles if borders are applied (see next section).

Float* places the entity at the left or right margin, effectively separating it from the regular flow of the page. Other elements will wrap around floating elements. *Dreamweaver displays floating images correctly, but not other elements.*

The **Clear*** setting determines the relationship of floating elements to the selected entity. A clear setting of *both* keeps objects from occupying the margins on either side of a selected entity. A clear setting of *none* allows floating entities to occupy either margin. Settings of *left* or *right* protect the respective margin. *Dreamweaver only displays this attribute correctly when it is applied to images.*

279

✔Tip

- To apply the *both* setting, you need to type the word "both" (without the quotes) in the Clear text box, because it is not available from the drop-down menu.

Padding* is similar to cell padding used in tables. Padding is blank space between an object and its margin or visible border. Padding is set as a unit value in pixels, inches (in), centimeters (cm), millimeters (mm), picas, ems, and exs, and percentage of the parent unit (%).

✔ Tips

- To set percentage values for any attribute other than height, you need to type the % directly into the code.

- Padding is only visible when you use a visible border (see the next section, *Border Attributes*).

- You can specify padding for the **top**, **bottom**, **left**, and **right** independently.

Margins* (**Figure 13.68**) are the location of the border around the box (whether or not that border is visible). Margins are set as either auto, or as a number of units, including pixels, inches (in), centimeters (cm), millimeters (mm), picas, ems, and exs, and percentage of the parent element (%). *Dreamweaver displays margins properly only when they are applied to block elements.*

✔Tips

- Setting top and bottom margins is a nice alternative to line spacing; you can subtly increase the spacing between paragraphs.

- You can set margins for the **top**, **bottom**, **left**, and **right** independently.

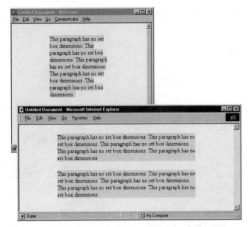

Figure 13.68 In this example, I added the following margins to the <p> tag: 100 pixels on the left and right, and 25 pixels at the top. I showed two different window sizes here (Navigator is at the top) to show how window size affects left and right margins.

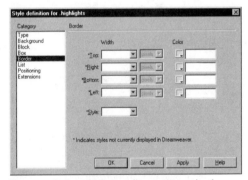

Figure 13.69 Box attributes allow you to make the border around the box visible.

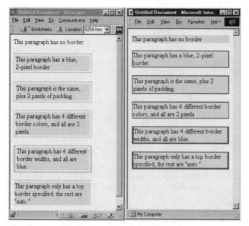

Figure 13.70 How Navigator (left) and Explorer (right) treat the same border settings. I set a box width of 200 pixels, which Navigator requires and Explorer ignores. You can't see this in black and white, but the border colors are treated differently by the two browsers.

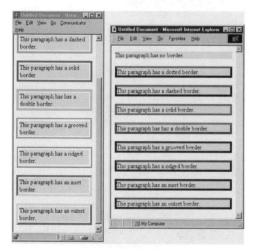

Figure 13.71 Border styles, displayed by Navigator (L) and IE(R). Neither browser displays all border styles as described: "dotted" and "dashed" don't look like their names.

Border Attributes

Border attributes are a subset of box attributes, but in the interests of space and neatness, Dreamweaver displays them in their own panel in the Style Definition dialog box (**Figure 13.69**).

*Border elements are not displayed by Dreamweaver in the Document window.

Borders are composed of four entities: the **top**, **right**, **bottom**, and **left**.

You can set a **width** and a **color** for each entity (**Figure 13.70**). In addition to setting a value for border width, you can set a relative value such as thin, medium, or thick. The auto setting will display the browser's default border width (generally a pixel or two).

☞ Navigator will display different border widths, but not different border colors. In fact, it may handle them pretty strangely.

☞ Navigator will only display box borders if a box width is specified (You can specify 100 percent). Explorer ignores box widths.

☞ Navigator and Explorer deal with color combinations differently.

You can also choose from a number of border **styles** (**Figure 13.71**). You *must* set a border style (solid is a good choice) in order for borders to show up at all.

✔ Tips

- Padding, a box property, starts doing its thing when you use visible borders.

- You can get interesting beveled effects by specifying borders for two of the four sides of the box and leaving the other two sides blank.

---

* Attributes with an asterisk (*) are not displayed in the Document window.

☞ Pointer items discuss how different browsers may treat an attribute.

List Attributes

List attributes are applied to ordered (numbered) and unordered (bulleted) lists, The List panel of the Style Definition dialog box is shown in **Figure 13.72**.

*List attributes are not displayed by Dreamweaver in the Document window.

The **Types*** of list attributes that apply to Ordered Lists (**Figure 13.73**) are *decimals* (1., 2., etc.) *lower-roman* (i., ii., etc.), *upper-roman* (I, II, etc.), *lower-alpha* (a., b., etc.), and *upper-alpha* (A., B., etc.).

For unordered lists, the Types* of bullets available include discs, circles, and squares (**Figure 13.74**).

You can also apply a **Bullet Image*** (**Figure 13.75**) to unordered lists, for which you supply an image URL. ☞ Navigator does not display bullet images.

The **Position*** of the list items applies to what the text will do when it wraps. Inside will indent all the text to the bullet point, while outside will wrap the text to the margin (**Figure 13.76**). ☞ Navigator does not display inside wrapping.

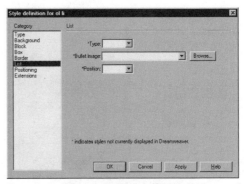

Figure 13.72 The List panel of the Style Definition dialog box lets you define the format of ordered (numbered) or unordered (bulleted) lists.

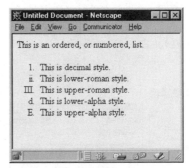

Figure 13.73 An ordered list, formatted with the five different types of ordered list styles.

Figure 13.74 An unordered list, formatted with the three different types of unordered list styles.

Figure 13.75 An unordered list, using bullet images.

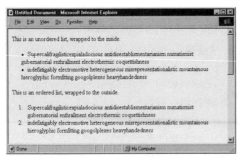

Figure 13.76 The first list is wrapped to the inside, and the second list is wrapped to the outside.

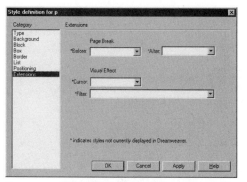

Figure 13.77 The Extensions panel offers extensions to the W3C style sheet specifications.

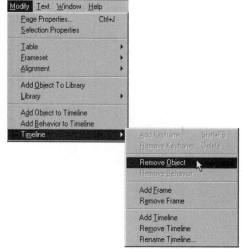

Figure 13.78 The visual effects filters are proprietary, unsupported gimmicks that only work in Internet Explorer.

Extensions

The attributes in the Extensions panel of the Style Definition dialog box (**Figure 13.77**) are not supported by most browsers.

The **Page Break** extension is a proposed style attribute that is not currently supported by any browser. This extension will allow you to recommend a page break before or after a given text block that would break the page when printing the document.

The **Cursor** extension is supported by MSIE 4 and 5. When the user mouses over a style callout, the cursor (pointer) changes into an icon other than the pointer.

The **Visual Effects Filters** are *supposedly* supported by MSIE 4 and 5. I had extremely mixed results using these filters, and I suggest you experiment with them rather than count on them. To apply a visual effects filter, choose it from the drop-down menu (**Figure 13.78**). You need to replace any question marks with values. I'm guessing that you use hex codes for colors; the units for the other values are anyone's guess, as these are not covered in the Dreamweaver manual or help files.

As with all things, in style sheets and in general Web design, experimentation is the key.

EXTENSIONS

---

*   Attributes with an asterisk (*) are not displayed in the Document window.

☞   Pointer items discuss how different browsers may treat an attribute.

LAYERS AND POSITIONING

Figure 14.1 This little collage is made with three layers, positioned so that they overlap in the browser window. Can't do *that* with tables!

Layers are part of the world of Cascading Style Sheets and Dynamic HTML. A layer is a container for HTML content, delineated by the `<div>` or `<span>` tag, that you can position anywhere on a page.

Layers are called layers because they can be positioned in three dimensions. You can set an absolute or relative location for a layer along the page's X and Y axes. The third dimension is called the Z-index and allows layers to overlap one another (**Figure 14.1**).

Designers really love layers for their versatility: You can hide layers (through visibility), or even parts of layers (with the Z-index or with clipping areas) when a page initially loads. Then you can write a script that will cause the hidden areas to appear after a certain amount of time or when a certain user event happens (see Chapters 15 and 16 for information on Behaviors and Timelines).

✔ Tip

- Browsers that don't support layers will display the content of a layer, but will ignore most layer properties, including positioning. See Appendix C on the Web site to find out how to accommodate older browsers.

CSS Positioning

Cascading Style Sheets Positioning, or CSS-P, allows the most specific positioning in HTML to date. Earlier methods, using tables, frames, and frame margins, don't approach the specificity you can reach with CSS-P.

You can apply CSS Positioning to a block of text, a block-type element, an image, or a layer. There are two ways to apply positioning: one is to create a style class and apply it to the selections or text blocks you want to position on the page (at which point, the object becomes a layer, for all practical purposes). The other is to create a layer in the Document window that you can modify independently of creating a style.

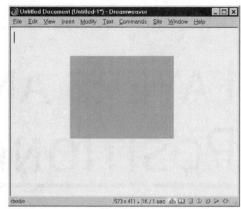

Figure 14.2 This layer is positioned 150 pixels from the left side of the window, and 70 pixels from the top of the window.

X and Y Coordinates

A layer or other positioned element is positioned using X and Y coordinates. X and Y correspond to Left and Top. This can be the left and top of the page itself or of another parent container, such as another layer or a text block (**Figure 14.2**).

The Z-index

The third property of a layer aside from positioning on the *X* and *Y* axes is the *Z-index*, or stacking order. This property is used when there are two or more layers on a page that overlap, and it indicates the order in which the layers stack on top of one another (**Figure 14.3**). The higher a layer's Z-index, the closer it is to the top of the stack.

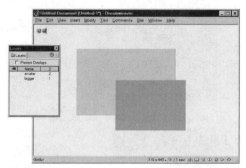

Figure 14.3 The smaller layer is positioned over the top of the bigger one. That means it has a bigger Z-index.

Layers and Animation

Dynamic HTML means that you can make layers change or move after the page is finished loading. Timelines, discussed in Chapter 16, are used to animate layers over time. The Show Layer Behavior and the Drag Layer Behavior both allow layers to change when the user performs an action. I describe both these behaviors in Chapter 15.

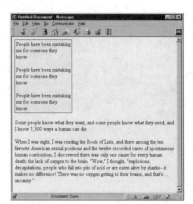

Figure 14.4 In static positioning, the layer is simply treated as a text block and thrown into the normal flow of text.

Figure 14.5 Relative positioning places the layer according to the specified *x* and *y* coordinates, but it still affects the flow of text. The <div> tag, for instance, causes a paragraph break after the layer. Compare to Figure 14.6.

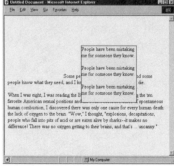

Figure 14.6 This code is exactly the same as in Figure 14.5 except it uses a <span> instead of a <div> tag.

Absolute vs. Relative Positioning

The position of an element in an HTML document can be either absolute, relative, or static.

Normal positioning is called *static*, and causes the element to be positioned within the normal flow of text. Specifying coordinates for static positioning does you no good, as they will be ignored (**Figure 14.4**).

Relative positioning means that a layer or other element is given a position relative to the top-left corner of the parent container. However, the relative element is included in the flow of the page, and is also inline—it does not automatically cause any line breaks (**Figure 14.5**). To guarantee the inline properties, a <span> tag should be used instead of a <div> tag (**Figure 14.6**).

An element such as a layer that is positioned absolutely is completely outside the flow of the document. The regular flow of the material on the page neither contains the layer, nor is it interrupted by the layer (**Figure 14.7**).

Figure 14.7 The layer is back to being a <div> now, and it's positioned absolutely. That means that the regular text flow once again starts at the top of the page, and the layer simply overlaps it.

Positioning Properties

Positioning properties can be applied to any object, but when you set these properties, the behavior of the object becomes similar to layer behavior, and Dreamweaver treats it as a layer, although the browsers may respond differently to positioned elements that are not enclosed in `<div>` or `<span>` tags.

To apply positioning to objects other than layers, create and apply a style, as described in Chapter 13, using the Positioning properties in the Style Definition dialog box (**Figure 14.8**). In general, it's easier to create layers individually using the steps detailed in this chapter. Once you have the hang of both layers and style sheets, you can create a style that you can use to create batches of layers.

The following properties are discussed more fully throughout this chapter in terms of layers.

Type lets you designate the positioning as *absolute, relative,* or *static.*

Visibility determines whether the element will be visible on load. You can declare an element as *visible* or *hidden,* or you can allow it to inherit its properties from the parent element. Using Behaviors (Chapter 15), you can make a layer's visibility change over time or when the user performs an action.

Z-Index (Figure 14.9) determines the stacking order of overlapping elements; the Z-index is the third coordinate, combined with X and Y, that determines the location of the layer on the page in three dimensions. The higher the number, the higher priority the element is given (a layer with a Z-index of 3 will be stacked on top of elements with a Z-index of 1 and 2).

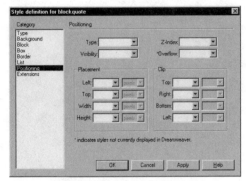

Figure 14.8 The Positioning panel of the Style Definition dialog box. I describe everything else to do with styles in Chapter 13; positioning is discussed in this chapter in terms of layers.

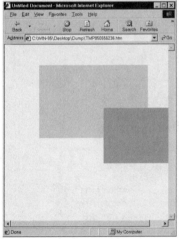

Figure 14.9 Two simple, rectangular layers. One is stacked on top of the other.

Figure 14.10 Each of these images is in a layer, and both images are transparent, so that each appears to float on the page.

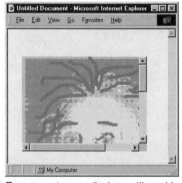

Figure 14.11 Internet Explorer will provide scrollbars for content that exceeds the dimensions of the layer. You can also designate this content as visible or hidden.

Figure 14.12 The clipping region allows you to define which areas of the layer are visible or hidden when the page loads. In this instance, only the top half of the image is being displayed on load.

If the layers have no background colors, and the images within the layers use transparency, you can stack layers so that images appear to overlap one another (**Figure 14.10**).

Overflow determines the behavior of the layer when the content exceeds the borders of the layer. You can designate the out-of-bounds content as *visible* or *hidden*; or the layer can be given scrollbars to make the rest of the content accessible (generally, auto also provides scrollbars) (**Figure 14.11**). *Overflow treatment is not displayed properly in Dreamweaver or supported by Navigator. In Navigator, overflow content is visible, even if another option is set.*

Placement (**Figures 14.9** and **14.10**) of a layer is determined by its distance from the *Left* and *Top* of the parent unit. The *Width* and *Height* measurements are related to placement in that they determine the position of the lower-right corner of the layer.

Clip refers to the clipping area of the layer; the area of the layer in which content shows through (**Figure 14.12**). You could give a layer an area of 200 pixels by 200 pixels, and then allow only a 100x100 pixel area to show through. You set a clipping area as a rectangular area comprised of four measurements (Top, Right, Bottom, and Left).

✔ Tip

- The clipping area is unrelated to overflow. Overflow is simply related to the layer's dimensions, regardless of whether a clipping region is defined.

Other CSS Attributes Related to Positioning

In Chapter 13, I described most style sheet attributes, except positioning attributes. I also relegated vertical alignment attributes to this chapter because you'll most often use them to align text and images within a layer. Vertical alignment attributes can be found in the Block panel of the Style Definition text box (**Figure 14.13**).

Superscript text is smaller text raised above the baseline text, as in $E=mc^2$.
Subscript text dips below the baseline, as in H_2SO_4.

The other vertical alignment options are used with text and images in combination (**Figure 14.14**), or with two images aligned within a parent layer.

The **baseline** is the imaginary line that text sits on. (*Descenders,* as in the letters *j* and *g,* dip below the baseline, while *ascenders,* as in the letters *l* and *d,* rise above lowercase text.) Baseline alignment makes text vertically align to the baseline of nearby text, or the bottom of an image align to the text baseline.

Top, **middle**, and **bottom** are self-explanatory.

Text-top and **text-bottom** align an object with the tallest ascender in the text or the lowest descender in the text, respectively.

✔ Tip

- Other style-sheet attributes are somewhat related to positioning, although they position text rather than other objects. Still, here's a list for reference: All Block attributes, particularly Text Align; Line Height, which is a Text attribute; the Position List attribute, which relates to indents; and most Box attributes, particularly Float, Clear, Margins, and Padding.

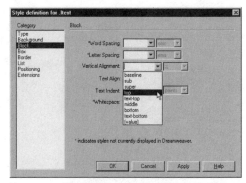

Figure 14.13 The Block panel of the Style Definition dialog box is where you apply vertical alignment attributes to text blocks or selections.

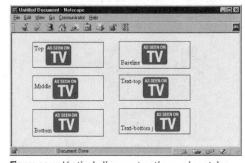

Figure 14.14 Vertical alignment options using styles.

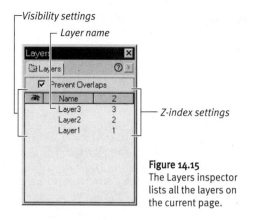

Visibility settings

Layer name

Z-index settings

Figure 14.15
The Layers inspector lists all the layers on the current page.

Figure 14.16 Viewing the grid can give you a better idea of the position of things.

Figure 14.17 View the rulers, with or without the grid, when you want to measure exactly where things are.

About the Layers Inspector

The Layers inspector (**Figure 14.15**) lists all the layers on the current page. When you create a new layer, its name will appear in the Layers inspector.

To view the Layers inspector:

◆ From the Document window menu bar, select Window > Layers.

or

Press F11.

Either way, the Layers inspector will appear.

About the Grid

The grid displays an incremental series of boxes that look like graph paper. You can use grid lines to guide you in positioning or resizing layers.

To view the grid:

◆ From the Document window menu bar, select View > Grid > Show.

The grid will appear (**Figure 14.16**).

About the Rulers

The rulers can be displayed along the top and left of the Document window to guide you in positioning and resizing layers.

To view the rulers:

◆ From the Document window menu bar, select View > Rulers > Show.

The rulers will appear (**Figure 14.17**).

✔ Tip

■ I discuss changing the preferences, snap-to settings, and units of the grid and rulers in *Customizing the Document Window* in Chapter 1.

Creating Layers

Before you can dig your fingers into all the nifty layer features, you need to put a layer on the page. You can insert a layer using the Objects palette, in which case you draw the layer on the page; or you can use the Insert menu, which places a default layer. In either case, you can modify the layer's size and location after placing it.

✔ Tip

■ You can modify the default layer properties. See *Layer Preferences*, near the end of this chapter.

To place a layer using the Insert menu:

◆ From the Document window menu bar, select Insert > Layer.

A default layer will appear at the top-left corner of the Document window (**Figure 14.18**).

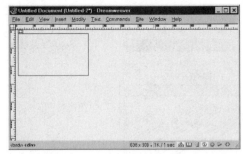

Figure 14.18 When you place a layer using the Insert menu, a default layer appears. You can change the properties of this layer after placing it.

Figure 14.19 After you click on the Draw Layer button, the pointer will turn into crosshairs you can use to draw the layer.

Layer marker

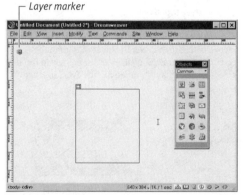

Figure 14.20 After you draw a layer, it appears exactly where you positioned it. A layer marker also appears in the window, indicating the layer's location in the code.

To place a layer using the Objects palette:

1. View the Objects palette, if necessary, by selecting View > Objects from the Document window menu bar.

2. Click on the Draw Layer button: 🖼. The cursor will appear as crosshairs in the Document window (**Figure 14.19**).

3. Click the cursor at the point where you want the top-left corner of the layer to begin, and drag the cursor to where you want the bottom-right corner to be.

4. Let go of the mouse button, and a layer will appear in the Document window (**Figure 14.20**).

Along with the layer, a layer marker will appear that shows where the layer's code appears within the code of the page.

✔Tip

■ If the layer markers aren't visible, view them by selecting View > Invisible Elements. You can toggle the markers on and off this way as often as you choose.

CREATING LAYERS

Selecting Layers

In order to delete, move, or resize a layer, you need to select it. Clicking within a layer does not select it. There are several ways you can select a layer.

To select a layer:

1. Click on the layer.

2. Click on the layer's selection handle at the top-left corner of the layer (**Figure 14.21**).

   or

   Click on the name of the layer in the Layers inspector.

   or

   Click the layer's border.

   or

   Click on the layer's marker in the Document window.

   or

   Click on the layer's tag (<span>, <div>, <layer>, or <ilayer>) in the tag selector at the left of the Document window's status bar (**Figure 14.21**).

Eight points, called *handles,* will appear on the edges of the layer (**Figure 14.22**), and the name of the layer will become selected in the Layers inspector. And, of course, our good old friend the Properties inspector will display Layer properties (**Figure 14.23**).

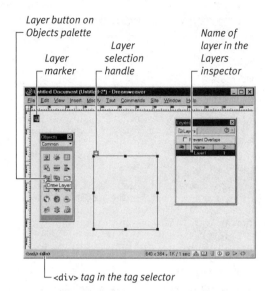

Layer button on Objects palette

Layer marker

Layer selection handle

Name of layer in the Layers inspector

<div> tag in the tag selector

Figure 14.21 To select a layer, you can click on the layer's selection handle; the layer marker in the Document window, the <div> or <span> tag in the tag selector; or the layer's name in the Layers inspector.

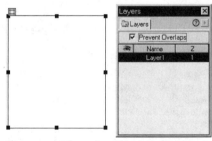

Figure 14.22 When a layer is selected, eight handles will appear around the borders of the layer, and its name will appear highlighted in the Layers inspector.

Figure 14.23 The Properties inspector, displaying Layer properties.

SELECTING LAYERS

Figure 14.24 Type a new name for your layer in the Properties inspector's Layer text box.

Figure 14.25 Type a new name for your layer in the Layers inspector.

Deleting a Layer

When a layer is selected, you can delete it if you choose.

To delete a layer:

1. Select the layer.

2. Press the Delete or Backspace key.

The layer will go away.

Renaming a Layer

Layer names are used by the browser and by any scripts that treat the layer as a script object. By default, Dreamweaver names each successive layer "Layer1," Layer2," and so on.

You may want to give your layers more meaningful names.

To rename a layer:

1. Select the layer.

2. In the Properties inspector, select the old layer name and delete it (**Figure 14.24**).

or

In the Layers inspector, click on the name of the layer and hold down the mouse button. The row holding the name of the layer will become highlighted, and the name of the layer will appear in a text box.

3. Type the name of the layer in the text box (**Figure 14.25**).

The layer will be renamed.

Choosing Tags

There are four tags used in creating layers. The <div> and <span> tags create what is called a *marquee layer*. The <div> tag uses absolute positioning; a paragraph break surrounds the <div> tag. If you prefer to create a layer that's inline, without paragraph breaks, then you want to use the <span> tag, which uses relative positioning.

To change tags:

1. Select the layer.

2. In the Properties inspector, choose either <div> or <span> from the Tag drop-down menu (**Figure 14.26**).

The tag will change to reflect your choice.

✔Tip

■ The other available tags, <layer> and <ilayer>, are Netscape tags. I discuss the special properties of those tags in *Netscape's Layer Tags*, near the end of this chapter.

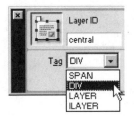

Figure 14.26 You can change tags by clicking on the Tag drop-down menu in the expanded Properties inspector.

— Layer selection handle

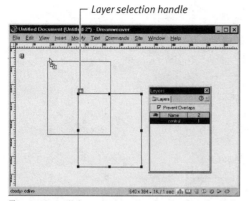

Figure 14.27 Click on the layer's selection handle and drag it to a new location.

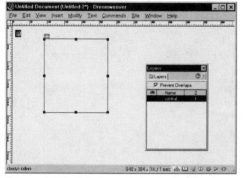

Figure 14.28 The layer is now in its new location.

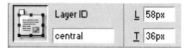

Figure 14.29 Type the X and Y (Left and Top) coordinates in the Properties inspector's L and T text boxes.

Moving Layers

The location of a layer on the page is measured by its distance from the top-left corner of the page (or the parent layer) to the top-left corner of the layer itself. You can change the location of a layer at any point—before or after you put content in it.

To change the layer's location by dragging:

1. Select the layer.

2. Click on the layer's selection handle (**Figure 14.27**) and drag it to its new location (**Figure 14.28**).

   or

   Use the arrow keys to move the layer in one-pixel increments.

✔Tip

■ To move the layer using the grid's snapping increment, select the layer and hold down the Shift key while using the arrow keys to move the layer.

To change a layer's location using exact measurements:

1. View the Properties inspector, if necessary.

2. Select the layer.

3. In the Properties inspector, type the distance of the layer from the left margin in the L text box, and the distance of the layer from the top margin in the T text box (**Figure 14.29**).

4. Press Enter (Return), or click on the Apply button.

The layer will change position on the page.

✔Tip

■ The default units for positioning are pixels, but you can use cm, in, and other units. See the sidebar *Units,* in Chapter 13.

Resizing Layers

You can change the height and width of a layer at any time, before or after you add content to the layer. You can resize a layer by clicking and dragging, by using the keyboard, or by typing exact measurements in the Properties inspector.

To resize a layer by dragging:

1. Select the layer. The handles will appear.

2. To change both the height and width of the layer, click on one of the corner handles and drag it (**Figure 14.30**).

   To change only one of the dimensions, click on one of the side handles and drag it (**Figure 14.31**).

When you let go of the mouse button, the layer will be resized.

To resize a layer using the keyboard:

1. Select the layer.

2. To resize by eyeballing it, press Ctrl+arrow (Option+arrow).

   To resize using the grid's snapping increment, press Shift+Ctrl+arrow (Shift+Option+arrow).

✔Tip

■ To find out how to change the grid settings, refer to *Customizing the Document Window* in Chapter 1.

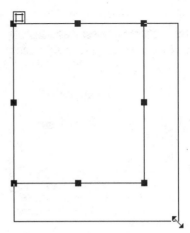

Figure 14.30 Click on the corner handle and drag it to resize two sides of a layer at once.

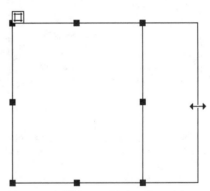

Figure 14.31 Click on a side handle and drag it to move one side of a layer.

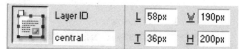

Figure 14.32 You can type new dimensions for your layer in the W(idth) and H(eight) text boxes in the Properties inspector.

To resize a layer using exact measurements:

1. View the Properties inspector, if necessary.

2. Select the layer.

3. In the Properties inspector, type the width of the layer in the W text box, and the height of the layer in the H text box (**Figure 14.32**).

4. Press Enter (Return), or click on the Apply button.

✔Tip

- If you resize a layer with content, such as an image or a piece of text, already inside it, you cannot make the layer visibly smaller than the content it contains. You can still resize the layer's measurements (as displayed by the Properties inspector), but the layer will expand, or rather, not shrink, to fit the content. See *The Clipping Area* and *Content Overflow* to find out how to manage content size.

RESIZING LAYERS

Nesting and Overlapping Layers

The neato thing about layers is that you can put a layer within a layer, or you can create two layers that overlap.

To overlap two or more layers:

All you need to do is move two layers so that they overlap, or create a layer that shares page area with another layer (**Figure 14.33**).

To nest a layer within a layer:

1. Create the first layer.

2. Click to place the insertion point within the existing layer.

3. Create a second layer inside the first (**Figure 14.34**).

The Layers inspector will display nested layers indented beneath the name of the layer that contains them (**Figure 14.35**). The *parent layer* is the one that holds the *child layer* nested beneath it.

✔ Tips

■ If you draw the layer, you may have to hold down the Ctrl (Command) key while you're drawing in order for the layers to be nested. See *Layer Preferences* for more details.

■ To prevent layers from overlapping or nesting at all, check the Prevent Overlaps checkbox on the Layers inspector. If you have already overlapped some layers when you check this option, if you want to un-overlap them, you'll need to do it manually, by dragging.

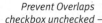
Prevent Overlaps checkbox unchecked

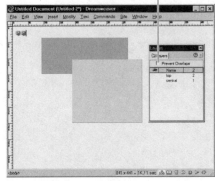

Figure 14.33 Two overlapping layers.

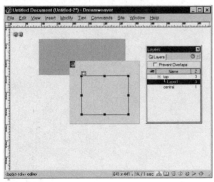

Figure 14.34 I drew one layer nested inside the other.

Figure 14.35 The Layers inspector displays nested layers indented beneath their parent layer.

Figure 14.36 Hold down the Ctrl (Command) key and click on the name of the to-be-nested layer in the Layers inspector.

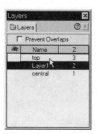

Figure 14.37 Drag the layer onto its parent layer's name.

Figure 14.38 Let go of the child layer, and it will become nested, and its name will be indented under its parent.

Figure 14.39 Click on the child layer that you want to un-nest.

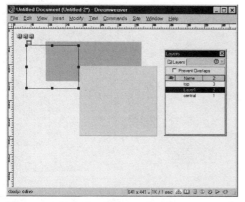

Figure 14.40 Drag the child away from its parent, and it will no longer be nested. Note that the new layer moved from its position in Figure 14.34 because its position is now relative to the upper-left corner of the page, not of its parent.

To nest two existing layers:

1. In the Layers inspector, click on the name of the layer you wish to nest inside another layer (the child layer). A layer icon will appear (**Figure 14.36**).

2. Hold down the Ctrl (Command) key and drag the name of the layer on top of the name of the parent layer. A box will appear around the name of the new parent (**Figure 14.37**).

3. Let go of the mouse button. The name of the child layer you dragged will appear indented beneath the name of the new parent (**Figure 14.38**).

You may decide that you don't want one layer to be nested inside the other.

To un-nest a layer:

◆ Click on the layer's name in the Layers inspector (**Figure 14.39**) and drag it so that it's no longer indented beneath the parent layer's name.

✔ Tips

■ When you nest or un-nest a layer, its position may change (in other words, it may move; see **Figure 14.40**), because nested layers' positions (on the X-Y axis) are based on the parent layer's position. Just drag it back to where you want it to be.

■ In the Layers inspector, you can collapse or expand the list of layers that are nested within the layer. Just click on the + sign next to the parent layer's name to expand the list, or the – sign to collapse the list.

■ When you're working with nested layers, the easiest way to select a layer is by clicking on its name.

■ You can also determine the stacking order of layers by dragging their names around. To find out about stacking order, refer to *Stacking Order*, later in this chapter.

NESTING AND OVERLAPPING LAYERS

Changing Layer Visibility

When you're working on a page with lots of layers, you may want to show or hide various layers depending on what area of the page you're working with. This is especially convenient when you're working with overlapping or nested layers.

Layer visibility also determines whether a layer will be visible when a page loads.

The layer's visibility is determined by its "eyeball status" in the Layers inspector. The eyeball is a three-way toggle switch:

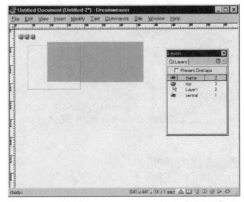

Figure 14.41 The layer that was on top and visible in Figure 14.40 has been hidden.

◆ A closed eye ![closed eye] means the layer is hidden.

◆ An open eye ![open eye] means the layer is visible.

◆ No eyeball means that the layer's visibility is determined by the status of the parent layer, if any.

To show or hide a layer:

1. In the Layers inspector, click on the name of the layer you wish to view or hide.

2. Click within the leftmost column until you change to the desired eyeball status: closed, open, or none.

The layers will appear or disappear (**Figure 14.41**), as indicated by the eyeball (**Figure 14.42**).

Figure 14.42 You can set the visibility of each layer individually by changing the status of the eyeball in the visibility column.

Figure 14.43 Click on the eyeball button at the top of the visibility column to show or hide all layers at once.

To show or hide all layers:

◆ Click on the eyeball button at the top of the leftmost column in the Layers inspector (**Figure 14.43**).

All the layers will appear with an open eyeball, or disappear with a closed eyeball.

✔ Tips

■ Layer visibility is not used simply in working with Dreamweaver; hidden layers will not appear on the page when viewed in the browser window.

■ You can use hidden layers with Timelines or Behaviors (see Chapters 15 and 16), so that layers become visible over time, or when certain actions are performed.

Stacking Order

The stacking order, or Z-index, of layers, determines the order in which the browser will draw them, as well as their stacking priority (**Figures 14.44–14.46**).

✔ Tips

- While Dreamweaver uses the term "stacking order" to describe the Z-index, that doesn't mean that it's an exclusive scale. If you have three layers on different parts of the page, you can make the Z-index 1 for all of them.

- If two layers with the same Z-index (or with no Z-index specified) overlap, the first layer listed in the code will be placed on the top of the heap.

Figure 14.44 The little person has the highest Z-index in this cheesy little montage.

Figure 14.45 In this version, I changed the overlap so that the gun has the highest Z-index, the sign is second, and the person is third. The money remains on the bottom.

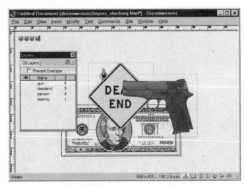

Figure 14.46 This is what the carnage looks like in Dreamweaver.

Figure 14.47 You can set the Z-index by typing a number in the properties inspector's Z-index text box.

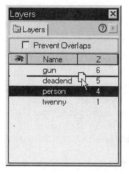

Figure 14.48 You can move the order of the layers in the Z-index by dragging their names in the Layers palette.

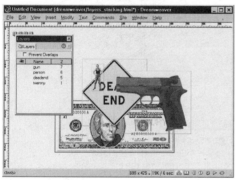

Figure 14.49 I dragged the "person" layer up through the stacking order. Its Z-index is now 6 (Dreamweaver gets sloppy with the numbering), and it's visible above the "deadend" layer.

You can change each layer's Z-index individually, or you can determine the stacking order of all the layers in the Layers inspector.

To change the Z-index of a single layer:

1. Display the Properties inspector, if necessary, by selecting Window > Properties from the Document window menu bar.

2. Select the layer.

3. In the Properties inspector (**Figure 14.47**), type a Z-index for the layer: the bigger the number, the higher the priority (a Z-index of 2 goes on top of a Z-index of 1).

To rearrange the stacking order in the Layers inspector:

◆ Click on the names of a layer in the Layers inspector, and drag it up or down to change its position (**Figure 14.48**).

The first layer listed in the Layers palette (and therefore, listed first in the code) has the highest priority in the stacking order, and so on down the line (**Figure 14.49**).

✔ Tips

■ Take care not to drag the layer's name onto the name of another layer; this will indent one layer beneath the other and thereby nest the layers (see *Nesting and Overlapping Layers*, earlier in this chapter).

■ The Layers inspector may renumber the Z-index strangely when you drag layers; you might start out with index numbers of 3, 2, and 1 and end up with 6, 4, and 1. You can reset these in the Properties inspector, if you like.

STACKING ORDER

305

Content and Layers

A layer can hold nearly any other kind of HTML content: text, images, tables, forms, multimedia content, and, as discussed previously, other layers.

To add content to a layer, click on the layer so that the insertion point appears within it, and then add content as you would to any other part of a Web page (**Figure 14.50**).

✔ Tips

■ You can drag content from outside a layer to within the layer's borders. Just select the object you wish to move, hold down the mouse button, and drag it within the borders of the layer.

■ You can put nearly anything in a layer, except a frame. You can put a form in a layer, but you cannot spread out form content over more than one layer.

■ If a layer contains less content than the layer's borders would indicate, Navigator 4.0 displays only the content (not the entire layer), but the layer's dimensions will still be considered in the layout. Explorer 4.0 or later and Netscape 4.5 or later display the entire layer dimensions, regardless of the content (**Figure 14.51**).

■ Pre-4.0 browsers will display the content of layers, but will ignore the positioning, overlap, and visibility attributes. The `<div>` tag acts like a `<p>` tag, and the `<span>` tag acts like a `<br>` tag (see **Figure 14.52**).

■ When drawing layers, Netscape has a resize bug for which Dreamweaver offers a JavaScript fix. See the sidebar, *Netscape Resize Fix,* later in this chapter.

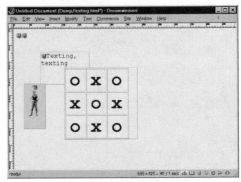

Figure 14.50 You can add any kind of content you want to a layer. Here we've added a table, some text, and an image to the various layers on this page. Just about the only thing you can't put in a layer is a frame.

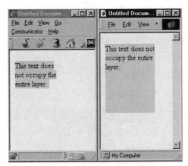

Figure 14.51 Navigator (on the left) displays only the part of the layer that contains content, not the entire layer.

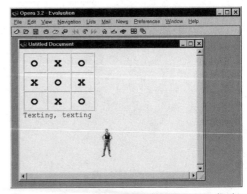

Figure 14.52 Pre-4.0 browsers such as Opera 3.2 display the content of layers, but ignore the positioning attributes. The person image was centered within the layer and is now centered on the page.

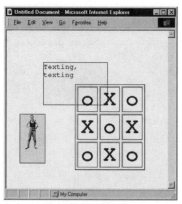

Figure 14.53 On this page, I redefined the `<div>` tag using style sheets so that all layers made with the `<div>` tag would have a one-pixel-wide black border.

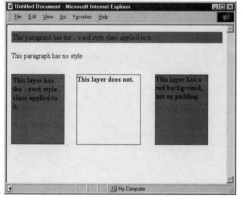

Figure 14.54 On this page, I assigned the .red class to the first paragraph and to the first of the three boxes. The third box has a red background color, but it is not modified by the .red class.

Layers and Styles

All the versatile style sheet attributes that I discussed in Chapter 13—not just positioning—can be applied to layers.

When you create a layer in Dreamweaver, the style attributes that guide the layer's behavior generally appear directly within the `<div>` tag (rather than as a class or tag redefinition, in which case the attributes would appear in the `<style>` area of the `<head>` tag).

You can, as I discussed in Chapter 13, redefine the `<div>` or `<span>` tag so that it attains new properties that will be applied to every layer you create using those tags (**Figure 14.53**).

You can also create a style class that you can apply to a layer by selecting the `<div>` or `<span>` tag and then applying the class to the tag (**Figure 14.54**).

Or, let's say you were playing along at home by following up your experiments with styles in Chapter 13 by viewing the source code and learning how to write style sheets on your own. You can type additional styles into the code for your layers.

Layer code—pre-content—might look something like this:

```
<div id="Layer2"
style="position:absolute;
left:23px; top:155px; width:358px;
height:33px; z-index:2;
background-color: #FFCC33">

</div>
```

All that stuff in the `<div>` tag is style sheet code. You can apply as many additional style attributes to a layer as you want.

The Clipping Area

Layers are somewhat like table cells in that they expand to fit the content you put in them. While you can specify an exact size for a layer, it will expand beyond those dimensions if you place larger content in it.

A layer is unlike a table cell, however, in that you can specify a clipping area for it. As I mentioned earlier, the clipping area is the part of the layer that is visible; it's somewhat like cropping an image, only the rest of the content remains hidden rather than being deleted out of the file. (The file size of clipped content remains the same as if you hadn't clipped it.)

You can make your clipping area the same size as the layer's area, or smaller than those dimensions. (You could make it larger, but that kind of defeats the purpose of having a layer of that size.)

To define the clipping area:

1. Display the Properties inspector and expand it so that all the properties are displayed, if necessary.

2. Select the layer.

3. Define the clipping area by typing the numbers that define the region in the Top, Left, Right, and Bottom text boxes (**Figure 14.55**).

4. Press Enter (Return), or click on the Apply button to apply the changes to the layer.

The area defined by the clipping area will be visible, and the rest will be hidden.

Figure 14.55 Define your clipping area using the Properties inspector.

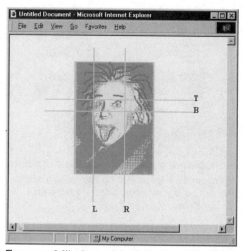

Figure 14.56 Clipping explained: The layer is the same size as the image. Lines T and B are measured from the top of the layer. T is is 70 pixels from the top, and B is 96 pixels from the top. Lines L and R are measured from the left of the layer. Line L is 20 pixels from the left, and Line R is 101 pixels from the left. The rectangular area framed by these lines is what will be left visible. (I drew these lines; you're not going to see them when you clip a layer.)

Figure 14.57 The layer as it looks post-clip (in Dreamweaver, so you can see the outlines of the layer).

✔ Tips

- The L and R measurements are from the left edge of the layer, and the T and B measurements are from the top edge of the layer (**Figure 14.56**).

- The clipping occurs as follows: The area from the left margin of the layer to the L measurement is clipped out, and the area from the R measurement to the right margin is also clipped out. The area between L and R, therefore, is visible. The same goes for T and B, respectively (**Figure 14.57**).

- Unspecified units are in pixels; you may define other units in the following format: 1.5cm (no space between the number and the unit).

- To find how to manage content that exceeds a layer's dimensions, see *Content Overflow* on the following page.

- For Navigator, you can define all four of these areas, or you can define only the bottom and right (the top and left will be set to zero, which is the top-left margin of the layer.)

- For Explorer, however, you *must* indicate a measurement of zero for the top and left, if that's what you want.

Content Overflow

When the content of a layer is larger than the layer's dimensions (independent of the layer's clipping area), you have what is called *content overflow*.

You can let the browser defaults take care of content overflow in their own ways, or you can set one of three properties for content overflow: hidden, visible, or scroll. The last option adds scrollbars to the layer so users can scroll to see the rest of the layer's content (**Figure 14.58**).

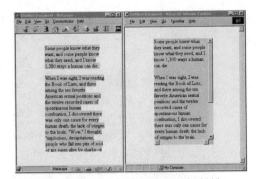

Figure 14.58 Navigator (left) displaying the hidden setting, and Explorer displaying the scroll setting for the same layer.

To control content overflow:

1. Select the layer.

2. In the expanded Properties inspector, choose *hidden*, *visible*, or *scroll* from the Overflow drop-down menu (**Figure 14.59**).

3. Click on the Apply button.

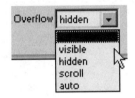

Figure 14.59 Select a content overflow setting from the Overflow drop-down menu on the Properties inspector.

Dreamweaver doesn't display content overflow—it always displays all the contents of the layer, regardless of whether they exceed the layer's dimensions.

✔ Tips

- If you don't choose a setting (if you leave the drop-down menu blank), the browser will display all the contents of the layer, regardless of the layer's dimensions.

- The *auto* setting translates as *hidden* in Navigator and *scroll* in Explorer.

- Navigator 4 does not support the *scroll* setting.

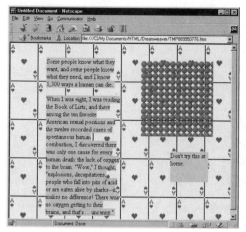

Figure 14.60 This self-consciously ugly page has a background image, over which the three layers are superimposed. In the layer at the upper right, the background image is a transparent GIF through which the background of the page shows.

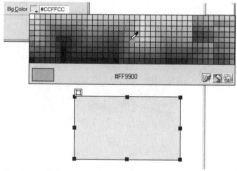

Figure 14.61 You can set a layer background color by clicking on the Color button and choosing a browser-safe color from the Colors palette.

Setting a Background

Layers, like tables, table cells, and CSS text blocks, can have their own background colors or background images. Layer backgrounds will be layered over other background colors or images on the page (**Figure 14.60**).

To set a layer background color:

1. Select the layer.

2. In the Properties inspector, type a hex code or color name in the Color text box.

   or

   Click on the Color button to pop open the Colors palette, and choose a color by clicking on it (**Figure 14.61**).

   or

   In the Color selection menu, click on the Colors palette button 🔘 to open the Color dialog box.

✔Tip

- For information about using the Color dialog box, see Chapter 2.

To set a layer background image:

1. Select the layer.

2. In the Properties inspector, type the URL of the background image in the Bg image text box.

   or

   Click on the folder icon to open the Select Image File dialog box. Browse through the files and folders on your computer until you find the image file you want to use; then click on Open to select the file.

✔Tip

- You can apply additional attributes to a background image using style sheets. See the section of Chapter 13 called *Background Attributes*.

Layer Preferences

When you insert a layer using the Insert menu, Dreamweaver plunks down a default layer whose properties you can then adjust (**Figure 14.62**). Of course, Dreamweaver being so clever, you can adjust those default properties, too. All the default properties except size properties will also be applied to layers you draw using the Draw Layer button on the Objects palette.

To set default layer properties:

1. From the Document window menu bar, select Edit > Preferences. The Preferences dialog box will appear.

2. In the Category list box at the left of the dialog box, click on Layers. The Layers panel of the dialog box will appear (**Figure 14.63**).

3. You can decide whether to use a `<div>`, `<span>`, `<layer>`, or `<ilayer>` tag for your layers by default. To change the default, choose one of these options from the Tag drop-down menu.

4. By default, visibility of the layers is controlled by the activity on the page. To make all layers visible or hidden by default, choose one of those options from the Visibility drop-down menu. You can also choose Inherit to have nested layers inherit their visibility from their parents.

5. The dimensions of a default layer are 200x115 pixels. To change these, type new dimensions in the Width and Height text boxes.

6. You can set a default background color or image for all new layers. Set these attributes as described in *Setting a Background,* earlier in this chapter.

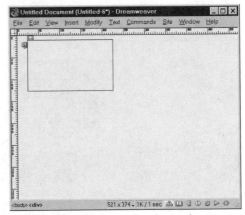

Figure 14.62 A default layer placed using the menu command Insert > Layer.

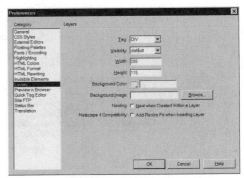

Figure 14.63 The Layers panel of the Preferences dialog box.

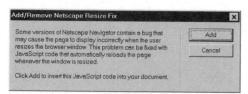

Figure 14.64 Click on Add to add the resize script to your page.

Figure 14.65 This is the complete script, in the HTML inspector.

7. The Nesting option, when checked, makes all overlapping layers nested by default.

8. The Netscape 4 Compatibility option automatically adds JavaScript to each page that features one or more layers. The script fixes a resize bug; to use it, check the Add Resize Fix when Inserting Layer checkbox. See the sidebar, this page, for more details.

9. When you're all hunky-dory with your choices, click on OK to close the Preferences dialog box. Your choices will be applied to your next new layer.

✔Tip

- You can toggle the automatic nesting of layers on and off by holding down the Ctrl (Command) key.

Netscape Resize Fix

Netscape Navigator version 4 and later display layers, but when you resize a Navigator window, any layers on the page may move around or scale improperly. Sometimes they disappear entirely.

Dreamweaver offers a small bit of JavaScript that detects whether the browser is Navigator 4, and if so, forces Navigator to reload the page when the window is resized, and therefore to redraw the layers properly.

To add this fix automatically to each and every page that uses layers, see step 8 in *Layer Preferences* (this page).

You can also add this fix to a single page, even if it doesn't use layers.

1. From the Document window menu bar, select Commands > Add/Remove Netscape Resize Fix. The dialog box in **Figure 14.64** will appear.

2. Click on Add to add the fix. The code is shown in **Figure 14.65.**

To remove the resize fix; for instance, if the page no longer uses layers or if you're saving a 3.0 version of the page, repeat these steps and click on Remove.

Netscape's Layer Tags

While layers are normally created by applying positioning attributes to <div> and <span> tags, the concept of layers is named after two proprietary tags introduced by Netscape with its first beta release of Navigator 4.

The <layer> and <ilayer> tags act similarly to CSS-P layers, although they also possess a few additional properties. The <ilayer> tag is for inline layers, which are embedded in the parent layer (**Figure 14.66**). You can also nest two layer tags; nesting behavior is somewhat different with Netscape layers (**Figure 14.67**).

Neither the <layer> nor <ilayer> tag is supported by Explorer. Their behavior in Dreamweaver is vaguely related to the way they appear in Navigator.

To create a layer or ilayer:

1. Create a layer as you normally would.

2. With the layer selected, choose Layer or Ilayer from the Tag drop-down menu in the Properties inspector.

The marquee layer will become a layer or Ilayer, and the Properties inspector will display additional properties for the layer (**Figure 14.68**).

Figure 14.66 An ilayer (inline layer) nested within a layer.

Figure 14.67 A layer nested within a layer.

Figure 14.68 The Properties inspector displays additional options for <layer> and <ilayer> tags.

Additional Netscape Layer Properties

The additional properties of Netscape's <layer> and <ilayer> tags are as follows:

When you're nesting two Netscape layers, you can choose between two x-y relationships for the two layers. Top, Left refers to the regular relationship a nested layer's position has to the top-left corner of its parent layer. Choosing PageX, PageY instead changes a nested layer's location so that it relates to the top-left corner of the page rather than to the parent layer. (Your mileage may vary.)

Netscape layers can also have a relative Z-index relationship. You can position a layer as appearing Above or Below a "sibling" layer—that is, a layer that shares a parent container, whether that's a parent layer or the page itself. Both layers must already exist when you create Above and Below settings.

✔ Tips

- When working with nested layers, parents automatically appear below children in the Z-index.

- Netscape Layers and <div> tag layers don't nest together very nicely.

You can display an entirely other HTML document as the content of the layer by specifying the URL of the document in the Layer Source text box.

To set Netscape layer properties:

1. Create the `<layer>` or `<ilayer>` and select it.

2. To set either the Top, Left or PageX, PageY relationship, click on the associated radio button in the Properties inspector.

3. To set the Above/Below relationship, choose Above or Below from the A/B drop-down menu, and then choose the name of the associated sibling layer from the drop-down menu to the right of the A/B menu.

4. To choose a source page for layer content, type the URL of the page in the Src text box.

   or

   Click on the folder icon to pop open the Choose HTML File dialog box, and browse through the files and folders on your computer to locate the file. When you find the file, click on Open to select it.

The `<nolayer>` Tag

Layers are proprietary, and importing layer source code is really, really proprietary.

Browsers that don't support the `<layer>` and `<ilayer>` tags, including Explorer 4, will display the content of a Netscape layer, completely devoid of positioning and of any scripting effects applied to it.

You can use a `<nolayer>` tag to either insult or "enlighten" users with browsers that don't support the `<layer>` and `<ilayer>` tags. Just add some code similar to the examples below.

For instance:

```
<LAYER SRC=monkey.html></LAYER>
<NOLAYER>
You could see my dancing monkey if
you had Netscape 4, but you don't.
Neener neener.
</NOLAYER>
```

Or you could be a bit nicer:

```
<LAYER SRC=monkey.html></LAYER>
<NOLAYER>
<img src=/images/monkey.gif>
This monkey would really put on a
show if you downloaded
<a href="home.netscape.com/">
Netscape 4</a>.
</NOLAYER>
```

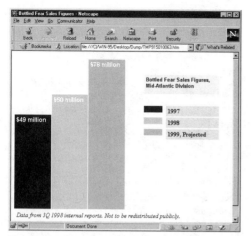

Figure 14.69 This page—bar chart, key, and all—was designed using layers and style sheets. Although it's convenient to be able to use HTML to present graphs, the design won't display in pre-4.0 browsers.

Figure 14.70 The Convert to 3.0 Compatible dialog box lets you save layers as tables, style sheets as font tags, or both.

Converting Layers to Tables (and Vice Versa)

As versatile a layout tool as layers are, it's still the case that only version 4 and later browsers display them properly—while the content may be visible, the positioning and Z-index properties will be ignored, which render the layers useless.

You can, however, export a layer-designed page into table format and then use a browser-detection Behavior (see Chapter 15) to send the browser to the layered or non-layered page. You can also use layers to create a mockup for a complex layout and then convert your design into a table-based layout without the time-intensive headaches involved in figuring out where all those empty cells should go.

✔ Tip

■ Dreamweaver cannot convert overlapping or nested layers. To prevent layers from overlapping before you begin designing, select the Prevent Overlaps checkbox on the Layers inspector. If you have overlapping or nested layers on your page, you must manually un-nest the layers and readjust their positions so they do not overlap.

To convert layers to tables:

1. If you have not done so, save (File > Save) your layers-based page (**Figure 14.69**). If you're using a local site, save the page to the site in which the page will appear.

2. From the Document window menu bar, select File > Convert > 3.0 Browser Compatible. The Convert to 3.0 Compatible dialog box will appear (**Figure 14.70**).

continues on next page

3. Click the Layers to Table radio button, or, if you have CSS text modifications you'd like to convert to `<font>` tags, click the Both radio button.

4. Click on OK. Dreamweaver will create a new, untitled document in the Document window that uses tables to replicate the layer-based design (**Figure 14.71**).

5. Save your new tables-based page (File > Save), optimally in the same directory in which you saved the original, layers-based page.

6. Preview the page by selecting File > Preview in Browser > Browser Name.

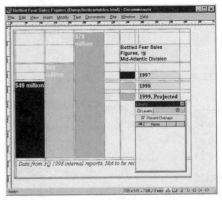

Figure 14.71 Dreamweaver automatically converted the layers-based design into a tables-based page. Each layer is a table cell; transparent GIFs also space the content.

✔ Tips

■ You can temporarily toggle off table borders to see the layout more clearly. From the Document window menu bar, select, View > Table borders (**Figure 14.72**).

■ You can also convert tables to layers in order to manipulate them for a more precise layout; you can later convert those layers back to tables, if you like.

■ Any layers already on the tables-based page will be left untouched when you convert tables to layers.

■ For more details on saving CSS pages as backwards-compatible pages, see the sidebar, *Saving CSS as Plain HTML*, in Chapter 13.

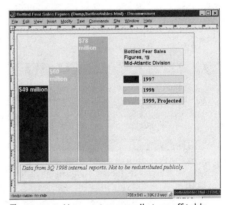

Figure 14.72 You can temporarily turn off table borders to see what the page will look like.

To convert tables to layers:

1. If you have not done so, save (File > Save) your tables-based page (**Figure 14.73**). If you're using a local site, save the page to the site in which the page will appear.

The tables-based layout in **Figure 14.73** is okay—but if I convert each cell into layers, I could use Behaviors (Chapter 16) or Timelines (Chapter 15) to animate individual layers.

Figure 14.73 Tables-based layout

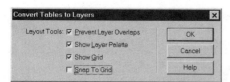

Figure 14.74 The Convert Tables to Layers dialog box offers options for creating and viewing your new layers page.

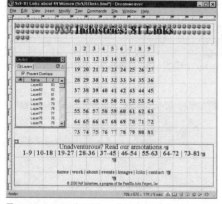

Figure 14.75 Each table cell in the original layout is now a layer, for a grand total of 83 layers (you can deselect View > Invisible Elements to hide the layer markers). Again, I wouldn't have wanted to position all those layers by hand.

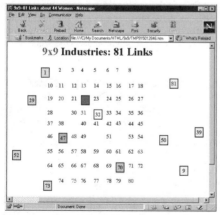

Figure 14.76 I twiddled with the layout using layers, and then converted the page back to tables and previewed it in Navigator 4.5. Using the same design in layers mode, I could create some interesting visual effects using the Drag and Drop Layers Behavior (Chapter 15) or Timelines (Chapter 16). I made the boxes using the Box and Border style sheet attributes (Chapter 13).

2. From the Document window menu bar, select Modify > Layout Mode > Convert Tables to Layers. The Convert Tables to Layers dialog box will appear (**Figure 14.74**).

3. The options in the dialog box let you preset options for the new window that will open.

   ◆ To automatically guard against overlaps, check the Prevent Layer Overlaps checkbox.

   ◆ Check the Show Layer Palette checkbox to make sure the Layers inspector is open when the page opens.

   ◆ Check the Show Grid checkbox to view the grid when the page opens.

   ◆ The last item, Snap To Grid, you may actually want to uncheck. This will make all the layers on the page snap to the grid.

4. When you've made your selections, click on OK to convert your tables page into a layers page, on which each previous table cell is a unique, individual layer positioned where the table cells were in the original layout (**Figure 14.75**).

Now, if you like, you can reposition the layers at will. Following your design tweaks, you can follow the steps starting on the previous page to convert the layers back into a table (**Figure 14.76**).

✔ Tip

■ You'll get a new page if you convert by File > Convert to 3.0 comp, but not if you use Modify > Layout > Convert layers to table (or tables to layers).

CONVERTING LAYERS TO TABLES

Using a Tracing Image

Some designers like to create page mockups in Photoshop (or another image editor) before production starts in on the HTML page itself. Wouldn't it be nice if the page hackers could view the mockup image behind the page and just drag and drop elements onto it?

Using Dreamweaver, you can do just that. You can display your mockup image (**Figure 14.77**) in the degree of transparency you prefer and then position layers on top of the image so that they line up exactly where God (or the designer) intended.

Then, of course, you can convert the exacting layers-based design into a tables-based page that the non-4.0 world can ooh and aah over.

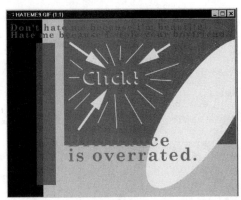

Figure 14.77 This is the image I created to start out with.

To set a tracing image:

1. From the Document window menu bar, select Modify > Page Properties. The Page Properties dialog box will appear (**Figure 14.78**).

2. In the Tracing Image area of the dialog box, type the location of the image or click on the Browse button to pop open the Select Image Source dialog box and locate the image file (.jpg, .gif, or .png) on your hard drive.

3. Drag the bar to set the transparency/opacity of your image so that you can work with it.

4. Click on Apply to preview your tracing image (so you can adjust transparency).

   or

5. Click on OK to close the Page Properties dialog box.

   Either way, the tracing image will appear in the Document window, behind any content already in the window (**Figure 14.79**).

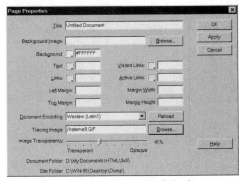

Figure 14.78 In the Page Properties dialog box, you can select an image file to use as a tracing image, and then set the opacity of that image. Tracing images will not show up in browser previews or on the Web.

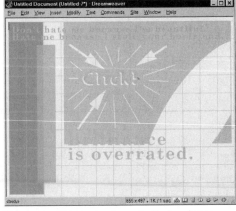

Figure 14.79 This tracing image is displayed at 40 percent opacity in the Document window.

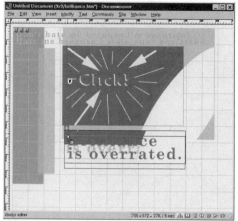

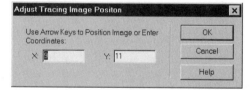

Figure 14.80 Using the tracing image as a guide, I'm placing GIF slices of the original image on the page, using layers to place them exactly. If I want to, I can replicate the tracing image and then convert the layers into tables.

Adjust Tracing Image Positon

Use Arrow Keys to Position Image or Enter
Coordinates:

X: 8   Y: 11

OK

Cancel

Help

Figure 14.81 With this dialog box open, you can move the tracing image's position in the Document window using the text boxes or the arrow keys on your keyboard.

Now you can create and drag layers onto the tracing image so that you can replicate the image's layout (**Figure 14.80**).

To toggle the tracing image on and off:

◆ From the Document window menu bar, select View > Tracing Image > Show.

To move the tracing image:

1. From the Document window menu bar, select View > Tracing Image > Adjust Position. The Adjust Tracing Image Position dialog box will appear (**Figure 14.81**).

2. Type the X (top) and Y (left) coordinates for your tracing image in the text boxes

   or

   With the Adjust Tracing Image Position dialog box open, use the arrow keys on your keyboard to move the tracing image in one-pixel increments.

3. When you're done, click on OK to close the dialog box and return to the Document window.

To reset the tracing image:

◆ From the Document window menu bar, select View > Tracing Image > Reset Position. The tracing image will resume its default coordinates.

To align the tracing image with an object:

1. Select the object in the Document window.

2. From the Document window menu bar, select View > Tracing Image > Align With Selection. The tracing image and the selected layer or image will line up by their upper-left corners.

✔ Tips

■ Because 0 percent opacity is invisible, and 100 percent is completely opaque, you'll probably find that between 40 and 60 percent works best for most images.

■ Fireworks, Macromedia's image editor for the Web, lets you create a page mockup and then carve it up into smaller images that you can export into GIFs. You can then use Dreamweaver to position the images on your HTML page using layers and line up the images so that they correspond exactly to their original locations on the mockup.

BEHAVIOR MODIFICATION

15

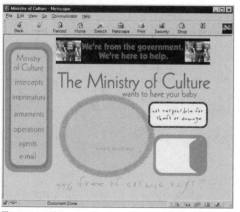

Figure 15.1 This page incorporates several behaviors, although you can't see them yet. In the background, the browser is pre-loading hidden layers and images.

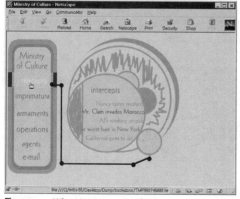

Figure 15.2 When I mouse over the button, the layers in **Figure 15.1** disappear and a new layer appears.

JavaScript behaviors can be used to make both flashy and actually useful gadgets, particularly when used in conjunction with CSS styles (Chapter 13) and layers (Chapter 14). These tools used together are called Dynamic HTML, in which the page can change after it loads (**Figures 15.1–15.3**).

You can make things happen on a page when a user loads the page, clicks an object, or moves the mouse around. Obviously, I'm simpifying—there are a lot of fancy things you can do with JavaScript (see the sidebar, *Learning JavaScript*). In this chapter I discuss the stock behaviors that Dreamweaver lets you apply—all without writing a line of code by hand.

You've already used some preset behavior tools if you've inserted an image rollover (Chapter 8) or a navigation bar (Chapter 9). In Chapter 16, you can get even fancier with Timelines.

✔ Tips

- All the actions that Dreamweaver provides work with version 4.0 and 5.0 browsers, and many also work with earlier browsers (as I note when explaining each action).

- Not all events are available to all browsers, and not all actions work in all browsers, so choosing which behaviors to use depend on which browsers you want to target.

JavaScript Concepts

A JavaScript behavior is sort of like an equation:

`Event + Object = Action`

or

If this event happens to this object, this behavior will happen.

You can see a simple example of this relationship in **Figure 15.4**.

An *object* is an HTML element on a Web page, such as an image, a link, a layer, or the body of the page itself.

An *event* is shorthand for both user event and event handler. A *user event* is what happens when the user, or the user's browser, performs a common task, such as loading a page, clicking on a link, or pointing the mouse at an image. An *event handler* is the JavaScript shorthand that designates a particular user event, such as onMouseOver or onLoad.

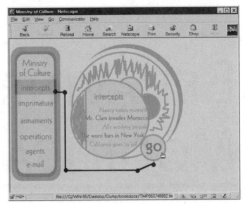

Figure 15.3 When I mouse over the image, a sound plays and another image appears (see the word, *go*?).

Pointer is "mousing over" the image — ⌐ Linked image

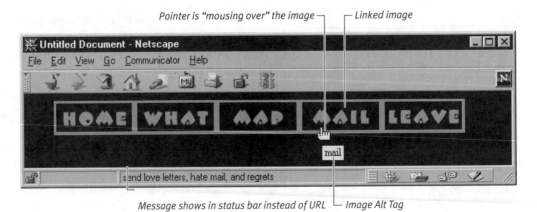

Message shows in status bar instead of URL └ *Image Alt Tag*

Figure 15.4 This button bar, shown in Navigator, is made up of five linked images (with image borders set to 0). The object is the link around the image. The event is onMouseOver, and the action is Show Status Message.

An *action* is where the JavaScript comes in. Normally, when you click on a link, you go to the page that's that link's target. That's a normal browser action that has nothing to do with a script. A JavaScript action might start with the click and then play a sound or pop open a dialog box.

In Dreamweaver, to add behaviors to a page, you choose an object and an event, based on which browsers you want to make the script available to. Then you choose an action that the object + event combination will trigger.

In this chapter, I'm first going to describe how to add a behavior to a page, which is a pretty darn simple process. The rest of the chapter will be dedicated to listing and describing the objects, events, and actions you can combine in Dreamweaver behaviors.

Learning JavaScript

You've probably gotten the idea by now that if you're not used to coding HTML by hand, Dreamweaver is a great way to learn how to do so. You just highlight the objects you're curious about in the Document window, open the HTML inspector, and, *voilà*, you can see what the code behind the page is.

You can do the same thing with JavaScript by creating Dreamweaver behaviors and viewing the code for them in the HTML inspector. If you feel lost looking at JavaScript, you might refer to one of the Web sites I link to in the supporting site for this book.

If you want a handy-dandy JavaScript reference, try *JavaScript for the World Wide Web: Visual QuickStart Guide*, Third Edition, by Tom Negrino and Dori Smith, also from Peachpit Press.

Making Scripts Go

Dreamweaver doesn't actually run any JavaScript behaviors. You need to preview your page in a browser to test your behaviors. You can preview in your default browser by pressing F12, or you can choose a browser from the preview list by selecting File > Preview in Browser > [Browser Name] from the Document window menu bar.

Appendix C on this book's Web site includes instructions on adding browsers to the Preview list.

JAVASCRIPT CONCEPTS

Adding Behaviors

Adding a behavior to a page is incredibly simple—the devil is in the details. All Dreamweaver behaviors are added and edited with the Behaviors inspector.

To view the Behaviors inspector:

◆ From the Document window menu bar, select Window > Behaviors.

or

Click on the Behaviors button (**Figure 15.5**) on the Launcher or the Document window Launcher bar.

or

Press F8.

The Behaviors inspector will appear (**Figure 15.6**).

To add a behavior:

1. In the Behaviors inspector, choose the browser or set of browsers you want the behavior to work in by selecting them from the Browser drop-down menu.

2. In the Document window, click on the object you want the behavior to act on, or choose an entire tag (such as <body>) by clicking on the tag selector at the bottom-left of the Document window (**Figure 15.7**).

3. At the left of the Behaviors inspector, click on the Add Action button ⊞ to pop up a menu of actions that are available for that particular browser-object combination (**Figure 15.8**).

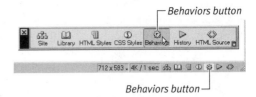

Behaviors button

Behaviors button

Figure 15.5 View the Behaviors inspector by clicking on the Behaviors button on the Launcher or the Launcher bar.

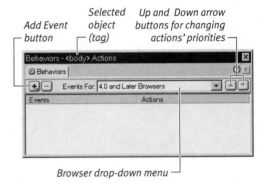

Add Event button — Selected object (tag) — Up and Down arrow buttons for changing actions' priorities —

Browser drop-down menu —

Figure 15.6 The Behaviors inspector is what you use to add JavaScript Behaviors.

Figure 15.7 The tag that's selected in the tag selector is the one that will be affected by the behaviors you apply in the Behaviors inspector.

ADDING BEHAVIORS

Figure 15.8 Click on the Add Action (+) button to pop up a menu and add an action to the selected event. The actions available depend on the selected browser + object combination.

Figure 15.9 Click on the Add Event (▼) button to pop up a menu and add or change an event for the selected object. The events available depend on the selected browser + object + action combination.

4. Choose your action from the menu (they're described later in this chapter). In most cases, a dialog box will appear.

5. Fill out the dialog box (guess what? I explain each of them later in this chapter), and click on OK. The name of the action will appear in the Actions list box.

6. Click on the arrow to the left of the Action name to drop down a list of available user events (**Figure 15.9**). The available events will depend on the object + browser + action combination you chose.

7. Choose your event from the menu (they're described later in this chapter). Its name will appear in the Events list box.

✔ Tips

- You can add more than one event to a single object. You might have different events for onMouseOver and onClick. Just repeat steps 3–7 for each additional event.

- You can also attach more than one action to a single event. Just repeat steps 5–7 to add additional actions to an event (each action will be listed separately). For instance, you might have onMouseOver trigger both a sound and a status message.

ADDING BEHAVIORS

To delete a behavior:

1. In the Document window (or the tag selector), click on the object to which you applied the behavior. The name of the event(s) associated with that object will appear in the Behaviors inspector (**Figure 15.10**).

2. In the Behaviors inspector, click on the behavior you want to delete.

3. Click on the Delete Action button ⊟. The name of the behavior will disappear (**Figure 15.11**).

To edit a behavior:

1. In the Document window, click on the object to which you applied the behavior. The name of the events associated with that object will appear in the Behaviors inspector (as we saw in **Figure 15.10**).

2. In the Behaviors inspector's Actions list box, click on the action you want to change.

3. To edit the action, double-click on its name. The associated dialog box will appear (**Figure 15.12**). (Dialog boxes for each of the actions are explained later in this chapter.) Make your changes and then click on OK to close the dialog box.

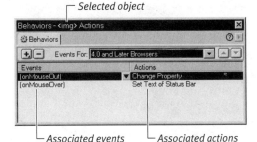

Figure 15.10 When an object is selected, its associated events appear in the Behaviors inspector.

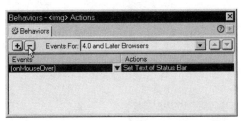

Figure 15.11 When I clicked on the Delete Action (-) button, the unwanted action disappeared.

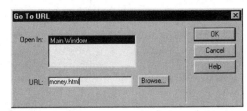

Figure 15.12 When you add a new action or double-click on the name of an existing action, a dialog box will appear in which you add or edit the variables for the action. This is the dialog box for the Go To URL action.

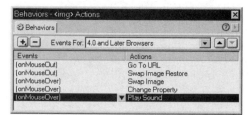

Figure 15.13 Select the proper object and then select the action whose position you wish to change.

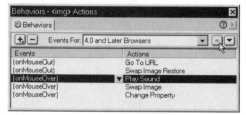

Figure 15.14 I moved the actions around by clicking on the up and down arrow buttons.

You can edit actions as often as you want. If you have an event that triggers more than one action, you may want to set the order in which the actions occur.

To change the order in which actions occur:

1. Select the object in the Document window or the tag selector.

2. Select the behavior in the Behaviors inspector (**Figure 15.13**).

3. Change the order of the action by clicking on the arrow buttons:

   - Click on the up arrow ▲ to move the action up in the list.

   - Click on the down arrow ▼ to move the action down in the list.

The order of the actions will change immediately (**Figure 15.14**), and the browser will perform the actions in order from the top down.

That's about it for adding and editing behaviors. The rest of the chapter is dedicated to the details.

✔ Tip

■ Behaviors are arranged in groups in the Behaviors inspector according to the user event they rely on. In **Figure 15.13**, the behaviors are grouped by onMouseOut and onMouseOver events. You can only move a behavior up and down within its group of like events. In **Figure 15.14**, I moved Play Sound as far up in the list as it would go.

Common Objects

You can attach a behavior to nearly any HTML element, although some are more versatile than others. I'm going to describe some of the more common objects here.

Anchors <a>

Many events are only available to the <a> tag that is usually used for links. Other objects can be attached to these events by surrounding the object with the <a> tag, which can be a null link that doesn't go anywhere.

For images that require a link tag, Dreamweaver will automatically supply an <a> tag for the object.

The anchor code for a null link will look like this:

```
<a href="#">foo</a>
```

The # (pound sign) basically means that the link doesn't go anywhere. You can replace the # later with an actual link, if you want.

✔ Tips

■ In the Behaviors inspector's Events pop-up menu, events that can be activated by applying the <a> tag appear (in parentheses).

■ You can use style sheets to remove the underlining or color changes from the added links on your page. See Chapter 13.

Body <body>

If you want to apply behaviors to an entire page, the <body> tag is what you select.

Images <img>

Images have some nifty properties, one of which is that they load. A popular trick the kids are playing with these days is the *rollover*, in which mousing over an image causes another image to load in its place.

Forms <form>

You can use special form behaviors with a form. The events available to a form include onSubmit and onReset.

Form Fields

You can attach behaviors to individual fields in a form, too, such as <option> (for items in a menu or list), <textfield>, and <checkbox>. One example is the Go to URL action, which can be applied to the <option> items in a drop-down menu, so that when you select an item from the menu, a new page loads.

Event Handlers

There are many different event handlers you can use in Dreamweaver behaviors. These events are detailed in **Table 15.1**.

✔Tips

■ Different events may appear in the Add Event menu in the Behaviors inspector depending on the browser and object you've selected.

■ Events surrounded (by parentheses) in the Add Event menu will become activated by adding an anchor to the selected object. Dreamweaver does this automatically.

■ Internet Explorer 4 and 5 include the most available events, but it's important to remember that only a fraction of your audience uses Explorer exclusively.

Table 15.1 User Events available in Dreamweaver. Events are arranged in logical sets rather than alphabetically. This table does not include all event handlers available to JavaScript, only those that Dreamweaver utilizes for behaviors.

Event Handlers

EVENT HANDLER NAME	DESCRIPTION OF THE USER EVENT *(The event handler may call any number of actions, including dialog boxes.)*	BROWSERS *(According to Dreamweaver.)*	ASSOCIATED TAGS *(Other tags may be used; these are the most common associated objects.)*
PAGE LOADING EVENTS			
onAbort	When the user presses the Stop button or Esc key before successful page or image loading	NN3, NN4, IE4, IE5	body, img
onLoad	When a page, frameset, or image has finished loading	NN3, NN4, IE3, IE4, IE5	body, img
onUnload	When the user leaves the page (clicks on a link, presses the back button)	NN3, NN4, IE3, IE4, IE5	body
onResize	When the user resizes the browser window	NN3, NN4, IE4, IE5	body
onError	When a JavaScript error occurs	NN3, NN4, IE4, IE5	a, body, img
FORM AND FORM FIELD EVENTS			
onBlur	When a form field "loses the focus" of its intended use	NN3, NN4, IE3, IE4, IE5	form fields: text, textarea, select
onFocus	When a form field receives the user's focus by being selected by the Tab key	NN3, NN4, IE3, IE4, IE5	form fields: text, textarea, select

(continues)

Event Handlers *(continued)*

EVENT HANDLER NAME	DESCRIPTION OF THE USER EVENT *(The event handler may call any number of actions, including dialog boxes.)*	BROWSERS *(According to Dreamweaver.)*	ASSOCIATED TAGS *(Other tags may be used; these are the most common associated objects.)*
FORM AND FORM FIELD EVENTS *(continued)*			
onChange	When the user changes the default selection in a form field	NN3, NN4, IE3, IE4, IE5	most form fields
onSelect textarea	When the user selects text within a form field	NN3, NN4, IE3, IE4, IE5	form fields: text
onSubmit	When a user clicks on the form's Submit button	NN3, NN4, IE3, IE4, IE5	form
onReset	When a user clicks on the form's Reset button	NN3, NN4, IE3, IE4, IE5	form
MOUSE EVENTS			
onClick	When the user clicks on the object	NN3, NN4, IE3, IE4, IE5 (IE3 only uses this handler for form fields)	a; form fields: button, checkbox, radio, reset, submit
onDblClick	When the user double-clicks on the object	NN4, IE4, IE5	a, img
onMouseMove	When the user moves the mouse	IE3, IE4, IE5	a, img
onMouseDown	When the mouse button is depressed	NN4, IE4, IE5	a, img
onMouseUp	When the mouse button is released	NN4, IE4, IE5	a, img
onMouseOver	When the user points the mouse pointer at an object	NN3, IE3, NN4, IE4, IE5	a, img
onMouseOut	When the user moves the mouse off an object they moused over	NN3, NN4, IE4, IE5	a, img
KEYBOARD EVENTS			
onKeyDown	When a key on the keyboard is depressed	NN3, NN4, IE3, IE4, IE5	form fields: text, textarea
onKeyPress	When the user presses any key	NN3, NN4, IE3, IE4, IE5	form fields: text, textarea
onKeyUp	When a key on the keyboard is released	NN3, NN4, IE3, IE4, IE5	form fields: text, textarea
INTERNET EXPLORER 4 EVENTS			
onHelp	When the user presses F1 or selects a link labeled "help"	IE4, IE5	a, img
onReadyStateChange	Page is loading	IE4, IE5	img
onAfterUpdate	After the content of a form field changes	IE4, IE5	a, body, img
onBeforeUpdate	After form field item changes, before content loses focus	IE4, IE5	a, body, img
onScroll	When the user uses the page scrollbars	IE4, IE5	body

EVENT HANDLERS

Common Actions

In this section of the chapter I describe how to set up some common JavaScript actions in Dreamweaver. This is not meant to be an all-encompassing JavaScript reference; the language is capable of much more than I'm able to sum up in a single chapter.

Setting up behaviors in JavaScript is very much like ordering Chinese food: you take one from Column A (objects), one from Column B (events), and one from Column C (actions).

Because it would be redundant for me to repeat every detail of how to set up a behavior for each of these actions, I'm going to skip some of the basic steps, like showing the Behaviors inspector. You can review the details in *Adding Behaviors,* earlier in this chapter.

✔Tips

■ The objects and events that I name in the instructions for these events are suggestions; many other combinations are possible.

■ Don't forget that JavaScript can crash older browsers. Heck, my computer crashed a half-dozen times just *writing about it*. Refer to Appendix C on the Web site for tips on writing pages for the masses.

Figure 15.15 Type your status bar message in the Message text box.

Status bar message   Link

Figure 15.16 When the user mouses over the link, a message appears in the status bar.

Set Text of Status Bar

A status bar message is a little bit of text that appears in the status bar of the browser.

Usage Example: Combine <a> and onMouseOver with Display Status Message. When the user mouses over a link, they'll see a message in the status bar such as "Explore the Invisible Cities." This is also a great trick for hiding the target URL.

To add a status bar message:

1. In the Behaviors inspector, select a browser (3.0+later).

2. In the Document window, select an object (a, body, img).

3. In the Behaviors inspector, add the Action Set Text of Status Bar (Set Text > Set Text of Status Bar). The Set Text of Status Bar dialog box will appear (**Figure 15.15**).

4. Type your message in the Message text box. Use a space to leave the status bar blank at all times.

5. Click on OK. The Set Text of Status Bar dialog box will close.

6. In the Behaviors inspector, choose an event (onMouseOver, onMouseOut, onLoad, onClick).

When you load the page in a browser, the message will appear in the status bar when you perform the user event you specified (**Figure 15.16**).

✔ Tip

■ If you specify a status message for onMouseOver, you may also want to specify a status message for onMouseOut. This can be a blank message. Just type a space in the Message text box.

SET TEXT OF STATUS BAR

Go to URL

You can open URLs with actions other than a click.

Usage Example: Have a link open two windows at once or open a document in each of two frames. You can also specify URLs in this way using JavaScript; older browsers get the regular old link, while the JavaScript user goes to the JavaScript page.

To add a URL:

1. In the Behaviors inspector, select a browser (3.0 + later).

2. In the Document window, select an object (a, img, body).

3. In the Behaviors inspector and add the action Go to URL. The Go To URL dialog box will appear (**Figure 15.17**).

4. Add your URLs as follows:

   ◆ To load a new URL in a single, non-frames window, simply type the URL in the URL text box.

   ◆ To load a single URL on a page with more than one frame and URL, select the name of the single frame from the Open In list box and type the URL in the URL text box.

   ◆ To load more than one URL on a page with more than one frame and more than one URL, repeat the preceding instruction for each single frame you want to load a document into.

5. Click OK. The dialog box will close.

6. In the Behaviors inspector, specify the event (onClick, onLoad, onMouseOver, onMouseOut). The URL(s) will open when the user performs the event, such as a click (**Figure 15.18**).

Figure 15.17 Select the windows (or frames) and type in the corresponding URLs that will load when the event happens.

✔ Tip

■ Be sure to test, test, and retest these links once they're on the server, particularly if you're targeting multiple frames.

Window Dressing

In the example in **Figure 15.17**, I can choose between opening my URL in the main page body or in any frame on the page. If you want the page to open in a new window, you can do that, too. One way is to set a target. Type this code in the URL text box, where path/file.html is the URL of your page:

```
path/file.html target="_blank"
```

Additionally, you can have the URL open in a custom-sized window, with or without toolbars. See *Open Browser Window*, later in this chapter. After you create a window, its name will appear in the Open In list box.

GO TO URL

Figure 15.18 When you click on many different links on the Dreamweaver help page, frames on both the left and right load new images.

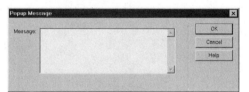

Figure 15.19 Type the message you want to appear in the dialog box in the Message text box.

Figure 15.20 A pop-up message created with Dreamweaver. This message appears when the user clicks on a link. I used this in combination with the Go To URL action; when the user clicks on OK, the browser will open a new page.

Popup Message

In the Popup Message action, when the user performs an action, a pop-up message or dialog box will appear. In Dreamweaver, the only choice in this dialog box is OK.

Usage Example: Combine this action with the result of another action, such as form validation ("You forgot to type your e-mail address") or plug-in detection ("You need Shockwave to properly appreciate this page").

To add a pop-up message:

1. In the Behaviors inspector, select a browser (3.0 + later).

2. In the Document window, select an object (*a*, *body*).

3. In the Behaviors inspector, add the action Pop-Up Message. The Popup Message dialog box will appear (**Figure 15.19**).

4. Type your message in the Message text box.

5. Click on OK. The Popup Message dialog box will close.

6. In the Behaviors inspector, specify the event (onClick, onMouseOver).

When you load the page in a browser, the pop-up message or dialog box will open when the user performs the event, such as a click (**Figure 15.20**).

✔Tip

■ Don't overuse this one. I've seen pages where the slightest mouse movement would open a dialog box, and it was truly annoying.

Open Browser Window

You know those little bitty JavaScript windows? You can pop one open using the Open Browser Window action—or you can pop open a regular-sized window. Incidentally, each of these pop-up windows has a unique URL that belongs to a distinct HTML document that you must create separately.

Usage Example: Pop open a floating toolbar, "control panel," or a window set to the exact size of a Shockwave applet or image map (**Figure 15.21**).

To add the Open Browser Window action:

1. In the Behaviors inspector, select a browser (3.0 + later).

2. In the Document window, select an object (a, img, body).

3. In the Behaviors inspector, add the Action Open Browser Window. The Open Browser Window dialog box will appear (**Figure 15.22**).

4. Type the URL of the content for the new window in the URL text box, or click Browse to select a local file.

5. If you want to specify a window width and window height, type these dimensions (in pixels) in the appropriate text boxes. If you don't specify these dimensions, a default-sized browser window will open.

6. The checkboxes allow you to display regular browser features such as navigation and location toolbars, the status bar, the menu bar, scrollbars, and resize handles. Leave all the boxes unchecked if you want a "featureless" window.

Figure 15.21 This sound control panel is set to pop open when a link in the parent window is clicked.

Figure 15.22 The open Browser Window dialog box. These are the attributes I set for the control panel in Figure 15.21.

Figure 15.23 Another floating toolbar. Note the extra space below the buttons—the window must be a minimum of 100 pixels high. If I were getting this control panel ready for prime time, I'd center the buttons within the window using a table, or I'd make bigger buttons.

Jump Menu Behaviors

Two actions listed in the Behaviors inspector, Jump Menu and Jump Menu Go, apply to jump menus. Jump menus, discussed in Chapter 12, are small drop-down menus from which the user can select a page to visit. A jump menu can operate with a Go button or without a button, in which case the browser activates the link in the menu as soon as the user selects it.

To insert a jump menu, see Chapter 12.

To edit a jump menu, select it, and then in the Behaviors inspector, double-click the action Jump Menu. The Jump Menu dialog box will appear (**Figure 15.24**, next page).

To add a Go button to a jump menu after you've inserted the menu, you must add a form button (Insert > Form Object > Button). In the Properties inspector, set the Action to Nothing, then label the button "Go," or whatever you like.

Then, in the Behaviors inspector, select the button, and give it the event onClick and the action Jump Menu Go. The Jump Menu Go dialog box will appear (**Figure 15.25**, next page). Keep in mind that the menu may still operate onSelect rather than by clicking the button. Unfortunately, the only reliable way to use a Go button is to add it while you're inserting the menu in the first place.

7. To specify a window name, type the title in the Window Name text box. (You can use these window names in other behaviors, such as Go to URL.)

8. Click on OK. The Open Browser Window dialog box will close.

9. In the Behaviors inspector, specify the event (onClick, onLoad, onMouseOver).

In the browser window, when the action (page loading, link clicking) occurs, the new window will open (**Figure 15.23**).

✔ Tips

- By trial and error, I've found that JavaScript windows must be at least 100 pixels high. The window in **Figure 15.21** is 115 pixels wide and 150 pixels high, and the window in **Figure 15.23** is 100 pixels high, although I'd like it to be about 50 pixels high.

- If you want links on your page to be able to load into this window, use the Go to URL Behavior, and from the Open In list box, select the window name you specified in step 7 as if it were a frame name.

- To set a page title for this window, open the separate HTML document in Dreamweaver (File > Open), and use the Page Properties dialog box (under the Modify menu).

Check Plugin

The Check Plugin action checks the user's browser to see if they have a particular plug-in installed. After the check, the action can load one of two URLs: one for Yes, and an alternate for No.

Usage Example: If the user has Shockwave installed, they will proceed to the Shockwave-enhanced version of the page. If not, they will be sent to a page that's designed to present the same information without Shockwave.

To add the Check Plugin action:

1. In the Behaviors inspector, select a browser (3.0+later).

2. In the Document window, select the <body> tag by clicking on it in the tag selector at the bottom left of the status bar, or select an <a> tag.

3. In the Behaviors inspector, add the action Check Plugin. The Check Plugin dialog box will appear (**Figure 15.26**).

4. Choose a plug-in from the drop-down menu.

   or

   If the desired plug-in is not available from the drop-down menu, type the name of the plug-in, *exactly as it appears in bold on Netscape's About Plug-ins page*. For example, to look for the latest version of the RealPlayer, you'd type `RealPlayer(tm) LiveConnect-Enabled Plug-In (32-bit)` (yes, the whole thing).

5. Type the URL for the Yes page in the URL text box (for example: `shock_index.html`).

6. Type the alternate URL for the No page in the Alt URL text box (for example: `noshock_index.html`).

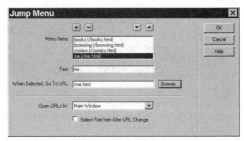

Figure 15.24 You can edit a jump menu after you insert it using the Jump Menu dialog box. See Chapter 12 for details.

Figure 15.25 If you have more than one jump menu on your page, select the correct one from the drop-down menu. You can apply this action to an existing menu or to a form button.

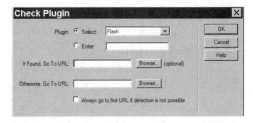

Figure 15.26 Choose your plug-in from the drop-down menu.

7. Click on OK to close the Check Plugin dialog box.

8. In the Behaviors inspector, specify the event (onLoad, onClick).

When the page loads or the link is clicked, the user will automatically be forwarded to the proper page.

✔ Tips

■ To view Netscape's About:Plug-ins page, select Help > About Plug-ins from Navigator's menu bar, or type about: plugins in the address bar and press Enter (Return).

■ For Internet Explorer, check the checkbox marked Go to URL if ActiveX is Available; deselecting the checkbox will send MSIE to the alternate URL. Many Netscape plug-ins have ActiveX counterparts for Internet Explorer; check the documentation for the plug-in to find out more.

■ I discuss plug-ins and ActiveX in Chapter 19. Appendix C on the Web site discusses making sites available to browsers other than the latest versions of Navigator and Explorer.

Check Browser

The Check Browser action checks the brand and version of the user's browser; different browsers do have different capabilities. After the check, the action can load one of two URLs: one for Yes, and an alternate for No.

Usage Example: If the user has a 4.0 browser, they can proceed to the layers-intensive version of the page. If they have a 3.0 browser, they will be sent to a page that's designed to present the same information using tables.

✔ Tips

- Browsers before Netscape 2 or Explorer 3 will not run this behavior, because they don't support JavaScript. Steps 3, 5, and 6 on the following page tell how to work around older browsers.

- It's a good idea to have the page on which this behavior appears contain the equivalent information for users with older browsers, and to use the Stay on this Page option for them.

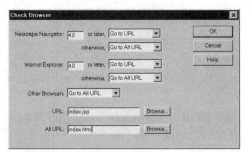

Figure 15.27 Specify different actions for different browsers using the Check Browser dialog box.

To add the Check Browser action:

1. In the Behaviors inspector, select a browser (3.0 + later).

2. In the Document window, select the <body> tag by clicking on it in the Tag Selector at the bottom left of the status bar, or select an <a> tag.

3. In the Behaviors inspector, add the action Check Browser. The Check Browser dialog box will appear (**Figure 15.27**).

4. For each of the three options, Netscape Navigator, Internet Explorer, or Other Browsers, choose an option from the drop-down menu: Go to URL, Go to Alt URL, or Stay on this Page. (Browsers that don't support JavaScript will use the last option by default.)

5. In the Netscape Navigator and/or Internet Explorer text boxes, type the *earliest* version number that supports the feature you're working around. If the feature is, say, layers, type 4.0 in both text boxes; for frames, type 2.0 in the Navigator text box and 3.0 in the Explorer text box.

6. Type the URL for the main page in the URL text box (for example, layers_index.html).

7. Optionally, type an alternate URL, for the alternate page, in the Alt URL text box (for example: nolayers_index.html). (If you don't specify an alternate URL, the user will stay on the current page or will use the non-JavaScript link.)

8. Click on OK to close the dialog box.

9. In the Behaviors inspector, specify the event (onLoad, onClick).

When the page loads or the link is clicked, the user will automatically be forwarded to the proper page.

CHECK BROWSER

Swap Image

Swapping images is the same as performing the famous rollovers I talked about earlier.

Usage Example: When the user mouses over the image, it's replaced with a "lit up" image (**Figure 15.28**) or another image entirely.

✔ Tip

■ You don't need to set up the Swap Image action in order to set up image rollovers. See the last section of Chapter 8 to find out how to use the Insert > Rollover Image object. This option inserts an image, pre-loads the secondary image, and automatically restores the original image onMouseOut.

Images must be named for image swapping to work properly.

To name your images:

1. Select the image.

2. In the Properties inspector, name the image by typing a name for it in the Image text box and pressing Enter (Return).

To add the Swap Image action:

1. In the Behaviors inspector, select a browser (Netscape 3.0 + later).

2. In the Document window, select an image (img; Dreamweaver will add the anchor tag if needed).

3. In the Behaviors inspector, add the Action Swap Image. The Swap Image dialog box will appear (**Figure 15.29**).

Figure 15.28 The Dreamweaver help page uses image rollovers to make the buttons "light up" when you mouse over them.

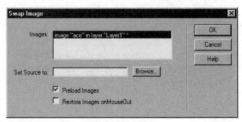

Figure 15.29 This is the Swap Image dialog box I used to set rollovers.

Figure 15.30 A popular way to implement image swapping is to use an image that's the reverse of the original. When the user mouses over the image on the bottom, it's swapped with an image that's the same size and shape, with reversed colors.

Figure 15.31 You can set the Swap Image action to swap several images at once. In this example, when the user mouses over the image on the bottom, all three images are swapped simultaneously.

4. The Images list box will display all the named images on your page. Click on the name of the image you want to swap.

   ◆ To swap the image you selected as an object in step 2, be sure to select the name of that image.

   ◆ To swap a different image when the user event occurs, select a different image.

5. Type the source for the new image (the one that will replace the named image when the action occurs) in the Set Source To text box, or click on Browse.

6. To have the images loaded with the page, select the Preload Images checkbox.

7. To automatically have the image revert to its original appearance when the user mouses out, select the Restore Images on MouseOut checkbox.

8. In the Behaviors inspector, specify the event (onClick, onLoad, onMouseOver, onMouseOut).When you view this page in a 3.0 or later browser, the images you selected will be swapped (**Figure 15.30**).

✔ Tips

■ If you select more than one image in a single action, all selected images will roll over when you mouse over the single image you selected in step 2 (**Figure 15.31**).

■ To set rollovers for individual images, you need to follow steps 2–7 for each consecutive image.

■ Image swapping onMouseOver is often combined with image restoring onMouseOut. You can set this up automatically, but you can also decide not to do so.

SWAP IMAGE

Preload Images

You can set up the Swap Image behavior to automatically preload images, but there are other instances in which you may want to preload images as well.

Usage Example: Preload a large image that appears in a DHTML/JavaScript window before the user ever gets there by adding this behavior to the home page.

To add the Preload Image action:

1. In the Behaviors inspector, select 4.0 and later browsers.

2. In the Document window, select the body of the page by clicking on the <body> tag in the tag selector.

3. In the Behaviors inspector, add the Action Preload Images. The Preload Images dialog box will appear (**Figure 15.32**).

4. Type the pathname of the image you want to preload in the Image Source File text box, or click on Browse to choose the image from your computer.

5. For every image you want to preload, click on the Plus button ⊞, and then repeat step 4.

6. To delete an image, select it and click on the Minus button ⊟.

7. Click on OK to close the Preload Images dialog box.

8. In the Behaviors inspector, make sure the onLoad event is selected.

Dreamweaver will write what's called an *array* in the head of the document. All image filenames that appear in this array will be preloaded when the browser loads the page.

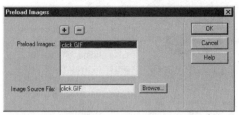

Figure 15.32 Set the source for all the images you want cached and ready in the Preload Images dialog box.

Set Navbar Image

The Behavior Set Navbar Image is used in conjunction with Navigation bars, described in Chapter 9. The behavior uses the same dialog box to change the image source for the navigation bar. You can also create additional user events using the Behaviors inspector for a navbar; for instance, you could add button images for onMouseDown or onAbort.

Figure 15.33 There's no good way to demonstrate rollovers in print, so let's pretend that the window on the left and the window on the right are the same window. On the left, we're mousing over the image. On the right, we've just moused out, and the image is restored.

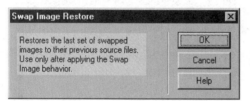

Figure 15.34 All you need to do with the Swap Image Restore dialog box is click on OK.

Swap Image Restore

When you set up an image rollover using either the Insert Rollover Image function or the Swap Image Behavior, you can select an option that automatically swaps the image back to its original source when the user mouses out (**Figure 15.33**).

However, if you have a different user event call the Swap Image behavior, or if you'd like a different event to swap the images back, you need to set up the Swap Image Restore Behavior.

This is simple: Just select the image for which you've previously set up a Swap Image or Rollover Image Behavior, and then add the action Swap Image Restore. The Swap Image Restore dialog box will appear (**Figure 15.34**). Just click on OK, and that's it. Then, specify a different event, if necessary.

Play Sound

You can use the Play Sound action to play a sound when a user performs an action such as a mouseover or a click.

Usage Example: Combine a small (<20KB) sound with image rollovers so that a beep of some kind occurs.

To add a sound:

1. In the Behaviors inspector, select a browser (Netscape 3, 4.0 + later).

2. In the Document window, select an object (a, body, img).

3. In the Behaviors inspector, add the Action Play Sound. The Play Sound dialog box will appear (**Figure 15.35**).

4. To play a sound onEvent, type the URL of the sound clip in the Play Sound text box.

   or

   Click on Browse. The Select File dialog box will appear. Choose the file from a folder in your local site.

5. Click on OK. The Play Sound dialog box will close.

6. In the Behaviors inspector, specify the event (onClick, onLoad, onMouseOver).

When you load this page in the browser you can play a sound clip (**Figure 15.36**).

Figure 15.35 Using the Play Sound dialog box, you can add a sound to an event.

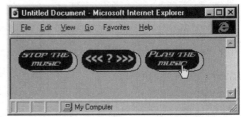

Figure 15.36 Using these images as the objects for the Play Sound behavior, you can let the user play a sound embedded using JavaScript.

The Fury of Sound

In past versions of Dreamweaver, you could purportedly use this behavior not only to play a sound but to stop one. You still can, if you're sneaky. For example, you may have a theme song set to play onLoad or onMouseOver. You can then attach a small (one second, even) sound to a button called, for example, Stop the Music (**Figure 15.36**). When the user mouses over the button, the sound that is currently playing will stop, and the short beep will play.

I cover plug-ins and sound files in Chapter 19. You can refer to that chapter for information on changing HTML or JavaScript code for hidden/visible sound controls, sound loops, and the like.

PLAY SOUND

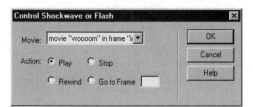

Figure 15.37 Using the Control Shockwave or Flash dialog box, you can provide controls to play, stop, rewind, or jump to a frame in a Shockwave movie.

Control Shockwave or Flash

You can use the Control Shockwave or Flash action to play, stop, rewind, or jump to a particular frame in a Shockwave or Flash movie.

Usage Examples: Provide buttons or links marked Stop and Play. For a Shockwave game, provide a Play Again link that jumps back to the particular frame in which the game starts.

✔ Tip

■ To use the Control Shockwave or Flash action, you must first embed a Shockwave or Flash object in the page using the <embed> or <object> tags. I discuss Shockwave, Flash, and other plug-ins in Chapter 19.

To add Shockwave Control:

1. In the Behaviors inspector, select a browser (3.0 + later).

2. In the Document window, select an object (a, img, input).

3. In the Behaviors inspector, add the Action Control Shockwave or Flash. The Control Shockwave or Flash dialog box will appear (**Figure 15.37**).

4. If there is more than one Shockwave or Flash movie on your page, select the correct object from the Movie dropdown menu.

5. Click on the radio button for the control you want to add: Play, Stop, Rewind, or Go to Frame. For this last option, type the number of the frame in the Frame text box.

continues on next page

6. Click on OK. The Control Shockwave or Flash dialog box will close.

7. In the Behaviors inspector, specify the event (onClick, onLoad, onMouseOver).

When you load this page in the browser you can control the Shockwave movie (**Figure 15.38**).

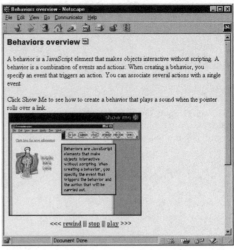

Figure 15.38 I modified the About Behaviors page from the Dreamweaver help files to add Shockwave controls that rewind, play, or stop the movie.

Error, Will Robinson!

You may get a JavaScript error in Dreamweaver when implementing this behavior. If a dialog box pops up mumbling something about Netscape and objects, follow these steps:

1. In the Document window, select the Shockwave object.

2. Display the Properties inspector by selecting Modify > Selection Properties from the Document window menu bar.

3. From the TAG drop-down menu, select OBJECT and EMBED.

Now both Navigator and Explorer will load both the Shockwave movie and the Control Shockwave script properly. I explain this more thoroughly in Chapter 19.

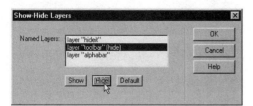

Figure 15.39 Set the (onEvent) visibility of your layers in the Show-Hide Layers dialog box.

Show-Hide Layers

The Show-Hide Layers action can make certain layers appear or disappear. You must already have the layers on your page to set up this behavior. The effectiveness of this behavior depends on the initial visibility setting you give your layers.

Usage Examples: When a user mouses over an image or clicks on a link, one layer will disappear and another will appear; we saw this in **Figures 15.1–15.3**. Because layers are loaded with a page, you can make several sets of content available on a single page and hidden in different layers.

To add the Show-Hide Layers action:

1. In the Behaviors inspector, select a browser (4.0 + later).

2. In the Document window that contains the layers, select an object (a, body, img).

3. In the Behaviors inspector, add the action Show-Hide Layers. The Show-Hide Layers dialog box will appear (**Figure 15.39**). Dreamweaver may take a moment or two to detect all the layers on the page, at which point their names (id="" or name="") will appear in the Layers list box.

4. Click on the name of the layer whose visibility you want the event to change, and then click on one of the three buttons: Show, Hide, or Default. Default will restore the layer's original visibility setting.

5. Repeat step 5 for all the layers you want this behavior to affect.

6. Click on OK to close the Show-Hide Layers dialog box.

continues on next page

Why Default?

The *Default* setting is most useful for a second Show-Hide Layers behavior.

For instance: Let's imagine a page with two layers. When the page loads, Layer Apple is showing, and Layer Banana is hidden—those are their default settings.

First behavior: When an onClick happens to a link called "Turn the Page" in Layer Apple, Apple hides and Banana appears.

Second behavior: When an onClick happens to a link called "Back to the Beginning" in Layer Banana, the Default settings of both layers are restored, and thus Apple appears and Banana hides.

Experiment with this; I got mixed results.

SHOW-HIDE LAYERS

351

7. In the Behaviors inspector, specify the event (onLoad, onClick, onMouseOver).

The page must be loaded in a 4.0 or later browser for this action to work, because earlier browsers don't show layers at all. **Figure 15.40** shows a page with all layers hidden. **Figures 15.41** and **15.42** show the same page with the layers showing.

✔ Tip

■ Another layer animation behavior, Drag Layer, is described later in this chapter.

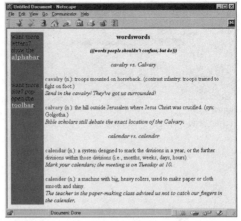

Figure 15.40 This page has two hidden layers. The links to them are in the table cell at the left.

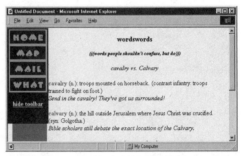

Figure 15.41 Click on the link that says Show Toolbar, and it calls a behavior that shows the Toolbar layer. Notice that that layer has a link called Hide Toolbar.

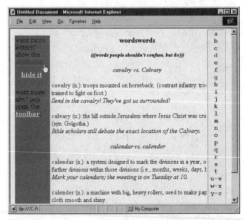

Figure 15.42 Here, we've hidden the toolbar again and are showing the layer called Alphabar. Notice the additional text in the left margin: that's yet another layer that has a link that will hide the Alphabar layer.

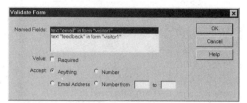

Figure 15.43 In the Validate Form dialog box you can restrict the input into text or text-area form fields.

Validate Form

Form validation is useful—you can have JavaScript validate a form before it's even sent to the form-handling script.

✔Tip

■ You must already have the completed form on your page, with all fields named, before you can apply this behavior.

Usage Example: You can require that certain fields be filled out, or require that data be in a certain format; for instance, a full e-mail address or only numbers instead of letters.

To add the Form Validation action:

1. In the Behaviors inspector, select a browser (3.0 + later).

2. In the Document window that contains the form, select the form (click on <form> in the tag selector).

3. In the Behaviors inspector, add the action Validate Form. The Validate Form dialog box will appear (**Figure 15.43**).

4. Dreamweaver may take a moment or two to detect all the named text form fields on the page, at which point their names will appear in the Named Fields list box.

5. Click on the name of the form field you want to validate.

6. To make the form field required, in which case the form will not be accepted unless this field is filled out, place a checkmark in the Required checkbox.

continues on next page

7. To restrict the content you'll accept, choose one of the following options:

- ◆ Number (content must be numbers)

- ◆ Number from *n* to *n* (range of numbers; type the range in the text boxes)

- ◆ E-mail address (text must be in the name@address.domain format)

8. Click on OK to close the Validate Form dialog box.

9. In the Behaviors inspector, make sure the onSubmit event is specified.

When users submit the form, they'll see a dialog box informing them if they failed to meet your validation standards (**Figure 15.44**).

✔ Tip

- ■ Before you unleash the form-validation script on your users, test it to make sure it does what you want it to.

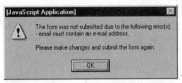

Figure 15.44 On my form, I required that the text in the e-mail field be in standard e-mail address format. If a user submits a form that doesn't conform to this validation requirement, they'll get a message telling them so.

The onBlur Event

The onBlur event is kind of confusing at best, but it makes a cute party trick. To "blur" a form field means that it "loses the focus" of its intent. To this end, you can mini-validate a single form field. Follow the instructions above, substituting the following variables:

In step 2, select a <text> or <textarea> tag as the object, instead of the <form> tag.

In step 9, use the onBlur event instead of the onSubmit event.

The easiest way to test out the onBlur event is to use numbers; in step 7, require a number between 1 and 10.

Now load the page in a browser, and try typing a number less than 1 or greater than 10 in the form field, and press Enter (Return). Your input will disappear. This doesn't work if you Tab out of the field, so it's only marginally useful.

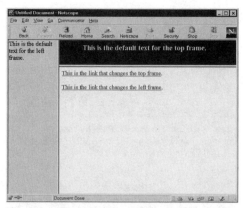

Figure 15.45 This is a mockup of a frames-based page that uses the Set Text of Frame behavior.

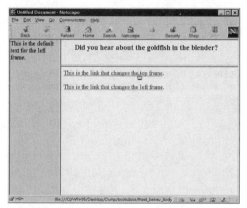

Figure 15.46 When the user clicks the link for the top frame, a simple text change occurs, and the background reverts to white.

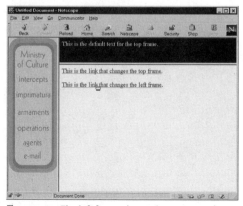

Figure 15.47 The left frame change is more complex, and includes a table, images, and links.

Set Text

Dreamweaver 3 offers a set of new behaviors that allow you to change the text or HTML in a frame, a layer, or a text field in a form. Any HTML content may be inserted dynamically, that is, after the page loads initially.

Usage Examples: When the user clicks on a link, selects an option from a menu, or mouses over a button, the new text appears.

Set Text of Frame

Normally, when you click on a link in a frame, a new page can appear in that frame or another frame. So what's the advantage of using a behavior? For one thing, you can specify a user event other than onClick. For another, the code for the new page is preloaded by the browser and therefore will appear faster than if the browser had to fetch a new page. The behavior is illustrated in **Figures 15.45–15.47**.

To set the text of a frame:

1. Create and save a frames-based page, as described in Chapter 11. Be sure to name each frame, or Dreamweaver will refer to them by arbitrary numbers.

2. In the Behaviors inspector, select a browser (3.0 + later).

3. In the Document window, select an object (a, body, img, select).

continues on next page

4. In the Behaviors inspector, add the action Set Text > Set Text of Frame. The Set Text of Frame dialog box will appear (**Figure 15.48**).

5. In the Set Text of Frame dialog box, you can edit the existing frame content, paste in text from another page, or write the page from scratch.

   To get the text of the current frame, click the Get Current HTML button. The text will appear in the New HTML text box, where you can edit it (**Figure 15.49**).

6. Otherwise, type or paste in the code.

7. Dreamweaver will entirely replace the code for the frame. If you want to preserve the current frame's background color, leave that box checked.

8. When you're finished, click on OK to close the Set Text of Frame dialog box.

9. In the Behaviors inspector, specify the event (onLoad, onClick, onMouseOver).

10. Preview your page in a browser and check to make sure your changes work properly.

Figure 15.48 Choose which frame you want to edit, and then supply the new text or HTML. The easiest way to do it is to paste it in.

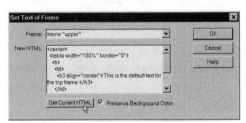

Figure 15.49 Here, I clicked on Get Current HTML for the "upper" frame; it includes the header formatting and the table.

SET TEXT

Figure 15.50 This is a layers-based page.

Figure 15.51 Mousing over the person layer pops up text and a link within a layer that wasn't even visible before.

Figure 15.52 Choose which layer you want to edit, and then supply the new text or HTML. The easiest way to do it is to paste it in.

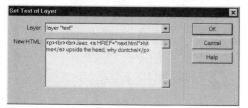

Figure 15.53 My new text for the layer includes a link.

Set Text of Layer

Setting the text and HTML of a layer allows you to make a layer useful by filling it with different things when different links are moused over or clicked. A layer can even be transparent and invisible on the page until this behavior acts on it (**Figures 15.50** and **15.51**).

To set the text of a layer:

1. Insert a layer on your page, as described in Chapter 14.

2. In the Behaviors inspector, select a browser (4.0 + later).

3. In the Document window, select an object (a, body, img, select).

4. In the Behaviors inspector, add the action Set Text > Set Text of Layer. The Set Text of Layer dialog box will appear (**Figure 15.52**).

5. In the New HTML text box, type or paste in the code for the new content (**Figure 15.53**). This can include image pathnames.

6. When you're finished, click on OK to close the Set Text of Layer dialog box.

7. In the Behaviors inspector, specify the event (onLoad, onClick, onMouseOver).

8. Preview your page in a browser and check to make sure your changes work properly.

Set Text of Text Field

You can use a text field in a form to display messages, almost like a frame within a page. You can also change a text field in an actual, working form when a user clicks on a link or a button. You can use a single-line (**Figure 15.54**) or multi-line (**Figure 55**) text field.

To set text field text:

1. Insert a text field and a form on your page, as described in Chapter 12.

2. In the Behaviors inspector, select a browser (3.0 + later).

3. In the Document window, select an object (*a*, *body*, *img*, *select*).

4. In the Behaviors inspector, add the action Set Text > Set Text of Text Field. The Set Text of Text Field dialog box will appear (**Figure 15.56**).

5. In the New Text text box, type or paste in the new text. This can include image pathnames.

6. When you're finished, click on OK to close the Set Text of Text Field dialog box.

7. In the Behaviors inspector, specify the event (onLoad, onClick, onMouseOver).

8. Preview your page in a browser and check to make sure your changes work properly.

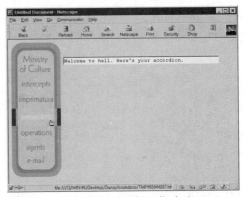

Figure 15.54 A single-line text box, displaying text during a mouseover.

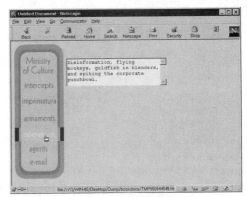

Figure 15.55 A multi-line text box, displaying text during a mouseover.

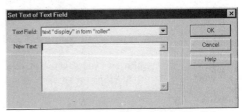

Figure 15.56 Type the text for the field in this dialog box.

Change Property

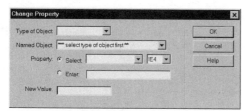

Figure 15.57 You can change several properties at once using the Change Property dialog box.

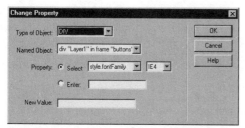

Figure 15.58 By selecting DIV, you can modify any named layer on the page, or a text block modified by a custom style. Modifiable properties include size, background color, and various style sheet attributes.

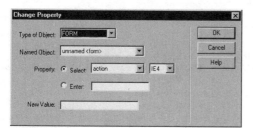

Figure 15.59 By selecting a form or a form field, you can change the functions of the buttons, the text fields, or the form itself.

This action has more variables than any other. You can have an event that's associated with one object change the properties of that object or a different object. See **Table 15.2** to find out the objects available to this Dreamweaver behavior, and their associated properties.

Usage Examples: Provide a drop-down menu from which the user can pick a layer background color. Change the dimensions or Z-index of a layer when the user clicks on a button image. Change the destination of a form if the user checks a particular checkbox.

To set up the Change Property behavior:

1. In the Behaviors inspector, select a browser (layer properties won't work in 3.0 or earlier browsers).

2. In the Document window that contains the layers, select an object (a, body, img, a form field, etc.).

3. In the Behaviors inspector, add the action Change Property. The Change Property dialog box will appear (**Figure 15.57**).

4. In the Change Property dialog box, choose the kind of object whose action you wish to change from the Type of Object drop-down menu (see **Table 15.2**) and **Figures 15.58** and **15.59**.

continues on next page

CHANGE PROPERTY

359

5. Dreamweaver may take a moment or two to detect all the named objects on the page, at which point their names (id="" or name="") will appear in the Named Object list box. Choose an object by selecting it from the list.

6. The properties you can change will be available from the Property drop-down menu (see **Table 15.2**). You may get additional properties by selecting a different browser from the Browser drop-down menu.

7. Repeat steps 4–7 for all the objects you want this behavior to affect.

8. Click on OK to close the Change Property dialog box.

9. In the Behaviors inspector, specify the event (onClick, onMouseOver, onBlur).

Table 5.2

Objects and Properties for Change Property action	
OBJECT AND TAG	**PROPERTIES**
Layer <div>, <span>, <layer>, <ilayer> (provided those tags have positioning and Z-index elements)	Position (top, left), Z-index, Clipping area, Background color, Background image (4.0 and later); Width and height (IE4 and later only)
Div <div>	Styles, including font family, font size, border width and color, background color and image, and text within the <div> tag (all IE4 and later only; use layer or span for NN4)
Span <span>	Styles, including font family, font size, border width and color, background color and image, and text within the <div> tag (all IE4 and later only; use layer or span for NN4)
Image <img>	Source (NN3, NN4, IE4, IE5)
Form <form>	Action (3.0+4.0 browsers)
Checkbox <input type=checkbox>	Status (checked/unchecked) (3.0+later)
Radio button <input type=radio>	Status (checked/unchecked) (3.0+later)
Text box <input type=text>	Value (will appear in text box) (3.0+later)
Text field <textarea>	Value (will appear in text field) (3.0+later)
Password text box <input type=password>	Value (will appear in text box) (3.0+later)
Menu or List <select>	selectedIndex (changes selection within menu, using index numbers for each <option> (3.0 + later)

CHANGE PROPERTY

360

✔ Tips

- In order to change an object's properties with this behavior, you must name the object. You can name any object by selecting it and typing a name for it in the Properties inspector. The Name text box is always at the top and left of the Properties inspector.

- You can also change additional properties by clicking on the Enter radio button and typing the property in the text box. There are too many variables for me to describe them all.

- If the object you're working with is a form field, you can provide a new value for the changed form field by typing it in the New Value text box. You can also type new values for layer attributes, etc. A little source-viewing should help you find the right format for things like stylesheet attributes.

CHANGE PROPERTY

Drag Layer

You can make layers on your page draggable by applying the Drag Layer action to the body of the page.

Usage Examples: Create a toy such as a paper doll, a jigsaw puzzle in which the pieces snap into place, a design in which users must drag layers in order to read them, or a slide control.

✔ Tip

■ Because each layer has its own coordinates, you need to add this behavior once for each layer you want to make draggable.

To add the Drag Layer action:

1. In the Behaviors inspector, select 4.0 and later Browsers.

2. In the Document window's tag selector, click <body> to select the entire page.

3. In the Behaviors inspector, add the action Drag Layer. The Drag Layer dialog box will appear (**Figure 15.60**).

4. From the Layer drop-down menu, select the layer you want to make draggable.

5. To allow the user to drag the layer anywhere in the window, leave the Unconstrained option selected.

   or

   To restrict movement of the layer within a specific area (**Figure 15.61**), select Constrained. A series of text boxes will appear (**Figure 15.62**).

6. The constrained movement values are relative to the top-left corner of the layer's original position and are in pixels.

   ◆ To restrict movement within a rectangular region, type values in all four text boxes.

   ◆ To restrict movement within a square, type the same value in all four text boxes.

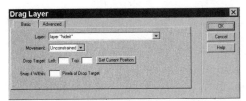

Figure 15.60 The Drag Layer dialog box allows you to make a layer draggable and to specify how and where a user can drag a layer.

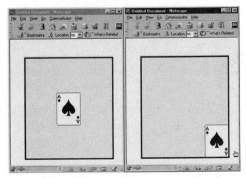

Figure 15.61 On this page, the user cannot drag the layer outside the box, which is another layer. I set a constrained area of 100x100x100x100.

Figure 15.62 When you select the Constrained option, text boxes appear that allow you to set a draggable area based on the layer's original top-left coordinates.

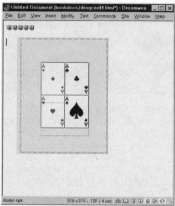

Figure 15.63 This is where I'd like the pieces to end up at the end of the puzzle. I put all the layers in place before I start setting up the Drag Layer behaviors, so I can use the Get Current Position feature to set drop targets.

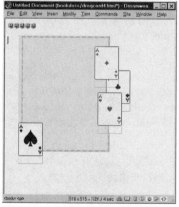

Figure 15.64 After I'm done setting up the behaviors, I put the layers where I'd like them to go when the page loads.

♦ To allow only vertical movement, type 0 in the Left and Right text boxes and a value in the Up and Down text boxes.

♦ To allow only horizontal movement, type 0 in the Up and Down text boxes and a value in the Left and Right text boxes.

7. If you would like the user to drag the layer to a particular spot, you must declare a drop target. The drop target coordinates are applied to the top-left corner of the layer and are measured from the left and top of the window.

To declare a drop target, type a pixel value in the Top and Left text boxes. To set the layer's current position as the drop target, click the Get Current Position button, and Dreamweaver will fill in those text boxes.

8. The layer can snap to the drop target if the user lets go of the mouse button when the top-left corner of the layer comes within a certain number of pixels of the drop target. Type a number of pixels in the Snap if Within text box, or clear this field if you don't want to snap to the drop target.

9. To modify only these options, click OK to return to the Document window. Otherwise, keep reading.

The following section assumes you have read the preceding one, *To add the Drag Layer action*. These instructions begin where the last set left off, in the Drag Layer dialog box.

✔ Tip

■ The easiest way to set the options for a puzzle-type game is to begin with all the pieces in their final resting places (**Figure 15.63**). Use the Get Current Position option to set the drop target for the layer, and then when you're done with the behavior, move the layer to its starting position on the page (**Figure 15.64**).

DRAG LAYER

To set more Drag Layer options:

1. To select further options, click on Advanced. The second panel of the Drag Layer dialog box will appear (**Figure 15.65**).

2. To allow the user to drag the layer by clicking on any part of it, set the Drag Handle option to Entire Layer.

   or

   To allow the user to drag the layer only if they click on a specific part of the layer (part of an image such as a button or a "window" title bar), select Area Within Layer from the Drag Handle drop-down menu. A series of text boxes will appear.

3. Type the area of the drag handle, in pixels, in the text boxes. This area will be a rectangle, measured from the top and left of the layer.

4. To change the Z-index of the layer so that it's on top while the user drags it, check the Bring Layer to Front checkbox.

   ◆ To leave the layer on top after dragging, select the Leave on Top option from the drop-down menu.

   ◆ To restore the layer's original Z-index after the user drops it, select Restore Z-Index from the drop-down menu.

5. To have the user's drag-and-drop actions call a JavaScript, see the *Calling Scripts by Dragging* sidebar.

6. When you're all set, click on OK to return to the Document window. Otherwise, keep reading.

✔ Tip

■ You must repeat these steps for each layer that you wish to make draggable.

Figure 15.65 The second panel allows you to set selection handles for your layers; to specify the Z-index of the layer while dragging and after dropping; and call a JavaScript based on the user's drag-and-drop actions.

Calling Scripts by Dragging

You can use the Drag Layer behavior can be used to call a JavaScript that performs additional actions when the layer is dragged to a certain location. This script would use the layer coordinates provided by the values of MM_UPDOWN, MM_LEFTRIGHT, or MM_SNAPPED.

For example, the script could be called when the value of MM_SNAPPED is true, or, for multiple layers, when a certain number of the layers reach a MM_SNAPPED value of true.

Or, for a slide control, the location of the dragged layer could determine speaker volume, background color, or font size.

Another option would be for the coordinates of a dragged layer to appear in form fields displayed on the page.

To call a JavaScript using this behavior, go to the second panel of the Drag Layer dialog box (**Figure 15.65**). Type the name of a JavaScript function in the Call JavaScript text box.

To call a script when the layer is dropped, type the name of a JavaScript function (such as, youWin()) in the When Dropped: Call JavaScript text box. Check the Only if Snapped checkbox if you want this script activated only if the layer has snapped to the drop target.

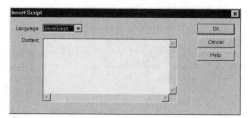

Figure 15.66 You can type a little script in the Insert Script dialog box.

Figure 15.67 The Properties inspector, displaying Script properties.

Adding New Scripts and Behaviors

If you're a veteran JavaScripter, and you want to set up your own scripts in Dreamweaver, you're more than welcome to. You can type or paste in a script using the Insert Script object, or you can set up your own actions to use in Dreamweaver behaviors.

To type in a script:

1. On the Objects palette, click on the Insert Script button. Or, from the Document window menu bar, select Insert > Script. The Insert Script dialog box will appear (**Figure 15.66**).

2. Type your script in the Insert Script dialog box, and click on OK. The Insert Script dialog box will close, and the Script icon will appear in the Document window.

3. Select the Script marker, if it isn't already selected, and display the Properties inspector, if necessary (**Figure 15.67**).

4. Select the type of script (JavaScript or VBScript) from the Language drop-down menu. If your script is in another scripting language, type it in the text box.

You can also insert a script from a file on your hard drive.

To insert a script from a text file:

1. Follow steps 1–3, above, but leave the Insert Script dialog box blank.

2. In the Properties inspector, type the source of your script in the Source text box, or click on the folder icon to browse your hard drive for the file.

You can type or edit longer scripts in the Script Properties dialog box.

To edit a script:

1. View the script properties in the Properties inspector.

2. Click on Edit. The Script Properties dialog box will appear (**Figure 15.68**).

   When you're finished typing or editing your script, click on OK to return to the Document window.

You can add actions to the Behaviors inspector that were written by other Dreamweaver developers. See the sidebar, this page, to find out how to add your own behaviors.

To add third-party actions:

1. In the Behaviors inspector, click on the Add Action button, and select Get More Behaviors. Dreamweaver will launch your browser and open the Dreamweaver Exchange.

2. Download the behavior that interests you, and unzip it.

3. Quit Dreamweaver.

4. Drop the new file into the Actions folder:

   ◆ On the PC: C:\Program Files\
   Macromedia\Dreamweaver\
   Configuration\Behaviors\Actions

   ◆ On the Mac: file:///Dreamweaver/
   Configuration/Behaviors/Actions

5. Launch Dreamweaver. The action will appear on the Add Action menu in the Behaviors inspector.

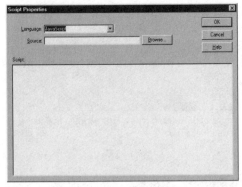

Figure 15.68 The Script Properties dialog box is like a script-editing window, except that it's a dialog box. In other words, you can't switch back and forth between the Script Properties dialog box and, say, the HTML inspector.

Adding Your Own Actions

If you write JavaScript, you can write your own actions and add them to the Behaviors inspector. However, this isn't quite as easy as just writing the HTML and JS files (as if that weren't hard enough!) and dropping them into the Actions folder. You need to work with the particular flavor of JavaScript that Dreamweaver uses.

To find out how to add the code that will make your JavaScript work with Dreamweaver and show up in the Behaviors inspector, consult the Extending Dreamweaver help files (Help > Extending Dreamweaver). These files include a sample behavior to get you started.

Figure 15.69 Type the JavaScript function, or the script itself, in the text box.

✔ Tip

■ Macromedia offers a script repository of behaviors written by Macromedia developers and Dreamweaver users. To get behaviors from the Web, click on the Add Action button in the Behaviors inspector, and select Get More Behaviors.

To Call a Script

Something tells me that if you can write JavaScript, you can tell the script when to happen. Nevertheless, Dreamweaver covers all the bases with the Call JavaScript behavior.

To add the Call JavaScript behavior to the page:

1. In the Behaviors inspector, select the browser you want to target.

2. In the Document window, select the object associated with the event.

3. Click the Add Action button, and from the pop-up menu, select Call JavaScript. The Call JavaScript dialog box will appear (**Figure 15.69**).

4. Type the name of a function, or a string of JavaScript, in the text box.

5. Click on OK to return to the Document window.

6. In the Behaviors inspector, specify the user event that you want to trigger the action.

Saves you a few lines of coding, anyway.

DRAWING TIMELINES

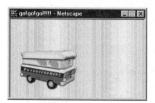

Figure 16.1
The magic bus at futurefarmers.com uses a Timeline in a JavaScript pop-up window.

Figure 16.2
It moves!

Figure 16.3 It keeps moving until it's off the screen, and then it starts over.

Figure 16.4 One click opens a new little window with a new Timeline.

Timelines are a way to add animation to a Web page using Dynamic HTML. As the people at Macromedia are so proud of saying, you don't need to write any code, and Timelines use no ActiveX, Java, or plug-ins.

Timelines use JavaScript to control layers (**Figures 16.1–16.4**). A layer can move, resize, appear, or disappear—and what happens when is controlled by a sequence of frames.

These frames are not the same as the frames I discussed in Chapter 11. These are *animation frames*. Just like the frames of footage in a movie, each frame can be slightly different from the last, which creates the illusion of movement over time on a 2-D surface. In this case, of course, the 2-D surface is a Web page projected on a computer screen rather than a film projected on a movie screen.

✔ Tips

- Because Timelines rely on layers in order to work their magic, they can only be viewed in 4.0 and later browsers.

- If you need information on layers, refer to Chapter 14. For information about Behaviors, turn to Chapter 15.

What Timelines Can Do

Timelines can incorporate three types of objects: layers, images, and Behaviors.

Layer properties that a Timeline can change include the following:

◆ **Moving** the layer's X+Y coordinates (position on the page or within the parent layer) (**Figure 16.5**).

◆ Changing **layer visibility**. You can switch between the three optional states: visible, hidden, or default (**Figure 16.6**).

◆ Changing the **stacking order,** or **Z-index** (**Figure 16.7**).

◆ Adjusting **layer dimensions** (**Figure 16.8**).

✔ Tip

■ Changes to a layer's dimensions are not supported by Navigator 4.

The only **Image property** that a Timeline can change directly is the image's source. This way, you can perform image rollovers during a Timeline without using additional JavaScript.

Timelines can also call a behavior from a particular frame. You can also use a behavior to start, stop, or skip to a particular frame within a Timeline.

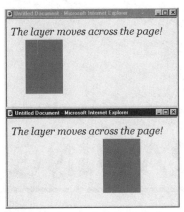

Figure 16.5 The Timeline moves the layer from left to right.

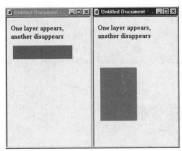

Figure 16.6 The Timeline shows one layer and hides another.

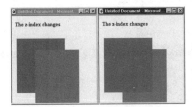

Figure 16.7 The Timeline changes the Z-index of the layers.

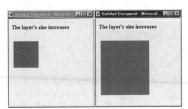

Figure 16.8 The Timeline increases the size of the layer.

The Timelines Inspector

The Timelines inspector (**Figure 16.9**) is the tool you use to create and modify Timelines in Dreamweaver.

To view the Timelines inspector:

◆ From the Document window menu bar, select Window > Timelines.

or

On the Launcher or the Launcher bar, click on the Timeline button.

or

Press F9.

In any case, the Timelines inspector will appear.

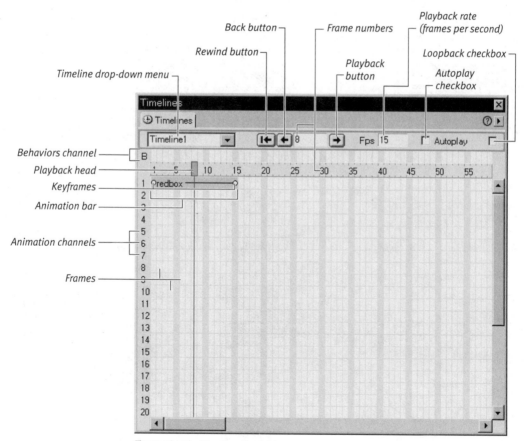

Figure 16.9 The Timelines inspector

Dissecting the Timelines Inspector

Each part of the Timelines inspector controls a different aspect of the Timelines on the page. Some of these elements won't really make much cognitive sense until you see them in operation, but you can use this page as a reference for what things do. Let's start at the top (**Figure 16.10**).

If you include more than one Timeline on a page, you can switch between Timelines by choosing the **Timeline** from the **Timeline drop-down menu**.

You can play Timelines in the Document window using the Timelines inspector's playback controls. The **Rewind button** rewinds the Timeline back to the beginning. The **Back button** rewinds one frame at a time; hold it down to play the Timeline backwards. The **Playback button** advances one frame at a time; hold it down to play the entire Timeline. The current frame is indicated in the **Frame number** text box.

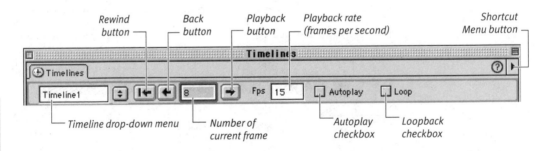

Figure 16.10 The top bar on the Timelines inspector

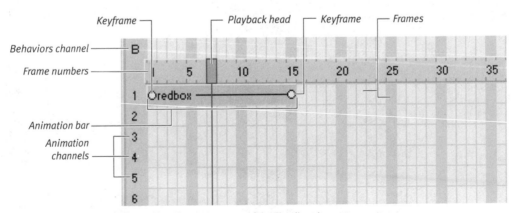

Figure 16.11 The content area of the Timelines inspector

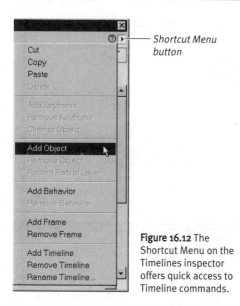

Shortcut Menu button

Figure 16.12 The Shortcut Menu on the Timelines inspector offers quick access to Timeline commands.

The **playback rate** is in frames per second (fps). The default is 15 fps; you can set it higher or lower depending on your content.

You can add Behaviors that will control how the document plays. The **Autoplay checkbox** adds a behavior that will make the Timeline start as soon as the page finishes loading. The **Loopback checkbox** adds a behavior that will make the Timeline play continuously while the page is in the browser.

Now we move to the part of the Timelines inspector that controls the content (**Figure 16.11**).

Use the **Behaviors channel** to add Behaviors that will be called from a certain frame in the Timeline.

Each numbered column in the Timeline inspector is a frame. Each frame is numbered. The **playback head** (the red bar) shows the advance of the playback. As the playback head passes over each frame, the frame number will appear next to the Playback button.

Each numbered row in the Timeline inspector is an **animation channel**. Different objects often occupy different animation channels.

When an object is added to a Timeline, the Timeline inspector displays an animation bar in its assigned animation channel. The little bullets at the beginning and end of the **animation bar** are **keyframes**. You can add other keyframes to an animation bar to add actions to the Timeline.

✔ Tip

■ In **Figures 16.10** and **16.12**, at the right side of the Timelines inspector, you can see a Shortcut Menu button. This button pops up a menu of commands (**Figure 16.12**) you can use when editing a Timeline.

DISSECTING THE TIMELINES INSPECTOR

Adding a Layer to a Timeline

You create a Timeline by adding an object to it. Once an object is added, Dreamweaver automatically adds the Timeline code to the page.

To add a layer to a Timeline:

1. Select the layer in the Document window (**Figure 16.13**).

2. From the Document window menu bar, select Modify > Add Object to Timeline.

   or

   Right-click (hold down the mouse button on a Mac) on the object's animation bar in the Timelines inspector, and select Add Object from the pop-up menu.

A new animation bar will appear in the Timelines inspector (**Figure 16.14**).

✔ Tips

■ The only objects you can add to a Timeline are layers and images. If you want other stuff to move or hide in a Timeline, create a layer and insert objects in it.

■ Before you add a layer or image to a Timeline, be sure that you name it properly in the Properties inspector. If you rename a layer or image after you add it to a Timeline, it may be deleted from the Timeline and you'll have to add it again.

■ To find out how to add images and Behaviors to a Timeline, see *To add an image to a Timeline* and *To add a behavior to a Timeline frame*.

■ You can also drag an object onto the Timeline. Click on the object and drag it to the exact location (channel and frame) where you want it to appear (**Figure 16.15**).

Figure 16.13 Select the layer in the Document window. Notice that the Timelines inspector doesn't have any objects in it yet.

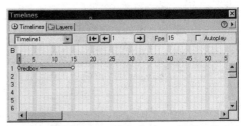

Figure 16.14 When you add the layer to the Timeline, an animation bar appears in the first available animation channel.

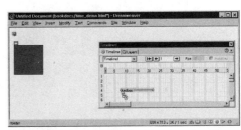

Figure 16.15 Dragging and dropping a layer into the Timelines inspector—it lands right where you drop it.

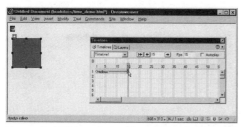

Figure 16.16 Click on the keyframe bullet at the end of the layer's animation bar to select that frame as well as the layer.

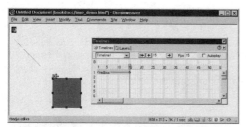

Figure 16.17 With the end keyframe selected, drag the layer to its new location and let go. The Timelines inspector will record the new position and draw a line from position 1 to position 2.

Setting the Playback Rate

The default playback rate for Dreamweaver Timelines is 15 frames per second. Macromedia advises not to set this rate much faster; the 15 fps rate is based on optimal performance on the average machine. Setting a faster playback rate might not actually make the animation go faster; while it might do so on your local machine, it's also the case that all the images and layers that you're playing with are stored in your memory cache. You can, however, set a lower rate for slower speeds.

Timeline Actions

Timeline actions were briefly described in *What Timelines Can Do* earlier in this chapter. In this section, I'm going to go over each action, step by step, starting with moving layers. As I go through each action a layer can perform, I'll describe the various modifications you can make to a Timeline.

The easiest way to start learning Timelines is to move a layer on the page.

To move a layer using a Timeline:

1. Add the layer to the Timeline.

2. In the Timelines inspector, click on the keyframe bullet at the end of the layer's animation bar (**Figure 16.16**). The playback head (the red bar) will move to that frame.

   The layer will be selected in the Document window automatically.

3. Click on the layer's selection handle and drag it to the position on the page where you want it to end up.

You'll see a line drawn from the layer's old position to its new position (**Figure 16.17**). The line connects the top-left corners of the layer in each position. This is the path that the Timeline will follow.

✔ Tip

- Notice in this section that I've stacked the Layers palette with the Timelines palette. I can flip back and forth between them easily and save desktop space. To move a palette onto or off of another one, click on its tab and drag it onto or away from the other.

TIMELINE ACTIONS

You can also track the movement of a layer while dragging it. You should start out with a layer that isn't in the Timeline yet.

To record a layer's path:

1. Select the layer you want to drag by clicking on its selection handle, and move it to its starting position.

2. From the Document window menu bar, select Modify > Timeline > Record Path of Layer.

3. Drag the layer by the selection handle wherever you want it to go. Loop-de-loops are allowed (**Figure 16.18**).

4. When you let go of the mouse button, the layer's path will be translated into an animation channel (**Figure 16.19**).

You can watch the layer move by playing back the Timeline.

To play back a Timeline:

1. In the Timelines inspector, click on the Rewind button [⏮] to move the playback head back to the beginning of the Timeline.

2. Move the Timelines inspector out of the way in the Document window.

3. In the Timelines inspector, click on and hold down the Play button [▶].

You'll see the layer move across the page (**Figure 16.20**).

✔ Tip

■ Recording the path of a layer adds it to the Timeline. If you have a layer and an animation channel selected when you record a path, you'll get this annoying error message (**Figure 16.21**). Basically, you can record a path for a layer not yet in the Timeline, or you can click just after the end of the layer's existing animation path and add the object again.

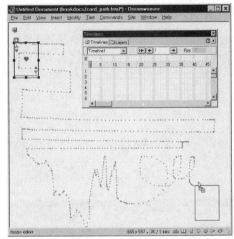

Figure 16.18 Using the Record Path of Layer option, I can drag a layer all over the place and the Timeline will follow. The little dots represent points the top-left corner of the layer has graced.

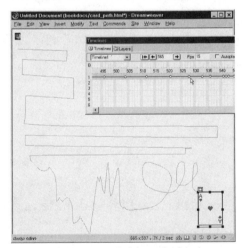

Figure 16.19 After I recorded the path of the layer, the layer appeared as an object in the Timelines inspector—with over 500 frames.

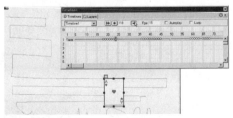

Figure 16.20 The Timeline in mid-play.

TIMELINE ACTIONS

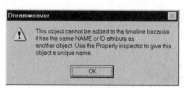

Figure 16.21 This error message may appear while you're trying to record the path of a layer—rename your object or click at the end of the current channel before recording.

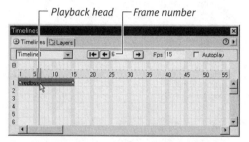

Figure 16.22 Click at the point on the animation bar where you want to add the new keyframe. The playback head will move, and the number of the frame will be indicated in the frame number text box.

Figure 16.23 Select Add Keyframe from the pop-up menu.

Figure 16.24 A keyframe bullet will appear on the animation bar.

About Keyframes

The Timeline inspector tracks the movement of a layer from one point to another frame by frame, and it paces the movement of an object so that the frame-to-frame transitions are smooth.

If there are only two points in a Timeline, the line is automatically straight. You can add a third point to a Timeline to make a layer move in an arc, or you can add multiple points to make it move wherever you want.

You do this by adding keyframes. A *keyframe* is a point on a Timeline where something happens. Each animation bar in a Timeline automatically has two keyframes: the beginning frame and the end frame.

To add a keyframe:

1. In the Timelines inspector, move the pointer to the place on the animation bar where you want the new action to happen, and click on that point (**Figure 16.22**). The playback head will automatically move to the new frame.

2. From the Document window menu bar, select Modify > Timeline > Add Keyframe.

   or

   Right-click (hold down the mouse button on a Mac) on the object's animation bar in the Timelines inspector, and select Add Keyframe from the pop-up menu that appears (**Figure 16.23**).

   or

   Press Shift + F9.

The Timelines inspector will add a keyframe bullet to the animation bar (**Figure 16.24**).

To add a new layer position to a keyframe:

1. In the Timelines inspector, click on the new keyframe. The layer will become selected automatically (**Figure 16.25**).

2. Move the layer to the position on the page where you want it to be when that keyframe is played (**Figure 16.26**).

The line drawn between the beginning position on the page and the end position on the page will now arc to fit the third point into the movement line (**Figure 16.27**).

✔ Tip

■ Play back the Timeline now to see how this movement looks.

Now you know how to change a layer's position, play back a Timeline, and add keyframes (and therefore, additional actions) to a Timeline. Let's look at some of the other things Timelines can do.

✔ Tip

■ How do you remove movement from a layer? What if you make a layer move and then want it not to do so? First, click on the frame in which the layer is where it is supposed to be. Then, open the Properties inspector and take note of the L(eft) and T(op) measurements. In the Timelines inspector, move to the keyframe where the movement changes. In the Properties inspector, type the numbers you jotted down in the L and T text boxes. Repeat for any additional keyframes where the layer's position attributes have changed.

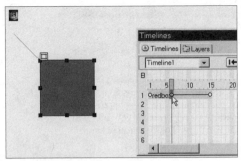

Figure 16.25 Select the keyframe, and the layer will automatically become selected. If for some reason it doesn't become selected, click on the layer's selection handle.

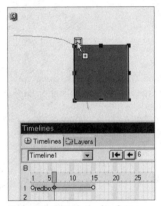

Figure 16.26 With the keyframe selected in the Timelines inspector, move the layer to its new location.

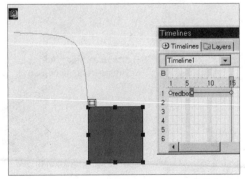

Figure 16.27 I fast forwarded to near the end of the Timeline so you could see the arc drawn by Dreamweaver between the three keyframes.

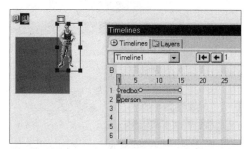

Figure 16.28 First, I add the new layer to the Timeline.

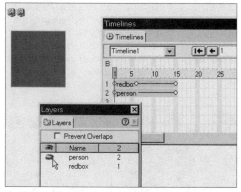

Figure 16.29 Then, I set its initial visibility to hidden on the first keyframe.

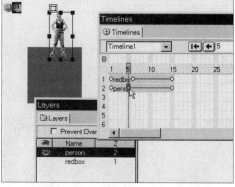

Figure 16.30 Finally, I added a new keyframe and set the layer's visibility to visible on the fifth keyframe. When the Timeline plays, the second layer will appear while the first layer moves.

Showing and Hiding Layers

You can show or hide a layer in a Timeline by changing its visibility to visible, hidden, or default.

To show or hide a layer during a Timeline:

1. If the layer is not already added to the Timeline, add the layer to the Timeline.

2. Click on the first keyframe on the layer's animation bar (**Figure 16.28**).

3. Using the Layers inspector or the Properties inspector, set the layer's visibility to the state you want it to be in when the Timeline begins playing (**Figure 16.29**).

4. On the layer's animation bar, add the keyframe where you want the visibility change to occur.

5. With the proper keyframe selected, change the visibility of the layer (**Figure 16.30**).

6. If you want the layer to change visibility again at the end of the Timeline, click on the keyframe at the end of the layer's animation bar, and change the layer's visibility.

To change the location of a keyframe:

1. In the Timelines inspector, click on the keyframe you want to move.

2. Hold down the mouse button and drag the keyframe bullet to a different frame.

3. Let go of the mouse button.

Voilà! The keyframe has moved.

✔ Tip

■ Images that are in hidden layers are automatically downloaded with the page. This is a good way to pre-load images for swapping image source. Or skip the source swapping altogether and just show or hide the layers that the new images are in.

Changing the Z-index

As you know, a layer's Z-index is what makes layers so layer-like. You can change the Z-index, or stacking order, of layers during a Timeline (**Figure 16.31**).

✔ Tips

■ Make sure all the layers have the Z-index you want them to have at their beginning keyframe(s) in the Timeline (**Figure 16.31**).

■ Z-index numbers affect the overlap of two or more layers; you can't make a layer hide under an image that isn't in a layer.

To change the Z-index of a layer during a Timeline:

1. In the Timelines inspector, add any keyframes you need to the layer's animation bar.

2. Click on the keyframe that marks the point at which the Z-index will change. The layer will be selected automatically.

3. Using the Layers inspector or the Properties inspector, change the Z-index number of the layer (**Figure 16.32**).

4. Play back the Timeline to watch the layer move over or under another layer on the page (**Figure 16.33**).

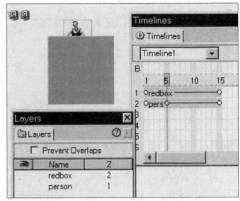

Figure 16.31 In this variant on the "appearing person and moving square" Timeline, I took out the movement of the box, but in the fifth frame, the person still appears. I set the Z-index in the first frame so that the box overlaps the person.

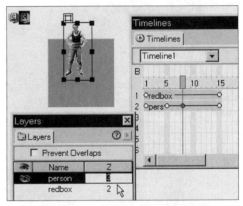

Figure 16.32 At frame 8, I added a keyframe and changed the Z-index of the person layer so that it would surface over the top square.

Figure 16.33 Three frames from a Timeline. In frame 1, the square is visible. In frame 5, the person appears, and the box is stacked on top of the person. In frame 8, the person's Z-index changes so that it's on top of the square.

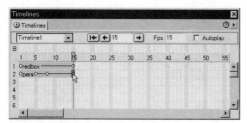

Figure 16.34 Click on the end keyframe and drag it to a new location.

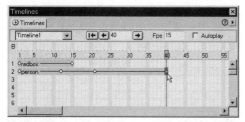

Figure 16.35 I lengthened the animation bar I selected in **Figure 16.34**. Notice how the keyframes in the middle of the animation bar are spaced out over the new length of the animation bar.

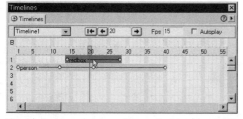

Figure 16.36 I moved the red box animation bar. It will both start and end later in the Timeline now.

Changing the Timing

You can change the length and duration of an animation bar if you want an action to start sooner or end later within the Timeline.

To move the beginning or end of an animation bar:

1. In the Timelines inspector, click on the beginning or ending keyframe on the layer's animation bar (**Figure 16.34**).

2. Drag the keyframe to a new frame number within the animation channel (**Figure 16.35**). You may notice the other elements in the Timeline moving around as you drag the keyframe.

3. Play the Timeline to see how it looks.

4. Repeat steps 1 and 2 as needed.

Longer Timelines allow for more actions and more gradual movement.

✔ Tips

- If you drag the end keyframe to lengthen the Timeline, any keyframes within the Timeline will be spaced out in proportion to their original position, to preserve the gradual arc of the Timeline (**Figure 16.35**).

- You can move an entire animation bar. Click on the middle of the bar (not on a keyframe) to select the whole thing, and drag it to a new location (**Figure 16.36**).

- See *To change the location of a keyframe* earlier in the chapter to find out how to move an individual keyframe.

Changing Layer Dimensions

Besides changing the visibility and Z-index of a layer, you can also use a Timeline to change the dimensions of the layer.

✔ Tips

- Layer size changes only work in Internet Explorer 4 and later, and not in Navigator 4.

- If you want to make a layer shrink in size, remember to change the layer's overflow setting to *hidden* or *scroll* in the Properties inspector; otherwise, the shrinking won't have any effect.

To change the dimensions of a layer using a Timeline:

1. In the Timelines inspector, click on the keyframe where you want the size change to occur. The layer will become selected automatically (**Figure 16.37**).

2. Change the size of the layer by dragging its handles, or by changing the W(idth) and H(eight) settings in the Properties inspector (**Figure 16.38**).

3. Play back the Timeline to see how it affects the size change.

Because the Timeline code makes layer properties change gradually rather than abruptly, the size change will begin a few frames before the set keyframe (**Figure 16.39**).

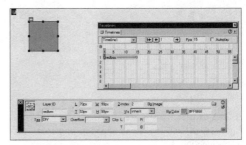

Figure 16.37 I added the layer to the Timeline.

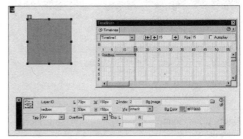

Figure 16.38 I selected the end keyframe and changed the size of the layer. If I click on each individual frame on the animation bar, the Properties inspector will display what size the layer will be in each succeeding frame leading up to the end frame's dimensions.

Figure 16.39 Three windows showing the progression in size from frame 1 to frame 8 to frame 15. I set two sizes: one in frame 1, and one in frame 15. With Dreamweaver Timelines, these changes happen gradually; for an abrupt change, make the size change happen in two adjacent frames.

CHANGING LAYER DIMENSIONS

Figure 16.40 Here I am in the Document window. I've just added the image of the person—this time independent of any layers—to the Timeline.

Adding an Image to a Timeline

You can also add an image to a Timeline, although the only available action for images that are not in layers is swap source.

To add an image to a Timeline:

1. View the Timelines inspector.

2. Select the image in the Document window.

3. From the Document window menu bar, select Modify > Add Object to Timeline.

   or

   Right-click (Ctrl+click or click and hold down the mouse button on a Mac) on the object's animation bar in the Timelines inspector, and select Add Object from the pop-up menu that appears.

A new animation bar will appear in the Timelines inspector (**Figure 16.40**).

✔ Tip

■ One way to pre-load images for source swapping is to place them in a hidden layer on the page. Another is to use the Preload Images Behavior described in Chapter 15.

Changing an image source with a Timeline is similar to using the Swap Image Behavior to create image rollovers, only the rollover will occur as time elapses rather than when triggered by a user event.

To change an image source using a Timeline:

1. Name the image using the Properties inspector.

2. Add the image to the Timeline.

3. Add any keyframes you need to the image's animation bar (**Figure 16.41**).

4. Click on the keyframe you want to use to change the image's source.

5. In the Properties inspector, change the source of the image to the source of the new image (**Figure 16.42**).

6. To make the image stay in its second state for the rest of the Timeline, select the end keyframe and set the source to be that of Image 2.

   or

   To make the image change back to its original state, add two keyframes: the first should be the end-stop for the source for Image 2, and the second should be the resetting of the source for Image 1.

7. Play back the Timeline to watch the effect (**Figure 16.43**).

✔ Tip

- If you use Autoplay with a Timeline, and the image changes source on the end keyframe, the image will only roll over for an instant to the new source. You can extend the end of the image's Timeline if you want to use Autoplay with this action. See *Making Timelines Go,* later in this chapter.

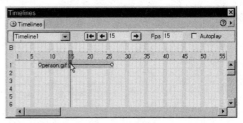

Figure 16.41 I added a keyframe to the image's animation bar; that's the point at which the source will change.

Figure 16.42 The two images side by side for comparison. With the keyframe selected, change the source in the Properties inspector. The image, which I selected with the mouse, shows the rectangular borders of the transparent image.

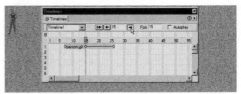

Figure 16.43 When the Timeline plays the keyframe, the source changes to the second image.

Behaviors channel　　Frame 20

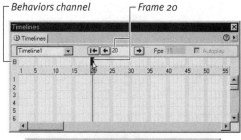

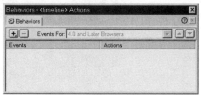

Figure 16.44 I double-clicked on the intersection of the Behaviors channel and frame 20, and the Behaviors inspector appeared. It's empty until you add an action.

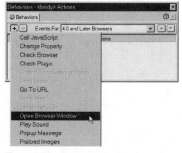

Figure 16.45 On the Behaviors inspector, click on the Add Action button ⊞, and choose an action from the pop-up menu.

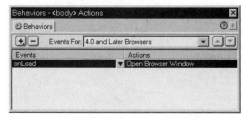

Figure 16.46 I added the Open Browser Window action to frame 20 of the Timeline; when the Timeline is played, the window will launch on frame 20. The event will be added automatically after you finish selecting the action.

Adding a Behavior to a Timeline

All the clever Behaviors I discussed in Chapter 15 can be added to a Timeline. For instance, you can make the Timeline execute an animation and then load a new page; you can play a sound at a certain frame in a Timeline; or you can use a Timeline to start playing a Shockwave movie at a certain frame.

To add a behavior to a Timeline frame:

1. In the Timelines inspector, click on the frame that will launch the behavior, to move the playback head to it.

2. Double-click on the frame number within the Behaviors channel (**Figure 16.44**). The Behaviors inspector will appear.

   The browser (4.0 and later browsers) will be preset.

3. In the Actions area of the Behaviors inspector, click on the Add Action button ⊞ to pop up the menu of available actions (**Figure 16.45**).

4. Choose the action you want to add. The associated dialog box will appear.

5. Fill out the dialog box and click on OK. The name of the action will appear in the Actions list box (**Figure 16.46**). The event, onFrameNumber, will be added to the Behaviors inspector automatically.

The behavior will be added to the Timeline. You'll see a little marker at that particular frame in the Behaviors channel.

✔ Tips

- For details about individual JavaScript Behaviors in Dreamweaver, see Chapter 15.

- Add a behavior to a frame by moving the playback head to that frame and selecting Modify > Add Behavior to Timeline from the Document window menu bar.

ADDING A BEHAVIOR TO A TIMELINE

385

Making Timelines Go

Timelines won't start playing in a browser unless another piece of JavaScript tells them to. There are two ways you can make a Timeline start playing, both of which use JavaScript Behaviors.

One way is to make the Timeline play automatically when the page is finished loading. The other way is to use a behavior, so that a user event such as a click or a mouseover triggers the Timeline.

The Autoplay behavior is an onLoad behavior; once the page loads, the animation will begin.

To make a Timeline play automatically:

◆ In the Behaviors inspector, place a checkmark in the Autoplay checkbox. A dialog box will appear (**Figure 16.47**) letting you know that Dreamweaver will add in the Autoplay code.

Simple, yes?

Figure 16.47 When you check the Autoplay checkbox, a dialog box will appear informing you that it's going to add the Autoplay behavior. Once you get the point, you can make this dialog box go away by checking the Don't show me this message again checkbox.

Behavior Modification

What sort of Behaviors could you add to a Timeline? The Timeline itself offers actions similar to Show/Hide Layer and Rollover Image. Here are some ideas to get you started.

◆ **Set Text of Layer**, **Set Text of Status Bar**, **Set Text of Text Field**, **Popup Message**: The user sees a message when a certain frame in the Timeline passes.

◆ **Open Browser Window**, **Popup Message**: During or at the end of the Timeline, a window or dialog box opens.

◆ **Drag Layer**: An animation plays in the Timeline, and after it's over, all the layers become draggable.

◆ **Play Sound**: On a certain frame, a sound plays. For example, when the mouse hits the cat in the head with a hammer, the user hears "Doink!"

◆ **Check Browser**: When the page loads (onLoad), the user is sent to a page with a Timeline if the browser is 4.0 or later, and to a page without the Timeline if the browser is 3.0 or earlier. (It would be a nice idea to detect the browser with a Timeline frame, but 3.0 browsers may or may not play the Timeline properly. If you want to try this, you should test it in the browsers you're targeting.)

Figure 16.48 I selected the link called Play It and added the Play Timeline action.

Figure 16.49 I chose Timeline > Play Timeline from the Add Action menu, and now I can select my Timeline in the Play Timeline dialog box.

Figure 16.50
After you select the Play Timeline (or other) action, specify the user event by choosing it from the drop-down list.

You can also make a behavior call a Timeline; when the user clicks on or mouses over a link or image, the Timeline will play.

To make a behavior play a Timeline:

1. In the Document window, click on the object you want to use to make the Timeline play (a, img, form button).

2. In the Behaviors inspector, select 4.0 and later Browsers from the browser drop-down menu.

3. In the Actions area of the Behaviors inspector, click on the Add Action button 🔢.

4. From the pop-up menu that appears (**Figure 16.48**), select Timeline > Play Timeline. The Play Timeline dialog box will appear (**Figure 16.49**).

5. If there is more than one Timeline on your page, select the Timeline you want to use from the Play Timeline drop-down menu.

6. Click on OK to close the Play Timeline dialog box.

7. To specify the user event that triggers the action, click on the arrow button and choose the event (onClick, onMouseOver) from the pop-up menu (**Figure 16.50**).

The event will call the Timeline when the page is loaded in a browser.

✔ Tip

■ To make a link that can play a Timeline and doesn't open a page, the content of the link should be "#".

You can also make a behavior stop a Timeline. This is a quite smart thing to do, especially if you're using the Loop function (I'll get to that in a minute). The browser's Stop button will not stop an in-progress Timeline.

To make a behavior stop a Timeline:

1. In the Document window, click on the object you want to use to make the Timeline stop (*a*, *img*, form button).

2. In the Behaviors inspector, select 4.0 and later browsers from the browser drop-down menu.

3. In the Actions area of the Behaviors inspector, click on the Add Action button.

4. From the pop-up menu that appears, select Timeline > Stop Timeline (**Figure 16.51**). The Stop Timeline dialog box will appear (**Figure 16.52**).

5. If there is more than one Timeline on your page, select the Timeline you want to use from the Stop Timeline drop-down menu.

   or

   Select ALL TIMELINES from the drop-down menu.

6. Click on OK to close the Stop Timeline dialog box.

7. Click on the arrow button and select the user event from the drop-down menu (onClick, onMouseOver, and so on).

✔ Tip

■ You cannot make the same link (or image) both play and stop a Timeline. An event that signals both a Play and a Stop event will only advance the Timeline one frame at a time. (If the order is Stop and then Play, it won't stop at all.) I have to admit, though, that this was a great way to get screen captures for this chapter.

Figure 16.52 In the Stop Timeline dialog box, I can choose to stop all Timelines or one selected Timeline.

Figure 16.51 Having selected the Stop It link, I chose Timeline > Stop Timeline from the Add action menu.

Figure 16.53 Click on the Loop checkbox, and this friendly dialog box will appear to tell you what's up and to which frame number it's adding the behavior. To make it go away, click on the Don't show me this message again checkbox.

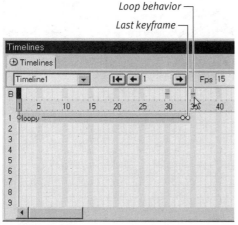

Figure 16.54 The Behaviors channel in this Timeline has two behavior markers. The one that follows the last frame is the one to double-click if you want to edit the Loop behavior.

Loop and Rewind

Some Timelines are so beautiful, you wish they'd go on forever. (Actually, the first 10 or so Timelines you make will automatically be that beautiful.) You can make a Timeline repeat indefinitely, or a certain number of times, by using the Loop feature.

To add the Loop:

◆ In the Timelines inspector, place a check-mark in the Loop checkbox. A dialog box will appear, letting you know that Dreamweaver will add the Go To Frame Behavior code (**Figure 16.53**).

The Loop behavior uses the Go to Frame action. In case of automatic loop, the Timeline reaches the end and returns to frame 1.

To modify the Loop:

1. In the Timelines inspector, locate the last frame in the Timeline. You'll see a marker in the Behaviors channel in the frame after that.

2. Double-click on the last Behaviors marker (**Figure 16.54**). The Behaviors inspector will appear.

3. Double-click on the action Go To Timeline Frame listed in the Actions list box. The Go To Timeline Frame dialog box will appear (**Figure 16.55**).

4. To make the loop pick up at a frame other than frame 1, type the frame number in the Go to Frame text box.

continues on next page

LOOP AND REWIND

5. To make the loop continue for a number of times less than infinity, type a number in the Loop text box.

6. Click on OK to close the Go to Timeline Frame text box.

Preview the Timeline in a 4.0 or later browser to see if it does what you think it will.

✔ Tip

■ You can move a behavior to a different frame if you want. Just click on the associated keyframe, if any, and move it to a different frame, and then click on the behavior (as in **Figure 16.55**) and move it to a different frame.

You can also add the Go to Frame Behavior from outside the Timeline. For instance, you can have a "Play Animation" button, a "Stop Animation" button, and a "Go Back to the Part with the Pie" button.

To add a Go to Frame behavior:

1. In the Document window, click on the object you want to use to make the Timeline jump to a particular frame (a, img, form button).

2. In the Behaviors inspector, select 4.0 and later browsers from the browser drop-down menu.

3. In the Actions area of the Behaviors inspector, click on the Add Action button 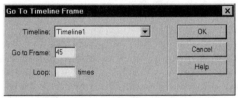.

4. From the pop-up menu that appears, select Timeline > Go to Timeline Frame. The Go To Timeline Frame dialog box will appear (**Figure 16.56**).

5. If there is more than one Timeline on your page, select the Timeline you want to use from the Timeline drop-down menu.

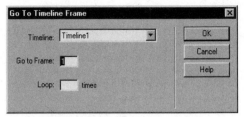

Figure 16.55 The Go To Timeline Frame dialog box controls the Loop behavior.

Figure 16.56 In the Go To Timeline Frame dialog box, I specified frame 45.

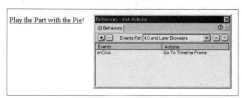

Figure 16.57 I added the onClick event and the GotoTimeline Frame action to the "Play the part with the pie" link.

6. To choose the frame to go to (the frame to rewind or fast forward to), type its number in the Go to Frame text box.

   You cannot set a loop from outside the Timeline.

7. Click on OK to close the Go To Timeline Frame dialog box.

8. Click on the arrow button and select the user event from the drop-down menu (onClick, onMouseOver, and so on) (**Figure 16.57**).

When the user commits the event, the action will cause the Timeline to jump forward or backward to a particular frame.

✔ Tip

■ You can add a Go to Timeline Frame action within a Timeline, too—not just at the end of the Timeline. Imagine this: On Frame 8, an image appears. On Frame 14, the Go to Timeline action makes the Timeline jump back to Frame 7. With the number of loops set to 3, the Timeline would go back to Frame 7 three times to make the image pop up before it continued to the end.

Adding and Removing Frames

I've already told you how to move the beginning and end of an animation bar, as well as the keyframes. You can also add or remove frames from the middle of a Timeline.

To add frames to a Timeline:

1. In the Timelines inspector, click on a frame to move the playback head to the place in the Timeline where you want to add a frame (**Figure 16.58**).

2. From the Document window menu bar, select Modify > Timeline > Add Frame.

   or

   Right-click (Ctrl+click on a Mac) on the object's animation bar in the Timelines inspector, and select Add Frame from the pop-up menu that appears (**Figure 16.59**).

The frame will be added to the right of the playback head (**Figure 16.60**).

You can also remove frames from a Timeline if you want to shorten the duration of the animation.

To remove frames from a Timeline:

1. In the Timelines inspector, move the playback head to the place in the Timeline from which you want to remove a frame.

2. From the Document window menu bar, select Modify > Timeline > Remove Frame.

   or

   Right-click (Ctrl+click on a Mac) on the object's animation bar in the Timelines inspector, and select Remove Frame from the pop-up menu that appears.

The frame the playback head is resting on will be removed.

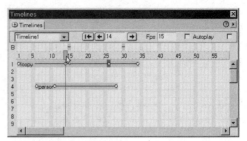

Figure 16.58 I placed the playback head one frame before a behavior on my Timeline.

Figure 16.59 Right-click on the frame, and select Add Frame from the pop-up menu.

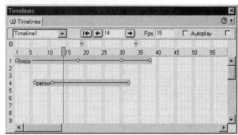

Figure 16.60 I added five new frames between the playback head and the behavior. If I want, I can move the keyframe back five frames by dragging it.

✔ Tips

■ Tinkering with the middle of the Timeline by changing the number of frames is easier than moving around all the keyframes, behaviors, and objects.

■ Adding and removing frames from the middle of a Timeline will remove any keyframes or behaviors that reside in those frames.

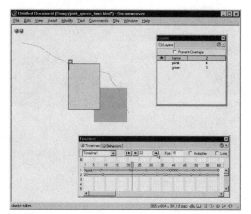

Figure 16.61 The Before Picture: Here's Timeline 1, in mid-play.

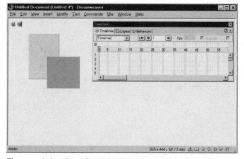

Figure 16.62 The After Picture: I just added Timeline 2. All traces of Timeline 1 are hidden.

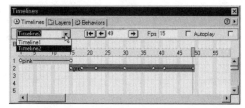

Figure 16.63 Choose which Timeline to work with from the drop-down menu on the Timelines inspector.

Using Multiple Timelines

You may want to use more than one Timeline if you want more than one animation to be available on the page. You can use the same objects in different Timelines, which could then be called by Behaviors attached to different links or buttons.

To add a Timeline:

◆ From the Document window menu bar, select Modify > Timeline > Add Timeline.

The Timeline inspector will reset, hiding the animation bars for the original Timeline; additionally, all the indicators of the Timeline will disappear from the Document window (**Figures 16.61** and **16.62**).

To toggle between Timelines:

◆ In the Timelines inspector, select the name of the Timeline you want to work with from the Timeline drop-down menu (**Figure 16.63**).

You can have as many Timelines as you want.

✔ Tip

■ Each Timeline should be fairly simple, or your page will take several days to load and will have more opportunities to crash browsers around the world.

USING MULTIPLE TIMELINES

Tired of "Timeline 1" and Timeline 2"?
Rename them.

To rename a Timeline:

1. View the Timeline you want to rename.

2. From the Document window menu bar,
   select Modify > Timeline > Rename
   Timeline. The Rename Timeline dialog
   box will appear (**Figure 16.64**).

3. Type the new name for your Timeline in
   the Timeline Name text box.

4. Click on OK. The Rename Timeline dialog
   box will close.

The new name for your Timeline will appear
in the Timeline drop-down menu in the
Timelines inspector.

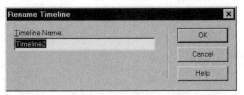

Figure 16.64 Type a new name for the Timeline in the
Timeline Name text box.

Figure 16.65 To remove an object, select Modify > Timeline > Remove Object. The Timelines inspector doesn't even need to be open for this.

Deleting Objects

Part of editing Timelines is removing objects from them.

To remove an object from a Timeline:

1. Select the object you want to remove.

2. From the Document window menu bar, select Modify > Timeline > Remove Object (**Figure 16.65**).

   or

   Right-click (hold down the mouse button on a Mac) on the object's animation bar in the Timelines inspector, and select Remove Object from the pop-up menu.

   or

   Click on the Shortcut Menu button on the right side of the Timelines inspector, and select Remove Object from the menu.

Either way, the object will be removed from the Timeline, but it will remain on the page.

✔ Tip

■ To remove a behavior from a Timeline, follow the steps above, substituting "Remove Behavior" for "Remove Object."

DELETING OBJECTS

Changing Objects

You might decide that the actions you've set up for an object are dandy, but that they describe the wrong object.

To change objects:

1. In the Timelines inspector, select the animation bar you wish to change.

2. From the Document window menu bar, select Modify > Timeline > Change Object. The Change Object dialog box will appear (**Figure 16.66**).

3. From the Object to Animate drop-down menu, select an object (a layer or an image).

4. Click on OK to close the Change Object dialog box. The animation bar will now describe the object you selected.

Figure 16.66 The Change Object dialog box allows you to transfer an animation channel from one object to another.

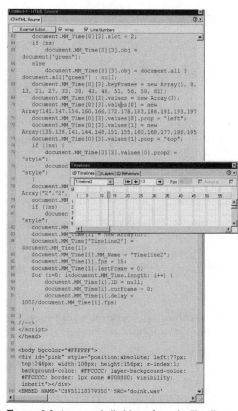

Figure 16.67 I removed all objects from the Timeline, but as you can see in the HTML inspector, the code for the Timeline is still there.

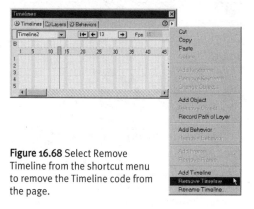

Figure 16.68 Select Remove Timeline from the shortcut menu to remove the Timeline code from the page.

Deleting a Timeline

Even if you remove all the objects from a Timeline, the JavaScript code may remain in the page. You need to "officially" remove a Timeline to remove all traces of the code (**Figure 16.67**).

To remove a Timeline:

1. Select the Timeline you want to remove.

2. Are you sure you want to remove the whole thing?

   From the Document window menu bar, select Modify > Timeline > Remove Timeline.

   or

   Click on the Shortcut Menu button on the side of the Timelines inspector, and select Remove Timeline from the menu (**Figure 16.68**).

Poof! It's gone.

✔ Tips

■ If you have a Timeline with objects and Behaviors already added to it, it might be a good idea to save a version of the document (File > Save As) so that you don't lose the entire thing. You might decide that you want to use a version of it later on.

■ If you accidentally remove a Timeline, remember the magic word: Undo. Select Edit > Undo from the Document window menu bar, or press Ctrl+Z (Command+Z).

Bringing It All Together

Timelines are quite versatile, although my simplistic examples might not do them justice. To wrap up this chapter, I'm going to visually dissect a quasi-useful Timeline I constructed using most of the Timeline's capabilities. Follow the figure captions for **Figures 16.69–16.77**.

One note about **Figures 16.74–16.76**: the Map layer doesn't do anything in the second Timeline, but I added it so it would be visible while working. Dreamweaver displays the default image rather than the one that's been swapped in.

Figure 16.69 The raw materials. The page contains five layers: the map, the person, and three "bubbles." The other layers need to be positioned relative to the map, so they're all nested within the map.

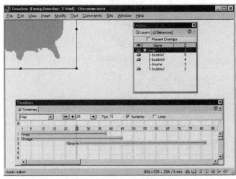

Figure 16.70 Frame 25 of the first Timeline, called Map. I want the window to begin blank. Then the first map is brought in from off screen.

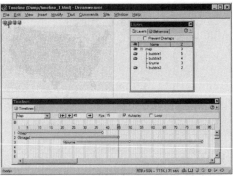

Figure 16.71 Frame 45 of the Map Timeline. A few frames after the map layer arrives, the image source changes into a different map (on frame 45, I changed the source in the Properties inspector). This map has a larger file size, but the image had been pre-loaded in a layer.

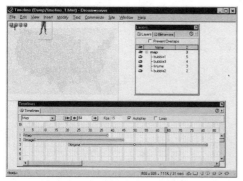

Figure 16.72 Frame 64 of the Map Timeline. The person layer ("tinyme") begins to arrive from off screen. Like the map layer, the person was given negative coordinates (L –400px,T –300px) at the start of the Timeline.

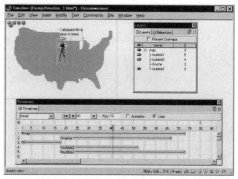

Figure 16.75 Frame 41 of the Travel Timeline. The person has moved halfway across the country. Bubble 1 is hidden and Bubble 2 appears. Note that the playback rate is 10 fps rather than 15; this Timeline moves more slowly.

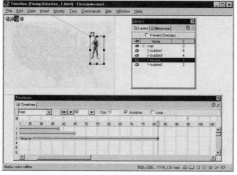

Figure 16.73 Frame 82 of the Map Timeline. The person has arrived. A few frames later, in frame 95, a behavior will play the second Timeline, called Travel.

Figure 16.76 Frame 73 of the Travel Timeline. At the end of the Timeline, the person is all the way across the map. Bubble 2 is hidden, and Bubble 3 appears. I also added a Loop behavior in frame 80; after a pause, the second Timeline will replay.

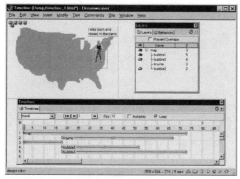

Figure 16.74 In frame 1 of the Travel Timeline, the layer "Bubble 1" appears above the person's head.

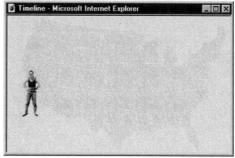

Figure 16.77 The work in action. I created a link to this Timeline in a JavaScript window the same size as the map images.

AUTOMATING DREAMWEAVER

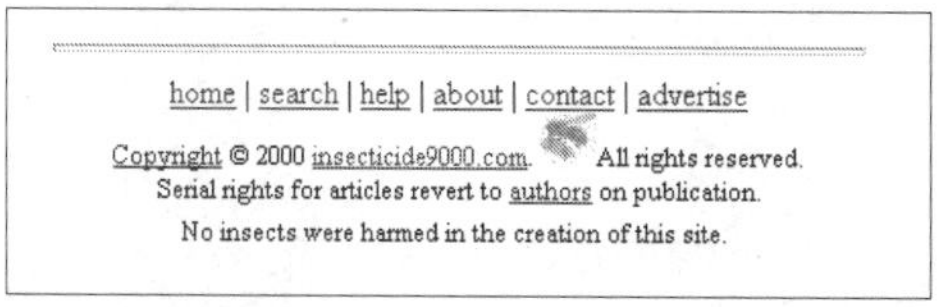

Figure 17.1 This page footer, including text, links, and the image and horizontal rule, is perfect fodder for a Dreamweaver library item. You can insert it onto any new or existing Web page in a matter of seconds. If one of the links changes or the information changes, you can automatically update all pages that use this footer.

Figure 17.2 Dreamweaver templates allow you to create a basic shell page on which some areas are editable and some are read-only.

Dreamweaver's automation features come into full effect with libraries and templates, both of which let you create your own automated HTML widgets that you can plunk onto pages whenever you like.

The Dreamweaver library is a custom-created storehouse of frequently used items that are updatable (**Figure 17.1**). Library items operate somewhat like server-side includes or imported style sheets; the HTML for the item is inserted into the page, along with a reference to the library item's URL. If you change a library item, you can then update the pages that reference it. (Library items don't update pages automatically, but it's trivial to execute an update.)

Besides the library, Dreamweaver offers "Dream Templates" (**Figure 17.2**). And speaking of templates, you can export editable regions of templates as XML and import XML into templates. That's in here, too.

In case you want to use Dreamweaver to insert actual server-side include tokens, I discuss those in this chapter as well.

One more way you can automate Dreamweaver is with the History palette, which lets you repeat actions you've performed during a session. You can even save sets of actions as macros to reuse later.

About Libraries

Libraries are HTML files with the extension .lbi that are stored in a specifically designated Library folder in a local site on your hard drive (**Figure 17.3**). As part of Dreamweaver's site management tools, the Library folder is stored in the site root folder of each site you use with Dreamweaver.

If you have more than one local site on your hard drive, each site will use a different Library folder.

Figure 17.3 A local site on my hard drive. The Library folder is highlighted.

✔ Tip

■ In Dreamweaver, a local site is the same as a folder or set of folders. If you designate a folder on your hard drive as a local site, Dreamweaver will then know how to code relative paths. For more on local sites, see Chapter 3.

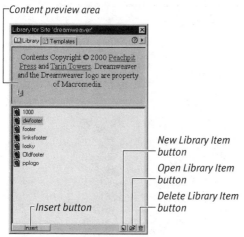

Content preview area

New Library Item button

Open Library Item button

Delete Library Item button

Insert button

Figure 17.4 Use the Library palette to create and insert library items.

You must save a page in a local site on your hard drive that Dreamweaver knows about before you can use library items on the page.

You create, edit, and place library items using the Library palette.

To display the Library palette:

◆ From the Document window menu bar, select Window > Library

or

On the Launcher or mini-Launcher, click on the Library button

or

Press F6.

Either way, the Library palette will appear (**Figure 17.4**).

So Which Is Which?

Libraries and objects (described in Chapter 18) do similar things, so which one do you use for your purposes? Think of it in terms of form and content: libraries are the content, and objects are the form.

Objects are good for inserting standard containers (like tables or layers) that you'll put content in later, or commonly used gizmos like JavaScript buttons or specially sized horizontal rules. However, they don't update automatically (as do libraries), and they aren't site-specific.

The superpower of libraries is that you can spread them over an entire site and still update them as often as you like. Libraries are best used for inserting content that may change over time. See the sidebar, "Bitchin' Examples," on the next page.

ABOUT LIBRARIES

What Library Items Do

Library items can contain HTML and JavaScript. Any items other than text (that is, images, plug-ins, and applets) will not be duplicated in a library item; the library item will contain links to those items.

Many big sites use CGI scripts to automatically replace text on page after page of a site, but library items can accomplish the same thing. They also act very much like server-side includes, described later in this chapter.

The main difference is that the HTML code itself is stored locally in each page, and you must execute an update to your files and then re-upload them in order for the change to take effect. However, if you fear UNIX and know nothing about setting the environment on your Web server so that server-side includes execute properly, library items are a user-friendly substitute.

Be sure to double-check the location of relative links and pathnames in library items if you move any documents that are linked to the library. You can have Dreamweaver automatically update library references when files are moved; see *Updating Your Site*, later in this chapter.

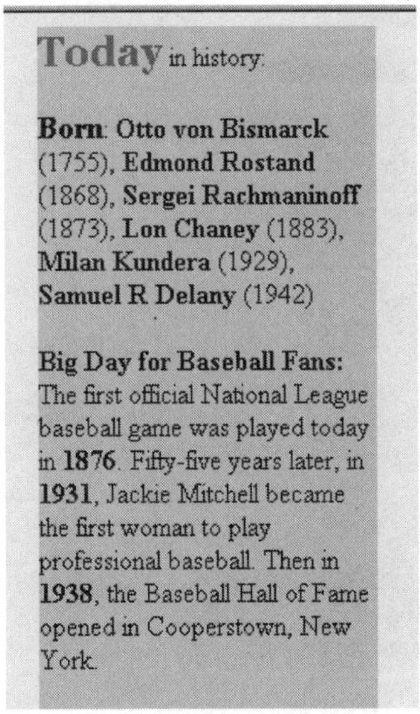

Today in history:

Born: Otto von Bismarck (1755), **Edmond Rostand** (1868), **Sergei Rachmaninoff** (1873), **Lon Chaney** (1883), **Milan Kundera** (1929), **Samuel R Delany** (1942)

Big Day for Baseball Fans:
The first official National League baseball game was played today in **1876**. Fifty-five years later, in **1931**, Jackie Mitchell became the first woman to play professional baseball. Then in **1938**, the Baseball Hall of Fame opened in Cooperstown, New York.

Figure 17.5 This "Today in History" sidebar gets updated daily. Making the whole chunk, including the layer containing the text, into a library item means you just update the library item to update the page—you don't even need to *open* the page.

Figure 17.6 If this navigation bar appeared on every page in your site, it would be a pain to replace every instance of it if you added a search function (and thus, a new toolbar button). Make it a library item, add a new image, and update the site automatically.

Bitchin' Examples

◆ The footer with copyright info at the bottom of every page in your site (like the one I showed you in **Figure 17.1**)

◆ "Daily" updates on pages that aren't otherwise updated (**Figure 17.5**)

◆ Navigation bars on sites that are still growing (**Figure 17.6**)

◆ Frequently used logo images, contact e-mail addresses, or mastheads

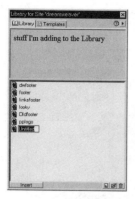

Figure 17.7 The Library palette. To display the Library palette without adding a new item to it, select Window > Library from the Document window menu bar, or press F6.

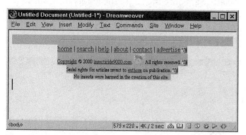

Figure 17.8 The elements you're adding to the library will be highlighted in yellow.

Creating a Library Item

You create a library item from existing HTML. You might create a page with the sole purpose of adding items to the library from that page, which you might do if you're creating the design and architecture for an entire site. Or you can select part of an existing page to add.

To create a new library item:

1. Open the page that contains the stuff you want to add to the library.

   If you are working with a new page, save the page in a Dreamweaver site folder.

2. Select the HTML for the desired objects. (You may want to do this in the HTML inspector to ensure proper tag selection.)

3. From the Document window menu bar, select Modify > Library> Add Object to Library. The Library palette will appear (**Figure 17.7**).

   or

   Drag the selection into the Library palette.

   or

   On the Library palette, click on the New Library Item button to add the selection to the library item.

4. Type a name for the library item in the text box, replacing the word *Untitled*.

The stuff you selected will be highlighted in the Dreamweaver window with a yellow box (**Figure 17.8**).

✔ Tips

- Once you designate a selection on a page as a library item, you will not be able to edit it freely. See *Editing Library Items,* later in this chapter for more on this.

- To add the content of a selection to a library item without replacing the selection with the new uneditable library item, hold down the Ctrl (Command) key while creating the library item.

Adding an Existing Library Item to a Page

Now that you've created a library item, you can add it to other new or existing pages in that site.

To insert a library item by dragging:

◆ The easiest way to add a library item to a page is to drag the library item icon from the Library palette to the Document window (**Figure 17.9**).

To add a library item at the insertion point:

1. Click to place the insertion point at the place in the Document window where you want the library item to appear.

2. In the Library palette, click on the icon for the library item you want to add.

3. Click on New Library Item button 🔲. The library item will appear at the insertion point (**Figure 17.10**).

To remove a library item from a page:

1. Click anywhere within the yellow box that surrounds the library item to select the entire thing (**Figure 17.11**).

2. Press Backspace or Delete. The library item will disappear.

✔ Tip

■ To add the contents of a library item without linking it to the library, hold down the Ctrl (Command) button and drag the library item onto the page.

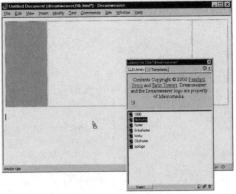

Figure 17.9 Drag a library item icon from the Library palette right onto the page. The library item will be inserted where you drop it.

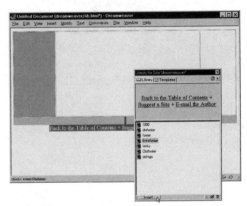

Figure 17.10 Click on the Insert button, and the library item will appear on the page at the insertion point.

Figure 17.11 Click anywhere on a library item to select the whole thing. Then you can delete it, or cut and paste it anywhere.

Figure 17.12 The Properties inspector, displaying library item properties.

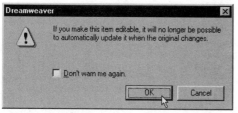

Figure 17.13 Dreamweaver warns you that the item will no longer be linked to the Library. To keep this dialog box from appearing, check off the *Don't warn me again* checkbox.

Figure 17.14 After making the item editable, the yellow highlighting is removed and the item is no longer linked to the Library.

Editing Library Items

There are two ways to edit a library item:

◆ Make the library item editable by disconnecting it from the library and then edit it on any page that contains the item (change is local).

   or

Edit the library item in its own window (change is global).

To make a library item editable:

1. In any document that contains the library item you wish to edit, select the library item by clicking on it (as we saw in **Figure 17.11**).

2. View the Properties inspector, if necessary (**Figure 17.12**), by selecting Modify > Selection Properties from the Document window menu bar or by double-clicking on the library item.

3. On the Properties inspector, click on Detach from Original. A dialog box will appear warning you that this will prevent the library item from being affected by future library updates (**Figure 17.13**).

4. Click on OK to close the dialog box. The item will be de-linked from the Site Library, and you can go ahead and edit it (**Figure 17.14**).

Making an item editable, or detaching it from the library, means that it has the same content as the library item had, but it is no longer connected to the library. This means that if you automatically update the entire site from the library, this page will not be affected by the update.

If you want to edit all instances of a library item, you need to edit the item in its own window.

To edit a library item globally:

1. In the Library palette, click on the icon for the item you want to edit. The current version will be displayed in the top frame of the Library palette (**Figure 17.15**).

2. Click on the Open Library Item button 📂.

   or

   Double-click the name of the library item, or the preview frame. Either way, a new document window will appear that contains only the HTML included in the library item (**Figure 17.16**).

3. Make your changes to the library item.

4. Save the changes to the library item using File > Save or Ctrl+S (Command+S). A dialog box will appear asking if you want to update all documents in your local site that contain the library item (**Figure 17.17**).
   - ◆ To update now, click on Yes.
   - ◆ To update later, click on No. (You may want to postpone this until you're finished editing and then update everything at once.)

5. Close the library item Document window.

✔ Tips

- ■ To find out more about updating pages that use library items, see *Updating Your Site*, later in this chapter.

- ■ You can make the preview area bigger or smaller by dragging the border between the two frames in the Library palette (**Figure 17.18**).

Figure 17.15 When you select an item in the Library palette, it is displayed in the frame at the top of the palette.

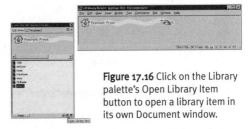

Figure 17.16 Click on the Library palette's Open Library Item button to open a library item in its own Document window.

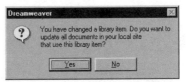

Figure 17.17 When you save the changes to the library item, a dialog box will appear asking you if you want to update the entire site.

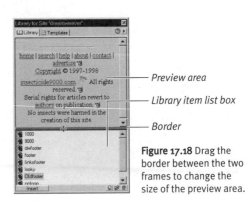

Preview area

Library item list box

Border

Figure 17.18 Drag the border between the two frames to change the size of the preview area.

EDITING LIBRARY ITEMS

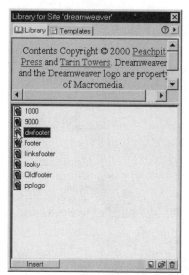

Figure 17.19 Select the item to rename in the Library palette.

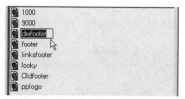

Figure 17.20 Click inside the name of the item, and then type the new name in the box.

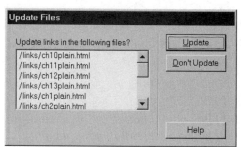

Figure 17.21 The Update Files dialog box will appear when you rename a library item. Click on Update to have Dreamweaver change all old references to the library item's new name.

Renaming a Library Item

You can rename a library item after you name it initially, and then Dreamweaver can update your site and fix any references to the old name. This feature is new in Dreamweaver 3; previously, if you renamed a library item, you had to update references to it manually.

To rename a library item:

1. In the Library palette, click on the item you want to rename (**Figure 17.19**).

2. Click on the item name. A box will appear around the name (**Figure 17.20**).

3. Type the new name in the box and press Enter (Return). A dialog box will appear, asking you if you want to update references to that library item. Click on Update to update the site, or Don't Update to skip it (**Figure 17.21**).

The library item will be renamed, and if you did not update the item, old references to the item will not link to the newly renamed one. It will retain its HTML content, but it will no longer be updatable.

✔ Tips

- You can rename a library item if you want to divorce it on purpose from the pages that reference the item. Then, you can create a new item with the old name, and old references will point to the new item.

- For example, say I have a library item called Toolbar. I want to completely change the toolbar, but I don't want to get rid of the library item entirely. I rename the old Toolbar OldToolbar. Then I create a new library item called Toolbar. The old references will point to the new item.

Deleting a Library Item

Deleting a library item removes the file from the library, but it doesn't remove any code from any of the pages that use the item.

To delete a library item:

1. On the Library palette, select the item you want to delete (**Figure 17.22**).

2. Click on the Delete Library Item button 🗑. A dialog box will appear asking you if you really want to delete the library item (**Figure 17.23**).

3. Click Yes. Poof! It's gone.

✔ Tip

■ Probably the easiest way to remove references to deleted library items is to select them and then make them editable. That removes references to the .lbi file, but leaves the content intact.

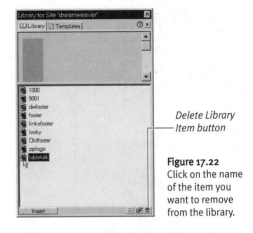

Delete Library Item button

Figure 17.22 Click on the name of the item you want to remove from the library.

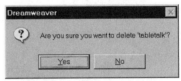

Figure 17.23 To commence deleting the item from the Library, click Yes.

Library Code

The code for a library item consists of two things: The code for the item itself, such as table tags, image paths, anchors, text, and font formatting; and the code that links the item to the library.

Code for a standard footer might look like this:

```
<!-- #BeginLibraryItem "/Library/tabletalk.lbi" -->
<center>
<font size="-1">Copyright &copy; 2000, Animalogic. All rights
reserved. <a href="/legal/">Legal Notices</a>.</font>
</center>
<!-- #EndLibraryItem -->
```

Dreamweaver keeps track of library-linked pages using the site cache (discussed in Chapters 3 and 20). When a library item is moved or renamed within the Library palette or the Site window, Dreamweaver looks in the cache for the #BeginLibraryItem marker in pages within your site.

If you want to remove all library item markers from a site, you can use Dreamweaver's Replace feature (Edit > Replace), discussed in Chapter 6, or the Clean Up HTML feature (Commands > Clean Up HTML; select Dreamweaver Comments), discussed in Chapter 4.

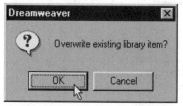

Figure 17.24 I accidentally edited the "Looky" library item so that it consisted of the text link on the bottom instead of the selected images. I still have a copy of the old library item on my page, so I select it.

Figure 17.25 I click on the Recreate button on the Properties inspector.

Figure 17.27 I have successfully rewritten the Looky library item with the old contents.

Re-creating a Library Item

If you delete an item from the Library palette, but it still exists on a Web page, you can re-create it.

Besides reinstating deleted library items, you can use the Recreate function to replace the contents of a library item with the contents of an edited library item (or vice versa). This is useful for renamed or mistakenly edited items.

To re-create a library item:

1. In the Document window, select an edited library item or an item that was deleted from the Library palette (**Figure 17.24**).

2. On the Properties inspector, click on the Recreate button (**Figure 17.25**). If you're overwriting an existing library item, a dialog box will appear (**Figure 17.26**).

3. Click on OK. The contents of the selected library item will overwrite the contents of the existing library item (**Figure 17.27**). (In the case of deleted items, the original name will be re-added to the Library palette).

✔ Tips

- You cannot overwrite a library item with the contents of another library item. In other words, you can't select the item July and overwrite it with the contents of June.

- The ability to re-create library items is one reason not to update your site immediately after you edit a library item. As long as the old library item content exists on a page somewhere, you can re-create the original. I like to update my library items just before quitting Dreamweaver or uploading pages. See *Updating Your Site*, the next section in this chapter.

Figure 17.26 caption: **Figure 17.26** A dialog box warns me that I'm about to overwrite the contents of the library item.

Updating Your Site

After you edit a library item, you can update single pages, selected pages, or entire sites that use that item. Then, the next time you upload pages to the site, they'll all have the new content in the place of the old library content.

To update a single page:

1. Open the page you want to update in the Document window.

2. From the Document window menu bar, select Modify > Library > Update Current Page.

3. A dialog box will appear telling you if any library items referenced on the page no longer exist (**Figure 17.28**).

4. Click on OK.

Any updated items will be re-posted to the page in their new form (**Figure 17.29**).

✔ Tip

■ If you want to add a previously deleted item to the library, you can re-create it. See the previous section. You don't need to re-create a library item unless you need it to be updatable.

Figure 17.28 When you update a site using Libraries, this dialog box appears if you've deleted a library item referenced on an updated page.

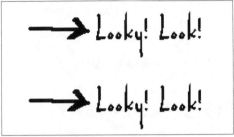

Figure 17.29 After I re-created the "Looky" item, I updated the page we saw in Figure 17.24, and now both items reflect the changes. (I'm not going to keep both of them here.)

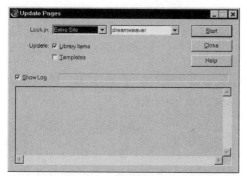

Figure 17.30 The Update Pages dialog box. You don't need to have any pages open to update your site.

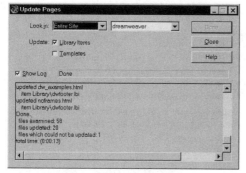

Figure 17.31 After the update is complete, a log file will display letting you know if any library items were missing, along with other useful data.

To update more than one page:

1. From the Document window menu bar, select Modify > Library > Update Pages. The Update Pages dialog box will appear (**Figure 17.30**).

2. The Update Pages window lets you update all library items in the entire local site, or only those pages that reference a specific library item. From the Look in drop-down menu:

   Select Entire Site to update all library items in this local site. If more than one site is open, you may select a different site from the second drop-down menu.

   or

   Select Files That Use to single out one library item, and then select that item from the second drop-down menu.

3. Click on Start. Dreamweaver will scan all the HTML files in the current site for references to library items.

4. When the update process is complete, a log file will appear in the Log box showing you how many files were scanned, which files were updated, and which library files, if any, are missing from the Library folder (**Figure 17.31**).

5. When you're done, click on Close to return to the Document window.

✔ Tip

■ You use the Update Pages dialog box to update templates, too. I describe templates later in this chapter.

Using Server-Side Includes

Server-side includes (SSIs for short), much like library items, are pieces of HTML that can be reused on any number of pages. Also like library items, any time the included file is edited, the changes will be reflected in the documents that reference the include.

Unlike library items, however, there is no additional update process necessary. The files are stored and processed by the Web server, so changes are automatic.

The Web document itself contains instructions for processing the included HTML files. These instructions, called *tokens,* include the pathname of the file on the server.

When you use the HTML inspector to view the source of a page that uses a server-side include, you'll see the token (**Figure 17.32**), but not the HTML of the include itself. However, when you view the file in Dreamweaver, or if you use Dreamweaver to preview the file in a browser, the include (if it's stored locally) will be displayed inline in the page (**Figure 17.33**).

Figure 17.32 The HTML inspector, displaying the code for a server-side include token. Note that the instructions are commented out so that they won't be displayed in the browser as is; also note that whatever HTML is in the file headlines.html is not displayed by the HTML inspector.

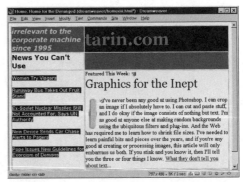

Figure 17.33 This is the Document window view of the same page seen in Figure 17.32. Again, the include is highlighted. As long as the included file is stored locally, Dreamweaver can process it and display it inline. Display options are covered later in this chapter.

✔ Tips

- Under most circumstances, a server-side include may use any HTML tags except `<HTML>`, `<HEAD>`, `<TITLE>`, or `</BODY>`. You also want to avoid `<FRAMESET>` and other associated tags, and embed frame instructions in the document rather than in the include.

- If you use Dreamweaver to create HTML files for server-side includes, be sure to delete the aforementioned tags.

- If your include file has HTML errors such as misordered or orphaned tags, these will show up as errors in the file that references the include; however, you should fix the errors in the include file instead.

Why Won't It Go?

If you upload both the file that contains the include token and the include file itself, and the contents don't show up on the live site, then you need to contact the Web server administrator. It's possible that a change to the Unix environment needs to be made before your server will process virtual or File includes.

And speaking of File includes, this option is available in the Properties inspector, but I couldn't get Dreamweaver to process these or deal with them at all, so I'm afraid I can't tell you much else about using them with Dreamweaver.

I can tell you that instead of `<!--include virtual`, the code says `<!--include file`, and the file is imported into the document. Either way, when you use an include and View Source in the browser window, you'll see the HTML source of the included file as well as the token.

Inserting SSIs

Inserting a server-side include is a gloriously simple process. First, however, let me review how to create the file to include.

To create a file to include:

1. Using Dreamweaver or another editor, create the file you wish to display in your document(s). Be sure to delete any ver-boten tags, as described on the previous page (**Figure 17.34**).

2. Save the file on your local site, in a location mirroring where it will be stored on the server.

To insert an SSI token:

1. Click to place the insertion point where you want the include to appear.

2. From the Document window menu bar, select Insert > Server-Side Include.

   or

   On the Objects palette's Common panel, click on the Server-Side Include button . Either way, the Select File dialog box will appear (**Figure 17.35**).

3. Select the file you wish to include.

4. In most cases, you'll want to use a docu-ment-relative path. If so, select Document from the Relative To drop-down menu.

5. Click on Select to select the file and close the Select File dialog box.

When you return to the Document window, the contents of the include file will be displayed.

✔ Tip

■ If the include file is not stored locally, or if it does not yet exist, a Comment icon will be displayed instead of the contents of the file.

Figure 17.34 The Document window and HTML inspector, displaying the contents of my include file.

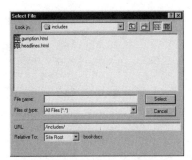

Figure 17.35 Select the file you wish to include.

Figure 17.36 Server Side Include properties.

Editing Server-Side Includes

In the Document window, select the server-side include by clicking anywhere on the text. (As with library items, when you select one part of an include, you select the whole thing.)

Display the Properties inspector, if neces-sary, by double-clicking the include. In the Properties inspector (**Figure 17.36**), click on Edit. Dreamweaver will open the file in a Document window. Make your changes and save the file. Any changes will be reflected on the pages that reference the file. Don't forget to upload it to the server if you change it locally!

INSERTING SSIs

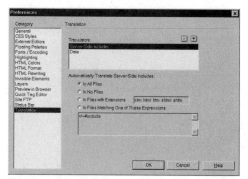

Figure 17.37 The Preferences dialog box, displaying Translation options for Server-Side includes. Note that the text boxes for the file extensions and regular expressions text boxes are grayed out.

Changing SSI Viewing Options

For one reason or another, you may not want to view server-side includes while you're working on your file.

To change SSI viewing options:

1. From the Document window menu bar, select Edit > Preferences. The Preferences dialog box will appear.

2. In the category box at the left, click on Translation. The Translation panel of the Preferences dialog box will appear (**Figure 17.37**).

3. If it's not already selected, select Server-Side Includes from the Translations list box.

4. Select one of the following options:
   - To display all includes, select In All Files.
   - To display no includes, select In No Files.
   - To display includes only in files with certain extensions, select In Files with Extensions. Includes will be displayed in files with only the specified extensions.
   - To display includes only in files that contain a particular regular expression, select In Files Matching One of These Expressions. Then type the expression in the text box.

5. When you're finished, click on OK to close the Preferences dialog box. Your changes will be reflected for all documents.

✔ Tips

- You can change these preferences as often as you like if you wish to turn viewing of SSIs off and on.

- Regular expressions are described in Chapter 6 and on the Web site for this book.

- The only way to view a server-side include inline in the browser window on a local page is to Preview (File > Preview > Browser Name) in the page with Dreamweaver. Opening the local page in the browser will not display the include contents.

Dream Templates

Macromedia calls the templates feature in Dreamweaver "Dream Templates," because they have some terrific features. For one, you don't just set up the page and let it go—you designate certain portions of the page as editable, and the rest is locked to the user. So as a site designer, you can give anyone a Dreamweaver template to use, and they won't be able to mess up your precious page design.

The other great feature of templates in Dreamweaver is that if you update the template design after it's been used on any number of pages, you can painlessly update all pages on your local site that use that template. Then you just re-upload the affected pages, and they'll have the changed template content.

For instance, if you suddenly want to change the page background of your site from blue to orange, or the copyright date from 1999 to 2000, you can change a single file—the Dreamweaver template—and then update all pages that use that template.

You can also attach existing pages to a template you just created.

Template Tools

Figure 17.38 Templates are stored in the templates folder in your local site, shown here in the Site window.

Figure 17.39 The Templates palette shows all the templates available in the current site, with previews.

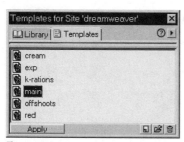

Figure 17.40 You can view or hide the preview pane by dragging the border between the two panes in the Templates palette.

As with library items, templates are stored in a folder called Templates in your local site (**Figure 17.38**). For more about managing local sites, see Chapter 3.

The tool you use to work with templates is the Templates palette (**Figure 17.39**). To display the Templates palette, select Window > Templates from the Document window menu bar, or press Ctrl+F11. The top half displays a list of all the templates available to your local site, and the bottom half displays a preview of the template's content.

You can hide the lower half to conserve screen real estate by clicking on the bottom border and dragging it until it meets the border between the two halves (**Figure 17.40**).

✔ Tips

- The Shortcut Menu button on the Templates palette offers quick access to options such as opening a template, applying a template to an existing page, and selecting a template in the Site window.

- In this chapter, I have the Library palette and the Templates palette stacked together, but you can separate the two by clicking on either name tab and dragging it elsewhere onscreen. To stack two palettes or inspectors, drag one palette's name tab onto another palette.

TEMPLATE TOOLS

Creating Templates

Before you can use a template, you must create a template file.

To create a template using an existing file:

1. Open the file you'd like to use as the template for other pages on your site.

2. From the Document window menu bar, select File > Save as Template. The Save As Template dialog box will appear (**Figure 17.41**). Any existing templates will be listed in the Existing Templates list box to inform you about overwriting.

3. If you have more than one local site, select the site the template will reside in from the Site drop-down menu.

4. Type the filename of the template in the Save As dialog box. The `.dwt` extension will automatically be appended to the file.

5. Click on Save to save the file as a template.

6. If you're overwriting an existing template, a dialog box will appear asking you to confirm this choice. Click on Yes to overwrite the old file.

The template will now be displayed in the Document window instead of the original HTML file.

To create a template from scratch:

1. On the Templates palette, click on the New Template button. A new Template icon will appear in the Templates palette (**Figure 17.42**).

2. Type a name for the new template in place of "Untitled," and press Return.

3. In the Templates palette, double-click the name of the template. A blank Document window will appear. You'll see the name of the template file (*nn*.dwt) displayed in the Document window title bar.

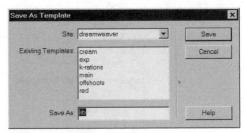

Figure 17.41 In the Save As Template dialog box, type the name of the new template, or choose a template to overwrite.

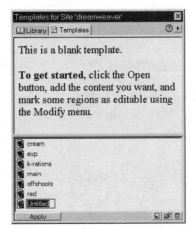

Figure 17.42 Click on the New Template button in the Templates palette, and type the name of your template in place of "Untitled."

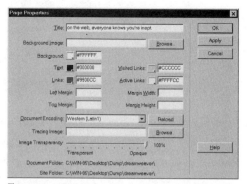

Figure 17.43 Remember to set any page properties for your template (Modify > Page Properties), such as the page background or text and link colors. The only page property that can be edited for a page based on a template is the page title.

Setting Template Page Properties

When users work with a page based on a template, they cannot edit any page properties other than the page title (**Figure 17.43**).

✔ Tip

- When a user tries to set page properties for pages based on a template, the locked properties are not grayed out, and there is no error message. The user will simply hear a beep when they close the Page Properties dialog box, and the properties will remain unchanged.

You should set page properties, such as the page background and text and link colors, in the template file itself. If you want some of your pages to have different page properties, then save the template with a different name and base the blue pages on the blue template and the orange pages on the orange template.

See Chapter 2 to find out more about page properties.

Using Styles and JavaScript in Templates

Because you cannot edit the <head> of a document that is based on a Dream Template, you cannot add or edit CSS styles, behaviors, or Timelines in these pages. It's certainly convenient to be able to create style sheets in a template and have them apply to all pages based on that template, but less convenient not to be able to use scripts.

An exception to the styles rule: you can create layers (which use unique instances of CSS) in pages based on templates.

✔ Tips

- To add dynamic content to a page based on a template, see *Detaching a Page from a Template*, later in this chapter.

- To add a style sheet to pages that use a template, you must return to the template itself and link to the style sheet from there.

Figure 17.44 Type the name of the new region in the Name text box.

Figure 17.45 The text you typed as the name of the new editable region will appear in the Document window at the insertion point, and its name will appear inside {curly brackets}.

Figure 17.46 The text you marked as editable will be highlighted in the editable region color in the Document window. Note how I edited both regions for font size and such.

Unmarking Editable Regions

To unmark an editable region, click on the region in the template's Document window to select it, and then from the Document window menu bar, select Modify > Templates > Unmark Editable Regions.

Setting Editable Regions

Everything you place on a template will be locked—that is, the user will not be able to edit that part of the page—unless you mark it as a named editable region.

To create a new editable region:

1. Click to place the insertion point where you want the new editable region to appear.

2. From the Document window menu bar, select Modify > Templates > New Editable Region. The New Editable Region dialog box will appear (**Figure 17.44**).

3. Type a name for the Editable Region in the text box. Avoid funky characters, and don't use quotation marks or <angle brackets>.

4. Click on OK to close the New Editable Region dialog box and return to the Document window. The name of the editable region will appear highlighted in the Document window (**Figure 17.45**). You can edit this text, if you like.

You can also create a page element and then mark it as editable.

To set an editable region:

1. Type a placeholder, such as **Headline** or **Image Goes Here**.

2. From the Document window menu bar, select Modify > Templates > Mark Selection As Editable Region. The New Editable Region dialog box will appear (**Figure 17.44**).

3. Type a name for the editable region in the text box. Avoid funky characters, and don't use quotation marks or <angle brackets>.

4. Click on OK to close the New Editable Region dialog box and return to the Document window. The editable region will be highlighted in the template's Document window (**Figure 17.46**).

Creating Pages Based on a Template

Once you've got your template set up, you can create pages based on that template.

To create a template page:

1. From the Document window menu bar, select File > New From Template. The Select Template dialog box will appear (**Figure 17.47**).

2. Select the name of the template on which you want to base your page.

3. Click Select. The Select Template dialog box will close, and a new document window will appear (**Figure 17.48**), including:

   ◆ The formatting of your template, including any HTML elements or page properties

   ◆ The locked regions of your template, highlighted in the locked highlight color.

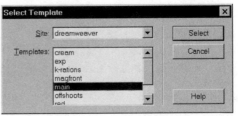

Figure 17.47 Select the template on which you want to base your page from the Select Template dialog box. You can also change sites by selecting a site from the drop-down menu.

Figure 17.48 A blank page based on the main.dwt template. The locked regions are marked in yellow, and the rest of the text is editable.

Detaching a Page from a Template

If you'd like to remove a template's format-ting from a page, you can detach the page from the template. This is what you need to do if you'd rather attach a page to a different template.

To detach a template:

◆ From the Document window menu bar, select Modify > Templates > Detach from [Template name].

The locked regions will still be visible on the page, but you'll now be able to edit or delete them.

After you detach a page from a template, you can add scripts and such to the page.

Once you detach a template from a page, it will no longer be updated automatically when you edit the template file.

Attaching an Existing Page to a Template

You can attach existing pages to a new template, too.

To attach a page to a template:

1. From the Document window menu bar, select Modify > Templates > Apply Template to Page. The Select Template dialog box will appear (**Figure 17.49**).

2. Select the name of the template to which you want to attach your page, and click on OK. The Choose Editable Region for Orphaned Content dialog box will appear (**Figure 17.50**).

3. Because templates only allow new content to appear in editable regions, you need to select the name of an editable region in which to stick your content. You'll be able to move it from region to region once the page is reopened, but for now, you have to pick one. Do so, and click on OK. (Clicking on None will throw away your content.)

4. When the dialog box closes, your content will appear in the region you selected. You can now resume editing your page.

✔ Tip

■ If a piece of placeholder text, for example "HeadingA," matches the name of a template region (in our example, it would also called "HeadingA"), Dreamweaver will automatically match the placeholder text with the editable region. That way, if the names of the editable regions on the blue template and the orange template are the same, it will be trivial to detach a page from one template and then attach it to another. You can leave "None" selected, and the placeholder content will remain in the correct regions.

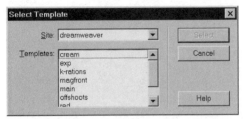

Figure 17.49 Select the template to which you want to attach the page.

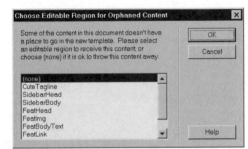

Figure 17.50 In the Choose Editable Region for Orphaned Content dialog box, pick an editable region to receive your content. If many different types of content are on the existing page, you can move the content from region to region after you convert the page.

Figure 17.51 All editable regions available to the current page are listed at the bottom of the Modify > Templates menu.

Figure 17.52 After you select an editable region from the list, it will become highlighted in the Document window so that you can type over it.

Figure 17.53 The image selected on this page is an editable region. If an image on a page will be rotating, you can mark it as editable. You can also insert images into editable regions (such as the highlighted body text in Figure 17.52) so they can be deleted or replaced.

Using Editable Regions

If you're working with a page with a number of editable regions and you want to make sure you put the right stuff in the right slots, Dreamweaver can help you locate them.

To find an editable region:

1. From the Document window menu bar, select Modify > Templates > [region name]. All editable regions appear at the bottom of the menu (**Figure 17.51**).

2. The editable region will become highlighted (**Figure 17.52**), and you can type away.

✔ Tips

- Images and other objects can be marked as editable regions, too. The page in **Figure 17.52** uses an image as a drop cap, and this image needs to be replaced with every story update. **Figure 17.53** shows the highlighted editable region, called FeatImg, in which the letter I has been replaced with the letter F. If the image were not an editable region of the document, it would be locked and permanent.

- If you're giving a batch of blank template pages to a webmonkey for filling in the blanks, you should point out this helpful feature so that your minions know for sure which content goes in which region. A printout of a mocked-up page with the region names clearly marked and labeled couldn't hurt, either.

Highlights for Templates

When you mark an editable region of a template, it will appear highlighted in the template, both in the Document window and in the HTML inspector (**Figure 17.54**). When you create a page based on a template, the locked regions will be highlighted, both in the Document window and in the HTML inspector (**Figure 17.55**). On templates, you can edit any region in either window. On pages based on templates, you can only edit editable—unhighlighted—regions.

You can also change the highlight colors of a library item.

To set the highlight colors:

1. From the Document window menu bar, select Edit > Preferences. The Preferences dialog box will appear.

2. In the Category box at the left, select Highlighting. The Highlighting panel of the dialog box will appear (**Figure 17.56**).

3. To set the color for either the locked or editable region, click on the Color button. The Colors palette will appear.

4. Select a color by clicking on it.

5. Repeat for any other elements whose highlighting you want to edit.

6. Click on OK to close the Preferences dialog box and return to the Document window.

✔ Tip

■ To turn off highlighting for a library or template entity, uncheck the Show checkbox for that item.

Figure 17.54 A template displayed in the Document window and the HTML inspector. Editable regions are highlighted in a template, and the default highlight color is blue.

Figure 17.55 This is a page based on a template. The page hasn't been edited yet. Locked, or uneditable, regions are highlighted. The default highlight color is yellow—similar to a library item.

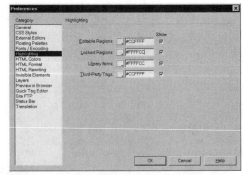

Figure 17.56 In the Highlighting panel of the Preferences dialog box, you can adjust the default highlight colors for editable and locked regions, as well as for library items and for third-party tags (such as new proprietary browser tags, tags introduced by other WYSIWYG editors, or RDF or XML tags).

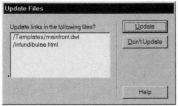

Figure 17.57 Click and hold on the name of a template in the Templates palette, and when the little box appears around the name, type over it.

Figure 17.58 Dreamweaver can update all pages that link to a template so that they link to its new name.

Renaming and Deleting Templates

You can rename a template and then update all pages in your site so that they refer to the new name. Or, you could skip the update and create a new template with the old name, and then the pages would refer to it.

To rename a template:

1. In the Templates palette, click on the name of the template so that a box appears around its name (**Figure 17.57**).

2. Type the new name and press Return. The Update Files dialog box will appear (**Figure 17.58**). Click on Update to update references to this template, or Don't Update to skip it.

3. Click OK. The template will be renamed.

✔ Tip

■ You can also rename a template using the Site window. Right-click on the template, and from the pop-up menu that appears, select Rename. When you rename the file, a dialog box will appear asking if you want to update references to the file. This is an excellent way to rename any file.

If you're utterly done with a template, you may delete it.

To delete a template:

1. In the Templates palette, select the template you wish to delete.

2. Click on the Delete button. A dialog box will appear asking you if you're sure you want to delete the template (**Figure 17.59**).

3. Click on Yes. The template will be deleted.

4. References to the deleted template will not be expunged; you'll need to attach affected pages to a new template.

Editing and Updating

You can edit templates at any time, even after you've attached pages to them. Once you've edited a template, you can then perform an update to reflect your recent edits.

To edit a template:

1. In the Templates palette, select the name of the template to edit (**Figure 17.60**).

2. Click on the Open Template button. The template will appear in a new Document window.

3. Make any changes you like, taking care to mark editable areas as such.

4. Save your changes. A dialog box will appear asking if you wish to update the pages that use this template (**Figure 17.61**).

   To update now, click Yes, and skip to step 2 on the next page. To update later, click No.

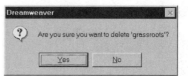

Figure 17.59 If you really want to delete that template, click on Yes.

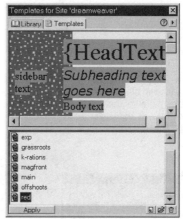

Figure 17.60 Select the name of the template to edit. (You can always do a File > Open, but this method is expedient when working with multiple templates and opening pages based on them.)

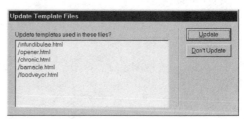

Figure 17.61 When you save changes to a template file, a dialog box will appear asking if you want to update your site.

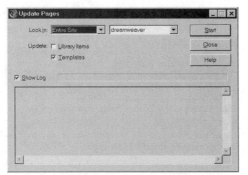

Figure 17.62 In the Update Pages window, you may decide to update the entire site or just those pages that use a certain template. You may also choose to update a different site than the one currently open.

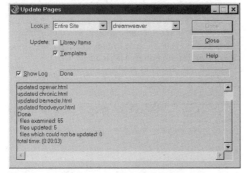

Figure 17.63 When you've finished updating the site or the selection of pages, a log file will appear telling you about pages updated, pages that couldn't be updated because they referred to deleted templates, and total pages reviewed.

To update your site:

1. In the Document window, open a page that uses a template or a template file.

2. From the Document window menu bar, select Modify > Templates > Update Pages. (You may select Update Current Page to modify a single page.) The Update Pages window will appear (**Figure 17.62**).

3. The Update Pages window lets you update all pages in the entire local site, or only those attached to a particular template. From the Look in drop-down menu:

   Select Entire Site to update all template pages in this local site.

   or

   Select Files That Use to single out one template, and then select that template from the second drop-down menu.

4. Click Start. When the update is complete, a log of updated pages will appear in the Log box (**Figure 17.63**).

Exporting as XML

XML stands for eXtensible Markup Language, which basically means you can create your own tags as you see fit for your own back-end scripts and database hooks to interpret. XML tags do not modify the behavior of what they contain in the browser setting. Rather, they're used as containers to mark content. An XML tag may be something like `<Headline></Headline>`, and the tag may be used as a container to import content into on dynamic pages; as a marker to export content out of into a database; or as a marker for a search robot to find particular types of content.

Because the editable regions of a Dreamweaver template are each named, you may name them the same things as XML tags you're using (or vice versa—name the tags for the regions). You may then export the content of a template-based file as an XML file, with the editable region names converted into XML tags.

To export editable regions as XML:

1. Open a page based on a template.

2. From the Document window menu bar, select File > Export > Export Editable Regions as XML. The Export Editable Regions as XML dialog box will appear.

3. You may use one of two formats for the exported XML tags:

    The Dreamweaver format (**Figure 17.64**):
    `<item name="RegionName"></item>`

    The editable region = tag name format (**Figure 17.65**):
    `<RegionName></RegionName>`

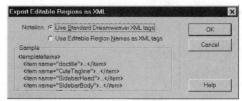

Figure 17.64 In the Export Editable Regions as XML dialog box, you may choose to save the editable regions of your template as Dreamweaver `<item>` tags or as self-referential XML tags.

Figure 17.65 In the second option in this dialog box, the tags themselves—true to XML's custom nature—are named for the editable regions.

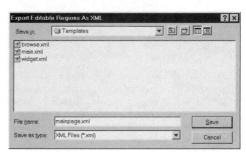

Figure 17.66 Type a filename for your new XML file in the second Export Editable Regions as XML dialog box.

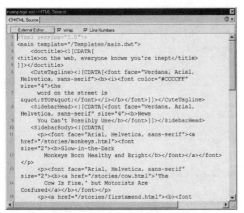

Figure 17.67 Here's the source of the XML file I just created, using the names of the editable regions as the names of the XML tags.

Figure 17.68 The Import XML dialog box. XML files must end in .xml.

Figure 17.69 If the XML file does not include a line of code specifying the template, you'll be prompted to choose one. The code looks like this: <TmpName template="Templates/TmpName.dwt">

Select the radio button for the format you wish to use, then click on OK. Another Export Editable Regions as XML dialog box will appear, this one looking like a Save As dialog box (**Figure 17.66** on previous page).

4. Select the directory in which to save the XML file, and type a name for the file in the File name text box.

5. Click on Save.

You now have an XML file containing the contents of your page, including both XML and HTML tags (**Figure 17.67**). You may edit this file in Dreamweaver's HTML inspector, or in another text editor.

Importing XML

You may also take an XML file you've previously created and import it to use with a Dreamweaver template. The XML or item tags will become the names of editable regions. You may then add other elements such as page properties, tables, and so on to the file.

To import XML into a template:

1. From the Document window menu bar, select File > Import > Import XML Into Template. The Import XML dialog box will appear (**Figure 17.68**).

2. Select an XML file to use, and click Open. If the XML file does not specify a base Dreamweaver template, a warning dialog box will appear (**Figure 17.69**).

continues on next page

3. Click on OK. The Select Template dialog box will appear (**Figure 17.70**).

4. Select a template into which you wish to import the XML tags, and click on Select.

5. A new, blank HTML window will appear. Dreamweaver will *merge* the XML file with the template regions, and you can view the result in the Document window (**Figure 17.71**) and the HTML inspector (**Figure 17.72**).

✔ Attention!

■ This method of importing works best if you first create a Dreamweaver template and export it as XML, using your desired XML tags as the names of editable regions.

Figure 17.70 In the Select Template dialog box, choose the template into which to import the XML.

Figure 17.71 The Document window, displaying the "blank" page created by merging an XML file with a Dreamweaver template. The locked region is highlighted.

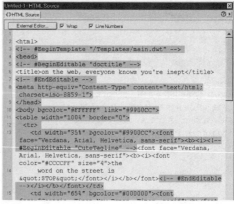

Figure 17.72 If you export a template as XML, then modify it and import it back into a template, the result will look much as it did before you exported it in the first place. I couldn't get any other sort of XML import to work.

What Good Is It?

If you look at it from just a Dreamweaver standpoint, it might seem kind of silly to go through these steps:

1. Create a page based on a Dreamweaver template.

2. Update the editable regions with actual content.

3. Export the content and the region names as XML.

4. Import the content and the region names, merge them with the structure of a Dreamweaver template, and create the same page you started with in step 1.

The more innovative use, of course, is to set database exports to create XML files that use those region names.

That way, you can do one of two things: First, you can use Dreamweaver to create templates for pages that will be served dynamically based on search results, customer profiles, cookies, and the like.

Second, you could use XML database exports for static pages when building a large site. For example, suppose you're building an enormous catalog. You can create a page like the one in **Figure 17.71** that has slots for item names and images rather than headlines and stories. Then you can create XML files for the feature pages from your database, and use Dreamweaver to import the XML onto the static pages.

To be sure the import-export process works properly, make sure the files use Dreamweaver's flavor of XML, especially including the name of the template to base the pages on.

EXPORTING AS XML

The History Palette

Just as a Web browser keeps track of the sites you've visited, Dreamweaver keeps track of the actions you've performed, and lists them in the History palette.

You can repeat or undo single or multiple actions using the History palette. You can also copy and paste actions or groups of actions. You can even save actions as commands to reuse later.

To view the History palette:

◆ From the Document window menu bar, select Window > History.

or

On the Launcher or mini-Launcher, click on the History button (**Figure 17.73**)

or

Press F9.

In any case, the History palette will appear (**Figure 17.74**).

What actions does the History palette store?

◆ Each Document window (and thus, each open document) has its own history list.

◆ On frames pages, each frame is a discrete document and has its own history list.

◆ When you close a Document window, the history list is cleared for that page.

◆ When you quit Dreamweaver, all history lists are cleared.

◆ The Site window has no history list.

Figure 17.73 Click on the History button on the Launcher or mini-Launcher to open the History palette.

Figure 17.74 The History palette, for a new document. No actions are listed because I haven't done anything on this new page.

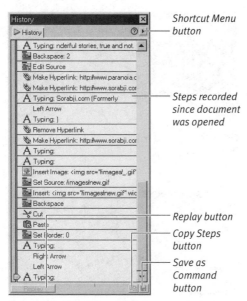

Shortcut Menu button

Steps recorded since document was opened

Replay button

Copy Steps button

Save as Command button

Figure 17.75 The History palette, for a page in progress.

When you open the History palette for a new document, it will appear blank (**Figure 17.74**). As you perform actions in the Document window (*not* the HTML inspector), they appear listed. If you open the History palette after you've done some work, you'll see your previous actions listed (**Figure 17.75**). See *Setting the Number of Stored Steps,* later in this chapter.

What Can You Replay?

Most actions can be replayed, including inserting objects such as tables and images; resizing and adjusting other object properties; typing text; modifying text; and copying, cutting, pasting, and deleting text or objects.

Sometimes an action will show up in the History palette with a red X over its icon. That means you can't replay, copy, or save it. These actions include dragging objects such as layers in the Document window, or selecting objects with the mouse.

You can repeat a selection action if you use your keyboard's arrow keys to select an object or some text. When you repeat several steps, if you include an arrow-key selection as the last repeated step, Dreamweaver will select the adjacent object as the last action in the series.

THE HISTORY PALETTE

Repeating and Undoing Actions

The History palette can repeat or undo single or multiple actions. Let's look at an example.

To repeat your last action:

1. In the Document window, select an object (**Figure 17.76**) and perform an action, such as making text bold (Ctrl+B or Command+B).

   The action will be listed in the History palette (**Figure 17.77**).

2. Now, select a different object on which you want to repeat the action. For example, select another piece of text (**Figure 17.78**).

3. In the History palette, click on the name of the action you want to repeat.

4. Click on Replay. In our example, the second piece of text would become bold. The action will also be listed again in the History palette (**Figure 17.79**).

Figure 17.76 I selected some text in the Document window.

Figure 17.77 I made the text bold, and the action Apply Bold appeared in the History palette.

Figure 17.78 I selected a second piece of text.

Figure 17.79 I clicked on Replay. The action was repeated on the new selection, and Apply Bold appeared listed again in the History palette.

Figure 17.80 I scrolled back one notch in the History palette. My action was reversed, and its name is grayed out in the History palette.

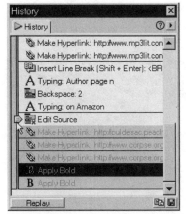

Figure 17.81 If I scroll back several notches, all those actions will be undone. To redo them, scroll back toward the bottom.

To undo your last action:

1. In the History palette, click on the slide-bar on the left side.

2. Scroll up one notch, and the action you just performed will become undone, and its name will be grayed out in the History palette (**Figure 17.80**).

To undo your last several actions:

◆ In the History palette, click on the slide-bar on the left side, and scroll up several notches (**Figure 17.81**). As you scroll, the actions you just performed will become undone in reverse order, and their names will be grayed out in the History palette.

✔ Tip

■ You cannot undo nonsequential steps in the History palette. They are arranged in reverse chronological order.

You can also redo any action you performed earlier.

To redo any action:

1. Select an object in the Document window. If you want to repeat a text insertion, click where you want the text to appear.

2. Click on the action's name in the History palette (**Figure 17.82**).

3. Click Replay. The action will be repeated (**Figure 17.83**).

Of course, you can undo and redo steps (singly or sequentially) in the Document window using keyboard shortcuts: Ctrl+Z (Command+Z) to Undo, Ctrl+Y (Command+Y) to Redo. These are also menu commands: Edit > Undo and Edit > Repeat.

The convenient thing is, you can repeat a *series* of steps on the next object you select.

Figure 17.82 I selected some text, and then I selected the "Make Hyperlink" step (for the correct URL) way back in the History palette.

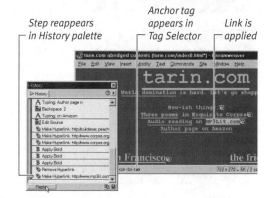

Figure 17.83 I clicked on Replay, and the link was made. The step also reappears as the last step in the History palette.

REPEATING AND UNDOING ACTIONS

Figure 17.84 I selected three sequential steps in the History palette, and I can replay them all at once.

Figure 17.85 I selected three nonadjacent steps in the History palette by holding down the Ctrl (Command) key while I selected. I can play these back as a group, too.

─Replay Steps action

┌Selected steps that were repeated

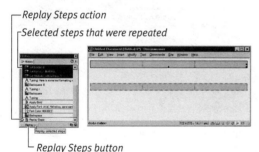

└ Replay Steps button

Figure 17.86 I selected the second table and replayed the selected steps. The "Replay Steps" action appeared in the History palette.

To redo a series of steps:

1. Select the object to which you want to apply the actions. In this example, I'm going to select a table.

2. In the History palette, select the steps you want to repeat. To select sequential steps, click and drag (**Figure 17.84**). To select nonadjacent steps, hold down the Ctrl (Command) key while you select the steps (**Figure 17.85**). For my table, I'm going to repeat the steps Set Border: 0, Set Bgcolor: #33FF33, and Set Attribute: cellpadding: 3.

3. Click Replay. The steps will be repeated on the selected object, and "Replay Steps" will appear as the last action in the History palette (**Figure 17.86**).

✔ Tip

■ To undo a set of actions like the one we just performed, you can undo the "Replay Steps" step. Just click on the last step and roll back the slidebar one notch.

Copying and Pasting Steps

Dreamweaver keeps a separate history list for each open Document window. If you want to share steps between documents, you can copy and paste steps.

To share steps between windows:

1. Display the Document window that includes the steps you want to share, and select the steps (**Figure 17.87**).

2. In the History palette, click on the Shortcut Menu button, and select Copy Steps from the menu (**Figure 17.88**).

   or

   Click on the Copy Steps button 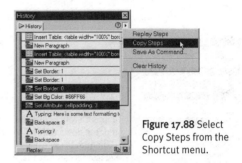.

3. Display the Document window (or open the document) that includes the objects you want to modify using the copied steps.

4. Select the object you want to modify, or click to place the insertion point where you want to insert an object (**Figure 17.89**).

5. From the Document window menu bar, select Edit > Paste.

   or

   Press Ctrl+V (Command+V).

   The steps will be replayed in the second window, and "Replay Steps" will appear in the History palette (**Figure 17.90**).

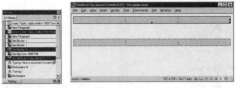

Figure 17.87 I selected three steps: inserting a table, setting the table border, and setting the cellpadding.

Figure 17.88 Select Copy Steps from the Shortcut menu.

Figure 17.89 In this example, I'm opening a new, blank document on which to insert the table, but you can open an existing document or display one that's already open.

Figure 17.90 I pasted the steps. The table appeared with the other modifications, and the single step "Paste Steps" appeared in the History palette.

✔ Tips

■ If you want to save steps permanently, see the next section, *Saving Steps as Commands*.

■ Do not attempt to copy and paste steps that include Copy or Paste as commands. You don't want to try to Paste a Copy, and you can't Paste a Paste that doesn't include a Copy, so just forget about it.

Pasting Steps into a File

Dreamweaver uses JavaScript as its native language for performing most actions. The steps stored in the History palette are little JavaScript widgets, not so different from the behaviors described in Chapter 15. If you copy a step or steps using the instructions on this page and then paste them into a text editor (or into the HTML inspector), they will appear as JavaScript. You can save them to reuse later or to rewrite if you're learning JavaScript.

To save steps as a command to reuse later, see the next section, *Saving Steps as Commands*.

For more about JavaScript and editing Dreamweaver commands, see Chapter 18.

COPYING AND PASTING STEPS

Saving Steps as Commands

If you come up with some handy multistep tricks you want to use again and again, you can save them as commands. That way, they'll be accessible—even after you quit and restart Dreamweaver—from the Commands menu.

To save steps as a command:

1. In the History palette, select the step(s) you want to save (**Figure 17.91**).

2. On the History palette, click on the Shortcut Menu button and select Save As Command (**Figure 17.92**)

   or

   Click on the Save As Command button: .

   The Save As Command dialog box will appear (**Figure 17.93**).

3. Type a name for your command. Spaces are okay.

4. Click on OK. The Command dialog box will close, and your command will be added to the Commands menu.

Figure 17.91 Select the steps you want to save as a command. They can be adjacent or nonadjacent.

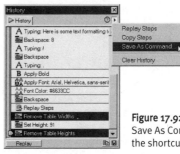

Figure 17.92 Select Save As Command from the shortcut menu.

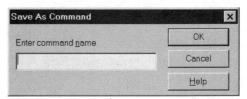

Figure 17.93 Type the name for your command in the Save As Command dialog box.

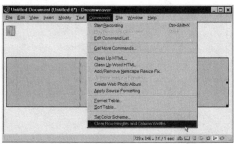

Figure 17.94 Your command will be available instantly from the Commands menu.

To use your new command:

1. Select the object to modify, or click to place the insertion point where you want to insert an object or text.

2. From the Document window menu bar, select Commands > [Your Command Name] (**Figure 17.94**). The steps will be repeated.

✔ Tip

- You can save as many commands as you like. These are HTML files containing JavaScript files, and they are saved in your Dreamweaver Configuration folder. To find out about editing menus and such using this folder, see Chapter 18.

Command Alternatives

What sorts of things make good commands? Well, the flip answer is, "Anything you do over and over again."

But as we've seen in this chapter, Dreamweaver offers other automation tools you can use instead of commands. For instance, bits of text, images, and other page components that you reuse can be stored as updatable library items. And if you're setting the look of an entire page, you may want to use an updatable template.

Text formatting that you use a lot, such as Bold + Courier + Size +1, can be saved as an HTML Style, described in Chapter 7.

In Chapter 18 I discuss custom objects, which allow you to add widgets you use a lot to the Objects palette and the Insert menu. Good examples of custom objects include tables, layers, horizontal rules, form fields, logos, and so on—with all the formatting intact.

You can also edit the names of commands or delete commands you added.

To rename a command you created:

1. From the Document window menu bar, select Commands > Edit Command List. The Edit Command List dialog box will appear (**Figure 17.95**).

2. Click on the name of the command you want to rename so that a box appears around the name (**Figure 17.96**).

3. Edit the existing name, or type a new name for the command.

4. Click on Close to close the dialog box and save your changes.

To remove a command you added:

1. From the Document window menu bar, select Commands > Edit Command List. The Edit Command List dialog box will appear.

2. Click on the name of the command you want to remove.

3. Click on Delete. A dialog box will appear asking if you're sure you want to delete it. Click on Yes.

   The command will be removed.

4. Click on Close to close the dialog box.

Figure 17.95 In the Edit Commands List dialog box, you can rename or delete commands you added.

Figure 17.96 Type a new name for the command, or edit the existing name.

Commanding Ideas

Here are some starter ideas for commands I've found useful:

◆ Clear Row Heights and Clear Column Widths (for tables).

◆ Set Vspace and Set Hspace (for images or tables).

◆ Set Page Properties (for a color scheme you use frequently).

◆ Insert Library Item [Name] (for frequently used library items—you don't even have to open the library!).

◆ Insert Copyright Mark.

◆ Adjust Cellpadding to n, Set Table Width to n, and so on (for adjusting tables to standard settings for your site).

◆ Set Bgcolor to [Teal] (for setting background colors of tables, cells, columns, and rows).

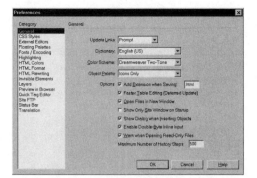

Figure 17.97 You can change the maximum number of stored steps in the General panel of the Preferences dialog box.

Setting the Number of Stored Steps

As you perform steps in the History list, the History palette stores them, but only as far back as the limit set in the preferences. As you perform more than this maximum number of steps, the oldest steps are erased. You can raise or lower this limit, but note that the more steps you store, the more memory is required by Dreamweaver.

To change the number of steps:

1. From the Document window menu bar, select Edit > Preferences. The Preferences dialog box will appear (**Figure 17.97**).

2. If it's not already selected, click on General in the Category box at the left.

3. The last item in the dialog box is Maximum Number of History Steps. The default number is 500; to change this, type a new number in the text box.

4. Click on OK to close the Preferences dialog box.

SETTING THE NUMBER OF STORED STEPS

Clearing the History List

If you want to start fresh after stacking up a lot of steps in the History palette, you can clear the history list. This doesn't undo any steps, but it erases all the steps from the History palette and from Dreamweaver's memory.

To clear the history list:

◆ On the History palette, click on the Shortcut Menu button, and select Clear History from the menu (**Figure 17.98**).

The history list will be cleared (**Figure 17.99**).

✔ Tip

■ You won't be able to Undo previous steps by pressing Ctrl+Z (Command+Z) after the history list is cleared, either.

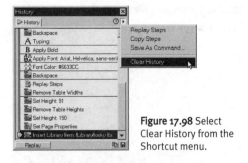

Figure 17.98 Select Clear History from the Shortcut menu.

Figure 17.99 The History palette was cleared of all its steps, but nothing was undone.

CUSTOMIZING DREAMWEAVER 18

Figure 18.1 You can create a custom panel in the Objects palette for storing custom objects.

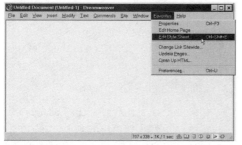

Figure 18.2 I added a custom menu to the Document window that includes all my most-used commands.

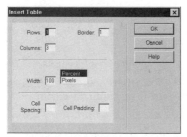

Figure 18.3 I changed the appearance of the Insert Table dialog box.

For all practical purposes, the entire Dreamweaver interface—that is, the back-end of the program itself—is written in JavaScript, HTML, and XML. That means you can customize the interface using a simple text editor.

If you know JavaScript, you can create your own dialog boxes, properties inspectors, palettes, menu commands, and so on. Unfortunately, that's beyond the scope of this book, but I'll point you toward some resources if you want to learn more.

Some Dreamweaver customization is simple and easy, however. You can add objects to the Objects palette and the Insert menu (**Figure 18.1**). You can edit Dreamweaver's menus and keyboard shortcuts (**Figure 18.2**). And you can edit the appearance of many of Dreamweaver's dialog boxes (**Figure 18.3**).

Custom objects are little widgets that tell Dreamweaver what to insert, and they may or may not use a dialog box. A line break, a comment, and a table are all objects, and you can add all sorts of HTML entities that you use over and over. You can also move, modify, or delete existing objects, and you can create your own panels in the Objects palette.

You can create custom menus, rename, move, or delete menu items, and change keyboard shortcuts by editing a single XML file. Working with existing XML isn't difficult if you're used to working with HTML, and most of it involves simple cutting and pasting.

And finally, you can edit the dialog boxes that Dreamweaver uses to insert and modify objects.

Other Customization Features

Other customizable features of Dreamweaver are discussed in the following chapters:

- Chapter 1: Stacking palettes

- Chapter 2: Customizing the Launcher, using the grid, using the rulers, setting page properties, and using the color dialog boxes

- Chapter 3: Customizing the Site window

- Chapter 4: Setting HTML formatting preferences

- Chapter 17: Using custom templates and library items, and adding to the Commands menu using the History palette

Many other chapters discuss modifying various preferences in Dreamweaver.

Figure 18.4 Our old friend the Objects palette. In this part of the chapter, we'll find out how to add objects to it.

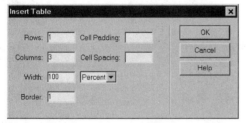

Figure 18.5 The Insert Table dialog box is called by a Dreamweaver object file. The dialog box takes user input before inserting the object.

Custom Objects

Object files, which appear in the Objects palette and the Insert menu, are simple HTML files that contain just snippets of HTML (without document formatting such as <HTML>, <head>, and <body> tags).

Once you create an object file, you add it to the Dreamweaver interface by adding an image to the Objects palette (**Figure 18.4**). Dreamweaver adds entries to the Insert Menu on your behalf.

Dreamweaver's pre-installed objects all use JavaScript to insert objects. Some objects, such as images and tables, use dialog boxes that you use to define the object before it's inserted (**Figure 18.5**), and these dialog boxes are also written in JavaScript. Other objects, such as horizontal rules and line breaks, include a single function, called the objectTag() function, that inserts the code onto the page.

For instance, the code for the Line Break object is as follows:

```
function objectTag() {
return "<br>";
}
```

You could also accomplish this with an HTML document that consisted of a single <BR> tag.

Modifying Dreamweaver Objects

Besides creating new custom objects, you can modify existing Dreamweaver objects. This involves modifying the HTML and/or the JavaScript that controls the insertion of each object—yet another good way to pick up some JavaScript fluency. (In particular, check out the JavaScript form tools used to create dialog boxes like the one in **Figure 18.5**.)

In some instances, this is simple; for instance, you could make the <br> object always have the "clear" attribute by editing the object so that it always read <br=clear> on insertion.

Before you start fooling around with the JavaScript, though, I recommend that you save a copy of the original object in a different folder, so you can restore it if you need to.

The first, and most important part of creating a custom object is creating the object file itself.

To create an object file:

1. Using Dreamweaver, another HTML editor, or a text editor, create a new, blank file.

2. Type or paste in the code for the object you want to create.

3. If the program automatically includes tags such as <html> and <body>, be sure to delete them (**Figure 18.6**).

4. Save the file as an HTML file (.htm or .html) in the Dreamweaver Objects directory:

   ◆ **Windows:** C:\Program Files\Macromedia\ Dreamweaver\Configuration\Objects\ [Object Folder Name]

   ◆ **Macintosh:** Dreamweaver/Configuration/ Objects/[folder name]

   You can also save the file in any of the folders within the Objects folder, including a new one (see the sidebar, facing page).

Before you can use your new object, you need to add it to Dreamweaver. After you add both the file and the image to an Objects folder, you need to restart Dreamweaver. Once you do this, the object will appear in both the Objects palette and the Insert menu.

✔ Tip

■ To download object files that other Dreamweaver users have made, select Insert > Get More objects. Your Web browser will take you to an objects clearinghouse on Macromedia's site.

Figure 18.6 A normal HTML file (left) includes <html>, <head>, <title>, and <body> tags. I deleted them in order to save the code as an object file, which in this case includes only the tags for the layer.

Figure 18.7 I created a custom panel in the Objects palette.

Figure 18.8 I created an 18x18 pixel image.

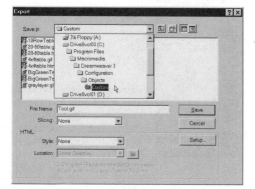

Figure 18.9 I saved the image in my Custom folder within the Objects folder. This is the same folder in which I saved the object file.

Now you need to add the Object to the Insert menu and the Objects palette.

You add the new object to the Objects palette by creating a 18-pixel by 18-pixel image with the same name as the object file. For instance, if the object file is named `GrayLayer.html`, the GIF should be named `GrayLayer.gif`.

You save this image in the same Objects folder as your file. If the object file is in the Forms folder, save your image in the Forms folder, too.

To add the new object to Dreamweaver:

1. Create an 18-pixel by 18-pixel GIF image (**Figure 18.8**).

2. Name it the same thing as the object file, and save it in the proper Objects folder (**Figure 18.9**).

    For example, if your HTML file is named `OrangeTable.htm`, you'd name the image `OrangeTable.gif`.

3. Quit and restart Dreamweaver.

Custom Object Panels

The Objects palette contains six panels: Characters, Common, Forms, Frames, Head, and Invisibles. These panels correspond to folders within the Dreamweaver Objects folder. To create your own custom panel in the Objects palette, just create a new folder within the Objects folder. **Figure 18.7** shows the Custom panel of the Objects palette, which I added by creating a folder called Custom in the Objects folder to hold my custom objects.

You can rename any of these folders, and the panel will be renamed. You can also move objects from folder to folder; just be sure to move both the image and the file.

You can create a new folder using Windows Explorer, the Finder in the Mac, or the Site window on either platform. The command is generally File > New Folder. To use the Site window to create an Objects folder, you have to designate the Configuration folder as a local site. See Chapter 3 if you need help.

To insert your object:

1. View the Objects palette (Window > Objects), and display the panel that contains your new object (**Figure 18.10**).

2. Click on the image to make sure it does what you want it to.

   or

   On the Document window menu bar, open the Insert menu, and select your object from the menu (**Figure 18.11**).

✔ Tips

- You'll find a starter image, called generic.gif, in the Objects folder. This image has the size specifications for an object image, as do the images in the different panel folders (Common, Forms, and so on.).

- If you create an image larger than 18x18, Dreamweaver will scale it down to that size.

- If you don't create an image file, Dreamweaver will use generic.gif as the button image on the Objects palette (**Figure 18.10**).

- To find out more about editing menus, see the next section in this chapter, *Editing Dreamweaver Menus.*

Figure 18.10 Now the image is on the Objects palette. Dreamweaver automatically shows the file's filename as a tool tip.

Figure 18.11 The objects I added are now available from the Insert menu. Later in this chapter, we'll find out how to edit the display names and rearrange the menu.

Don't Do Images?

Not a big image person? Try creating a 16-pixel by 16-pixel GIF that consists of a color and a letter: W.

Another solution is to take an existing image from the Objects folder and invert or colorize it using an image editor:

If you're frightened by image editors, I recommend using Jasc Paint Shop Pro or Macromedia Fireworks.

Editing Dreamweaver Menus

You can edit any menu in Dreamweaver. You can rename, move, or delete items, and you can add or change a keyboard shortcut for any item. You can also add items, but that requires firm knowledge of JavaScript.

The Dreamweaver menu commands are all stored in a file called menus.xml, which is stored in the Menus folder, inside the Configuration folder. The location of this file is

◆ **Windows:**
C:\Program Files\Macromedia\ Dreamweaver\Configuration\Menus\ menus.xml

◆ **Macintosh:**
Dreamweaver/Configuration/Menus/ menus.xml

Before you do anything to this file, make a backup copy of it. The file menus.bak is a pre-installed backup copy, as well, but one can never be too cautious when it involves editing application code.

✔ Tip

■ To add items to the Commands menu using the History palette, see the sections about History in Chapter 17.

About XML

The eXtensible Markup Language, affection-ately known as XML, is a markup language based on SGML, just as HTML is.

XML uses tags as containers to mark up text, just as HTML does. Most tags have an opener and a closer. For instance, in HTML, the <I> tag opens and closes like so:

```
<i>italic text</i>
```

The extensibility of XML means that developers can create new tags for specific purposes. So, in the Dreamweaver menus.xml file, you'll see tags called <MENU>, <MENUITEM>, <SEPARATOR>, and <MENUBAR>.

In HTML, if you use a tag that doesn't have a closer, you simply don't close it:

```
<img src="/images/image.gif">
```

In XML, if you use a tag that doesn't have a closer, you need to add a closing slash to the end of the tag:

```
<menuitem attributes="" />
```

Notice that there's a space before the closing slash.

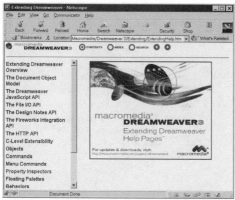

Figure 18.12 The help files called *Extending Dreamweaver* cover basic concepts behind adding inspectors, palettes, objects, commands, and so on.

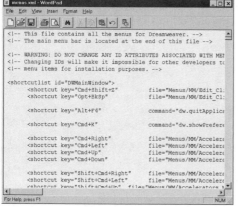

Figure 18.13 The menus.xml file is a behemoth.

Extending Dreamweaver with the JavaScript API

If you have a firm grasp of JavaScript, you can do much more than rearrange menu items. You can add palettes and inspectors, you can add and customize dialog boxes, and you can add translators for XML (like the one that translates server-side includes into inline HTML) or other content. You can modify the way the Site window works, the way code is written, the function of design notes, and more. Dreamweaver uses an extensible application programming interface (API) and allows modification of its Document Object Model (DOM).

Dreamweaver includes a second set of help files, called *Extending Dreamweaver,* which consists of instructions for people who want to add their own elements to the interface (**Figure 18.12**). This involves editing the source code, which means that commands must be written with JavaScript or C++ and then added to the interface using the JavaScript API. The location of the Extending Dreamweaver help files is:

Windows:
C:\Program
Files\Macromedia\Dreamweaver
3\Extending\ExtendingHelp.htm

Mac:
Hard Drive/Macromedia/Dreamweaver
3/Extending/ExtendingHelp.html

If you're learning how to write JavaScript, one way to begin extending the code is by starting with elements other people have written. You can find a repository of code additions on Macromedia's Web site at:

http://www.macromedia.com/exchange/
dreamweaver/

Be sure you keep plenty of backup copies of any files you modify.

About the Menus.xml File

The menus.xml file (**Figure 18.13**) contains several sections. First is the list of keyboard shortcuts, for the Document window as well as for the shortcut menus found on some of the inspectors and palettes. Second, for Windows users only, is the menu bar for the Site window (the Mac version uses the same menu bar for both). This is followed by the shortcut menus for the palettes and inspectors that use them.

✔ Attention!

- Do not use Dreamweaver to open or edit the menus.xml file. Use another text editor to open it. On Windows, you can use WordPad or HomeSite, for example. (I found that the file is too large to open with NotePad). On the Mac, you can use SimpleText or BBEdit. (BBEdit's versatile Find feature may help you out.)

- If you haven't created a backup copy yet, be sure to do a File > Save As when you open the file, so you don't accidentally delete anything vital.

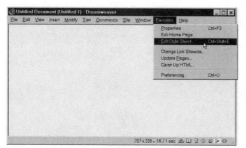

Figure 18.14 I added a menu called Favorites to the Document window menu bar.

The menus.xml file ends with the menu bar for the Document window. You can scroll to the near the end of the document and look for this line of starting code:

```
<menubar name="Main Window"
id="DWMainWindow">
```

Or, you can do a Find (Edit > Find in your text editor) for this code or for part of it, such as id="DWMainWindow".

Tags in the menus.xml file are nested, just as they are in HTML. So the outline of the code looks something like this:

```
<menubar>
    <menu name="Menu Name">
        <menuitem name="Menu Item" />
        <menuitem name="Menu Item 2" />
    </menu>
</menubar>
```

Menus that are nested within menus, such as the Table menu within the Modify menu, are similarly nested in the code:

```
<menu name="Menu Name">
    <menuitem name="Menu Item" />
    <menuitem name="Menu Item 2" />
    <menu name="Nested Menu Name">
        <menuitem name="Nested Menu Item" />
    </menu>
</menu>
```

You can add a new menu to the interface, within another menu or on a menu bar. Make sure to use both opening and closing <menu> tags; give the menu a unique name; and give the menu a unique ID. For the Favorites menu I added in **Figure 18.14**, I used the following code:

```
<menu name="_Favorites"
id="DWMenu_Favorites">
<menuitem name="" />
</menu>
```

Of course, in my menu, I used actual menu items.

About Menu Items

Each menu item is represented by an individual tag within the menus.xml file. The command Insert > Table is within the menu named "Insert," and it looks like this:

```
<menuitem name="_Table"
key="Cmd+Opt+T" file="Table.htm"
id="DWMenu_Insert_Table" />
```

Attributes for each item include name, key, file, and ID. The *name* is the name of the item, as it appears in the menu, and preceded by an underscore. *Key* is the keyboard shortcut, if any. *File* is the name of the file that contains the HTML and/or JavaScript for performing the menu command. And *ID* is the attribute that Dreamweaver uses to identify the menu item.

✔ Attention!

- Do not change the ID attribute of any menu item, or Dreamweaver may not be able to perform the menu command.

Figure 18.15 The Text menu, in its original state.

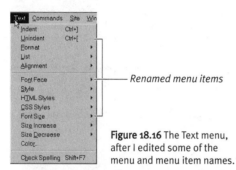

— Renamed menu items

Figure 18.16 The Text menu, after I edited some of the menu and menu item names.

Renaming menus and menu items

You can rename any menu or menu item. Let's look at the Text menu for examples (**Figures 18.15** and **18.16**). You might want to rename the Font menu Font Face, or the Size menu Font Size. Or you might want to rename Outdent "Unindent" instead.

To rename a menu or menu item:

1. Quit Dreamweaver.

2. Open your working copy (not the pristine backup) of menus.xml in your favorite non-Dreamweaver text editor.

3. Locate the menu or menu item you want to rename, and make sure it's within the correct menu bar (**Figure 18.17**).

4. Type a new name for the menu or menu item. If it's preceded by a underscore, leave the underscore there (**Figure 18.18**). If the underscore appears elsewhere in the name, don't worry about placing it.

5. Don't touch the ID attribute.

6. Save your file as menus.xml in the Menus folder.

Launch Dreamweaver and look for the new name.

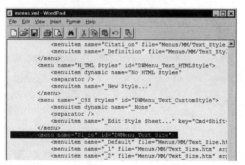

Figure 18.17 I located the menu name I wanted to change.

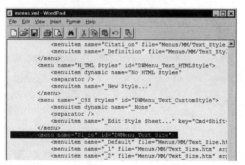

Figure 18.18 I typed a new name for the menu.

ABOUT MENU ITEMS

Rearranging Menu Items

If you want, you can move a menu item from one menu to another, or you can rearrange the order of items within a single menu. For instance, you might want to move a frequently used item to the top of a menu; you could move Properties to the top of the Window menu, or Launcher to the bottom.

Or, you might want to create a new menu and move or copy your favorite menu items there (**Figure 18.19** and **18.20**).

To move a menu or menu item:

1. Quit Dreamweaver.

2. Open your working copy (not the pristine backup) of menus.xml in your favorite non-Dreamweaver text editor.

3. Locate the menu or menu item you want to move or duplicate, and select it (**Figure 18.21**). When selecting an entire menu, make sure to include both its opening and closing tags.

   ◆ To move the menu item, cut it (Ctrl+X/Cmd+X).

   ◆ To duplicate the menu item elsewhere, copy it (Ctrl+C/Cmd+C).

4. Place the insertion point where you want the selection to appear, whether it's in the same menu or a different one.

5. Paste the menu item (Ctrl+V/Cmd+V) into its new location (**Figure 18.22**).

6. Don't touch the ID attribute.

7. Save your file as menus.xml in the Menus folder.

8. Launch Dreamweaver and look for the new arrangement (**Figure 18.23**).

Figure 18.19 I created a custom menu called Favorites simply by adding a menu tag and copying and pasting my most-frequently used menu items into it.

Figure 18.20 This is the XML code for my custom menu in the menus.xml file.

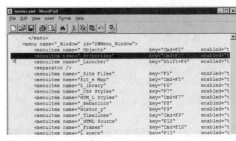

Figure 18.21 Select the menu item you want to move.

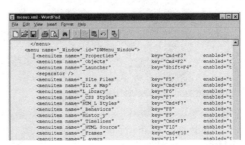

Figure 18.22 I moved the Properties inspector line above the Objects palette line in the Window menu.

Figure 18.23 Now my Window menu on the Document window menu bar lists the Properties inspector first.

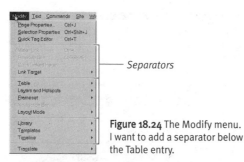

Figure 18.24 The Modify menu. I want to add a separator below the Table entry.

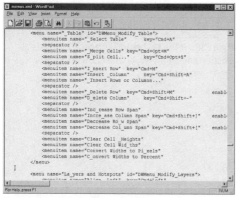

Figure 18.25 This is where I want the separator to go.

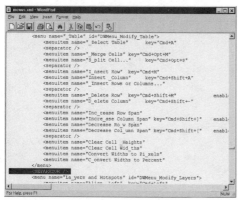

Figure 18.26 I added the separator tag.

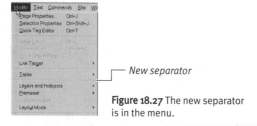

Figure 18.27 The new separator is in the menu.

Deleting a Menu Item

You can remove a menu item entirely if you never use it. Or, for example, suppose you find yourself using the Insert > Layer command instead of drawing a layer with the Objects palette. You can remove the option.

To delete a menu item:

1. Follow steps 1-3, above, and cut the menu item.

2. Follow steps 7 and 8, above.

Remember that your backup copy retains the old menu item, should you want to restore it.

Adding a Separator

Separators, similar to horizontal rules, divide areas on a menu (**Figure 18.24**).

To add a separator:

1. Quit Dreamweaver.

2. Open your working copy (not the pristine backup) of menus.xml in your favorite non-Dreamweaver text editor.

3. Locate the place where you want your separator to appear (**Figure 18.25**).

4. On a new line, insert the following code (**Figure 18.26**):

   ```
   <SEPARATOR />
   ```

5. Save your file as menus.xml in the Menus folder.

6. Launch Dreamweaver and look for the separator (**Figure 18.27**).

✔ Tip

To remove a separator, simply remove the appropriate <SEPARATOR /> line from the menus.xml file.

DELETING A MENU ITEM/ADDING A SEPARATOR

Changing Keyboard Shortcuts

You can change keyboard shortcuts in Dreamweaver either by using a previously unused shortcut or by reassigning an existing shortcut to a different menu item.

✔ Tip

■ The Dreamweaver help files include a Keyboard Shortcut Matrix (**Figure 18.28**) that displays standard key combinations and the command attached, if any. The location on your computer is something like this:

Windows:
`C:\PROGRAM FILES\MACROMEDIA\DREAMWEAVER 3\ Help\html\17shortcuts23.html`

Mac:
`Hard Drive/Macromedia/Dreamweaver 3/ Help/html/17shortcuts23.html`

To change a keyboard shortcut:

1. Quit Dreamweaver.

2. Open your working copy (not the pristine backup) of menus.xml in your favorite non-Dreamweaver text editor.

3. If you're adding a new keyboard shortcut that doesn't need to be reassigned, skip to step 6.

   If you need to remove references to your shortcut first, locate, in the menus.xml file, the menu command that contains the shortcut you want to use, and copy the shortcut (Ctrl+C/Cmd+C).

4. Open the Find feature of your text editor, and paste (Ctrl+V/Cmd+V) the shortcut into the Find What text box.

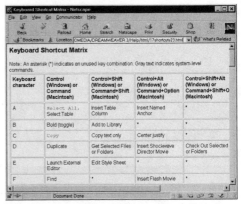

Figure 18.28 The Keyboard Shortcut Matrix lists all existing and empty keyboard shortcuts in Dreamweaver.

Figure 18.29 I'm changing every reference to the Properties inspector to indicate my new shortcut. By using "Cmd" instead of "Ctrl," my shortcut will work on both Windows and the Mac.

Figure 18.30 You can see, in the Window menu, that I changed the keyboard shortcut for displaying the Properties inspector. Note that "Cmd" shows up as "Ctrl" on the PC. On the Mac, it would be displayed as the butterfly symbol that's on the Command key.

5. Find each instance of the shortcut in the menus.xml document, and delete each one. The key attribute will read key="".

6. Find the menu item to which you want to assign the new shortcut.

If the menu item already has a shortcut, select it and paste the shortcut over it (**Figure 18.29**).

If the menu item does not have a shortcut, you need to add the key attribute:

key="Ctrl+Shift+P"

7. Don't touch the ID attribute.

8. Save your file as menus.xml in the Menus folder.

9. Launch Dreamweaver and test the new shortcut. The menu item should also indicate the new combination (**Figure 18.30**).

✔ Tip

■ If a shortcut is assigned to two different menu items, the first pairing listed in menus.xml will be the working combination. That means it's especially important to make the changes in the keyboard shortcuts section at the top of the menus.xml file.

Mama's Little Baby Likes Shortcuts

Some people like clicking on buttons, some people prefer to do their selecting with menus, and others like the quick convenience of keyboard shortcuts. I don't know about you, but I have a lot of standard keyboard shortcuts memorized, and not so many non-standard ones. I remember that F10 opens the HTML inspector, but if I want to open any other palette or inspector, I'm pretty much wedded to the Window menu.

You can, however, change keyboard shortcuts so that they work for you.

For instance, the Properties inspector didn't even get a keyboard shortcut in Dreamweaver 1.2, and I can't seem to remember Ctrl+F3. So I decided to make it more like P, for Properties. Ctrl+P is paste, and I don't want to change that. So I open the Document window, press Ctrl+Shift+P, and look at the History palette. It looks like Ctrl+Shift+P is Format: Paragraph. I don't use that shortcut, anyway. So first, I'm going to divorce that shortcut from that command, and then, I'm going to add a new line, wedding it to my command, Window > Properties.

A key such as a number or a letter is a regular key; a key such as Control or Command is a modifier. The modifiers are as follows:

◆ **Ctrl** Ctrl, both platforms

◆ **Cmd** Command on the Mac, Ctrl on Windows

◆ **Alt, Opt** Interchangeable for Alt on Windows and Option on the Mac

◆ **Shift** (Shift key, both platforms)

To combine modifiers and keys, use their names and a plus sign:
Shift+Ctrl+P

Other keys, including function keys (F1, F2) and keys such as Home, PgUp, and PgDn, are typed as they are spelled on the keyboard. *Space* is spelled Space.

Figure 18.31 Open the file you want to modify. Its name will be similar to its menu command name.

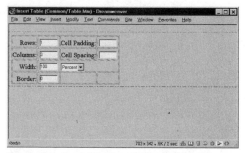

Figure 18.32 Doesn't look much like a dialog box, does it?

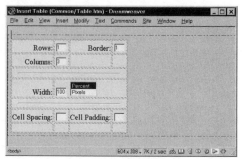

Figure 18.33 I modified some of the menus in the Insert Table dialog box.

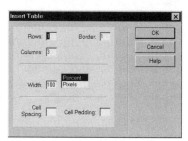

Figure 18.34 After quitting and restarting Dreamweaver, this is what the dialog box looks like.

Customizing Dialog Boxes

You can customize the appearance of dialog boxes in Dreamweaver, too. These include the dialog boxes you use to insert objects and modify behaviors, as well as other commands. You can rearrange menu items, change the size of text boxes, relabel form fields, and remove unused items.

✔ Tips

■ To find out about modifying forms-based interfaces, see Chapter 12.

■ You cannot add an item to a dialog box unless you also add the name of the object in the JavaScript API. See *Extending Dreamweaver with the JavaScript API*.

■ In Chapter 12, the first thing we did when we added a form field was to name it. The names of form fields in Dreamweaver dialog boxes are linked to their functionality, so don't change them.

To customize a dialog box:

1. Locate the .htm or .html file for the dialog box you want to modify. It will be found in the Configuration folder, and then in either the Commands, Behaviors, or Objects folder (**Figure 18.31**).

2. Make a backup copy of the file in a different folder. I keep a Backups folder in the Configuration folder.

3. Open the file in Dreamweaver (**Figure 18.32**).

4. Use Dreamweaver's form tools to modify the file (**Figure 18.33**).

5. Save the file with its original name in its original folder. Make sure you're keeping a pristine backup, too.

6. Quit and relaunch Dreamweaver, then open the dialog box to test it (**Figure 18.34**).

Plug-ins
and Active Content

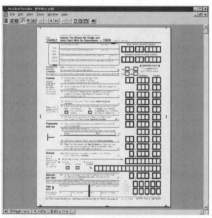

Figure 19.1 All sorts of documents, in every format, can be accessed over the Web.

Figure 19.2 Plug-ins such as Shockwave turned the Web into a multimedia experience. Without Shockwave, online gaming wouldn't be nearly as cool. And I wouldn't be able to abduct aliens at http://www.shockwave.com.

Before Mosaic, any file that wasn't text or HTML had to be downloaded and saved to open later with a separate application. When Mosaic hit the scene, some images could be viewed inline, but other forms of media were still "save and play." (Many computers back then weren't true multitaskers, and most people didn't do a lot of simultaneous audio, much less video.)

Netscape Navigator 1.1 could automatically launch helper applications to play these downloaded files. Audio started becoming part of the life of the Web, and programs like Adobe Acrobat came onto the scene (**Figure 19.1**).

Navigator 2 went a step further and forever changed the face of the Web. Plug-ins could play or view darned near any type of file you could think of. Now, not only could you view Shockwave movies inline (**Figure 19.2**), but music could also be embedded invisibly into Web pages, and RealAudio could even play these files while they downloaded. Netscape 2 also introduced Java and VRML capabilities to the mainstream world.

Microsoft's answer to plug-ins was ActiveX, a scripting language that used Visual Basic and OLE technology to duplicate the plug-in idea and take it a step further.

Dreamweaver makes it easy to insert the code for these multimedia objects onto your pages. Dreamweaver tries to be as cross-platform as possible about these doo-dads.

✔ Tips

■ You can insert any of these objects using the Common panel of the Objects palette (Window > Objects) and you can modify them using the Properties inspector (Window > Properties or Modify > Selection Properties). I'm just refreshing your memory, in case you'd forgotten.

■ In previous versions of Dreamweaver, canceling out of inserting a media object inserted a placeholder anyway. This odd behavior has been fixed in Dreamweaver 3.

■ To skip the Select File dialog box for inserting media objects, change your preferences. From the Document window menu bar, select Edit > Preferences. In the General panel of the Preferences dialog box (**Figure 19.3**), deselect the Show Dialog when Inserting Objects dialog. Then click OK to close the dialog box and save your changes.

■ You can set up external editors for working with media objects in Dreamweaver. See the sidebar, *Image Editor Integration*, in Chapter 8 or the section of Appendix D, on the Web site, about setting up external HTML and text editors. Follow the instructions and specify your file type and application (instead of image or HTML files).

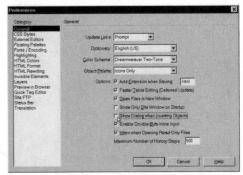

Figure 19.3 Deselect the *Show Dialog When Inserting Objects* checkbox to skip the Insert dialog boxes.

The Sound of Downloads

When linking to sound files, it's a good idea to let your users know what they're in for. Unless the sound is very small, it's good practice to indicate the file type and file size of sound files so that users know whether to download them. For instance, some older Mac browsers don't support .WAV files, and some older PC browsers don't support .AIFF files. And any user on a 14.4 kbps modem wants advance notice before they start downloading a 100K+ sound file.

A line like this near the link should do the trick:

They Killed Kenny! (10K .WAV)

or even better:

They Killed Kenny! (10K .WAV, 9K .AIFF)

Figure 19.4 Type the location of the sound file in the Properties inspector's Link text box.

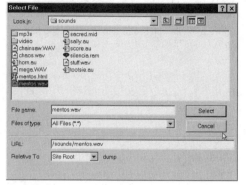

Figure 19.5 Select the sound file in the Insert File dialog box (this is the Mac view).

Using Sound Files

Sound files come in more flavors than ice cream (see the sidebar, *Sound File Types*). Not all browsers support all sound files, but any browser that supports plug-ins or ActiveX (Navigator or Explorer versions 2 or later) should be able to play most sound files. Navigator 3 or later's pre-installed LiveAudio plug-in plays nearly every common sound file type.

There are two ways to add a sound file to your page. One way is to link to the sound file, so that the user downloads and plays it when they click on a link. The other way is to embed the sound file so that it begins to load when the page loads, and a plug-in will play it automatically when the sound file finishes loading.

A sound link is like any other link.

To link to a sound file:

1. In the Document window, select the text or image that you want to make into the link.

2. In the Properties inspector, type the pathname for the sound file in the Link text box (**Figure 19.4**).

   or

   Click on the folder icon, and use the Select File dialog box to choose a sound file from your computer (**Figure 19.5**). Be sure to select All Files (*.*) from the Files of type drop-down menu.

3. Press Enter (Return). The selection will be linked to the sound file.

continues on next page

When the user clicks on the link, they'll download the sound file (**Figure 19.6**).

When the user clicks on the link on your page, one of three things will happen:

◆ An external program, or "Helper App," will launch to play the sound file (**Figure 19.6**); or

◆ The browser will play it using its own capabilities or those of a plug-in; or

◆ If the browser doesn't support or recognize the file type, an error will occur. Sometimes a dialog box will open that says "Unrecognized file type," and sometimes the browser will open the file as if it were text.

Figure 19.6 WinAmp is one kind of helper app that plays sound files.

Embedding a sound file is similar to linking to an image. You can add the <embed> tag by inserting the sound file as plug-in content, or you can add the code by hand.

To embed a sound file:

1. View the document you want to attach the sound file to in the Document window.

2. Click to place the insertion point at the place in the document where you want the sound controller to appear. For invisible sound files, you can place the file anywhere, although at the top or bottom of the document is usually more convenient.

3. View the HTML source for the page in the HTML inspector by selecting Window > HTML from the Document window menu bar (or by pressing F10).

4. For a sound file with no controls showing, type the following line of code:

```
<embed src="sounds/yoursound.wav"
autoplay="TRUE" hidden="TRUE">
</embed>
```

Where sounds/yoursound.wav is the pathname of the sound file.

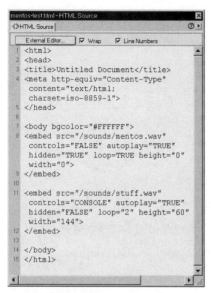

Figure 19.7 The code for a standard, non-visible Netscape controller (top), and for a standard visible controller.

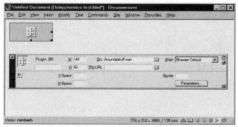

Figure 19.8 This is the same page we saw in Figure 19.7. Note that the hidden controller is not displayed at all in the Document window.

5. Save your changes to the page (**Figures 19.7** and **19.8**).

6. Preview the page in a browser to make sure it works.

✔ Tip

■ You can embed a sound file with or without the use of the plug-in dialog box. Because Dreamweaver's Insert > Plug-in feature doesn't include all the stuff you need for embedding sounds in a page, I'm going to discuss embedded sound and plug-ins as if they were two different entities.

Explorer's <bgsound> Tag

Versions of Internet Explorer before 4.0 do not support embedded sound files. Explorer uses a proprietary tag called <bgsound>. You can use the <embed> and <bgsound> tags on the same page.

A <bgsound> tag goes in the body of the document and looks like this:

```
<bgsound src="sounds/mysound.wav" loop="infinite" autoplay="true" volume=0>
```

The loop parameter can be either infinite or a number. Volume can be 0 (full) to –10,000 (lowest). There are no user controls to display with the <bgsound> tag.

Sound File Parameters

Embedding a sound requires a plug-in, which is no sweat for browsers that support such things. If you want to use Dreamweaver to insert these parameters into a sound plug-in file (rather than typing them into the code), see *Extra Parameters*, later in this chapter.

Here's the skinny on some of the different parameters you can use with sound files that use the `<embed>` tag:

- `src=""` (required)
  The source of the file.

- `name=""`
  Name the embedded file if you want to call it from a script. If you use the `name` value, you must also include the `mastersound` attribute (no value).

- `controls=console|smallconsole|true|false`
  (Required for visible controllers.)

- `hidden=true|false`
  Determines whether the controller is visible.

- `autoplay=true|false`
  Determines whether the sound begins playing as soon as it loads.

- `volume=0%–100%`
  Percent of system volume used.

Sound File Types

.AIFF: Macintosh Audio format.

.AU: Sun Audio format.

.DCR: Shockwave audio (also used for Shockwave movies). Requires Shockwave plug-in.

.LA, .LAM, .LMA: Netscape streaming audio. Handled automatically by Netscape 4 and over.

.MID, .MIDI: MIDI electronic music format. Requires plug-in in Netscape 2.0.

.MOD, .RMF: Beatnik audio format. Requires Beatnik plug-in. (Note: once Beatnik is installed, it will also handle .AIFF, .AU, .MID, and .WAV by default.)

.MOV: QuickTime audio (also used for QuickTime movies). Requires QuickTime plug-in.

.MPG: MPEG, or MP3 files, which provide CD-quality sound. Requires an audio plug-in such as RealPlayer or QuickTime or a helper app such as WinAmp.

.RAM, .RPM: RealAudio (also used for RealVideo). Requires RealAudio or RealPlayer plug-in.

.WAV: Windows Audio.

Figure 19.9 The standard Netscape LiveAudio sound controller, embedded in a page. LiveAudio plays .AIFF, .AU, .MID, and .WAV files, among others.

Figure 19.10 The same controller in Explorer. Note that it ignores the given dimensions.

It's a good idea to include the URLs of the plug-in and your favorite browser.

◆ `loop=true|false|n`

Determines whether the sound will loop continuously. A setting of `loop=3` would make the file loop three times.

◆ `height` and `width` (Required for visible controllers.)

Determines the height and width of the controller. For console: `height=60 width=144`. For smallconsole: `height=15 width=144`.

When you adjust the height and width of an embedded controller, its placeholder changes shape in the Document window.

◆ `align="LEFT|RIGHT|TOP|BOTTOM"`

Defines alignment for visible controllers.

◆ `HSPACE="n" VSPACE="n"`

Sets space around visible controllers.

◆ `type="MimeType"`

Use for listing the mime type of a plug-in.

A standard audio controller (**Figures 19.9 and 19.10**) would have the following settings:

```
<embed src="sounds/yoursound.wav"
height="60" width="144"
controls="CONSOLE" autostart="FALSE"
loop="FALSE"></embed>
```

✔ Tips

■ If the source for the sound file isn't correct, the console will not show up in Navigator.

■ Quotation marks are not essential for anything but SRC, but Dreamweaver prefers them.

Noembed

If you want to provide a description of a sound or other plug-in for browsers without plug-in capability, use the NOEMBED tag:

```
<noembed>
```

```
This page contains content available
only with the DorkBlast plug-in and
a plug-in capable browser.
```

```
</noembed>
```

Netscape Plug-ins

Netscape plug-ins work in Netscape 2 or later. Many plug-ins can be set either to run inline or to launch a helper app. They can also be set to play different qualities of content depending on the computer or modem speed. The RealPlayer is a good example of both of these traits.

There are some ActiveX equivalents to Netscape plug-ins; see *ActiveX*, later in this chapter, and the documentation for the specific plug-in.

To insert a Netscape plug-in:

1. In the Document window, click to place the insertion point at the place on the page where you want the plug-in to appear.

2. From the Document window menu bar, select Insert > Plug-in.
   or
   Click on the Insert Media Plug-in button on the Objects palette.

3. Either way, the Select File dialog box will appear (**Figure 19.11**). When you locate the file, click on Open.

4. When the pathname of the plug-in appears in the Plug-in Source text box, click on OK. The dialog box will close and a plug-in placeholder will appear in the Document window: 🧩.

✔ Tip

■ You can use the behavior called Check Plug-in to determine whether a user has a particular plug-in installed. See Chapter 15 for more details.

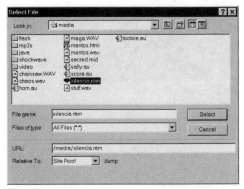

Figure 19.11 Browse for the plug-in files on your computer. Remember that you're looking for the media file to be played, not the plug-in component (DLL) that plays it.

Playing Plug-ins in Dreamweaver

Dreamweaver now supports some plug-ins, which means you can play them inline in the Document window. You must have the plug-in installed in Netscape's (or Dreamweaver's) plug-ins folder for Dreamweaver to be able to play the plug-in.

There are two ways to play a plug-in with Dreamweaver. First, on the Properties inspector for a selected plug-in, there's a green Play arrow on the expanded inspector. Press this button to play the selected object. The button will turn into a red Stop button, whose use you can guess.

Alternately, you can select View > Plug-ins > Play (and Stop). You can also select View > Plug-ins > Play All (or Stop All) for pages that have multiple plug-ins.

Your mileage may vary. A couple notes: Don't do this with ActiveX. The Play button's there, but Macromedia doesn't recommend doing so. I had problems getting Dreamweaver to play even a simple `.WAV` file.

Figure 19.12 The Properties inspector, displaying plug-in properties

Plug-in Properties

Properties you can set for Netscape plug-ins include the following:

Name the plug-in by typing a name for it in the text box.

Set dimensions for the plug-in by typing the **W**(idth) and **H**(eight) in the associated text boxes.

Change the **Source** by typing it in the Src text box. Click on the Folder icon to browse for the file on your computer.

If a user doesn't have the plug-in installed, they can be directed to an installation page. Type the URL for this page in the **Plg URL** text box.

Set the **alignment** of the plug-in on the page by selecting an alignment from the Align drop-down menu. These alignment options are the same as for images. (I discuss image alignment in Chapter 5.)

To provide an **alternate image** for browsers without plug-in capabilities, type the Image source in the Alt text box. Click on the Folder icon to browse for the image on your computer.

V space and **H space** denote an amount of space around the plug-in. **Border** describes a visible border around the plug-in. (I discuss these options further with regard to images in Chapter 8.) The units for these options are in pixels. Type a number without units in the appropriate text box.

After you insert the placeholder, you can set additional properties for the plug-in.

To set Plug-in properties:

1. Select the Plug-in placeholder in the Document window. The Properties inspector will display Plug-in properties (**Figure 19.12**).

2. Change any properties in the Properties inspector, and click on the Apply button.

3. To set extra parameters, click on the Parameters button. (See *Extra Parameters,* later in this chapter.)

✔ Tip

■ If you change the source for the plug-in by clicking on the folder icon, you'll need to select the appropriate file type, or **All Files**, from the Files of Type drop-down menu.

Shockwave and Flash

Shockwave and Flash Player are Netscape plug-ins, but you get more up-front ability to set their attributes by using the Insert > Media > Shockwave and Insert > Media > Flash tools. Director, Flash, and Dreamweaver are all made by Macromedia, after all, and integration of the three is one of Dreamweaver's big selling points.

To insert a Shockwave or Flash file:

1. In the Document window, click to place the insertion point at the place on the page where you want the Shockwave or Flash movie to appear.

2. From the Document window menu bar, select Insert > Media > Shockwave Director or Insert > Media > Flash.

   or

   Click on the Insert Shockwave 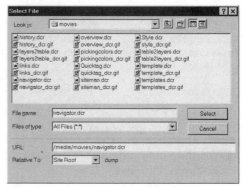 or Insert Flash button on the Objects palette.

3. The Select File dialog box will appear (**Figure 19.13**). Locate the file on your computer. Click on Open when you find the file.

4. When the filename of the movie appears in the Movie Source text box, click on OK. The dialog box will close and an icon will appear in the Document window: .

✔ Tip

- Behaviors for detecting whether a browser has Shockwave or Flash installed and for inserting Shockwave or Flash controls are discussed in Chapter 15.

Figure 19.13 Choose a .DCR file or a .SWF (Flash) file from your computer.

Using Aftershock with Dreamweaver

Aftershock is an HTML tool used with Director and Flash to create HTML files using Shockwave. You can open files created with Aftershock and edit them in Dreamweaver. You can also select the relevant HTML and paste it into other Dreamweaver documents.

If you want to edit Aftershock object files that have been inserted into Dreamweaver HTML documents, view them in the Properties inspector and click on Launch Aftershock. Edit the Aftershock file, close the program, and accept the This File has Been Edited dialog box. For more on using Dreamweaver with external editors, see the Tip earlier in this chapter.

Figure 19.14 The Properties inspector, displaying Shockwave for Director properties.

Figure 19.15 The Properties inspector, displaying Flash properties. Note that Flash has a few extra attributes.

Once you've gone through the motions of inserting a Shockwave or Flash file, you can change the properties.

To set Shockwave properties:

1. Select the Shockwave or Flash placeholder in the Document window. The Properties inspector will display Shockwave properties (**Figure 19.14**) or Flash properties (**Figure 19.15**).

2. Change any properties in the Properties inspector, and click on the Apply button.

3. To set extra parameters, click on the Parameters button. (See *Extra Parameters,* later in this chapter.)

SHOCKWAVE AND FLASH

Shockwave and Flash Properties

Properties you can set for Shockwave for Director and Shockwave Flash include the following:

Name the plug-in by typing a name for it in the text box.

Set dimensions for the Shockwave or Flash movie by typing the **W**(idth) and **H**(eight) in the associated text boxes.

Change the **Source** by typing it in the File text box. Click on the Folder icon to browse for the file on your computer.

Set the **Tag** by selecting it from the Tag drop-down menu. The `<object>` tag is used by Internet Explorer, and the `<embed>` tag is used by Netscape Navigator. By default, Dreamweaver inserts code for both tags so the object shows up in both browsers. If you're making browser-dependent pages, choose the appropriate tag.

Set the **alignment** of the movie file on the page by selecting an alignment from the Align drop-down menu. These alignment options are the same as those for images. (I discuss image alignment in Chapter 8.)

To set the **background color** that will fill the dimensions before the movie loads and after it finishes playing, type a hex code for the color in the Bgcolor text box, or click on the Color button to choose a color. (I discuss choosing colors in the most detail in Chapter 2.)

ID sets the ID parameter for the Shockwave or Flash ActiveX control.

V space and **H space** denote an amount of space around the plug-in. **Border** describes a visible border around the plug-in. (I discuss these options further with regard to images in Chapter 8.) The units for these options are in pixels. Type a number without units in the appropriate text box.

To provide an **alternate image** for browsers without plug-in capabilities, type the Image source in the Alt text box. Click on the Folder icon to browse for the image on your computer.

Additional Flash Properties:

Quality sets the quality of Flash movies according to processor speed. Anti-aliasing is used to smooth the appearance of frame-to-frame playback in Flash, and that requires a fast machine. *Low* turns off anti-aliasing in favor of playback speed. *High* turns on anti-aliasing in favor of appearance. *Autohigh* starts out using anti-aliasing and turns it off if the machine's performance isn't keeping up. *Autolow* starts off without anti-aliasing and turns it on if possible.

Scale is used if the H and W settings are different from the original movie size. *Default (Show All)* scales the movie using its original aspect ratio and may fill in the blanks using borders. *No borders* makes these borders invisible. *Exact fit* abandons the original aspect ratio to make the movie fit the dimensions. You can also set the H and W values to % instead of pixels to scale the Flash movie to the window size.

Autoplay causes the Flash movie to begin playing as soon as it loads. **Loop** makes the Flash movie loop as long as the page is in view.

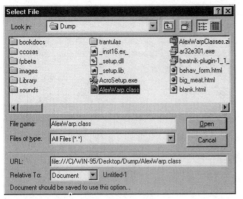

Figure 19.16 Select the class file from your computer. The file will probably have the .CLASS extension.

Java Applets

Java is an object-oriented programming language based on C++ and developed by Sun Microsystems. The goal of Java is to be as cross-platform as possible. Currently, most Java applets (little applications) are run inline inside a Web browser, although standalone programs—and even operating systems—have been written for Java.

Java applets run on Netscape 2 or later for PCs, Netscape 2.2 or later for the Mac, and Internet Explorer 3 or later.

To insert a Java applet:

1. In the Document window, click to place the insertion point at the place on the page where you want the Java applet to appear.

2. From the Document window menu bar, select Insert > Media > Applet.

   or

   Click on the Insert Applet button on the Objects palette 🐢.

   Either way, the Select File dialog box will appear (**Figure 19.16**).

3. Locate the applet on your computer. When you locate the source file, click on Open.

4. When the pathname of the applet appears in the Java Class Source text box, click OK. The dialog box close and a placeholder will appear in the window 🐢.

✔ Tip

■ Some applets will run on your computer; others must be on a Web server, depending on how many additional classes they require to run.

After you insert the placeholder, you can set additional properties for the Applet.

To set Applet properties:

1. Select the Applet placeholder in the Document window. The Properties inspector will display Applet properties (**Figure 19.17**).

2. Change any properties in the Properties inspector, and click on the Apply button.

3. To set extra parameters, click on the Parameters button. (See *Extra Parameters,* later in this chapter.)

Figure 19.17 The Properties inspector, displaying Applet properties.

Applet Properties

Properties you can set for Java Applets include the following:

Name the applet by typing a name for it in the text box.

Set dimensions for the applet by typing the **W**(idth) and **H**(eight) in the associated text boxes.

Change the Source by typing it in the **Code** text box. Click on the Folder icon to browse for the .CLASS file on your computer. When you set the source for an applet, the **Base** text box is automatically filled in. This indicates the home directory for the applet.

Set the **alignment** of the applet on the page by selecting an alignment from the Align drop-down menu. These alignment options are the same as for images. (I discuss image alignment in Chapter 8.)

V space and **H space** denote an amount of space around the plug-in. (I discuss these options further in regard to images in Chapter 8.) The units for these options are in pixels. Type a number (without units) in the appropriate text box.

To provide an **alternate image** for browsers without Java capabilities, type the Image source in the Alt text box. Click on the Folder icon to browse for the image on your computer.

ActiveX

ActiveX is a software architecture developed by Microsoft for use in Internet Explorer 3 or later. An ActiveX control can act like a plug-in and invisibly play multimedia content, or it can act like Java or JavaScript and serve as a miniature program that runs inside the Internet Explorer Web browser.

There is a plug-in for Netscape 4 that plays some ActiveX controls, but support is not built into the program and the plug-in should not be counted on to work. Dreamweaver tries to be as cross-platform as possible about this; you can insert an ActiveX Control and specify the Netscape plug-in equivalent, and Dreamweaver will write code for both programs simultaneously.

To insert an ActiveX control:

1. In the Document window, click to place the insertion point at the place on the page where you want the ActiveX control to appear.

2. From the Document window menu bar, select Insert > Media > ActiveX.

   or

   Click on the Insert ActiveX button 🖼 on the Objects palette.

3. Either way, an ActiveX placeholder will appear in the Document window at the insertion point 🖼.

✔ Tips

- You can use JavaScript to have the browser go to one URL if the browser is ActiveX capable and to a different URL if it's not. See the section in Chapter 15 called *Check Plugin*, and use the ActiveX checkbox.

- Macromedia recommends that you refer to the documentation for the ActiveX control to determine the requisite IDs and parameters needed.

ActiveX Properties

Properties you can set for ActiveX controls include the following:

Name the control by typing a name for it in the text box.

Set dimensions for the control by typing the **W**(idth) and **H**(eight) in the associated text boxes.

Set the **Class ID** for the control by selecting it from the drop-down menu or typing it in the Class ID text box. (See step 3 in *To set ActiveX properties* for information about Shockwave and ActiveX.) If you change your mind about the selected ID, select the text and press Delete. Clicking on the Minus button will permanently remove the ID from the list of options.

If the class is not on the list, type the URL from which Explorer can download the ActiveX control in the **Base** text box.

To set up the Netscape equivalent of the control using the <embed> tag, place a checkmark in the **Embed** checkbox. Once you've selected this option, the **Src** (source) text box will become available. Type the URL for the plug-in file source in the Src text box.

Data sets the source for a data file used by some ActiveX controls.

ID sets the ActiveX ID parameter. This optional number can be used to pass information from control to control; it can also be used for security purposes.

Set the **alignment** of the control on the page by selecting an alignment from the Align drop-down menu. These alignment options are the same as for images. (I discuss image alignment in Chapter 8.)

To provide an **alternate image** for browsers without ActiveX capabilities, type the Image source in the Alt text box. Click on the Folder icon to browse for the image on your computer.

V space and **H space** denote an amount of space around the plug-in. **Border** describes a visible border around the plug-in. (I discuss these options further in regard to images in Chapter 8.) The units for these options are in pixels. Type a number without units in the appropriate text box.

Figure 19.18 The Properties inspector, displaying ActiveX properties

After you set up the placeholder, you can set additional properties for the ActiveX control.

To set ActiveX properties:

1. Select the ActiveX placeholder in the Document window. The Properties inspector will display ActiveX properties (**Figure 19.18**).

2. Change any properties in the Properties inspector, and click on the Apply button.

3. Control IDs for RealPlayer, Shockwave, and Shockwave Flash are pre-installed. If you select Shockwave or Shockwave Flash, the placeholder will change from ActiveX to Shockwave because Dreamweaver automatically writes ActiveX code for those programs.

4. To set extra parameters, click on the Parameters button. (See *Extra Parameters*, next.)

✔ Tip

■ Frequently used ClassIDs are stored in the Properties inspector. To delete one permanently, click on the Minus (-) button on the Properties inspector for ActiveX.

ACTIVEX

485

Extra Parameters

Some multimedia objects require other parameters for optimal performance. These parameters may be indicated in the documentation for the language or program you're using. Of course, if it's an applet or object you wrote yourself, you'll know all about it already. (See the sections on sound for details about embedded sound parameters.)

Figure 19.19 Add any extra attributes for your multimedia files in the Parameters dialog box.

To set additional object parameters:

1. In the Document window, select the placeholder for the object. The Properties inspector will display the object's properties.

2. On the Properties inspector, click on the Parameters button. The Parameters dialog box will appear (**Figure 19.19**).

3. Click on the Plus (+) button. The Parameter text field will become available.

4. Type the name of the parameter in the Parameter text field (such as **loop**).

5. Press the Tab key. The Value text field will become available.

6. Type the value of the parameter in the Value text field (such as **TRUE**).

7. Repeat steps 3–6 for any additional parameters.

8. When you're all set, click on OK to close the dialog box and return to the Document window.

Figure 19.20 shows the Parameters dialog box displaying parameters for an embedded sound file.

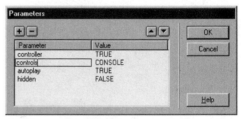

Figure 19.20 These are the parameters for an embedded sound file. I find it more expedient to type the parameters in the HTML inspector and then proof them in the Parameters dialog box.

Removing and Reordering Parameters

You can change the operation order of parameters by clicking on the name of the parameter in question and clicking on the up or down arrow buttons to move the parameter through the list. You can also delete a parameter:

1. Follow steps 1 and 2 in the list on this page to open the Parameters dialog box.

2. Click on the name of the parameter you want to delete.

3. Click on the Minus button. The parameter will be deleted.

MANAGING YOUR WEB SITES

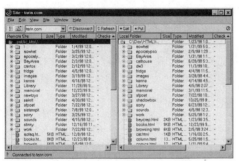

Figure 20.1 The Site window is not only a file management tool, but also a full-fledged FTP client.

Once you're ready to put a page—or an entire site—up on the Web for the whole world to see, you don't have to leave Dreamweaver. The Site window (**Figure 20.1**) is a full-fledged, handy-dandy FTP client. That means it's a built-in tool for *putting* files on the Web, or *uploading* them. You can also use Dreamweaver to *get* files from the Web, or *download* them.

✔ Tip

- If you skipped Chapter 3, go back and use it to help you set up a local site. You can't use Dreamweaver's site management tools without setting up a local site.

Once you set up your site information, including both the local site paths and the name of your Web host, you can connect to a remote server—the place where your Web site will live. As you move files back and forth from place to place, Dreamweaver makes sure that the directory structure of the two versions of the site mirror one another. Dreamweaver doesn't make automatic updates, but if you delete or add a file in one location, it can scan for changed links automatically, as described in Chapters 3 and 9.

Also in this chapter, you'll find out about other site management tools, such as the site map (**Figure 20.2**), design notes (**Figure 20.3**), and file synchronization. If you're working with a team, you can also find out how to set up the check-in and checkout features.

Setting up remote site info

Remote site information allows you to connect to an existing Web site. You will be connecting either to an FTP site or to a local network. If you're not sure which, ask your network administrator.

If you're on a dialup account, it's likely you'll use an FTP (file transfer protocol) site. Even if you're on a local network, you may be using FTP.

To set up remote site info (FTP):

1. From the Site window menu bar or the Document window menu bar, select Site > Define Sites. The Define Sites dialog box will appear (**Figure 20.4**).

2. Select the local site you want to set up, and click on Edit. The Site Definition dialog box will appear (**Figure 20.5**).

3. In the Category box at the left, click on Web Server Info. That panel of the dialog box will come to the front (**Figure 20.6**).

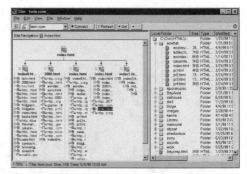

Figure 20.2 The site map lets you see the link relationships in your site at a glance.

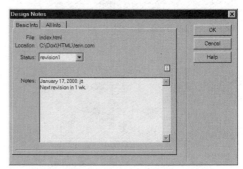

Figure 20.3 Design notes let you leave love notes for your web design team.

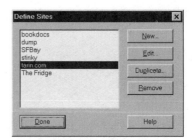

Figure 20.4 Choose which local site to set up for prime time in the Define Sites dialog box.

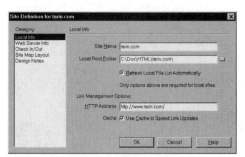

Figure 20.5 The Site Definition dialog box is where you set up and edit both local and remote site management information.

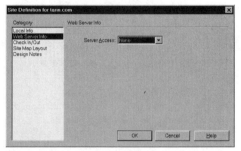

Figure 20.6 The Web Server Info area of the Site Definition dialog box starts out blank.

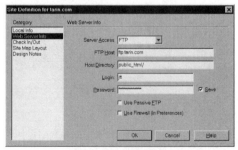

Figure 20.7 If your server access is through FTP, you'll enter all your account information here.

4. From the drop-down menu, select FTP. The dialog box will display FTP information (**Figure 20.7**).

5. In the FTP Host text box, type the alphanumeric address for the Web server (for example, ftp.site.com or www.site.com).

6. In the Host Directory text box, type the name of the initial root directory for the site (e.g., public_html or html/public/personal).

7. In the Login text box, type the username for the ftp or www account. In the Password text box, type the password for the ftp or www account.

8. To save the username and password, place a checkmark in the Save checkbox.

9. When both the local and remote site information are filled out, click on OK to close the Site Definition dialog box. You'll return to the Site window, where you'll see your local site displayed.

✔ Tip

■ If you use the same FTP host for several different sites, you can avoid having to repeat these steps again and again. In the Site Definition dialog box, you can select a site with remote information already set up, and then click on Duplicate to make a copy of it. Then, rename the site and edit the local root folder information.

Setting up for a local network

If you're on a local network at work, a DSL (Digital Subscriber Line), or cable modem account at home, you may connect to your Web server via a local network. Even if you use a local network, you may still use FTP to put files on the external or internal Web servers. If that's the case, use the previous section in this book on FTP servers. In the case of a truly local intranet Web server, you connect using the Network Neighborhood (Windows) or AppleTalk (Macintosh) to choose a machine to put files onto.

To set up remote site info (local):

1. **Windows users:** Log into your Network Neighborhood as yourself.

   Mac users: Use the Chooser to connect to the local server using AppleTalk.

2. Follow steps 1-3 in the previous section.

3. From the Site Definition dialog box drop-down menu, select Local/Network. The dialog box will change to reflect your choice (**Figure 20.8**).

4. In the Remote Folder text box, click on the Folder icon, and the Choose Remote Folder dialog box will appear (**Figures 20.9** and **20.10**).

5. **Windows:** Choose Network Neighborhood from the Select drop-down menu, and then browse through the computers on the network as if they were regular folders. When you find the right machine and folder, click on Select.

   Mac: Select Desktop from the drop-down menu, then select the server from the ones displayed. When you find the right machine and folder, click on Choose.

6. Click on OK to close the Site Definition dialog box. You'll return to the Site window, where you'll see your local site displayed.

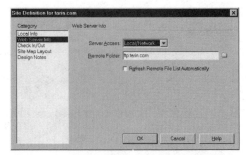

Figure 20.8 If you're using a local network via the Windows Network Neighborhood or Macintosh AppleTalk, you can choose your local machine here.

Figure 20.9 The Choose Remote Folder dialog box. It's just like selecting a folder, only it happens to be on a different computer.

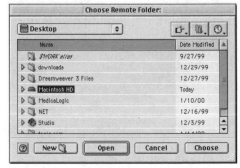

Figure 20.10 The Mac's Choose Remote Folder dialog box. By default, it starts you out on the Desktop, which is where your remote computer is after you connect with the Chooser.

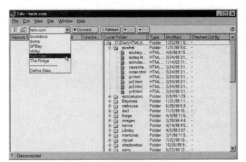

Figure 20.11 Choose the site you want to connect to from the Remote Site drop-down menu.

Figure 20.12 A series of dialog boxes will briefly appear while Dreamweaver connects you to the remote site.

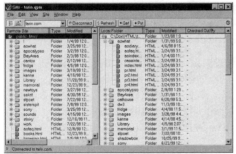

Figure 20.13 You'll know you're connected when Dreamweaver says so. The Connect button will be a Disconnect button. Oh, yeah, and the files will be displayed in the Remote Site pane of the Site window. (They do stay in view after you've disconnected, however.)

Connecting to a Remote Site

Before you can download an existing remote site or upload to it, you need to connect to it.

To connect to a remote site:

1. Set up a remote site profile.

2. In the Site window, select the site you want to connect to from the Site drop-down menu (**Figure 20.11**).

3. Click on the Connect button. Dreamweaver will use the host and other information you gave it to connect to the remote Web server.

4. A Connecting to [host name] dialog box will appear while Dreamweaver contacts the Web server (**Figure 20.12**) .

5. When you've successfully connected to the remote server, the Connect button will change to a Disconnect button (**Figure 20.13**), and the remote file list will appear.

After you've finished getting and putting files, you can disconnect from the remote site.

To disconnect from a remote site:

1. In the Site window, check in the status bar to make sure there aren't any files being transferred. If the window is idle, the status line should read "Connected to [site name]."

2. Click on Disconnect. The status line will read *Disconnected* and the Disconnect button will again read *Connect*.

✔ Tip

- If you don't move a file for a period of 30 minutes, Dreamweaver will disconnect for you. To change this, see *Site FTP Preferences*, later in this chapter.

Getting and Putting

Now you're ready to download (get) stuff from and upload (put) stuff to your local and remote sites. If the files you download are in a directory on the remote site that doesn't yet exist on the local site, the directory will be created on the local site; and vice versa.

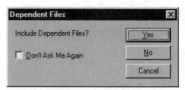

Figure 20.14 The Dependent Files dialog box can automatically get or put images or other files attached to the page.

To download files from a remote site:

1. Connect to the remote site as described on the previous page.

2. In the Site window, select the file(s) or folder(s) you want to download.

3. Click on Get. The Dependent Files dialog box will appear (**Figure 20.14**) . Click on Yes or No (see the sidebar, *About Dependent Files*, this page).

4. The progress of the download will appear in the status bar of the Site window while the files are being retrieved.

To upload files to a remote site:

1. Connect to the remote site.

2. In the Site window, select the file(s) or folder(s) you want to upload.

3. Click on Put. The Dependent Files dialog box will appear (**Figure 20.14**). Click on Yes or No (see the sidebar, *About Dependent Files*).

4. The progress of the upload will appear in the status bar of the Site window while the files are being sent to the remote server.

✔ Tips

■ Right-click (Ctrl+click) on a file and select Get or Put from the pop-up menu.

■ To stop the current transfer, click on the Stop Current Task button, or press Esc (Command+. (period) on the Mac).

About Dependent Files

When you get or put a file in the Site window, the Dependent Files dialog box will appear, asking you if you want to include dependent files (**Figure 20.14**).

Dependent files include images, sound files, plug-ins, and other objects the page links to. Dependent files also include all the files in a frameset.

This feature can be really convenient; you can click on the frameset document and then click on Yes in the Dependent Files dialog box, and all the files and images in the frameset will be uploaded to the site.

On the other hand, if you do most of your dealing in single documents, you may find this feature annoying. Just place a checkmark in the Don't Ask Me Again checkbox and you won't see the dialog box any more.

You can show and hide dependent files in the Site Map view, which is described later in this chapter.

To set preferences for dependent files, see *Site FTP Preferences*, at the end of this chapter.

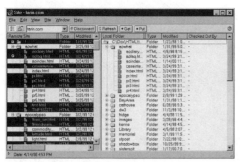

Figure 20.15 The newer files are automatically highlighted in the Site window.

Figure 20.16 The Synchronize Files dialog box lets you select batches of newer files to get, put, or both.

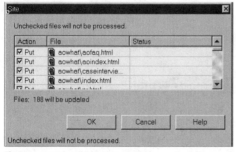

Figure 20.17 This dialog box lets you uncheck files out of a big batch to be left alone.

✔ Tip

■ I strongly discourage checking the *Delete remote files not on local drive* checkbox. If you get files, any ones on your local site that don't exist on the remote site will be deleted from your computer. If you put files, any ones on the remote site that are not on your local site will be deleted from the Web server. Yes, that goes both ways, even though the Synchronize Files dialog box doesn't show it.

Synchronizing

Dreamweaver can automatically select a batch of newer files in a directory or entire site, so that you can be sure you're not overwriting the latest version of a file during a transfer.

To select newer files:

1. Select the proper local site and connect to the associated remote site.

2. From the Site window menu bar, select Edit > Select Newer Local or Edit > Select Newer Remote, depending on the pane in which you want the newest files to be highlighted. Dreamweaver will compare the dates of the local and remote files.

3. When the comparison is complete, the files that are newer than the ones on the other site will be highlighted (**Figure 20.15**). After double-checking, you can get, put, or synchronize the selected files.

The Synchronize feature selects newer files and then gets or puts them automatically, as a batch. You may want to make backups first.

To synchronize files:

1. From the Site window menu bar, select Synchronize. The Synchronize Files dialog box will appear (**Figure 20.16**).

2. From the Synchronize drop-down menu, choose whether to sync the entire site or just a selection.

3. From the Direction drop-down menu, choose whether to Get, Put, or Both.

4. Click on OK to prepare to sync up. The Site dialog box will appear (**Figure 20.17**). Uncheck any files you don't want to include.

5. When you're ready, click on OK. The specified, newer files will upload or download, and the progress of the transfers will appear in the Site window status bar.

Refreshing and Switching Views

If you move files around on your local site using a local file management program, or if you move them around on the remote site using a different FTP program, the Site window might not accurately reflect what's where. You can refresh the view—just like reloading a page in a browser window.

To refresh the Site window:

◆ From the Site window menu bar, select View > Refresh Local (Shift+F5) or View > Refresh Remote (Alt+F5 (Option+F5)). On the Mac, the command is Site > Site Files View > Refresh Local or Refresh Remote.

Or, just click on the Refresh button.

Dreamweaver will check the displayed directory info against the actual directory info and display the latest file and folder paths.

More Site View Tips

◆ The fourth possible view is the Site Map, which I describe later in this chapter.

◆ Drag the lower-right corner of the Site window to change the window size. Drag the frame border between the two window panes to adjust the space given to each.

◆ To hide floating windows that may cover the Site window, press F4. Press F4 again to show only the windows open before.

◆ To change which view is always showing, Local or Remote, see *Site FTP Preferences*, at the end of this chapter.

Expander arrow

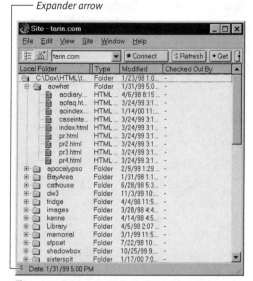

Figure 20.18 Conserve your desktop: Show only one view at a time in the Site window by clicking the Expander arrow. This is the Local view.

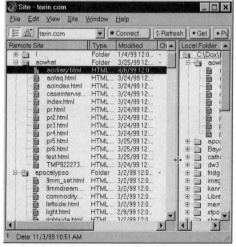

Figure 20.19 The Remote view in the Site window. I dragged the frame border to show only the Remote pane. You can reverse the way these figures work by changing the Site FTP Preferences.

Changing site views

There are three different site views you can use when working with site files: Local, Remote, or Both. The default view is Both.

To change the site view:

◆ Show the Show Always portion of the site, Local or Remote, by clicking on the Expander arrow (**Figure 20.18**).

or

Drag the border between the panes to view only one frame at a time in the Site window (**Figure 20.19**).

The window will expand or contract into the view option you selected (**Figures 20.18** and **20.19**).

Checking In and Checking Out

If several people are collaborating on a site, it might be helpful to know who put which file where, and when they did it. (If there are only one or two of you, you should already know the answer.)

Checking out a file marks the file with a green checkmark, assigns your username to that file, and locks it in the Dreamweaver Site window. Other team members who use Dreamweaver will not be able to overwrite locked files (files checked out by another person). These files can be overwritten by any other FTP client, however. This is a simpler, user-based, and less secure approximation of CVS checkout, a Unix-based tool used in production groups.

Files other people have checked out are marked in the Site window with a red checkmark and the person's checkout name appears in the Checked Out By column (**Figure 20.20**).

Setting up file check-in

Before you can check files in or out, you must enable that option in the site's definition.

To enable check-in and checkout:

1. From the Site window menu bar, select Site > Define Sites. The Define Sites dialog box will appear (**Figure 20.21**).

2. Select the site for which you want to set check-in and checkout options, and click on Edit. The Site Definition dialog box will appear (**Figure 20.22**).

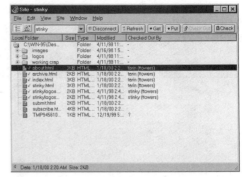

Figure 20.20 The files with checkmarks have been checked out; you can see the checkout names in the Checked Out By column.

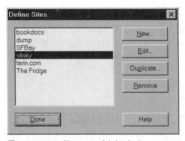

Figure 20.21 Choose which site's check-in preferences to modify in the Define Sites dialog box.

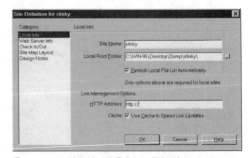

Figure 20.22 The Site Definition dialog box.

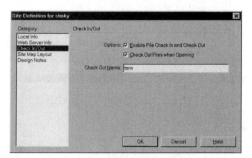

Figure 20.23 Enable file checkouts and set your checkout name in the Check In/Out panel of the Site Definition dialog box.

3. In the Category box at the left, select Check In/Out. That panel will move to the front of the dialog box (**Figure 20.23**).

4. To enable check-in and checkout, click that checkbox.

5. If you want to mark files as checked out when you open them in the Document window, check the Check Out Files When Opening checkbox.

6. Type the name you want others to see when you check out files in the Check Out Name text box. This can be your full name or your username (e-mail address).

7. Click on OK. Now, each time you get a file from the remote server, it will be marked as checked out, and each time you put a file, it will be marked as checked in.

✔ Tips

- If you access your files from a different computer and cannot perform an upload because the files are checked out, you can still upload or download them by using a different FTP client, such as Telnet/CVS, WS_FTP, Fetch, or Cute FTP.

- If you're using the Check-in/Out feature to prevent others on your team from overwriting each other's work, make sure they are using Dreamweaver to manage their FTP sessions.

CHECKING IN AND CHECKING OUT

Checking in a file unlocks it on the remote server, but makes it read-only on your local site so that you don't accidentally edit a file that is not checked out.

Think of it like a library book: When you check out a book, no one else can borrow it until you return it. When you check it back in, anyone can access it but you.

To check out one remote file:

1. Connect to the appropriate site in the Site window.

2. Click on Check Out.

3. Respond to the Dependent Files dialog box.

The file will be copied to the local site (**Figure 20.24**), but it won't open.

You may have to refresh the Local site view to see the file (or its folder, if that was freshly created, too).

✔ Tip

■ You can also double-click on a file in the Site window to both open and check out the file at the same time.

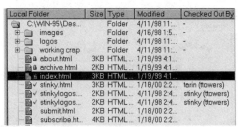

Figure 20.24 When files have been checked into the site, they appear locked in the Local pane of the Site window. That's because you're supposed to check out a file before you edit it locally.

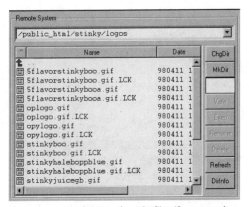

Figure 20.25 You can see the .LCK files if you examine the site with an FTP client other than Dreamweaver's.

To check out more than one file:

1. Connect to the appropriate site in the Site window.

2. Select the files or folders you want to check out in the remote site.

3. From the Document window menu bar, select File > Check Out (Site > Site Files View > Check Out on the Mac).

4. Respond to the Dependent Files dialog box.

About .LCK Files

When you check out a file using Dreamweaver, a lock is placed on the file in the Dreamweaver Site window. This lock is a text file with the .LCK extension. .LCK files are invisible in the Dreamweaver Site window, but you can see them in a different FTP client (**Figure 20.25**).

An .LCK file contains the username of the person who checked it out. This file also shows the date and time of the checkout in the time stamp.

You can see the date and time of a .LCK file in most FTP clients in the date and time column. The .LCK files I examined were only 7 bytes each (there are 1000 bytes in 1 kilobyte), so they aren't going to make you run out of server space any time soon.

The files will be transferred to the local site, but they will not automatically open in the Document window. The files will get a green checkmark and a .LCK file on the remote server. Your checkout name will appear in the Checked Out By column in the Local Sites pane of the Site window.

To undo a file checkout:

◆ After checking out the files, select File > Undo Check Out (Site > Site Files View > Undo Check Out) from the Site window menu bar.

To check in files:

1. Connect to the appropriate site in the Site window.

2. In the local site, click to select the files or folders you want to check in.

3. From the Document window menu bar, select File > Check In (Site > Site Files View > Check In on the Mac). Or, just click on the Check In button.

4. Respond to the Dependent Files dialog, as well as the Overwrite dialog box in **Figure 20.26** or **20.27**, if one appears.

The file will appear with a locked icon on the local site. The Checked Out status and the .LCK file will be removed from the remote server (**Figure 20.28**), and your name will disappear from the Checked Out By column.

Figure 20.26 You may get a dialog box like this if you try to overwrite a newer, single file.

Figure 20.27 You may get a dialog box like this if you try to overwrite a batch of files.

Figure 20.28 The padlocks on the remote site are gone now that the files have been checked in.

✔ Tips

■ When a file is checked out, a checkmark will appear in the Checked Out column when the file is selected. If there isn't a checkmark there already, you can check out a file by clicking in this column.

■ To turn off the read-only feature for checked-in files, select File > Turn Off Read Only (Macintosh: Sites > Site Files View > Turn Off Read only) from the Site window menu bar.

CHECKING IN AND CHECKING OUT

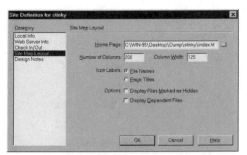

Figure 20.29 The Site Map Layout panel of the Site Definition dialog box. Go here first to set up a home page for your site map.

Figure 20.30 Choose your home page. This is just like an Open dialog box in Windows.

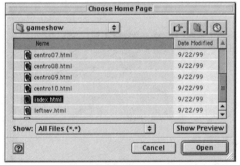

Figure 20.31 Choose your home page. This is just like an Open dialog box on the Mac.

Using Site Maps

Dreamweaver offers visual site maps for use in viewing the relationships of files, not only in the sense of what's in what directory but also regarding what links to what.

To use a visual site map, you must first select a file to be the home page file. This can be the default index page of a particular site. You may also decide to display a site map for a subsection of a site, in which case you would change the home page view to make that page the focal point of the site map.

To set the home page:

1. In the Site window, select Define Sites from the Sites drop-down menu. The Define Sites dialog box will appear.

2. Choose the site you want to edit, and click on Edit. The Site Definition dialog box will appear.

3. In the Category box at the left, click on Site Map Layout. That panel of the dialog box will come to the front (**Figure 20.29**). If your site root has a file called index.html, Dreamweaver will assume it's the home page and fill in the Home Page text box.

4. In the Home Page text box, type the path of the file to set as the home page, or click on the Browse button to open the Choose Home Page dialog box (**Figures 20.30** and **20.31**).

5. Select the file, and click on Open to close the Choose Home Page dialog box and return to the Site Definition dialog box.

6. Click on OK to close the Site Definition dialog box and return to the Site window.

Now you can view the site map.

To view the site map:

1. On the Site window, click on the Site Map View button (**Figure 20.32**) ⚒ . The Site window will display the site map (**Figure 20.33**).

2. You can drag the lower-right corner of the window to enlarge it, and you can drag the border between the two frames.

To adjust the site map layout:

1. Follow steps 1-3 on the previous page to bring up the Site Map Layout panel of the Site Definition dialog box (**Figure 20.29**, previous page).

2. Set the maximum number of columns by typing a number in the Number of Columns text box.

3. Set the column width in pixels by typing a number in the Column Width text box.

4. You can use either filenames or page titles as the labels for each page icon.

   ◆ To view file names, select the File Names radio button.

   ◆ To view page titles, select the Page Titles radio button.

5. To display all files, including those that would normally be hidden (such as .LCK files and FTP logs), check the Display Files Marked as Hidden checkbox.

6. To display all dependent files, such as all files in a frame family, check the Display Dependent Files checkbox.

7. Click on OK to close the Site Definition dialog box and return to the Site window (**Figure 20.34**).

✔ Tip

■ You can toggle the last three options on and off by selecting them from the View menu on the Site window menu bar.

Figure 20.32 Click on the Site Map View button to view the site pane of the Site window. To view *only* the site map in the Site window, click and hold down the button, and from the pop-up menu that appears, select Map Only.

Figure 20.33 The site map. Ta-da! You can examine, visually, the relationships between pages on your site.

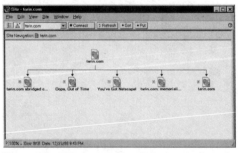

Figure 20.34 This site is in Map-Only view. I adjusted the site map layout so that page titles instead of filenames are visible. I also changed the number of columns to 250 and the column width to 150.

Site Map Icons and Tips

In Site Map view, various icons are used to represent different types of pages or links. These icons are described in **Table 20.1**. Lower levels of the site use smaller versions of the same icons.

In Dreamweaver 2, the site map displayed only two levels of the site at a time. Dreamweaver 3 lets you expand the site map almost infinitely.

To view more levels:

◆ In the site map window, pages with more levels are marked by a + (plus) sign. Click on the plus sign to view the subsidiary links for that file (**Figure 20.35**).

To view the map from a branch:

◆ From the Site window menu bar, select View > View as Root (Macintosh: Site > Site Map View > View as Root). The map will rearrange as if the selected page were the site root (shown in **Figure 20.37**, next page).

To save the site map as an image:

1. From the Document window menu bar, select File > Save Site Map As. The Save Site Map dialog box will appear (**Figure 20.36**, next page).

2. Type a filename for the graphic in the File Name text box.

3. From the Save as Type drop-down menu, select Bitmap (BMP), Ping (PNG), or PICT (on Mac).

✔ Tip

■ If you want to put this graphic up on a Web page, you must first use an image editor to convert it into a GIF. You can then create an image map so that it's clickable, (see Appendix A on the Web site).

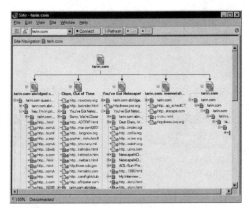

Figure 20.35 Click on the plus signs (+) to expand the links for each document in your local site.

Table 20.1

Site Map Icons

Icon	What it Means
index.html	Green checkmarks indicate files you have checked out.
stinkylogos.html	Red checkmarks indicate files someone else has checked out.
about.html	Padlocks indicate locked or read-only files.
index.html	The broken icon indicates a broken link—that is, a link to a local file that there is no copy of on the local site.
http....com/index8.html	A blue globe indicates a file whose link can be found, or a link to a script or e-mail address.
fridge.html	A page icon.
stinky.gif	An image icon.
mailto...mckinley.com	A mailto link icon.
http://www.tarin.com	A Web URL icon.
stuff.wav	A media or text file icon.

Drawing Links in the Site Map

If you view the site map and select a page in it, the Link Tool icon appears next to the page: ⊕ .

To use the Link tool:

1. Click and drag this icon to any page in the Site Map pane (**Figure 20.37**) or the Local Sites pane (**Figure 20.38**) to put a link onto the page you're drawing *from,* which links *to* the page you're pointing to.

2. You'll see a straight line while you're drawing. If you draw to a page in the Local pane, the page will appear in its new location in the site map. Additionally, a link to the page's title or the media file will appear at the bottom of the page.

To edit the new link:

1. Double-click the page you drew the arrow *from*. It will open in the Document window.

2. Locate the link at the bottom of the page (**Figure 20.39**). You can drag it anywhere you want, edit its text, or copy the location and link it to existing objects.

Figure 20.36 Save your site-map data as an image, a bitmap, png or PICT graphic file.

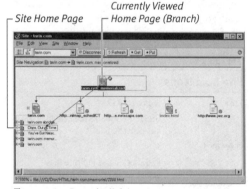

Figure 20.37 From the link icon next to any page, draw a line to another page to make a link. Notice that I'm viewing the map from a branch here.

Figure 20.39 The link I drew appears in the Document window on the bottom of the page I drew the link from. The text is either the filename or page title of the page I drew the link to.

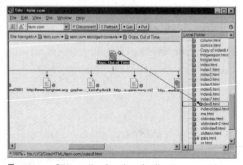

Figure 20.38 Here, I'm drawing the line to a page in the Local Sites pane.

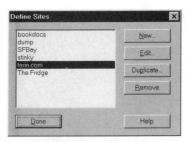

Figure 20.40 Choose your local site in the Define Sites dialog box. If you haven't set up a local site yet, turn to Chapter 3 for instructions on how to do so.

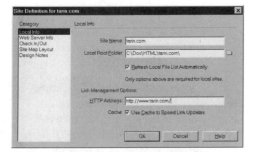

Figure 20.41 The Site Definition dialog box.

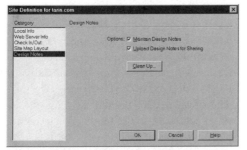

Figure 20.42 Enable design notes by checking the first box in the Design Notes panel of the dialog box.

Setting Up Design Notes

Design notes are a new tool in Dreamweaver 3 that allow you to save workflow information about a file. Using design notes, you can flag files that need attention, keep track of who's worked on a file, and store notes regarding just about anything.

In order to use design notes, you need to enable the use of them with your local site.

To enable design notes:

1. Open the Site window by pressing F5.

2. From the Site window menu bar, select Sites > Define Sites. The Define Sites dialog box will appear (**Figure 20.40**).

3. Click on the name of the site for which you want to enable design notes.

4. Click on Edit. The Site Definition dialog box will appear (**Figure 20.41**).

5. In the Category box at the left, click on Design Notes. That panel of the dialog box will appear (**Figure 20.42**).

6. If the Maintain Design Notes checkbox is checked, leave it alone. If it's unchecked, check the box to enable Design Notes.

7. If everyone in your workgroup is using Dreamweaver to produce a site, you may want to upload design notes along with their files. To enable automatic uploading of design notes, check the Upload Design Notes for Sharing checkbox.

✔ Tip

■ If you're working alone on a project or if your group isn't using Dreamweaver as a team, you should make sure to uncheck the Upload Design Notes for Sharing checkbox, or the server will be cluttered with files useless to everyone but you.

SETTING UP DESIGN NOTES

Using Design Notes

A design note is basically a hidden text file that stores information about another file. You can use design notes not only with Web pages, but also with images, multimedia files, CSS or HTML style sheets, library items, templates, and any other file in your local site.

To create a design note:

1. Select the appropriate file in the Site window, or open it in the Document window. Then, select File > Design Notes from the Site window menu bar *or* the Document window menu bar.

2. Either way, the Design Notes dialog box will appear (**Figure 20.43**), displaying the name of the file and its site path/location.

3. The Status drop-down menu allows you to flag a file with the following labels: draft; revision 1, 2, or 3; alpha, beta, or final; or needs attention. You may select any of these or leave the menu blank.

4. To stamp the current date in the design note, click on the Date button above the vertical scrollbar in the Notes text box. The date will appear in the Notes text box.

5. Type additional notes in the Notes text box.

6. To have Dreamweaver pop open the design notes whenever the file is opened, check the Show When File Is Opened box.

7. To add specific notes to be used consistently from file to file, click on the All Info tab to make that panel of the dialog box visible (**Figure 20.44**).

8. To add a note, click on the + button. In the Name and Value text boxes, type the information, such as **Project** and **Intranet** or **Author** and **ttowers**.

9. When you're done, click on OK to close the dialog box and save your design notes.

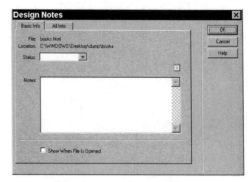

Figure 20.43 Leave notes for yourself or your coworkers in the Design Notes dialog box.

Honestly?

Design notes are a great idea. The implementation, however, is a different story. No flag or icon or pop-up appears to tell you which files have design notes. You can't search design notes specifically using Find and Replace. And you can't specifically export or upload only those files that have design notes.

So what good are they? Well, if you're a developer, you can use XML and JavaScript to extend Dreamweaver to include a Design Notes inspector or to use a status flag in a design note to change tags within a file. If you're a regular old user, you might just want to use them to keep track of things for yourself.

The only current advantage to using design notes over simple comments in the file itself is that design notes remain hidden and private. In future versions of Dreamweaver (let's have a collective groan), design notes may actually be implemented usefully rather than showing up as the germ of a good idea that leaves all the work to the user.

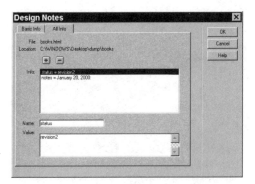

Figure 20.44 Add formatted notes (name=value) in the All Info tab of the Design Notes dialog box.

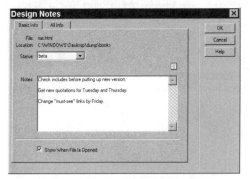

Figure 20.45 The Design Notes dialog box displays information I saved earlier about the progress of the page.

Accessing Design Notes

Opening a design note for a Web page or other file is similar to creating one. You open the same dialog box, and then you can read and edit the design notes.

To open a design note:

1. In the Site window, select the file whose design notes you want to read.

2. From the Site window menu bar, select File > Design Notes. The Design Notes dialog box will appear (**Figure 20.45**).

Now you can read, update, or edit the notes.

Where Are They?

The first time you create a design note, Dreamweaver creates a folder called Notes. Unfortunately, there isn't one central folder—Dreamweaver creates a Notes folder for each separate location of each separate file. For instance, if you create a design note for a page in the site root folder, and then another note for an image in the /images folder, Dreamweaver creates a Notes folder in each place.

What's more, the Notes folders are not visible using the Site window; to open the folder, you need to use your regular file manager (Windows Explorer or the Finder).

Inside the Notes folder, each design note is named for its file, plus an additional extension, .MNO (Macromedia Notes). So if your file is called calendar.html, the design note is called `calendar.html.mno`.

Cleaning up design notes

After you delete a file, Dreamweaver does not automatically delete its associated design notes. You can clean up orphaned design notes easily.

To clean up design notes:

1. From the Site window menu bar, Sites > Define Sites. The Define Sites dialog box will appear.

2. Click on the name of the site for which you want to clean up design notes.

3. Click on Edit. The Site Definition dialog box will appear.

4. In the Category box at the left, click on Design Notes. That panel of the dialog box will appear (**Figure 20.46**).

5. Click on the Clean Up button. A dialog box will appear (**Figure 20.47**) asking you if you really want to do that. Click on Yes.

6. Dreamweaver will remove all orphaned design notes from the selected site.

✔ Tip

■ If you disable the Maintain Design Notes option, Dreamweaver will remove all design notes from your site.

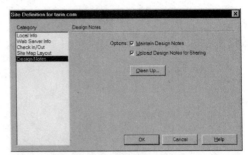

Figure 20.46 The Design Notes panel of the Site Definition dialog box.

Figure 20.47 After I clicked on Clean Up, the dialog box asked me if I was really sure I wanted to clean up.

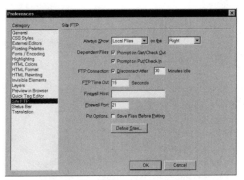

Figure 20.48 The Site FTP panel of the Preferences dialog box.

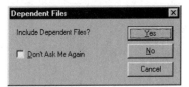

Figure 20.49 Our old pal, the Dependent Files dialog box.

Burn, Burn, Burn—A Wall of Fire

A firewall is a piece of security software that sits on the server and prevents outsiders and people without privileges from so much as viewing the stuff on all or part of a server. If your server uses a firewall, you need to set up your remote site information in Dreamweaver to get around the firewall. You set this up in the Preferences for Dreamweaver. Press Ctrl+J to view the Preferences dialog box, and click on Site FTP to view that panel of the dialog box. Enter the hostname of the proxy server in the Host text box, and if the server uses an FTP port other than 21, enter that in the Port text box.

For any sites that use this proxy server, check off the Use Firewall checkbox in the Site Definition dialog box.

Site FTP Preferences

You can change a variety of preferences for the Site window, including the timeout limit, whether the Dependent Files dialog box shows up, and the appearance of the Site window.

To change Site FTP preferences:

1. From the Site window menu bar, select Edit > Preferences. The Preferences dialog box will appear, with the Site FTP panel at the front (**Figure 20.48**).

2. By default, remote files appear on the left, and local files appear on the right in the Site window. If you'd prefer a different setup, select Local Files or Remote Files from the Always Show drop-down menu, and select Right or Left from the second drop-down menu. This setting will also affect the position of the site map in the Site window.

3. The Dependent Files dialog box (**Figure 20.49**) will appear whenever you get, put, check in, or check out a file. You can turn off the dialog by checking the Don't Ask Me Again box . To turn off the dialog, or to reinstate it, select or deselect the Dependent Files checkboxes.

4. By default, Dreamweaver will disconnect after 30 minutes of idling. To change this number, type it in the Minutes Idle text box. To turn off automatic timeouts (for instance, if you have a direct network connection), deselect the Disconnect After checkbox.

continues on next page

5. If the server is not responding, the connect, view file list, get, or put process will
   time out. The default timeout period is 15
   second but 60 seconds is recommended.
   You can set a different limit by typing it in
   the FTP Time Out text box.

6. To automatically save files when uploading them, check the Save Files Before
   Putting checkbox.

7. When you're satisfied, click on OK to save
   the changes to the preferences and close
   the Preferences dialog box. You'll return
   to the Site window.

Making a Mirror Site

A mirror site is a more-or-less exact copy of an existing site that resides on a different
server. Mirror sites are used for three main reasons:

♦ Testing

♦ Providing faster access to different physical locations

♦ Spreading the pain of downloads around to more than one site.

For instance, big, popular sites like TUCOWS, WebMuseum, and the Internet Movie
Database have mirror sites positioned around the world so that everyone who uses the
site can have speedier access.

Setting up a mirror site is easy using the Site window.

1. If you don't have a local copy of the original site, Site 1, create one. You can download
   an entire site by selecting everything in the remote Site window and "get"ting it into
   the local site folder.

2. Disconnect from the remote site.

3. Change the site information for the local site so that the Web server and username
   correspond to the Web server at Site 2.

4. Connect to Site 2.

5. Put the contents of the local site onto the Site 2 Web server.

Now you have three copies of the site: one local, one on Site 1, and one on Site 2.

INDEX

INDEX

INDEX

INDEX

INDEX